Equality Deferred

PATRONS OF THE OSGOODE SOCIETY

Blake, Cassels & Graydon LLP
Gowlings
Chernos Flaherty Svonkin LLP
McCarthy Tétrault LLP
Osler, Hoskin & Harcourt LLP
Paliare Roland Rosenberg Rothstein LLP
Torys LLP
WeirFoulds LLP

The Osgoode Society is supported by a grant from
The Law Foundation of Ontario.

The Society also thanks the Law Society of Upper Canada
for its continuing support.

LAW AND SOCIETY SERIES
W. Wesley Pue, General Editor

The Law and Society Series explores law as a socially embedded phenomenon. It is premised on the understanding that the conventional division of law from society creates false dichotomies in thinking, scholarship, educational practice, and social life. Books in the series treat law and society as mutually constitutive and seek to bridge scholarship emerging from interdisciplinary engagement of law with disciplines such as politics, social theory, history, political economy, and gender studies.

A list of titles in the series appears at the end of the book.

Equality Deferred

Sex Discrimination and British Columbia's Human Rights State, 1953-84

DOMINIQUE CLÉMENT

PUBLISHED BY UBC PRESS FOR
THE OSGOODE SOCIETY
FOR CANADIAN LEGAL HISTORY

UBC Press • Vancouver • Toronto

© UBC Press 2014

All rights reserved. No part of this publication may be reproduced, stored in a retrieval system, or transmitted, in any form or by any means, without prior written permission of the publisher, or, in Canada, in the case of photocopying or other reprographic copying, a licence from Access Copyright, www.accesscopyright.ca.

22 21 20 19 18 17 16 15 14   5 4 3 2 1

Printed in Canada on paper that is processed chlorine- and acid-free.

Library and Archives Canada Cataloguing in Publication

Clément, Dominique, 1975-, author
    Equality deferred : sex discrimination and British Columbia's human rights state, 1953-84 / Dominique Clément.

(Law and society series)
Includes bibliographical references and index.
Issued in print and electronic formats.
ISBN 978-0-7748-2749-2 (bound). – ISBN 978-0-7748-2750-8 (pbk.). – ISBN 978-0-7748-2751-5 (pdf). – ISBN 978-0-7748-2752-2 (epub)

    1. Sex discrimination against women – Law and legislation – British Columbia – History – 20th century. 2. Equality before the law – British Columbia – History – 20th century. 3. Women – Legal status, laws, etc. – British Columbia – History – 20th century. 4. Human rights – British Columbia – History – 20th century. 5. British Columbia. Human Rights Act. 6. Human rights – Canada – History – 20th century. I. Title. II. Series: Law and society series (Vancouver, B.C.)

| KEB458.C54 2014 | 342.71108'78 | C2014-900716-7 |
| KF4483.C57C54 2014 | | C2014-900717-5 |

Canada

UBC Press gratefully acknowledges the financial support for our publishing program of the Government of Canada (through the Canada Book Fund), the Canada Council for the Arts, and the British Columbia Arts Council.

This book has been published with the help of a grant from the Canadian Federation for the Humanities and Social Sciences, through the Awards to Scholarly Publications Program, using funds provided by the Social Sciences and Humanities Research Council of Canada.

UBC Press
The University of British Columbia
2029 West Mall
Vancouver, BC V6T 1Z2
www.ubcpress.ca

DEDICATED TO JILL

Contents

List of Illustrations / ix

Foreword / xi

Preface / xiii

Acknowledgments / xvii

Additional Resources / xix

Introduction / 3

1 Sex Discrimination in Canadian Law / 22

2 "No Jews or Dogs Allowed": Anti-Discrimination Law / 46

3 Gender and Canada's Human Rights State / 66

4 Women and Anti-Discrimination Law in British Columbia, 1953-69 / 86

5 Jack Sherlock and the Failed Human Rights Act, 1969-73 / 94

6 Kathleen Ruff and the Human Rights Code, 1973-79 / 109

7 Struggling to Innovate, 1979-83 / 134

8 Making New Law under the Human Rights Code / 157

9 The Politics of (Undermining) Human Rights: The Human Rights Act, 1983-84 / 169

Conclusion / 197

Notes / 217

Bibliography / 270

Index / 284

Illustrations

FIGURES

1. Anti-discrimination legislation / 61
2. Equal pay legislation / 73
3. Sex discrimination amendments to human rights legislation / 74
4. Human rights legislation / 78
5. Human rights complaints, 1969-73 / 107
6. Settlements / 141
7. Human rights complaints, 1974-82 / 141
8. Disposition of complaints, 1970-82 / 160
9. Combined funding for provincial human rights programs in Canada, 1975-83 / 172
10. Provincial funding for human rights programs, 1977, 1981, and 1985 / 173
11. Budgets for human rights programs in Canada, 1975-83 / 173
12. Boards of inquiry appointed, 1974-81 / 175
13. Complaints of discrimination on the basis of race and gender, 1976-81 / 175
14. British Columbia human rights program budget / 177
15. Determination of human rights complaints under the NDP (1972-75) and Social Credit (1970-72, 1975-85) governments / 185

Photographs

Kalmen Kaplansky, 1951 / 51
JLC poster session conference, 1947 / 51
Jewish Labour Committee anti-discrimination poster / 59
Jack Sherlock, 1972 / 97
Hanne Jensen and Aileen Cassidy, 1972 / 102
Human Rights Commission, 1969 / 103
Kathleen Ruff, 1975 / 111
Lady Godiva ride, UBC, 1981 / 131
Student protests at the Lady Godiva ride, UBC, 1981 / 132
Nola Landucci, 1980 / 139
Hanne Jensen, 1983 / 139
Remi De Roo, 1977 / 144
Robert McClelland and protesters, 1983 / 191
Andrea Fields, 1984 / 194

Foreword

The Osgoode Society for Canadian Legal History

One of the most profound changes to our law in the second half of the twentieth century was what is often termed the "rights revolution." The same period also saw the rise of a plethora of administrative agencies to administer law and policy in many areas. Professor Clément's pioneering study combines these two phenomena, providing a history of the origins and operation of human rights law and the human rights commission in British Columbia. It focuses particularly on sex discrimination, and documents the political debates surrounding human rights law, analyzes the role of social movements in developing the law, and discusses the working of the tribunals and human rights investigators who put the law into practice.

The purpose of the Osgoode Society for Canadian Legal History is to encourage research and writing in the history of Canadian law. The Society, which was incorporated in 1979 and is registered as a charity, was founded at the initiative of the Honourable R. Roy McMurtry, and officials of the Law Society of Upper Canada. The Society seeks to stimulate the study of legal history in Canada by supporting researchers, collecting oral histories, and publishing volumes that contribute to legal-historical scholarship in Canada. It has published ninety-two books on the courts, the judiciary, and the legal profession, as well as on the history of crime and punishment, women and law, law and economy, the legal treatment of ethnic minorities, and famous cases and significant trials in all areas of the law.

Current directors of the Osgoode Society for Canadian Legal History are Robert Armstrong, Kenneth Binks, Susan Binnie, David Chernos,

Thomas G. Conway, J. Douglas Ewart, Violet French, Martin Friedland, John Gerretsen, Philip Girard, William Kaplan, C. Ian Kyer, Virginia MacLean, Patricia McMahon, Roy McMurtry, Dana Peebles, Paul Perell, Jim Phillips, Paul Reinhardt, Joel Richler, William Ross, Paul Schabas, Robert Sharpe, Lorne Sossin, Mary Stokes, and Michael Tulloch.

The annual report and information about membership may be obtained by writing to the Osgoode Society for Canadian Legal History, Osgoode Hall, 130 Queen Street West, Toronto, Ontario, M5H 2N6. Telephone: 416-947-3321. E-mail: mmacfarl@lsuc.on.ca. Website: Osgoodesociety.ca.

R. Roy McMurtry
President

Jim Phillips
Editor-in-Chief

Preface

Equality Deferred is a history of human rights law in Canada, with a special focus on sex discrimination in British Columbia. Canada has created the most sophisticated human rights legal regime in the world, and for a brief period between 1974 and 1984, British Columbia boasted the most progressive human rights legislation in the country. This book explores how Canadian law has discriminated against women since the nineteenth century; traces the origins of human rights legislation; documents political debates regarding BC human rights law in 1953, 1969, 1973, and 1984; examines the role of social movements; reveals how human rights tribunals were used to create new law (and the judiciary's response to it); and provides a glimpse into the activities of the human rights investigators who put the law into practice. A central theme throughout this book is how governments can inhibit the application of their own laws. The existence of a law is no assurance that it will be enforced. At times, the task of creating, promoting, and enforcing the law fell to non-state actors.

Human rights law is currently the focus of intense public debate, which largely revolves around whether or not to retain the original model of human rights adjudication documented in these pages. British Columbia and Ontario have implemented sweeping reforms in recent years, and Saskatchewan eliminated its Human Rights Tribunal. Newfoundland, on the other hand, kept the traditional model when its government introduced new legislation in 2011. In addition, the Canadian Museum for Human Rights – the first national museum to appear in decades – will open in 2014. This is an ideal time to be examining Canada's human rights history.

Perhaps the greatest obstacle to writing this book was Canada's wretched freedom of information regime. There is plenty of evidence to demonstrate that provincial and federal law is more effective at concealing government records than providing access. After more than a decade of using freedom of information legislation, I still cannot fathom why the law must be so broad as to encompass such mundane materials as cabinet ministers' speeches or grants to community groups. This book is based in large part on an extensive collection of pre-1985 records from British Columbia's Human Rights Branch and Human Rights Commission. I was the first person to gain access to these records. But it took two years, and I spent those years drafting a contract for access in cooperation with the attorney general's office, which had never before been faced with such a request. Far more disturbing was the British Columbia Archives' response to my request for government records relating to all aspects of my study. The archives decided to begin enforcing an obscure provision of the provincial freedom of information statute that requires users to permit civil servants to "audit" (inspect) their offices, including their computers, to confirm security measures. This is remarkably invasive for documents that are over forty years old. At least I had an office; graduate students have been forced to allow archives staff to inspect their homes. The staff can be intimidating, uncooperative, and poorly informed regarding the legislation they are implementing. In my case, the enforcement officer insisted that access was a *privilege,* whereas, in fact, the law states quite clearly that it is a *right.* I cannot help but wonder how much of British Columbia's history remains unwritten because of the burdensome regulations for accessing government documents. This is truly unfortunate, given the province's rising prominence in Canada.

I originally conceived of this book as a history of second-wave feminism in British Columbia, with a particular focus on the way in which activism is shaped by rights discourse. To document this process, I sought to examine how feminists engaged with human rights law. As sometimes happens, I discovered a wealth of material on human rights law in British Columbia and decided that there was an important story to tell on this topic alone. So much of human rights work, from individual investigations to conciliation or settlements, remains hidden. One of my goals with this book was to secure documentation and conduct interviews to make this process more transparent and to understand the origins of the current model. I also hope that readers will find Chapter 1, which provides an overview history of how Canadian law has discriminated against women since the nineteenth century, a useful resource. The chapter has extensive commentary in the endnotes, and I would encourage readers who are interested in the history of the law and gender to refer to those citations.

One of this book's key themes is how the women's movement made the law possible. A history of the women's movement in British Columbia is yet to be written. Indeed, a great deal more remains to be written. Too much of the literature on human rights in Canada focuses on Ontario and Quebec, and historians are latecomers to this field of study. *Equality Deferred* is certainly not exhaustive. For me, it is only the beginning.

Acknowledgments

The longer I am an academic, the more I realize how easily we accrue debts in the production of a single book. As I think of the five years during which I worked on this study, I am amazed at the willingness of people to share their valuable time to help me along. On my own, I could never have produced the book you are about to read.

I should begin with those who lived this history. I interviewed many people, and I would like to thank them first and foremost for taking the time to share their life stories. Their names are listed in the Bibliography. But I want to extend a special thanks to Linda Sproule-Jones, who spent hours helping me get started, and Bill Black, who provided documentary evidence on human rights investigations in the early 1970s. My trip to the northern town of Smithers was for no other reason than to spend two days with Kathleen Ruff. She stands alongside Dan Hill as a key pioneer of Canada's human rights state.

Many others contributed to this project. Ramona Rose at the University of British Columbia Rare Books and Special Collections went the extra mile to uncover collections that were essential to my research. My two-year odyssey to access restricted files from the attorney general's office was made easier by its liaison, Linda Canham, whose professionalism gave me some faith in the freedom of information regime. Several research assistants at the University of Alberta also contributed to this study: Greg Eklics, Tyler Moroniuk, Will Silver, and Dan Trottier. When I had to travel and needed research assistance, Constance Backhouse (University of Ottawa), Lynn

Marks (University of Victoria), Tamara Myers (University of British Columbia), and Eric Sager (University of Victoria) put me in contact with dependable graduate students. As any historian knows all too well, archival research presents myriad challenges, especially now that new technologies enable thousands of documents to be copied in a single visit. As for those students – Ted, Ben, and Falon – it was tedious work, but you were each exemplary.

I am especially grateful to those who took the time to review drafts. Constance Backhouse, Donica Belisle, Bill Black, Linda Kealey, and Veronica Strong-Boag provided helpful feedback on individual chapters. Sarah Carter and Carmela Patrias read the entire manuscript and helped me shape the book into its final form. I must also commend the anonymous peer-reviewers who clearly spent a great deal of time on the text with an eye for details, which has made this book so much better. As did Deborah Kerr, the copy editor, who did an exceptional job editing the manuscript. Finally, I'm indebted to the staff at UBC Press, including Ann Macklem and Randy Schmidt for their support and feedback.

I began this project when I arrived at the University of Alberta in 2008. I've spent the past five years working with one of the best department chairs in the university, Harvey Krahn, and I've received invaluable career advice from my colleague Kevin Haggerty. The university is serious about supporting the research of new scholars. I am indebted to the University of Alberta's Killam Fund for providing generous seed-money for this study, as well as the Social Sciences and Humanities Research Council and the Osgoode Society for Canadian Legal History for the funding to complete my research.

There is a small but growing cohort of human rights historians in Canada. Human rights constitute an exciting field of study but one that is daunting for any historian because, until very recently, it was dominated by political scientists and legal scholars. Carmela Patrias and Ruth Frager, in particular, have made critical inroads in charting the early history of law and discrimination, and I depended greatly on their scholarship for Chapter 2. For proof that the study of human rights history has enormous potential, we need look no further than the new Canadian Museum for Human Rights. I have been privileged to be deeply involved in its development, and it will undoubtedly inspire further scholarship on human rights.

Additional Resources

Canada's Human Rights History
www.HistoryOfRights.com

Canada's Human Rights History is a site dedicated to exploring every aspect of Canada's rights revolution. It is a research and teaching portal for the study of social movements, state policy, and law. In addition to providing information on critical human rights moments and controversies throughout Canadian history, the site provides access to an extensive collection of archival materials. It also contains detailed reading lists, links to other resources, and information on conferences, publications, research funding, and recent events. Unlike most historical websites, this site is not static but, rather, new content is added as the author's scholarship evolves.

Equality Deferred

Introduction

Like most flight attendants in 1975, Jacqueline Culley was in her twenties, white, attractive, earning about ten dollars an hour, and working twenty or so hours a week. On 15 June, Canadian Pacific Airlines forced her to go on leave without pay. The reason: she was thirteen weeks pregnant. That same day, Culley walked into the offices of the Human Rights Branch in Vancouver. She found the one-page form for human rights violations, sat down, and began writing: "I allege that I was discriminated against by Mr. E. Stones and Mr. G. Manning of Canadian Pacific Airlines because of my sex." Her complaint file includes a copy of a company memorandum informing female flight attendants that they were required to notify the airline immediately if they were pregnant. Ajit Mehat, a human rights officer, met with Manning, the vice-president of customer service, a few weeks later in the airline's downtown Vancouver office. Mehat asked if there was any possibility that the policy could be changed. Canadian Pacific Airlines, Manning insisted, was not willing to make any adjustments.[1]

Culley faced sex discrimination every day at work, even though women dominated the profession. At Air Canada, for instance, 80 percent of flight attendants were women. And yet, the industry divided flight attendants into two categories: pursers and stewardesses. No matter how long she worked for the airline, Culley would never become a purser, who was always a man and in charge during flights. Male pursers had attempted to organize separately in the 1940s, and although the National War Labour Board forced male and female flight attendants into the same union, it also authorized separate wage and seniority scales. Between 1965 and 1973, female flight attendants were required to sign an agreement allowing Air Canada to arbitrarily dismiss them after ten years of employment.[2] They had to quit if they married or became pregnant, and they were automatically fired once they turned thirty-two. This was a common practice in Canada's airline industry. Pacific Western Airlines even refused to hire divorced women. Culley, who was married, would never have been hired except that, following a protracted political campaign by the Canadian Airline Flight Attendants Association, Air Canada had lifted its ban on married women (and had integrated salaries and seniority lists) by 1972. Other airlines soon did the same.[3] But as Culley discovered, airlines were determined to retain their ban on pregnant flight attendants.

Gail Anderson, also a pregnant flight attendant facing an obligatory leave of absence, tried to sue British Columbia–based Pacific Western Airlines (PWA) in 1975 for violating the Canada Labour Code.[4] For Anderson and Culley, being forced out of work was a financial burden: they had to leave after thirteen weeks, but despite modifications to the federal unemployment insurance program in 1971, pregnant women could submit claims only after twenty-eight weeks. PWA executives insisted that their policy was for passenger safety, although, as Joan Sangster argues, it is far more likely that pregnant women undermined the companies' attempts to promote a highly sexualized image of flight attendants:

> [Pacific Western Airlines] attendants, perhaps more than others, were convinced their employer intended to use their bodies as a marketing lure for leering customers, since they had already fought a grievance over "sexualization" issues. In 1971, two BC-based PWA attendants refused to wear the Stampeder cowboy costume which the airline had already introduced on its Vancouver to Calgary run. With a very short, fringed skirt and prominent red bloomers underneath, they argued it simply invited male groping. When an attendant was "grabbed and pawed" on a flight to the BC Interior, she refused to don the "red panties," resulting in charges of insubordination, her suspension, and a threat of dismissal. A grievance ensued which the union won on the basis that this was not the "standard uniform" noted in the attendants' job description.[5]

PWA fought a lengthy legal battle with the Canadian Airline Flight Attendants Association over pregnancy in the 1970s. No federal law banned women from working or flying while pregnant, and the company's own policy did not bar female pilots from flying. Its position was that pregnant women were not laid off, but instead given a leave of absence. PWA was aware that the Canada Labour Code prohibited businesses from refusing to employ women *solely* on the basis of pregnancy, so it resorted to arguing that pregnant women were physically incapable of working.[6] To make its case, it played on the public's fears regarding airline safety and brought to the witness stand a steady stream of medical and aviation experts who testified that pregnant women would be unable to help passengers in distress or during emergencies. The presiding judge was confronted with images of eight-months pregnant flight attendants attempting to reach across a narrow aisle as the plane plummeted to earth or shook violently in the air. Sangster writes,

> As if this scare testimony was not enough, PWA produced a number of doctors, including their own company expert on health and aviation, all of whom confirmed that pregnant flight attendants were safety risks because of their girth, the possibility of miscarriage, the extra dangers of jet lag effect and fatigue, their inability to get immunizations for foreign travel, vein problems, swollen legs, and their emotional state of mind.[7]

Culley's human rights complaint was a non-starter. PWA convinced the British Columbia Supreme Court that the case fell under federal jurisdiction, and as a result, it could not be brought before a provincial human rights board of inquiry (there was no federal human rights law in 1975).[8] Anderson's lawsuit failed in court. PWA relented in 1981, albeit only partially, and allowed pregnant women to continue working longer while providing supplementary benefits. Not until 1985, following amendments to the Canada Labour Code and the federal Human Rights Act, as well as a critical Supreme Court of Canada decision, were prohibitions on employing pregnant women considered sex discrimination.[9] This book is an attempt to understand the nature and pervasiveness of sex discrimination, and to what degree human rights law succeeded (or failed) in addressing gender inequality in the past.

Human Rights and the Law

Jacqueline Culley's initial reaction to her employer's discriminatory policy was probably not to think of it as a violation of human rights. For most people, a rights-claim begins with the belief that they have been treated unfairly. Culley probably talked to friends, family, and her union representative about options for redress, and someone suggested that she make a complaint to the Human Rights Branch. In essence, she sought redress for being treated unfairly, and she used the language of rights to frame her grievance. By this time, rights-talk had become the dominant language that people used to articulate claims against the state and society.

Human rights are the rights one has simply by virtue of being human. They are the "highest moral rights, they regulate the fundamental structures and practices of political life, and in ordinary circumstances they take priority over other moral, legal, and political claims."[10] If it is to exist, a right must be recognized by other people and must be secured through human action. It is an entitlement premised on a widely held set of beliefs about the nature of the entitlement; even if it is not recognized in law, a right emerges from a moral or ideological belief.[11] With every human right comes a correlative duty from others to respect and help realize that right. Furthermore, human rights are grounded on the presumption of the equal worth and dignity of all human beings. The right to life (or physical security) and the freedom to determine our own destiny are elemental human rights principles. These principles are not absolute, but they are universal and inalienable, and they exist prior to law.[12]

This book begins with British Columbia's first equal pay legislation in 1953 and ends in 1984, with the collapse of the country's most progressive human rights legal regime. Its focus on women and sex discrimination is easily explained. Whereas in the United States, racial minorities employed civil rights legislation more than others, human rights legislation in Canada was for a long time overwhelmingly associated with discrimination against women. It is difficult to exaggerate the significance of gender in the history of Canadian human rights law. Gender (sex) discrimination dominated debates regarding human rights by the 1970s, and women's issues were inextricably linked to public discourse about such rights. The women's movement rallied around human rights law and was often integral to its creation, promotion, and enforcement. And although a dozen different grounds for discrimination existed in most jurisdictions, more than half of the complaints received every year dealt with only one: gender.

This book is as much a history of women's lived experiences as it is about law. It is filled with bitter recollections from women whose experiences of discriminatory treatment are transposed with memories of successful challenges to seek redress. These life stories range from absurd, almost unbelievable, acts of discrimination to profound philosophical disagreements about equality: Janice Foster, a five-foot-tall 105-pound woman who was denied a chance to work in a sawmill because of her size; Jean Tharpe, a trained laboratory technologist who had to drive along a dangerous northern logging road to work every day because Lornex Mining Company refused to provide the same free accommodations it offered men; Dutchie Mathison and her daughter, who were not allowed to play golf with her husband before 11:00 a.m. because they were women, although the ten-year-old son of another player was welcome to play; Andrea Fields, a waitress who had to endure constant sexual overtures and groping from her boss, Wilhelm Ueffing; or Kathleen Strenja, a mother of three whose husband was unemployed and who was prevented from driving a taxi because United Cabs-Comox feared she might be raped. In this way, a study of human rights law is a unique window into understanding gender inequality.

This book, however, largely explores individual acts of discrimination. It goes without saying that inequality is far more pervasive, and the law addressed only one aspect of gender inequality. It is curious that, except for a few complaints from Aboriginal women, most formal inquiries into sex discrimination in British Columbia during the period of this study involved white women. An important recent development in the scholarship on human rights law has been the problem of naming, or intersectionality: recognizing that discrimination is not always based on a single factor, such as sex, but is instead a product of intersecting qualities, such as disability or race and sex.[13] Unfortunately, because only a few cases from minority women and women with disabilities existed in British Columbia by 1984, this issue is difficult to address. Finally, although human rights law certainly touched on the lives of a wide range of women, there were limits to its reach. Becki Ross's study of burlesque in Vancouver documents the lives of women who faced sexual harassment and unequal pay every day.[14] But their voices are silent in this book. They, and undoubtedly many other women, experienced discrimination but did not engage with human rights law.

Human rights laws are among the most significant legal innovations in twentieth-century Canada. A book on the subject is, therefore, a study of social policy. Some of the questions explored in these pages include, What was the success rate of people who submitted complaints? Was the process fair and equitable? What remedies were provided? What role did social movements play in enforcing the legislation? How did victims' conception of their rights conflict with the response by the state and people accused of discrimination? Moreover, this book is about how we conceive of discrimination. Should intent be a factor in prosecuting someone for discrimination? Are neutral practices that indirectly harm groups of people, such as height and weight requirements for police officers, biased? Should state policy go beyond addressing individual discriminatory acts and confront systemic discrimination? How much accommodation is reasonably expected for employers and service providers? For example, is it unfair for a school board to refuse to employ someone with a criminal record?

This is also a study of how law is enforced. Joseph Katz, a member of the British Columbia Human Rights Commission, declared in 1979 that women were not needed on the commission because its members could consult their wives. Women's rights organizations quickly condemned his comment. In fact, advocacy groups were often critical of human rights law, yet women's organizations vigorously defended the system. Human rights law depended on the participation of social movement actors, particularly in promoting awareness of it, filing complaints, and lobbying for legislative reform. The idea of human rights has historically been highly statist, but grassroots activism has been at the heart of the most profound human rights advances. Social movements are defined by the beliefs they propagate, but they are composed of people who articulate, sometimes imperfectly, those beliefs. Ideas of rights evolve within a particular social context. The study of human rights must begin locally.

The Human Rights State

By the 1960s, a profound shift was under way in Canada: a genuine rights revolution that would affect virtually every aspect of social, cultural, political, and economic life. It transformed the state, which increasingly regulated private activities. It also transformed social movements, which were playing a greater role in enforcing state policy. Human rights law was one product of the rights revolution.

Laws that bind the state to advance human rights principles, as well as the associated enforcement apparatus, constitute the "human rights state." The human rights state is premised on the belief that governments should create mechanisms to help alleviate social inequality. It is analogous in this way to the welfare state. And as in the case of the welfare state, a broad consensus has evolved regarding its necessity, although specific policies may be contested. Human rights statutes were introduced in every Canadian jurisdiction between 1962 and 1979 to prohibit discrimination in housing, employment, and accommodation. The human rights state is composed of a system of similar provincial and federal statutes and commissions. To a lesser degree, Canada's Charter of Rights and Freedoms (1982) and legislation dealing with multiculturalism, official languages, and privacy are also pillars of the human rights state. All share the same principle: they oblige the state to defend and promote human rights. But it is human rights legislation, enforced by commissions, that is the most visible manifestation of the human rights state.

In essence, the human rights state is public policy. Canada's version began in the 1930s, with a few minor amendments to existing legislation that prohibited differential treatment on the basis of race or religion. Later, in the 1950s, several provinces passed anti-discrimination statutes. These laws were based on a formal equality model: everyone should be treated in the same manner irrespective of their membership in an identifiable group. Anti-discrimination legislation, according to historian James W. St. G. Walker, was premised on the assumption that discriminatory acts sprang from the aberrant behaviour or psychological problems of pathological individuals. The behaviour of these individuals influenced popular notions of what was right and moral. The solution, therefore, was to stop the disease at its source by mobilizing the state to punish discriminatory acts. But as we will see, such laws were largely ineffective. They were poorly designed and rarely enforced.

In 1962, human rights legislation began to replace anti-discrimination laws, a process that dramatically expanded the scope of the human rights state. Over time, the latter came to symbolize a profound change in the role of the state and the law. The first anti-discrimination statutes referred only to race, religion, and ethnicity; by 1984, human rights laws also prohibited discrimination on the basis of sex, sexual orientation, pardoned criminal conviction, social condition, disability, political affiliation, and age. In this way, the human rights state reflected changing values and beliefs about human dignity and equality. As Brian Howe explains in his study of Canadian human rights commissions, these institutions epitomize a fundamental alteration in how the law was enforced and experienced:

> Rights to equal concern and respect are held to be basic. They stand above the ebb and flow of ordinary politics and cannot depend for their enforcement on benevolence or the good will of majorities or politicians who represent majorities. Rights require special recognition and they require

effective protection. Such protection cannot be achieved adequately through the ordinary political process, but through the courts or special administrative and quasi-judicial bodies (e.g., human rights commissions and tribunals). At the same time, rights are not simply claims on the state without corresponding responsibilities; they involve responsibilities among rights-bearers to tolerate and respect the rights of others.[15]

Human rights laws were further designed to "correct systemic conditions that produce discriminatory results even in the apparent absence of overt prejudicial acts."[16] They were premised on the belief that prejudice could be unspoken and systemic. In this way, they signalled a shift from formal to substantive equality: "A substantive equality approach asks whether the same treatment in practice produces equal or unequal results ... Substantive equality requires taking into account the underlying differences between individuals in society and accommodating those differences in order to ensure equality of impact and outcome."[17] The move toward substantive equality was apparent in several innovations in human rights law: these included exemptions for ventures (such as equal opportunity programs) designed to assist certain classes of people; the focus on education; scrutinizing seemingly neutral policies for indirect harm; and rejecting honest belief or lack of intent as a defence for discrimination. The principle of equality before the law had evolved to include both the law's form and its impact in practice.

For women, human rights were one way of articulating their grievances by appealing to a universal discourse of accepted norms. Canadian human rights law first banned discrimination on the basis of sex in 1969. At a time when British Columbia's leading newspaper could claim that "matrimony is the only career for women," and as *Chatelaine* editor Doris Anderson suggested, "some men simply assumed sexual harassment was a perk of being boss," the human rights state was truly revolutionary.[18] However, it was not transformative. Its history suggests that there are limits to how far the law can facilitate radical social change. To be sure, the human rights state marked a profound departure from a time when discrimination against women was pervasive and entrenched in law. In this way, human rights law was revolutionary. Nonetheless, it was not transformative, because, although it acknowledged systemic discrimination, in practice it poorly addressed the root causes of gender inequality.

It is easy to assume that human rights are the natural and inevitable way of framing a vision for social change. And yet, not too long ago, appeals to socialism or Christian values were more common.[19] Some labour historians, for instance, lament that the labour movement has abandoned the principles of industrial democracy in favour of advocating for human rights.[20] Industrial democracy "was a direct challenge to the unaccountable power of employers to determine working conditions: democracy meant having a 'say' over those conditions."[21] Rights discourse, according to Nelson Lichtenstein, is an individualist rather than a collective advancement of mutual interests. Human rights "are universal and individual, which means that employers and individual members of management enjoy them just as much as workers ... A discourse of rights has subverted the very idea and the institutional expression of union solidarity."[22] Human-rights-based activism "has had virtually no impact on the structure of industry or employment, in either the United States or abroad. A rights-based approach to the democratization of the workplace fails to confront capital with demands that cannot be defined as a judicially protected mandate."[23]

Feminists have raised similar concerns in response to the way that "gender neutrality serves to obfuscate the gendered relations of social power."[24] Appealing to human rights requires women to frame their grievances in a gender-neutral language. Such an appeal has consequences. In her analysis of sexual assault laws, Judy Fudge argues that "instead of directly addressing the question of how to best promote women's sexual autonomy under social relations which result in women's sexual subordination, feminists who invoke the *Charter* must couch their arguments in terms of the rhetoric of equality rights ... Feminist discourse about power is translated into a discourse of rights."[25] As a result, the social construction of sexuality and the power relations that produce sexual inequality are neglected or ignored.[26] Moreover, rights discourse "can be exploited by groups with opposition political agendas."[27] In 1972, for instance, the New Democratic Party was elected in British Columbia, and its Women's Rights Committee insisted on the creation of a Ministry of Women's Rights. Premier David Barrett, however, rejected the idea and famously stated, "I believe in human rights, not women's rights."[28] So human rights can be used as a gender-neutral discourse to the detriment of advancing women's equality.

Framing grievances in the language of human rights raises the possibility of ignoring women's lived experiences and history of oppression. Human rights legislation, as we will see, was a useful tool for confronting overt forms of discriminatory behaviour. However, it was less effective at addressing systemic discrimination. Appeals to a neutral discourse of rights can obscure entrenched patterns of gender-based bias. They decontextualize the social position of women who are victims of rights violations, thus benefitting those men who do not need to overcome systemic barriers. In other words, laws that are not premised on gender differences might indirectly reproduce gender inequalities. Lori Chamberson, Judy Fudge, Hester Lessard, and Wanda Wiegers have demonstrated how men have used the equality section in the Charter of Rights and Freedoms to challenge laws regulating child support, social assistance for single mothers, affirmative action programs, sexual assault, and women's right to name or place their children with adoptive parents.[29] There is a disturbing trend toward formal rather than substantive equality in recent Charter litigation that has acted to the detriment of gender equality. The father's rights movement has scored several victories, most notably the 2003 *Trociuk* decision wherein the Supreme Court of Canada ruled that a law giving mothers the final authority on naming their children violated the rights of the biological father.[30] If human rights are shared by everyone by virtue of their humanity, women's rights are specific to women's distinct history and lived experience. The need for a vision of human rights that goes beyond universal qualities to rights that are specific to certain forms of oppression has inspired the rallying cry in recent years that "women's rights are human rights."[31] Women's rights might take the form of a right to name children or a prohibition against using a woman's sexual history in assault trials. Gender-based violence is another example of a rights violation that affects women in a unique way.[32] In other words, women have their own human rights needs.[33]

A central theme in this book, therefore, is the limits of human rights law as a vehicle for pursing gender equality. The law was not an effective tool for overcoming generations of inequality or addressing unspoken assumptions about gender. Equal pay provisions, for example, prohibited differential pay for women who worked in the same jobs in the same places as men. It did not apply to the sexual division of labour that was the root cause of unequal pay for many female employees. Women's workplace inequality was also a product of disadvantages arising from childcare obligations, yet human rights legislation never imposed positive obligations on the state, such as providing affordable childcare or parental leave for fathers. Over time, human rights legislation came to recognize equal pay for work of equal value, as well as systemic discrimination, but it remains haunted by its formal equality origins. As Wiegers suggests, human rights law has to date been relatively ineffective in dealing with systemic inequalities in the workplace, in transforming the standards of evaluation or "merit," and in addressing subtle issues of climate ... The removal of formal barriers to equality (and the apparent success of a few visible women) has apparently convinced many women students, and certainly many more young men, that women presently enjoy equal opportunity.[34]

The failure of the human rights state in addressing systemic discrimination is an important theme of this study.

Human Rights History

The emergence of the Canadian human rights state coincided with similar developments around the world. Anti-colonial movements swept across the globe in the two decades following the 1948 United Nations Universal Declaration of Human Rights (UDHR), many of which drew on the language of the UDHR.[35] Twelve new African nations incorporated part of the UDHR in their constitutions. Several new regional treaties committed sovereign states to human rights principles, including the American Declaration of the Rights of Man (1948), the European Convention on Human Rights (1950), and the American Convention on Human Rights (1969). The first international human rights treaties were also established during this period, including the Convention on the Prevention and Punishment of the Crime of Genocide (1948), the International Covenant on Civil and Political Rights (1967), and the International Covenant on Economic, Social and Political Rights (1967). Inspired by international developments, and responding to pressure at home, several Western governments produced laws to protect human rights. The United States, for example, introduced civil rights legislation in 1957 (Voting Rights Act), and anti-discrimination legislation also appeared in Australia and the United Kingdom. Meanwhile, the international human rights system was supported through a growing network of social movement organizations. Amnesty International (1961) and Human Rights Watch (1978) were among the most prominent of these but were certainly not unique. Regional associations such as the Asian Coalition of Human Rights Organizations and the Inter-African Network for Human Rights reported on human rights abuses. In Canada, at least forty human rights and civil liberties groups were founded during the 1960s and 1970s.[36] As a result of these and similar developments, human rights "reached consensual (prescriptive) status on the international level."[37]

Nevertheless, historians have been slow to write about the history of human rights. In a contribution to the *American Historical Review,* Kenneth Cmiel lamented their lack of engagement with the subject, as did Samuel Moyn, who insists in his recent book that "historians in the United States started writing the history of human rights a decade ago."[38] Since 2000, historians in Canada have begun to address this lacuna with studies on racial and ethnic minorities, organized labour, law, social activism, and other topics, written from a human rights perspective. The present volume is the first historical study of human rights law in Canada.

Studies of Canadian human rights law are rare.[39] Anyone who is interested in the subject must consult a limited scholarship that focuses mainly on Ontario.[40] And yet, the law is an essential element of Canada's human rights history. In several recent studies, Janet Ajzenstat, Michel Ducharme, and Christopher MacLennan have examined both the impact of rights-talk on political discourse and the post-1960s proliferation of legislation to protect rights.[41] MacLennan also posits that the declining influence of parliamentary supremacy on Canadian politics and law set the stage for a constitutional bill of rights in 1982. Stephanie Bangarth, Ruth Frager and Carmela Patrias, Ross Lambertson, Shirley Tillotson, and James W. St. G. Walker have documented how twentieth-century rights discourse spawned new social movements or transformed old ones.[42] Frager, Lambertson, MacLennan, Patrias, Miriam Smith, Tillotson, and Walker have further argued that grassroots mobilization has been central to legal reform.[43] By contrast, R. Brian Howe and David Johnson's book credits the state with innovations in human rights law. The present volume complements the existing literature by addressing similar themes: the relationship between human rights agencies and social movements; the impact of human rights laws; and the challenges facing the human rights state.

This book also contributes to the literature on Canadian human rights history by insisting that the human rights state must be considered in a local context. Abigail Bakan, Sonia Cardenas, Andrée Côté and Lucie Lemonde, Shelagh Day, James Kelly, Lucie Lamarche, Rosanna Langer, and Hester Lessard have produced tentative studies on human rights law. Still, they provide only a thin discussion of the role of social movement actors, few account for the political and ideological divisions that have shaped human rights policies, and none offer a detailed study of human rights law in practice. This book, in contrast, reveals the ways that local events, actors, and issues have influenced the adoption and enforcement of human rights law. Even in the international literature, far too many scholars focus on treaties and international institutions to the detriment of local studies. In her book on national human rights institutions, American human rights scholar Julie Mertus makes a strong case for the need to focus on how human rights principles are implemented locally: "Among human rights advocates, the dominant wisdom is that the promotion and protection of human rights rely less on international efforts and more on domestic action." For this reason, "establishing national-level human rights mechanisms has emerged as a core part of the international human rights agenda."[44] A study of a provincial human rights regime helps us to understand the strengths and weaknesses of human rights law, and how ideas of rights have evolved in a specific context.

The regional bias in the literature is especially disturbing. The current framework for human rights law in Canada was pioneered in Ontario, and most studies reflect this origin. A study of British Columbia provides an opportunity to expand the scope of the literature and address many issues that have yet to be fully explored. Unlike Ontario, for instance, British Columbia was the site of intense ideological conflicts surrounding the human rights state. The province also introduced several legal innovations. For this reason, it is crucial for scholars to consider the human rights state in British Columbia as distinct from that in Ontario.

Geography, economics, culture, history, and politics can shape law in practice. The history of BC politics, for example, exemplifies the need for local studies of human rights law. Between 1956 and 1991, BC politics was sharply divided between the Social Credit Party (Socreds) and the New Democratic Party (NDP). The Socreds ruled almost continually from 1956 to 1991, with the NDP briefly forming government from 1972 to 1975. W.A.C. Bennett, a former Conservative MLA and Kelowna hardware merchant, led the pro-business Socreds, who relied on votes from rural British Columbia. Still, although dedicated to free enterprise, the Socreds were committed to government intervention in the economy. Bennett believed that private business should guide the economy but that government should intervene in large projects when the private sector failed, or had no interest, in developing them.[45] His administration built thousands of kilometres of highways and rail, created several Crown corporations including BC Ferries and BC Power, dramatically expanded post-secondary education, and developed hydroelectric power on the Columbia River.

Bennett was premier until 1972, when the NDP, led by David Barrett, defeated the Socreds. The two men could not have been more different. A former social worker and MLA since 1960, Barrett described himself as a poor Jewish boy from Vancouver's East Side. The NDP had built a solid electoral base in urban British Columbia, especially among the professional middle class in the service sector. The party pursued a vision that was "more moderate, concerned to strengthen social policies, lessen foreign ownership, and exercise state control over public utilities and the exploitation of natural resources."[46] Barrett moved quickly after the election to introduce hundreds of new programs and policies. One statute passed during the NDP interregnum was the Human Rights Code, which was the most progressive human rights law in Canada. In contrast, the Socreds were loath to impose excessive state regulations on private business: the Human Rights Act they had introduced in 1969 was among the weakest in the country. Barrett's ill-fated decision to call a snap election in 1975 allowed the Socreds, led by Bill Bennett (son of the former premier), to return to power. Once again the province was in the hands of a pro-business government, except this time the Socreds had a stronger electoral base in Vancouver. They remained in office until 1991, when they were defeated by the NDP; soon afterward, they were eclipsed by a resurgent Liberal Party.[47]

The two-party system produced profound philosophical disagreements regarding the human rights state. The limitations of the Social Credit government's weak Human Rights Act led the New Democratic Party to introduce a far more expansive Human Rights Code in 1973. A decade later, another Socred government introduced a variation of its original Human Rights Act. Not to be outdone, when the NDP returned to power in 1991, it replaced the Socred legislation with a variation of its original Human Rights Code. Lasting less than a decade, this law was replaced in 2002 by the Liberal Party's Human Rights Act, which had a great deal in common with the Socreds' 1969 and 1984 statutes. In no other province – and indeed few other countries in the world – were ideological divisions surrounding human rights law so apparent. Provincial government support for the human rights state in British Columbia was lukewarm at best, except when the NDP was in power.[48]

Another theme throughout this book, therefore, is how governments can inhibit the application of their own laws. Only a case study approach, with a focus on the law in practice at the local level, can reveal how human rights law was open to abuse from a government that rejected the underlying principles of the human rights state. In sum, the existence of a law is no assurance that it will be enforced. One the one hand, the human rights state was innovative public policy that people used to resist discrimination. On the other hand, the system was plagued by delays, costs, and innumerable other obstacles to enforcing the law. The intervention of social movements helped overcome some of these impediments, but the system was far from perfect. This tension is evident throughout the book, which attempts to strike an important balance in the analysis: that the limitations of the human rights state should not vitiate its significance as progressive social policy.

British Columbia and Sex Discrimination

An in-depth study of human rights law at the local level is clearly needed. British Columbia has a history of being at the forefront of human rights innovation. It was one of the first jurisdictions to enact human rights legislation and the first to prohibit sex discrimination. It also set precedents in areas such as gay rights and sexual harassment. The province has historically possessed a diverse workforce in manufacturing and primary resources, and it has extraordinarily high rates of unionization. Between 1961 and 1968, the provincial labour force grew faster than in any other province. In 1981, two-thirds of all BC jobs were in service industries (up from one-quarter in 1911). Women worked many of these jobs, particularly the low-paid ones. Employment in healthcare, education, and government services expanded from 7.6 percent of the provincial labour force in 1941 to 18.5 percent in 1971; women held half of these jobs and accounted for 46 percent of unionized workers in these sectors.[49] By the early 1980s, a majority of adult women were working outside the home, and almost half the provincial labour force was female. The province was also a leading immigrant destination and the site of decades of conflict regarding Asian immigration. Vancouver was unlike other major Canadian cities such as Halifax, Montreal, and Toronto in that it had a small black population, but a large number of Indo-Canadians and Chinese Canadians. Ninety percent of Chinese immigrants to Canada lived in British Columbia. The province's demographics, labour force, and political culture informed many of the debates on human rights and undoubtedly contributed to the creation of remarkably progressive – and remarkably regressive – human rights laws.

Sex discrimination played a prominent role in the human rights state. In every Canadian jurisdiction, sex discrimination in the workplace represented the largest number of complaints received by human rights commissions for much of their history (except in Nova Scotia and Ontario, where slightly more complaints involved racial discrimination). It is perhaps not surprising that British Columbia was the first jurisdiction to prohibit discrimination on the basis of sex: the province has often led the country on women's issues. Historians Angus McLaren and Arlene Tigar McLaren point out that British Columbia "can claim to be the province in which the birth control movement in Canada was, thanks to Margaret Sanger's initial prodding, first launched."[50] Furthermore, in 1918, British Columbia was among the first provinces to elect women to public office after they had secured the right to vote (it was also the first province, in 1873, to enfranchise women for municipal elections). And it was in British Columbia in 1921 where a woman was appointed to cabinet for the first time in Canada's history, and in 1949, the legislature appointed the first female Speaker of the House. The BC legislation for mothers' pensions, introduced in 1920, was "the most progressive Mothers' Pension policy of its era in North America."[51] It was also the first province, in 1924, to legislate maternity leave for women. By the 1960s, women in British Columbia continued to lead the country on many fronts. According to Jean Barman, BC

> women were in the forefront in moving back out of the home, if not into the work-force at least to pursue further education. Not only did their fertility rate remain the lowest in Canada, but average age of marriage, while falling, was still the highest in English Canada. The province, alongside Ontario, possessed the lowest average number of children per family in 1966 at 1.7 compared with a high of 2.6 in Newfoundland.[52]

Social movements play a crucial role in the history of the human rights state and have been especially prominent in British Columbia. As McLaren and McLaren note, the province "served, in the early decades of the twentieth century, as a spawning ground for a host of radical movements." It "found itself with an aggressive and sophisticated trade union movement ... Vancouver, moreover, was home to an active women's movement and to a wide range of other reformist groups – theosophical lodges, the Women's Labour League, the Women's International League for Peace and Freedom, the Anti-Vaccination and Medical Freedom League – all seeking to ensure a better future."[53] In the 1960s, a period long associated with social activism in Canada and abroad, British Columbia was again a locus of engagement. It was host to the country's first gay rights organizations; the first gay pride parade; Greenpeace; widespread anti-war protests during the 1950s and 1960s; no less than twelve civil liberties groups and eleven Aboriginal advocacy groups (in both cases, more than in any other province except Ontario); and dramatic student protests.[54] Union density in British Columbia outgrew that of every other North American jurisdiction except Quebec: by 1972, more than 54 percent of workers were unionized.[55] The result was increased labour militancy. One of every three unionized workers walked the picket line in 1972.

In a province with a tradition of social movement activism, it is not surprising that the women's movement flourished. Women's groups – especially the Council of Women – played a prominent role in the campaign for mothers' pensions in 1920 and in their administration.[56] Women in Vancouver launched the Canadian birth control movement and, in 1939, the country's first branch of the Elizabeth Fry Society.[57] The Vancouver Council of Women was the second-largest of all the provincial councils by the 1950s. The BC branch of the Voice of Women contributed 40 percent of the national organization's budget in the 1960s, equal to its Ontario counterpart (the rest of Canada provided only 20 percent). By the mid-1970s, there were more than seventy-six local advocacy groups throughout the province. This was a remarkable increase from the 1960s, when the Voice of Women and the Council of Women were among its only women's rights groups. There were also at least forty-six women's centres, fifteen transition houses, twelve rape crisis centres, thirty-six service-oriented organizations (health centres, self-defence programs), and twenty artistic initiatives (women's music festivals, bookstores). None of these had existed before the 1970s. And this is a conservative estimate, which does not capture spontaneous grassroots protest activities, events such as Take Back the Night, or women's involvement in school boards and municipal councils. By the 1970s, the province hosted the country's first rape crisis centre, the first feminist newspaper *(Kinesis)*, the first transition house, the first black woman elected to a provincial legislature (Rosemary Brown), the only female member of Parliament from 1968 to 1972 (Grace McInnis), and one of the first women's liberation groups in the country (Vancouver Women's Caucus); as mentioned, it was also the first province to legislate against sex discrimination. It was also the first to fund rape relief centres, transition houses, and women's health collectives. The Vancouver Women's Caucus led the most visible protest against the abortion laws in Canadian history: a caravan carried a coffin from Vancouver to Ottawa to symbolize the deaths of women from backstreet abortions. In 1991, BC premier Rita Johnston, the first woman to lead a Canadian government, established the country's first stand-alone Ministry of Women's Equality.

Several observers have noted the unique radicalism of the BC women's movement at this time. There is no question that, much as the Voice of

Women and the Vancouver Council of Women were highly active, the Vancouver Status of Women was among the leading women's rights groups in Canada. Whereas lesbians struggled to gain recognition among mainstream feminist organizations in the 1970s, the British Columbia Federation of Women at least had a lesbian rights committee from its inception in 1974.[58] Jill Vickers suggests that "experience with right-wing governments in British Columbia ... has made Vancouver feminist groups much more anti-system than many of their eastern counterparts."[59] Rosemary Brown, who was herself a key figure in the BC women's movement during the 1970s, also recalled that "feminists in the rest of Canada looked on in disbelief at the audacity of the actions and pronouncements of the Vancouver Status of Women. It contributed to the Canadian myth of British Columbians as unusual, and although they admired our organization no province moved to duplicate it; all were convinced that such an organization could not survive outside BC."[60] No other jurisdiction perfectly combines a widespread and influential women's movement with a progressive (and regressive) human rights regime.

Although the following study focuses on sex discrimination and human rights law in British Columbia, it places the provincial human rights state in national and historical context. Chapter 1, for instance, provides a historical survey of federal and provincial legislation as it affected women in British Columbia. It is impossible to appreciate the impact of the human rights state without a clear understanding of how gender inequality was entrenched in law. Chapters 2 and 3 document the origins of the human rights state in Canada. Social movements, especially those of organized labour and Jewish activists, were at the vanguard of campaigns to ban discrimination on the basis of race, religion, and ethnicity. However, neither these campaigns nor the legislation they spawned included sex discrimination. The only recognition for women came in the form of weak equal pay laws.

Chapters 4 to 9 are divided by key periods of human rights legal innovation in British Columbia. The province's first anti-discrimination law was the 1953 Equal Pay Act, which was soon followed with legislation banning discrimination in employment and accommodation. Certainly, this was an important stage in the evolution of the human rights state, but as Chapter 4 (1953-69) reveals, these laws were largely ineffective. Chapter 5 (1969-73) examines the next stage in the genesis of the province's human rights state. The Socred Human Rights Act of 1969 was a notable milestone: British Columbia became the first province to add sex to its list of prohibited grounds of discrimination. But the poor design and weak enforcement of the legislation quickly became apparent. The NDP government's 1973 Human Rights Code, however, transformed the human rights state in British Columbia. Chapter 6 explains why it was remarkable for its time and explores the first five years after its enactment, when Kathleen Ruff was director of the Human Rights Branch. Ruff created a separate agency to deal with complaints – the Human Rights Branch – hired the province's first human rights investigators, developed procedures for filing and scrutinizing complaints, and fostered productive relationships with social movements. This was a period of genuine innovation as the fledgling branch struggled to confront many issues such as sexual harassment. Chapter 7 examines the period of Ruff's successors (1979-83), who presided over a dramatic expansion of the human rights state. It discusses the branch's increasing reliance on social movements, the effort to define a role for the Human Rights Commission, and the attempt to extend the human rights state into rural British Columbia. Chapter 8 reveals how the province set key precedents in human rights law while simultaneously acknowledging its limitations, especially with respect to equal pay. Finally, Chapter 9 chronicles the human rights state under attack, describing developments throughout Canada and demonstrating that the Social Credit government – re-elected in 1975 – disdained the law and did everything in its power to restrict its enforcement. Chapter 9 also examines the Socreds' 1984 Human Rights Act to compare competing visions for the human rights state. The dispute over the human rights state in British Columbia became a national issue, as the entire country debated the legitimacy of the province's reforms. In this way, the history of the human rights state in British Columbia constitutes an ideal case study for Canada, if for no other reason than because it was the epicentre of a conflict on the nature and legitimacy of the human rights state.

I
Sex Discrimination in Canadian Law

> *By marriage, the husband and wife are one person in law: that is, the very being of legal existence of the woman is suspended during the marriage, or at least is incorporated and consolidated into that of the husband ... A man cannot grant anything to his wife, or enter into covenant with her: for the grant would be to suppose her separate existence; and to covenant with her, would only be to covenant with himself ... The husband also, by the old law, might give his wife moderate correction.*
>
> – William Blackstone, Commentaries on the Laws of England

At the birth of the human rights state in the mid-twentieth century, the unequal treatment of Canada's female citizens was pervasive and entrenched in law. The law reflected common sense notions about gender and women's roles in public and private life. Male legislators created laws that restricted women's opportunities and choices or imposed greater obligations on them. Nineteenth-century law often gave husbands control over their wives. Alternatively, some laws "privileged" women, such as protective labour laws that provided opportunities for women that did not exist for men. However, they were rooted in the belief that women were dependants or defined them as mothers whose reproductive responsibilities needed regulation. In other words, they marginalized women in the workforce and promulgated unequal gender roles.

The widespread legal discrimination against women in British Columbian and federal law provides the context for the emergence of the human rights state. And yet, even a survey of statute law as it affected women in British Columbia does not capture those social and economic policies such as taxation, prisons, social assistance, or healthcare that also contributed to gender inequality. Nonetheless, reforms in statute law were an essential precursor to the human rights state. In British Columbia, these reforms occurred in two stages, which reflected similar developments across Canada. The first phase, from the nineteenth century to the mid-twentieth century, addressed fundamental rights of *citizenship*. The most visible campaign for reform was for the female franchise, but there were also changes to the law on property and work. However, legal distinctions based on gender were still prevalent, and a renewed effort for legal reform sprang up in the mid-twentieth century. This second phase was designed to achieve *formal legal equality*. By the 1980s, most of the explicit legal distinctions based on gender had been eliminated from statute law.

Equal Citizenship

Under the law, women in nineteenth-century Canada were denied even the most fundamental rights. Before universal suffrage was granted, women sometimes voted, usually if they were property owners, but they were gradually disenfranchised as the nineteenth century progressed. In 1832, Prince Edward Island became the first colony in British North America to prohibit them from voting, followed by New Brunswick (1836), the Canadas (1849), and Nova Scotia (1851).[1] Female property-owners (single or widowed) could vote for school trustees as early as 1850 in Ontario and in BC municipal elections as of 1873.[2] And they could serve on school boards: the first woman elected to a BC school board held office in 1901 (however, between 1913 and 1922, the Public Schools Act banned women from serving as school trustees in rural districts).[3] Otherwise, until 1920 the provinces determined eligibility for voting in federal elections, and no province allowed women to vote (nonetheless, the Dominion Elections Act of 1906 insisted that "no woman, lunatic or criminal shall vote").[4] Women could also be denied the franchise because they belonged to a certain class of people. British Columbia disenfranchised men and women of Chinese and Aboriginal descent in 1874, a restriction that eventually applied to Japanese people (1895) and East Indians (1907); teachers were banned from voting between 1878 and 1883, and civil servants could not vote between 1899 and 1900. Between 1914 and 1946, women who married non-citizens lost their citizenship, and Ottawa disenfranchised Japanese Canadians in 1946. British Columbia even denied the right to vote to Doukhobours (1931), Hutterites (1947), and Mennonites (1947).

Because they could not vote, women were unable to become legislators, coroners, magistrates, or judges. Not a single woman was appointed as judge, coroner, justice of the peace, police constable, or police magistrate in the nineteenth century. In 1905, a New Brunswick Supreme Court judge, reflecting on the role of women in society, insisted that "the paramount destiny and mission of women are to fulfil the noble and benign offices of wife and mother. This is the law of the Creator."[5] Universal suffrage was first granted in 1916 in Manitoba, and British Columbia followed soon afterward in 1917.[6] With the vote came the right to run for public office. Women were elected for the first time to the British Columbia Legislative Assembly (1918) and Vancouver City Council (1937). Mary Ellen Smith, elected in 1918, was also the first woman in the Commonwealth appointed to cabinet, in 1921.[7]

The franchise also offered the opportunity for (white) women to become more active in public life, although most provinces continued to ban them from serving on juries or allowed them an exemption based on their gender. In the nineteenth century, law societies prohibited women from becoming lawyers, partly because they were not deemed "persons" under the constitution, which also prevented them from serving as senators. British Columbia passed legislation in 1877 to prevent women from working in mines, and it regulated their work above ground (by determining their hours and meal breaks).[8] Explicit legal restrictions on women in occupations were admittedly rare. Nonetheless, "they acted in the name of protecting women from especially dangerous working conditions as well as particularly long hours and night work. Even though these measures were not well enforced, they reinforced the notion that certain jobs were solely for men."[9]

Slowly, access to professions began to open. In 1912, when a BC court rejected Mabel French's attempt to practise law in the province, even though she had been admitted to the New Brunswick bar six years earlier, the legislature had to pass a statute to permit women to become lawyers.[10] By 1926, only Quebec still prohibited women from practising law, a restriction it maintained until 1940. Meanwhile, women were still unable to become senators, because the constitution restricted senate appointments to "qualified persons," a description that was assumed to apply solely to men. The Supreme Court of Canada affirmed in 1928 that women were not eligible, but the Judicial Committee of the Privy Council overruled the decision and determined in 1929 that women were indeed "persons," as stated in the constitution.[11] By this period, women were challenging barriers in all sorts of ways. In British Columbia, for the first time in provincial history, they became a licensed pilot (1929), an ordained United Church of Canada minister (1940), a broadcaster at a Vancouver radio station (1942), and a lifeguard on a Vancouver beach (1943). The BC government also appointed the first female parliamentary Speaker in the Commonwealth in 1949.

In addition to depriving women of the vote and access to certain professions, nineteenth-century law denied them basic property rights. "Marriage," as one historian has described the legal reality for women under nineteenth-century common law, "meant civil death."[12] A woman lost her legal status when she married, and her husband was assumed to control her person. She also took on his nationality and domicile upon marriage. Under the common law, he controlled her earnings and could prohibit her from working for wages. He could legally rape her, confine her, and mete out physical punishment, or "discipline." Until the 1850s, he owned the family farm, including everything in the home; in 1876, Canada's Dominion Lands Act also proscribed married women from homesteading (single women were barred as well).[13] Without property, women could not hope to support themselves independently of their husbands. A lifetime of work on the farm did not ensure a woman any degree of ownership when her husband died; in fact, the land usually went to the son (leaving her dependent on her children), and a widow could lose any claim to property if she remarried.[14] A married woman had no control over property. Her income and profits belonged to her husband; she could not be sued and could not contract with or sue another person in her own name; her husband's consent was required for her to start a business; and all her personal property (including wages) transferred to him. In return, a husband was liable for his wife's debts and contracts.[15] In a 1913 speech before the Local Council of Women, Vancouver lawyer F.G.T. Lucas explained that, although a husband was obliged to support and maintain his family, his obligation was "more moral than legal. There has never been and there is not now any legal obligation on the part of the father to maintain his wife and children unless neglect to do so should bring the case within the Criminal Code."[16]

Legal reform was incremental.[17] On Vancouver Island, an 1862 statute protected the property and wages of a deserted wife from her husband's creditors (as long as she demonstrated her chaste and moral character, and refrained from entering into a relationship with another man).[18] The Homestead Act, passed in 1865, permitted couples to protect up to $2,500 in property from creditors, a provision that was later amended to allow a widow to keep the property for the duration of her children's minority as long as she did not remarry.[19] A far more comprehensive Married Women's Property Act became law in 1873 (following Ontario's precedent of a year earlier), permitting a wife to hold and dispose of any property she brought to the marriage or acquired thereafter, including any profits deriving from the property.[20] Any wages she earned *separately from her husband* belonged to her. She could also become a stockholder in a company, deposit her own money in a bank, and write her own cheques. At the same time, the law protected her husband against any debts arising from her property before marriage, and it immunized him from liability for debts she incurred from her business or employment. Property law was not "motivated by any desire to emancipate women ... Formal legal equality did not challenge the economic and social inequality central to nineteenth century marriage."[21]

Nineteenth-century law not only denied women property rights, it deprived them of rights over their children. Helen Gregory MacGill, the famous Vancouver Juvenile Court judge, wrote in 1913 that "domestic legislation can scarcely be called modern or reasonable."[22] Fathers determined their children's education and religion. A man could disinherit his wife; children were his sole property; he could consent to the marriage of his twelve-year-old daughter without his wife's consent; he could appoint a guardian for children under seven years old without the mother's consent (nor was her consent required after their seventh birthday unless they were sent "beyond the seas"); a father inherited the estates of all children under twenty-one; and in his will, he could even appoint a guardian for his children, including those born after his death. In those rare circumstances when a woman left her husband, custody battles often favoured him. As Constance Backhouse notes in her seminal study of nineteenth-century law,

> Women were subordinate to men, and children were subordinate to adults. Within this vision, children were, for all practical purposes, regarded as property or economic assets, which could gainfully contribute to household production or family income through waged labour. Since the male head of the household generally controlled family property, it seemed only logical that he should have sole authority and control over the children.[23]

Only in extreme cases involving abuse would a judge have taken children from their father.

In 1897, following Ontario's 1855 precedent, British Columbia passed the Guardians Appointment Act. The legislation authorized judges to grant mothers custody of children under seven years old, and to grant custody even in cases where the father had specified in his will that a different guardian be appointed after his death.[24] Women who had committed adultery, though, were automatically denied custody. Nineteenth-century law did not provide any relief for women and children abandoned by the father, except for the 1862 Vancouver Island statute that conferred limited rights on women after abandonment. In the 1910s, however, many provinces introduced legislation for deserted wives and children. British Columbia's Deserted Wives Act (1911) empowered a magistrate to order a husband to provide money to his wife for her basic necessities if he abandoned or severely beat her.[25] Once again, women who had committed adultery could not sue for maintenance.

Several other family law reforms were implemented in the early twentieth century. As of 1914, a woman could gain custody of her children if her husband was living permanently outside the province or if the courts declared him to be a lunatic.[26] In 1917, British Columbia was the first province to enact legislation that provided mothers with rights and obligations equal to those of fathers for the care, custody, and education of their children.[27] In 1920, the legislature also enacted a statute for mothers' pensions that was among the most progressive in North America. Introduced in Alberta, British Columbia, Manitoba, Ontario, and Saskatchewan between 1916 and 1920, the laws conferred "pensions" (in British Columbia) or "allowances" (elsewhere) to support women who were raising young children.[28] The BC legislation allowed widows, unwed and divorced mothers, and those whose husband was imprisoned, incapacitated, or had deserted them to collect pensions. It afforded some of the most generous grants in North America, and it included a discretionary clause allowing the superintendent to include anyone deemed worthy of assistance.[29] Nonetheless, mothers' pensions defined women as nurturers, mothers, and dependants. They were discontinued when children turned sixteen.[30]

BC law provided few protections for dower rights.[31] To address instances when men died without a will (intestate), or a will did not provide for the proper maintenance of a widow and/or her children, the 1920 Testator's Family Maintenance Bill allowed a judge to redistribute the proceeds of an estate.[32] However, a 1924 amendment to the Administration Act prevented a woman from inheriting her intestate husband's property if she had left him and was committing adultery or if she had left him "without cause" at least two years before his death.[33] In 1922, the BC government passed the Children of Unmarried Parents Act, which permitted the superintendent of neglected children to take custody of children born out of wedlock, to legitimize children of unmarried parents, and to sue the father for the cost of maintenance. The law also allowed the father to enter into a private agreement with the superintendent to provide support without acknowledging his paternity (perhaps to encourage married men to secretly support their illegitimate children).[34] Similar laws were passed in other Canadian jurisdictions in the late nineteenth century to remove children from the custody of abusive parents. Finally, in 1924, the province set a Canadian precedent with An Act Respecting the Employment of Women Before and After Childbirth.[35] It provided women with basic maternity leave from work (before and after birth) and prohibited employers from dismissing a woman because of her absence to give birth.

British Columbia's unprecedented maternity leave legislation represented a broad shift in the law, which was slowly adapting to the harsh realities of an industrial economy. Farm wives received little credit or recognition for their work: in the census, they were listed as having no occupation. As industry expanded, women entered the paid labour force in increasing numbers. They often did piecework at home or were hired to work in "garment industries, textile factories (cotton, wool, and silk), boot, shoe, tobacco, book-binding, and leather manufacturers, and canning plants for fish, fruit and vegetables."[36] In 1901, 16 percent of Canada's female population above the age of fifteen worked in this way; in 1931, this figure had increased to 22 percent and to 23 percent in 1941.[37] By the 1940s, a growing number of women were employed in white-collar professions, especially teaching, nursing, social work, clerical work, and retail sales. True, the law did not prohibit them from entering male professions. It did not need to. A gendered division of labour emerged that largely segregated men and women, with women's work seen as an extension of their traditional labour at home. In the case of male professions, "employers would not hire them, and women themselves would not apply because they shared the conventional assumptions that they were by nature unsuited to such work."[38]

The law directly contributed to marginalizing women in the workforce. The Vancouver Local Council of Women determined in 1914 that a young woman needed at minimum ten dollars per week to survive; the average female shop or factory worker earned only three to seven dollars weekly, and many women made as little as a dollar a week.[39] They invariably earned less for doing the same jobs as men, or they were concentrated in certain occupations and paid less. British Columbia was the second province, after Alberta, to introduce a female minimum wage law in 1918, followed soon after by the other provinces except New Brunswick and Prince Edward Island (Alberta had implemented the same minimum wage for men and women in 1917).[40] However, it excluded farm workers and domestics, who made up almost half the female labour force. The law allowed lower pay (often no more than half the minimum wage) for women who were under eighteen, inexperienced, or "physically defective."[41] The female minimum wage was also kept lower than that of men. Women comprised approximately 19 percent of Vancouver's labour force by 1931 and earned 56 percent of the average male wage.[42] To make matters worse, during the Great Depression many were banned outright from receiving municipal relief. In 1930, only 155 women (rising to 900 in 1933) were on Vancouver's relief rolls, compared to 9,757 men.[43] Many politicians reasoned that as long as domestic service jobs were available to single healthy women, they should be denied relief. In February 1939, Vancouver City Council went so far as to introduce a resolution to prohibit married women from paid work in stores, offices, and factories.[44]

Protective labour legislation was another form of legal discrimination. As Ruth Frager and Carmela Patrias point out, it represented a dichotomy for reformers: "Those female activists who were particularly concerned about the plight of women workers spearheaded a debate that continues to engage feminists to this day: was full legal equality the only means to ensure the equality of women in society, or was differential legal treatment called for since women are the bearers of children?"[45] Most female employees in the nineteenth century were young and unmarried, often working in factories with no lunchrooms or even washrooms (or sometimes sharing washrooms with men). In the 1880s, Ontario and Quebec introduced their first laws to protect women and child workers on the basis "that female workers needed greater protection than male workers because of their presumed physical frailty and moral vulnerability."[46] British Columbia's Factories Act was passed in 1908.[47] In addition to restricting children to certain types of work (such as canning fish), it contained several provisions dealing with female employees: they were to be provided with a seat for any work that could be performed while seated; "resilient material" was to cover concrete flooring if their work required constant standing; they could not eat near machinery or clean it while it was in motion; and their work was limited to eight hours a day or forty-eight hours per week, with one hour at noon every day for a break (and no night shifts).[48] Employers could be imprisoned or fined for treating female staff in any way that might adversely affect their health. The need for protective labour legislation for women was routinely framed in terms of their reproductive capabilities. According to Helena Gutteridge, one of the most celebrated feminists in British Columbia, "short hours are far more essential to women than they are to men ... The injurious physical and mental effects of such work are plainly visible ... and the rapid aging of the working women has its injurious effects on the next generation."[49]

Rather than genuinely protecting women, such laws defined them as a dependent category of workers who required state regulation. As Frager and Patrias state,

> The emphasis on protecting women's childbearing capacities buttressed the view that women's primary role was as the bearers and rearers of children and hence that their participation in the paid labour force was temporary and of secondary importance. The protective labour laws also reinforced gender segregation in the workplace by underlining the presumed differences between male and female workers. The law legitimated the view that there were certain types of jobs that women could not do.[50]

In this way, although state legislation may have vitiated some of the harshest workplace conditions, it more probably restricted women's access to the paid labour force.

At times, protective labour laws went to extremes. Between 1912 and 1919, Saskatchewan banned "Chinese, Japanese or other Oriental persons" from employing white women.[51] Manitoba (1913) and Ontario (1914) implemented a similar measure, as did British Columbia, with a 1919 amendment to the Municipal Act.[52] Even more extraordinary was British Columbia's 1924 Act for the Protection of Women and Girls in Certain Cases. In essence, it empowered a chief of municipal police, by the simple expedient of posting a certificate in his office, to prohibit any employer from providing lodging for or hiring an Indian woman or white woman if the police deemed that doing so might undermine "the morals of such women and girls."[53] A year later, following a sensational murder case involving a Chinese male and a white woman, MLA Mary Ellen Smith introduced legislation to ban households from employing Chinese men and white women simultaneously (the law was later found unconstitutional).[54] Restrictions on women's participation in the labour force were not always clearly spelled out in statute law but were nonetheless implemented through agencies of the state. In 1914, a *Vancouver Sun* editorial criticized the Vancouver Police Court for sending a man to jail for one year because he showed an "indecent" photograph to a young woman working at a cigar stand. The newspaper insisted that it was "contrary to the moral good of the public that girls should fill these positions." In response, the Board of License Commissioners passed an order banning female employment in cigar stands. Women who owned and worked at cigar stands immediately "created a stir by threatening to publicly horsewhip the editor unless their jobs and businesses were restored ... By mid-March a compromise had been hammered out, and cigar stand proprietors were advised that they could 'hire only male help should one of the girls voluntarily resign.'"[55]

Minority women experienced discrimination as both women and minorities. British Columbia went to extraordinary lengths to deny visible minorities the right to vote: the first law passed after the province joined Confederation barred First Nations and Chinese people from registering their vital statistics under the Registration of Birth, Deaths, and Marriages Act (this information was used to create lists of eligible voters). As Timothy J. Stanley explains, "race joined gender as one of the readily visible, easily determinable markers of alleged fitness to participate in the public realm."[56] Few provinces outdid British Columbia in attempting to discourage visible minorities from emigrating to Canada. A head tax implemented in 1885 prohibited Chinese women from entering the country. Those who did reach British Columbia often faced major obstacles in securing employment and were usually restricted to working in small restaurants, laundries, or fish canneries. Aboriginal women worked in canneries as well, although at lower pay and with fewer hours than men. Those few Aboriginal girls who did attend school were segregated according to race. Prostitution laws targeted Chinese and Aboriginal people.[57] Chinese prostitutes were explicitly banned under the 1885 head tax legislation, and in the 1880s Parliament passed a series of laws to impose harsher sentences and lower evidentiary standards for Aboriginal prostitutes.[58] The 1880 Indian Act prohibited the owner of a house from allowing Aboriginal prostitutes on the premises and applied tougher penalties to keepers of bawdy houses.[59] African Canadian women throughout Canada struggled to find jobs other than as domestics.[60] Retail sales work was simply not an option for most visible minority women. Jewish women found themselves unable to get hired at Eaton's or Woodward's, and women who did not come from Anglo-Celtic backgrounds might also find office work barred to them. In fact, white-collar work in general was usually off-limits to minority women, unless perhaps a segregated school needed to hire a black teacher.[61] Racism also infected state policy. Fears surrounding the rising numbers of visible minorities led the BC government to restrict funding for Asians by requiring British citizenship or English-language proficiency.[62]

Finally, sex discrimination was also integral to criminal law. In her study of women and nineteenth-century law, Backhouse documents their "differential treatment and prejudice within the irrefutably male legal system."[63] Criminal law reflected an almost obsessive need to regulate female sexuality. In 1892, for example, the Criminal Code prohibited an employer or manager from seducing a female employee who was under his direction. In 1900, the clause was extended from factories, mills, and workshops to apply to shops and stores, and then to all places of work in 1920.[64] Chastity laws were introduced in the nineteenth century, and the practice of separately incarcerating female convicts was common by the 1870s. In 1910, the federal government also deemed it necessary to prohibit contact between female immigrants and male crew members during a sea voyage.[65] It was also a crime, as of 1918, for a woman with a venereal disease to have sex or solicit sex with a member of the armed forces.[66]

Women were usually arrested for drunkenness, petty theft, and vagrancy.[67] Vagrancy laws targeted them for prostitution, punishing them rather than their customers.[68] Between 1810 and 1847, Montreal police arrested more than 2,500 women for vagrancy but only 1,300 or so men, who usually received more lenient sentences.[69] By the early twentieth century, prostitutes faced increasingly harsher sentences and sweeping prohibitions.[70] Parliament amended the Criminal Code in 1913 so that abducting an immigrant girl for a brothel, exerting control over a woman for prostitution, and concealing a woman in a bawdy house became illegal. The enforcement of the law was also gendered. In 1924, as Amanda Glasbeek explains, Helen Gregory MacGill

> lamented the bad enforcement of a good law to the readers of *Social Welfare*: How curious that usually male patrons are allowed to go, or to pay their forfeitable bails or fines, even when taken in the same raid where the women are required to submit to medical examination ... The pity of it is that both man and woman should not stand at least equal in the eyes of the law.[71]

In rape trials, which were rare in nineteenth-century Canada, judges and juries favoured women who fit a model of chastity. A woman's sexual history was often a key issue at trial: "The message was explicit ... Women who were raped could expect little sympathy from criminal courts ... For women whose sexual lives were condemned by nineteenth century mores, this meant that they would never obtain legal protection from rape, regardless of what rhetoric the law professed."[72] Chastity was also an issue in seduction, which Parliament criminalized in 1886. Previously, seduction had been a civil crime, a fact that permitted fathers to sue men who had "carnal knowledge" of their daughters. If the daughter were pregnant, and the man refused to marry her, the fathers would sue for the cost of maintaining both mother and child, which essentially meant "asserting parental property interests in the sexual behaviour of their female offspring."[73] This law (except in Quebec) recognized only the father's right to sue, not the woman who had been seduced. When seduction was criminalized, a man who had sex with a girl between the ages of twelve and sixteen could be sent to jail for two years. In 1887, the law was changed so that men under twenty-one years old could not be prosecuted for seduction even though women could not press a charge of seduction if they were over eighteen years old. And the law applied only to women who could prove that they were of previously chaste character, and that the sexual act was committed under the promise of marriage.[74]

Criminal law regarding infanticide and abortion also targeted women. Murdering a child was a felony, but when the cause of death could not be established as homicide, convicting the mother was virtually impossible. So, male legislators in British North America passed laws between 1810 and 1840, allowing prosecutors to substitute a verdict of "concealment of birth" when a mother was acquitted of murdering her newborn, a crime that carried a punishment of two years in jail. But this measure was generally ineffective, partly because guilt was difficult to prove and because male judges or juries sympathized with female defendants.[75] Still, British Columbia inherited this criminal legal regime when it joined Confederation in 1871. An 1892 amendment to the Criminal Code also criminalized "failing to obtain reasonable assistance for childbirth," an offence that carried the severe sentence of life imprisonment if a prosecutor could prove that a woman had deliberately not sought assistance so that the child would die.[76] Procuring an abortion became a crime in British North America in New Brunswick in 1810, and soon afterward the other colonies followed suit; previously, under common law, abortion was not illegal if it occurred before the fetus quickened (became capable of movement). Abortion trials were infrequent during the nineteenth century, but the vast majority produced a guilty verdict.[77] If the abortion predated quickening, the abortionist could be sent to jail for several years; an abortion after quickening was punishable by death. By the 1850s, the distinction regarding quickening had been eliminated. The death penalty was also removed, although doctors faced severe punishment, which ranged from more than a decade in jail to life in prison. In New Brunswick and Nova Scotia, a woman who obtained an abortion committed a criminal offence. When British Columbia joined Confederation, the federal government had incorporated all of these far-ranging provisions into the Criminal Code. In 1892, it went even further and banned the sale, distribution, and advertisement of any material relating to contraception or abortion.

Despite reforms in several areas, whether voting or property rights, women and men were not equal before the law. It restricted women's opportunities to work and was infused by a desire to regulate their sexuality (or to impose a sexual double standard in cases of adultery). Protective labour legislation was in many ways a misnomer.[78] It constructed women as mothers, nurturers, dependants, and second-class workers. Women challenged legal discrimination and achieved some notable successes during this period, albeit often to the benefit of a privileged few. Many women who demanded the right to vote or mothers' pensions simultaneously advocated denying similar rights to minorities. Minority women suffered even further marginalization as a result of legislation targeting racial and religious groups. For instance, the law did not recognize First Nations women's cultural traditions, and the Indian Act contained explicit provisions that discriminated against women.

The legacy of nineteenth-century law is best exemplified in divorce. Marriage and divorce law was premised on male dominance in the family: a husband "was entitled to [his wife's] sexual services and could use the courts to seek compensation from anyone having sexual relations with her, encouraging her to leave him, or providing her sanctuary if she did leave him."[79] Nineteenth-century law in Upper and Lower Canada made it virtually impossible to divorce: in Upper Canada, an act of Parliament was required, and in Lower Canada, marriage was indissoluble until death![80] A man who wished to secure a divorce could do so by proving that his wife had committed adultery; the wife had to prove adultery as well as desertion without reason, extreme cruelty, incest, or bigamy. Judges often applied a cruel double standard, blaming wives for giving up too quickly if they left a spouse after one incident of abuse, or alternatively accusing battered wives of accepting or encouraging the abuse if they waited too long. BC law reflected the same double standard, although in 1877, the province began to adopt a practice from the Maritime provinces of establishing divorce courts (rather than requiring an act of the legislature). Women could also seek damages and separation rather than divorce. When they did secure a divorce, they often faced ostracism and poverty. Divorce law would remain largely unchanged in Canada until the late 1960s.[81]

By the twentieth century, the law touched on almost every aspect of women's lives: birth (infanticide), childhood (maintenance, child custody), work (labour laws, professions), courtship (seduction, marriage), sexual relations (rape, prostitution), marriage (property), parenting (maternity leave, abortion, adoption, legitimacy), divorce or separation (maintenance, child custody, pensions, desertion), and death (inheritance). Even after decades of reforms, the law reinforced male privilege and patriarchal power in the family. To be sure, many reformers, including feminists and male legislators, were sincerely devoted to advancing women's rights and gender equality. Nevertheless, nineteenth- and early-twentieth-century legal reform should be seen primarily as an attempt to maintain traditional gender roles. And the fact that it benefitted white middle-class women should not be forgotten. In his exhaustive account of nineteenth- and early-twentieth-century legal reform as it affected women in British Columbia, Chris Clarkson asserts that BC "legislation was dedicated to three constant objectives: providing political and economic opportunities to settlers, expanding the liberal-capitalist economy, and encouraging the formation of white, heterosexual nuclear families in order to stimulate population growth."[82]

Formal Legal Equality

By the mid-twentieth century, women were no longer prohibited from voting or owning property unless they belonged to a minority group such as Aboriginal peoples.[83] British Columbia's 1931 Sex Disqualification (Removal) Act reaffirmed that, by virtue of marriage or sex, no person would be disqualified from a profession or holding public office.[84] In 1953, all references to race were removed from provincial electoral law, and in 1960, Ottawa enfranchised Aboriginal people. But the sudden absence of a legal prohibition did not vitiate the legacy of generations of legal discrimination. Between 1919 and 1972, women never held more than 5 percent of seats in the House of Commons, and by 1972, only 10 percent of the provincial legislature was female (as it turned out, 10 percent between 1972 and 1975 was actually a high point for the next twenty years).[85] Not until 1973 did women constitute more than 20 percent of enrolments in law schools, albeit less than 5 percent of practising lawyers were female; by 1986, only 22 percent of lawyers were women, and the first appointment of a woman to the Supreme Court of Canada was in 1982.[86] In fact, university enrolment in general remained stubbornly low for women. In 1920, there were 3,716 female university graduates in Canada, compared with 19,580 male graduates; in 1960, the ratio was 26,629 to 80,582; and by 1975, there were 140,268 female and 190,696 male university graduates.[87]

Women born in British Columbia during the 1940s inherited an inadequate, outdated, and patronizing legal regime for property, labour, family, and criminal law. An Industrial Home for Girls Act, introduced in 1912, created institutions for the "custody and detention, with a view to their education, industrial training, and moral reclamation, of such girls as are lawfully committed for detention therein."[88] The legislature passed a law in 1933 to forcibly sterilize people who were mentally ill (only Alberta had similar legislation). In practice, the law disproportionately targeted women and Aboriginal people.[89] That the state continued to define women in terms of rigid gender roles in the 1960s was exemplified in a 1966 federal Department of Citizenship and Immigration publication, which explained that "winter weather is a limiting factor [for Canadian women's political activity] as well as household duties and farm chores."[90]

Nonetheless, another phase of legal reform, oriented toward the elimination of formal legal distinctions based on gender, was under way by the 1940s. The BC mothers' pension was replaced with the federal family allowance in 1944. The latter imposed less scrutiny on women, and the money went directly to them. Jury duty was still a predominantly male activity even after the province removed its ban against women in 1964 (following Ontario and Manitoba in 1951).[91] British Columbia remained the only jurisdiction with legislation for maternity leave (1924) until New Brunswick and the federal government followed suit in 1964 and 1971.[92] The Married Women's Property Act and the Factories Act were largely unchanged, although the sterilization legislation was repealed. Differential minimum wage laws had been revoked in Alberta, Manitoba, New Brunswick, Ontario, Quebec, and Saskatchewan by 1970, but they remained in force in British Columbia. The Industrial Home for Girls Act and the Women and Girls Protection Act were repealed in 1963 and 1968, respectively, and the Family Relations Act was amended in 1972 to remove the differing obligations placed on wives and husbands.[93] Women and men were given equal legal responsibility for maintaining their children, and both wives and husbands were permitted to sue for alimony or maintenance.[94]

The situation facing Aboriginal women remained bleak.[95] When they secured the right to run for band leadership in 1951, the final legal barrier to women running for office had been removed. However, they continued to face discrimination under the Indian Act. In addition to the innumerable provisions of the original statute that discriminated against all Aboriginal people (e.g., up to one month in jail for being drunk off-reserve), the 1887 legislation gave the superintendent-general of Indian Affairs the power to "stop the payment of the annuity and interest money of ... any woman who has no children, and who deserts her husband and lives immorally with another man."[96] The 1887 Indian Act further specified that Aboriginal widows must be of "moral character" to inherit property. The most contentious section was the provision that Aboriginal women lost their Indian status if they married a non-Aboriginal male. The same did not apply to men; in fact, Aboriginal men could confer status on their wives. When they lost their status, Aboriginal women forfeited their right to live on Aboriginal lands, own band property, inherit land or a house on a reserve, and to be buried on a reserve (yet, as one observer has noted, non-Aboriginals could bury dead dogs in a pet cemetery on a reserve).[97] Nor could they regain their status, and therefore return home, if their marriage dissolved or they divorced. This provision, which remained in place until 1985, was just one of the many forms of sex discrimination under the Indian Act that survived until the mid-1980s: if a status Indian man was enfranchised, his wife and children involuntarily were as well; his wife automatically belonged to his band even if she came from another; illegitimate children of Aboriginal descent were denied status; and children lost status when they reached the age of twenty-one if their mother did not have status before her marriage.[98]

In the 1960s, perhaps the most profound legal reform as it related to woman occurred in the area of divorce. Canada's draconian divorce laws had remained largely unchanged since the nineteenth century. The 1968 federal Divorce Act expanded the grounds for divorce beyond adultery to homosexuality, physical and mental cruelty, and marriage breakdown (causes of breakdown included a jail term, drug or alcohol addiction, a three-year separation, non-consummation, and desertion).[99] It streamlined the divorce application process and reduced costs and delays, which had been a particular hardship for women. Canada's divorce rate doubled during the first year following the Divorce Act, and most of those flocking to the courts were women.[100] However, the law was not a panacea. In a report for British Columbia's Provincial Status of Women coordinator, Lynne Pearson recalled that many of the women she interviewed "talked about how they or their friends had gone through a separation and divorce and discovered that they had no idea of the legal rights and responsibilities related to marriage. They had assumed, as well, that they would receive half of any matrimonial property, even though their name might not be on the title."[101]

Meanwhile, the federal government appointed the Royal Commission on the Status of Women (RCSW) in 1967. The RCSW identified a plethora of discriminatory laws. According to the commissioners, "Canadian citizens have not been equal before the law or been treated equally in its application."[102] Some of the more blatant forms of sex discrimination identified in the commission's report, which was published in 1970, included the following:

- Women were banned from enlisting in the Royal Canadian Mounted Police. Moreover, women in the military were, in practice, restricted to certain low-level trades, and those with children were released from service. They were not admitted to military colleges.
- Minimum wage: Like Newfoundland, Nova Scotia, and Prince Edward Island, British Columbia maintained separate minimum wage scales for men and women (its Industrial Relations Board began enforcing the same minimum wage for men and women in 1971, and the separate wage scale for women was repealed in 1972).
- National housing loan regulations: When lending institutions determined debt service for married couples, they assumed that the husband would own the property.
- Passports: Federal law required a woman to secure a new passport when she married, which had to use her husband's surname. She could request that her maiden name appear instead but nonetheless had to give her husband's name on the passport. (He did not have to indicate her name.)
- In most provinces, including British Columbia, before the 1968 Divorce Act married women were not allowed to have a separate legal domicile.
- The provinces and Ottawa had "maintenance laws" that required fathers to support wives and children. Only in Alberta and Yukon were wives obliged to support their husbands, and only British Columbia, Manitoba, Ontario, and Quebec imposed equal obligations on wives to support children under the age of sixteen.
- Citizenship: Until 1947, a woman who married a non-citizen and adopted his citizenship lost her Canadian citizenship. By 1970, wives of non-citizens were experiencing longer wait times to secure their husband's citizenship; their children did not automatically receive Canadian citizenship; when families applied for citizenship for a minor, only the father's citizenship was recognized; and adoptions favoured

fathers in determining citizenship. Policies implemented under the Immigration Act presumed that, when couples applied for citizenship, women were dependants and men were heads of the household.
- Jury duty: Newfoundland and Quebec banned women from serving on juries; Alberta, New Brunswick, Nova Scotia, and Saskatchewan allowed them to opt out of service solely because of their gender (or required them to nominate themselves to be placed on the jury list).
- Prisons: The federal Prisons and Reformatories Act discriminated on the basis of sex in determining age for sentencing, the type of immutable offences, and the length of sentence. In some provinces, a woman's religion determined the type of institution in which she would serve her sentence.
- Under the Canada and Quebec Pension Plans, the husband and children of a female pension contributor were not entitled to the pension if she died unless she was disabled or declared a dependant. Under the federal civil service pension plan, a widow received benefits if her husband died, but the same did not apply to the husband of a deceased female civil servant.
- Provincial workmen's compensation laws applied to wives of deceased men, but not to husbands of deceased women.
- Unemployment insurance: The unemployment insurance program did not consider men as dependants. In addition, before they applied for unemployment insurance, pregnant women were required to work longer than ordinary applicants.

The RCSW study of criminal law was especially revealing. Women were most commonly convicted for theft, prostitution or keeping a bawdy house, abortion or attempted abortion, infanticide, concealing the body of a child, and child neglect. Their convictions for narcotics offences, vagrancy, and attempted suicide disproportionately outnumbered those for other crimes.[103] The Criminal Code did not consider them capable of committing sexual offences except incest, buggery, indecent assault on another female, and gross indecency (the latter was added in 1954). Women could not sexually assault or seduce men, or be charged for having illegal sex with a male under a certain age. A man who indecently assaulted another man could go to jail for ten years, but a woman who indecently assaulted a woman could be sentenced to only five years in prison. For incest, men could be sentenced to whipping, a penalty that did not apply to women, who could be exonerated if they proved that the offence was committed under restraint, duress, or fear. Moreover, the law did not consider males under the age of fourteen capable of incest, but because it did not refer specifically to girls, a thirteen-year-old girl could be tried for incest. Only males were capable of seduction, a crime that was defined solely in terms of their age: if the boy was under eighteen or if the girl was older than eighteen, seduction was not an offence. The basis of several offences continued to rest on a woman's "previously chaste character"; if she was younger than twenty-one, the burden was on the accused to prove that she was unchaste. For instance, sexual intercourse with a girl under fourteen was a criminal offence, but a man could be found innocent for having sex with a girl who was between fourteen and sixteen if he could show that she was not of previously chaste character. And criminal law simply did not conceive of the possibility that sexual abuse in a marriage could be construed as rape.

The RCSW submitted 167 recommendations for legislative reform. The federal government responded with wide-ranging reforms, most notably the 1974 Statute Law (Status of Women) Amendment, which amended ten federal statutes dealing with immigration, the military, unemployment insurance, pensions, elections, and the public service.[104] The Criminal Code was amended to recognize a spouse's (rather than a husband's) responsibility to provide necessities of life, and the Citizenship Act was changed to apply equally to men and women. Other legal reforms soon followed.[105] Women were permitted to enlist in the RCMP beginning in 1974 and to enrol in military colleges after 1979. In 1972, vagrancy laws directed at prostitution were changed to focus on solicitation, and they applied equally to men and women, although, in practice, women continued to be the primary targets for arrests. In 1983, Parliament repealed the section of the Unemployment Insurance Act that denied benefits to pregnant women.[106] In the same year, rape was removed from the Criminal Code and replaced with gender-neutral sexual assault provisions, which "eased the evidentiary requirements for convictions on sexual assault, narrowed the opportunities for the defence to question a victim on her past sexual conduct and placed restrictions on the publication of a victim's name. In addition, maximum penalties were increased and several loopholes for sexual misconduct with young adults from 14 to 16 years old were dropped."[107] Marital rape became a crime. And in 1986, Parliament passed the Employment Equity Act to enhance the representation of women and minorities in any federally regulated workplace with more than a hundred employees.[108]

British Columbia's Social Credit government, on the other hand, expressed little interest in the RCSW. It never created a status of women advisory council to oversee implementation. As documented below, the Socreds often refused to acknowledge sex discrimination as a social problem. The Status of Women Action Group concluded in 1978 that, of all the "recommendations from the Royal Commission on the Status of Women in 1970 which fall under Provincial jurisdiction, almost none have been implemented in BC."[109] Only sixteen of sixty-eight recommendations had been implemented by 1980.[110] Still, the RCSW report was not completely ignored. Rosemary Brown and other Opposition MLAs introduced several failed private member's bills arising from the report. The RCSW also inspired the formation of new women's rights organizations in British Columbia. In fact, many women's associations embraced the report as the foundation for their activism throughout the 1970s. In this way, the RCSW did have an impact on British Columbia: it informed a generation of women's rights activism while at the same time instigating some legal reforms. For instance, in 1971 the Board of Industrial Relations stopped using separate minimum wage scales for women, and within a year, the legislation was repealed. The Department of Labour revised its publications to eliminate sex stereotyping.[111] The British Columbia Teachers' Federation successfully lobbied for the implementation (full or partial) of many RCSW recommendations on education, such as new textbooks for schools and expanding education programming in rural areas. New services were created with provincial funding, including family planning clinics, transition houses, and women's centres. Still, the RCSW's direct impact on legal reform was minimal.[112] The NDP government (1972-75), which was more amenable to legal reform, established a provincial coordinator for the status of women, a committee to study sex discrimination in the school curriculum, and a Women's Economics Rights Branch. Within a couple of years, however, the new Socred government eliminated the first two and reduced the branch to a division within the Ministry of Economic Development.[113]

Moreover, despite the wide-ranging nature of the RCSW recommendations, innumerable provincial laws were never addressed by the commission.[114] So when Canada ratified the United Nations Convention on the Elimination of All Forms of Discrimination against Women in 1981, British Columbia still had some legal house cleaning to do. To ensure their compliance with the convention, the Ministry of Intergovernmental Affairs reviewed every provincial law.[115] The ministry's final report on amending provincial legislation was a testament to the longevity of discriminatory laws informed by gender roles. Most of the recommendations involved simply amending the gendered language of existing legislation (changing "male" to "person," or "husband" to "spouse"). But in other cases, the law contained explicitly discriminatory provisions. For instance, in what the report described as the "high point of absurdity," under the Name Act (as amended in 1972), a woman who took her husband's name upon marriage could not change it later, but she could use her maiden name if she kept it when she married. If her marriage dissolved, she could apply to a court for a change of name but only if she had no children under the age of twenty-one, and she could change her children's surname only if she was widowed or divorced. Some minor revisions in 1977 permitted a married person to alter her name with the permission of her spouse, but her choice was restricted to his surname, her maiden name, or her surname immediately prior to marriage.[116] Provincial laws included other discriminatory clauses:

- Vital Statistics Act: Children of a married woman had to be registered under their father's surname.
- Workers Compensation Act: A widow could continue to receive compensation benefits arising from her husband's workplace injury. If she remarried, however, the payments were discontinued. However, if a male widower remarried, he was still entitled to the benefits. Moreover, if a widow or common law wife was found to be cohabiting with someone else "as man and wife," the benefits were discontinued. Once again, the same did not apply to men.[117]
- Children younger than nineteen who were protected under the Family and Child Services Act (e.g., orphans) lost the benefits of state guardianship if they married someone who did not come under the act. If two orphans married each other and were both under nineteen, only the female lost her benefits.
- The restriction on married women holding a separate legal domicile from their husband created problems with regard to wills, estates, immigration, and adoption.
- Factories Act: Employers were required to provide female factory workers with seats or special flooring of a resilient material if their work required constant standing on a hard surface.
- Several statutes also specified "widow" or "wife," presuming that, for example, the director of an insurance company would invariably be male, and benefits to his wife were regulated.[118]

Within two years, only the Family and Child Services Act and the Insurance Act had been amended. As late as 1984, most of these laws were still on the books, including provisions in the Barber's Act and Hairdresser's Act that prevented female staff from cutting the hair of a girl or boy under the age of seven! However, when the equality clause (section 15) of the Charter of Rights and Freedoms came into force in 1985, the legislature was finally compelled to enact widespread amendments to provincial law.[119] In British Columbia, a 1985 omnibus bill eliminated the remaining discriminatory laws and changed the language in over a dozen statutes that referred to "wife" or "widow" rather than "spouse" (of the forty-nine amended statutes, fifteen dealt with women; the others referred to illegitimate children or restricting privileges to British subjects).[120] The Married Women's Property Act was repealed, and the Factories Act was replaced with new legislation lacking the paternalistic provisions for female workers.

Still, simply changing statute law was not enough. State *policy*, including regulations enforced through dozens of state agencies, was also discriminatory. Policies governing day care (or its lack), healthcare (including abortion), education (including textbooks), pensions, and adoption were gendered. For example, the British Columbia Liquor Control Board mandated in 1942 that beer parlours in Esquimalt, Prince Rupert, and Vancouver had to erect partitions separating men from women and that they must have separate entrances with signs reading "Men's Entrance" and "Ladies and Escorts." The policy was eliminated in 1963, although many parlours retained the partitions for another decade.[121] Until 1972, the board also prohibited women from serving liquor in public houses or lounges unless they owned the liquor licence. Another (in)famous state policy of the 1970s was the spouse-in-the-house rule. Several provinces, including British Columbia, denied social assistance to single women if evidence revealed that they were living with a man. The policy, which lasted into the 1980s, presumed that a sexual relationship entailed an economic one (the rule did not apply to men). In this way, state law was discriminatory even if it was not explicitly written in statute law.

Judge-made law could also be discriminatory. When BC judges were faced with interpreting property law in the early twentieth century, they "shied away from an expansive reading of the new rights provided by the statutes."[122] Courts were more likely to convict young girls for moral rather than criminal offences and would impose longer sentences on girls than on boys who were guilty of the same act. Sangster's scholarship reveals that, from the late nineteenth century to the mid-twentieth century, the judiciary used the law to regulate female sexuality. Women were routinely jailed for "immoral behaviour," which was often a pretext for using "incarceration as a means to regulate the sexual and moral behaviour of women perceived to be 'out of sexual control.'"[123] Judges and juries applied a cruel double standard, not only in divorce cases, but in sexual assault as well. Judges interpreted the doctrine of corroboration in a way that was "deeply suspicious of testimony of women and girls." By 1927, courts commonly quashed convictions for intercourse with young girls "because of mandatory statutory corroboration provisions that were interpreted narrowly by judges who professed greater concern over the plight of men potentially falsely accused than they did over sexual crimes involving females."[124] Property distribution after divorce favoured men and penalized women for working in the home, and rape trials favoured the accused over the accuser. Even the 1960 federal Bill of Rights, which purported to ban sex discrimination, was undermined through judicial interpretation: the judiciary rejected every sex discrimination claim under the legislation.[125] And as late as 1975, the Supreme Court of Canada ruled that a lifetime of labour on a farm did not entitle a woman to an equivalent division of assets after divorce.[126]

Far more difficult to quantify or document was the sexism that, at times, appeared to be rampant throughout the predominantly male judiciary. In 1977, an Ontario judge sentenced a twenty-one-year-old man to six months in jail for breaking into the home of a sixteen-year-old woman and forcibly seizing her. In justifying the light sentence, the judge explained that

> women don't get much brains before they're thirty anyway ... But at the age of eighteen or so, they make some stupid mistakes, mostly because we males who know better lead them into it ... I don't think under the circumstances of this case I'd be entitled to give him five years because he got mixed up with a silly, little bunch of girls.[127]

The Canadian Judicial Council investigated hundreds of complaints against judges in the 1980s. Oftentimes the complaints involved sexist comments such as "rules are like women, they are meant to be violated," or that a man who sexually abused his daughter should have hired a prostitute instead. Other complaints focused on sentencing. A judge in the Northwest Territories fined a man $1,000 instead of sending him to prison because "a man who beat his wife deserved a lighter sentence because she provoked him wearing a T-shirt."[128] A Manitoba judge reprimanded a female lawyer for requesting an adjournment because her nursing infant was unwell and suggested that her client find someone "who is not trying to be a mother and a lawyer at the same time."[129]

Legal reform was, therefore, a slow, complex, and highly contested process. For example, in 1969, the federal government had decriminalized the dissemination of birth control information, and it legalized abortion *if* a hospital-appointed Therapeutic Abortion Committee approved the procedure. The abortion law remained in place until 1988, when the Supreme Court of Canada finally struck it down because, among other reasons, access to such committees was inequitable. The military had an informal ban on women serving in combat roles until a 1989 federal Human Rights Tribunal ruling forced its full integration (service in submarines was included in 2000).[130]

Securing formal legal equality for women would span generations, although by the late 1980s there was clearly a shift toward gender-neutral statute law. Although the law had undergone profound changes, legal discrimination against women remained pervasive in Canada. This fact made it apparent that more systemic and institutional legal reform was required, rather than formal legal equality as expressed in statute law. The human rights state was created, in part, to address this social problem. Human rights law emerged at a time when governments had already begun to remove explicit inequalities embedded in statute law.

2
"No Jews or Dogs Allowed"
Anti-Discrimination Law

You will be pleased to know that for the first time in the history of this area [Sydney, Nova Scotia], colored girls have been employed in some of the larger shops: one at the Metropolitan and two at Eaton's. I was waited on yesterday at Woolworths by the colored girl there, and she seemed to be a very capable girl. I called up the manager later to commend him for what he had done, and he was delighted to receive my call. He indicated that he was pleased with her performance, and he intends to give permanent employment to her and others in the future. He said that he told his staff before hiring her, and found that they were 99 percent in favour, and that the one who was reluctant, has not done anything to impede the experiment. The colored girl is getting along well in her work, and with her fellow workers, and though the general public has not commended him for his move, neither have they shown any objection or hostility. I have not yet seen the girls at the other two stores, but I intend to do so, and compliment the managers, and endeavor to have others do so.

*— Jim McDonald, Canadian Labour Congress,
to Sid Blum, Jewish Labour Committee,
17 December 1957*

Canada's human rights state originated in the 1930s, but a genuine human rights legal regime did not emerge for a generation afterward. In many ways, the defining feature of this era was what *did not* occur. By 1960, not a single statute had banned discrimination against women. The period witnessed the rise of the first civil liberties organizations in Canadian history and the first sustained campaigns for anti-discrimination law. The women's movement also gained influence. And yet, most passionate advocates for the rights of racial, religious, and ethnic minorities expressed little interest in legislating a ban on sex discrimination. Jim McDonald's 1957 observation to the director of the Jewish Labour Committee, quoted above, is a useful example. His concern for her race, rather than her gender, typified rights campaigns at this time. Activists and policy-makers alike largely ignored the widespread discrimination that women experienced in their daily lives. Nonetheless, this was a formative period in the history of the human rights state. Women would use the foundations established during it to later expand the scope of the human rights state. The lack of any substantial debate regarding sex discrimination says a great deal about this era and partly explains why anti-discrimination law was a failure.

It is worth remembering that race-based discrimination was a fact of life in Canada by the mid-twentieth century. Immigration policies were explicitly racist. Thousands of Canadian citizens of Japanese descent were deported to Japan in the aftermath of the Second World War. During the war, Canada was among the world's least hospitable destinations for Jewish refugees, barely five thousand of whom were allowed to enter the country. Recruiting centres rejected visible minorities who sought to enlist. Barbers refused to serve blacks; taverns posted signs reading "No Jews or Dogs Allowed"; golf courses banned racial and religious minorities; hotels banned Aboriginal people; blacks were refused service in bars and segregated in theatres; and landlords refused to rent apartments to visible or ethnic minorities. Aboriginal people were not permitted to hire legal counsel to sue the government, a prohibition that was not eliminated until 1951. The federal ban on Aboriginal political organizing and land claims, instituted in 1927, was also lifted in that year. Minorities were regularly denied licences to operate businesses. Ontario and Saskatchewan prohibited white women from working for Chinese employers. Schools in Nova Scotia and southern Ontario segregated blacks and whites. Most visible minorities could not vote, and in 1945 the BC legislature rejected a Co-operative Commonwealth Federation (CCF) motion to enfranchise

Asian Canadians (meanwhile, the federal government *dis*enfranchised Japanese Canadians). Jehovah's Witnesses, whose pamphlets referred to the Catholic Church as the "whore of Babylon," were routinely persecuted and jailed.[1] An economic campaign in Quebec during the war, *achat chez nous,* encouraged French Canadians to boycott Jewish businesses. Such was the pervasiveness of anti-Semitism that even Jewish businesses sometimes refused to hire Jews.[2]

In 1948, *Maclean's Magazine* published an article based on a test of forty-seven employers in Toronto. Two women with almost identical qualifications had applied for the same job. One gave her surname as Greenberg, and the other used Grimes. The former received seventeen offers, the latter forty-one.[3] Employers routinely asked applicants about their race or nationality, religion, and place of birth. In 1951, when several Toronto employers were asked why they had no blacks on staff, explanations varied from "negroes are lazy" to "we never put them on milk routes because the ladies would complain," "they couldn't sell to a white person," "if you had a nigger policeman dealing with white people you wouldn't have confidence in him," and "they can't stand work with heavy stamping machines."[4] Few instruments better exemplify discrimination than restrictive covenants – agreements among a group of people to ban religious or racial minorities from purchasing property, usually houses, but also plots in a cemetery. The following restrictive covenant, for instance, was signed by a group of homeowners in an Ontario neighbourhood in 1951:

> The ownership of no lot on plan 269 and no part of the low-water beach aforesaid shall be transferred by sale, inheritance, gift or otherwise, nor rented, licensed to or occupied by any person wholly or partly of negro, Asiatic, coloured or Semitic blood, nor to any person less than four generations removed from that part of Europe lying south of latitude 55 degrees and east of longitude 15 degrees east. Relationship, however slight, to any class forbidden as aforesaid shall be deemed sufficient to prevent transfer to or occupancy by such persons of northern and western European descent, other than Jews. Such restrictions, however, shall not apply to bona fide domestic servants of actual occupants during the period of such occupancy. The land and premises herein described shall never be sold, assigned, transferred, leased, rented or in any manner whatsoever alienated to and shall never be occupied or used in any manner whatsoever by any person of the Jewish, Hebrew, Semitic, negro or coloured race or blood, it being the intention and purpose of the Grantor, to restrict the ownership, use, occupation and enjoyment of the said recreational development, including the

lands and premises herein described to persons of the white or Caucasian race not excluded by this clause. No building shall be erected on these premises except by a person who is a white Gentile, nor by any limited company whose shareholders are not entirely Gentile.[5]

Several developments came together in the 1940s to produce a movement for anti-discrimination legislation. The CCF's growing popularity forced a host of new issues onto the public agenda. Since adopting its founding program in 1933 (Regina Manifesto), the CCF had been an outspoken proponent of federal and provincial bills of rights, and by the 1940s it was an advocate for anti-discrimination legislation.[6] Moreover, virulent manifestations of anti-Semitism made many political leaders uneasy: Jews faced economic boycotts, bans on purchasing property, prohibitions on entering university programs, and immigration restrictions; they were also targets of violence. The Second World War served to further highlight the ugly consequences of anti-Semitic state policy. It did not take long for people to begin commenting on the fact that many of those who encountered prejudice at home had served their country faithfully on the battlefield. Canada's own wartime record and its government's vicious abuses of human rights before, during, and after the war rankled many who might have opposed human rights legislation.

According to James St. G. Walker, the Second World War "produced a sensitivity to racial issues, making the public more receptive, and legislators more inclined, to the legal protection of human rights in Canada."[7] The United Nations Charter (1945) declared the equality of all human beings and provided the institution with a mandate to promote human rights. War rhetoric, atrocities on the battlefield, the Holocaust, and the creation of an international body with a mandate to promote human rights deeply affected Canadians. Then, in 1948, the Universal Declaration of Human Rights "set out both the rationale and the direction for human rights programs in the postwar world."[8] Of course, minorities had been demanding legislative reform long before the war. But the war and the emerging international consensus emboldened activists, helped solidify popular support domestically, and provided advocates with new tools for their campaigns.

Support for anti-discrimination legislation continued to increase long after the war, and it often coalesced around an organization called the Jewish Labour Committee (JLC). The JLC and the Joint Public Relations Committee (an alliance of the Canadian Jewish Congress and B'nai Brith) were established in 1936 and 1938, respectively. Working together, they created Joint Labour Committees to Combat Racial Discrimination in Montreal, Toronto, Vancouver, Windsor, and Winnipeg, which were "jointly" funded by the Canadian Congress of Labour and the Trades and Labour Congress.[9] A central figure in this movement was Montreal-based Kalmen Kaplansky. A war veteran born in Poland and fluent in Yiddish and English, Kaplansky was appointed national director of the JLC in 1946. He essentially ran the committees. His ties to the International Typographical Union and the CCF were invaluable assets for forming alliances with politicians, unions, and religious and minority organizations. He also had close ties to the American Jewish Labour Committee, and in fact spent several weeks in New York, learning how to manage labour committees.[10] Over time, the JLC leadership included Sid Blum, another war veteran and an American citizen who served as secretary of the Toronto labour committee after working for the Canadian Labour Congress, and David Orlikow, a respected CCF MP from Winnipeg. The JLC was an extraordinarily influential organization and one of the few social movement bodies in Canada with a genuine national reach.

Finally, rights discourse was increasingly pervasive in post-war political, social, economic, and cultural debates. Michael Dawson draws attention to this phenomenon in his study of discussions of commercial store hours.[11] "In fact, the postwar era," Dawson argues, "witnessed a blossoming of rights-based rhetoric ... Supporters and opponents of store-hour regulations incorporated rights-based rhetoric into their public campaigns and pronouncements."[12] In this case, opponents articulated their opposition to bans on Sunday shopping with reference to a right to *shop* or a right to *sell*, whereas supporters claimed that workers had a right to *leisure*. In the post-war period, as Shirley Tillotson also suggests, workers drew on rights rhetoric to express a sense of entitlement to leisure, a belief that was not widely voiced before the 1940s.[13] Furthermore, support for equal pay and anti-discrimination legislation was growing among leading media outlets. In 1951, for example, the *Toronto Globe and Mail* published several editorials supporting fair employment and equal pay legislation.[14]

Anti-Discrimination Legislation

The first anti-discrimination provisions in Canadian law began with a few, virtually unnoticed, minor reforms to existing statutes. British Columbia introduced the Unemployment Relief Act in 1931 to distribute relief during the Depression. Section 8 of the act prohibited discrimination on the basis

Anti-Discrimination Law 51

Kalmen Kaplansky, 1951 | LAC PA-139571

JLC poster session conference, 1947 | LAC PA-149148

of political affiliation in the distribution of relief; a year later, the government amended the act to expand the prohibition to race and religion.[15] The Ontario government amended its insurance law in 1932 to ban racial and religious discrimination in the assessment of insurance.[16] Soon after, in 1934, Manitoba amended the Libel Act to include a new section prohibiting "the publication of a libel against a race or creed likely to expose persons belonging to a race or professing the creed to hatred, contempt or ridicule, and tending to raise unrest or disorder among the people."[17] None of these initiatives addressed sex discrimination.

Aboriginal people and women, as well as racial, religious, and ethnic minorities, had a long history of attempting to address their marginalization through the courts, albeit often unsuccessfully.[18] Minorities were also at the forefront of campaigns for protective legislation. Jewish groups, including B'nai Brith, the Canadian Jewish Congress, and the JLC, and Jewish labour unions such as the International Ladies Garment Workers, were especially prominent in these early campaigns. In Manitoba, Ontario, and Quebec, Jewish elected officials attempted numerous times to amend existing statutes during the 1930s.[19] Kaplansky and Blum often sought alliances with African Canadian associations (such as churches and youth clubs) as well as with Japanese Canadians in protesting discrimination throughout the Second World War.[20] Organizations representing ethnic minorities, many of whose members were all too familiar with the sting of bigotry, added their support to campaigns.[21]

The political left and the labour movement, including the CCF and the Communist Party of Canada, were also key players in these fledgling human rights campaigns. The CCF founding document, the Regina Manifesto, was in fact the first public declaration for a bill of rights by a Canadian political party. The first civil liberties organizations also materialized during the 1930s. The Association for Civil Liberties (Toronto) played a key role alongside the JLC in mobilizing the first delegations to lobby Ontario premier Leslie Frost in the 1940s.[22] Although support for protective measures was far from widespread by the late 1940s, the idea that state legislation should prohibit discrimination was certainly not new.

Still, politicians hesitated to act. For some people, anti-discrimination legislation represented an unwarranted restriction on the rights of merchants to operate their business (the "freedom of commerce" principle). This was certainly the predominant attitude in the courts, as a 1930s case revealed. In 1936, Fred Christie and two friends, Emile King and Steven St. Jean, entered the Montreal Forum's York Tavern for a beer. As they sat down to order a drink, a waiter quietly informed them that they had to leave. The tavern was under new management, he said, and the owners did not want blacks in the bar. Christie, a chauffeur and avid Montreal Canadiens fan who had been to the tavern many times in the past, was indignant and refused to leave. Eventually, the police arrived and escorted Christie and his friends off the premises. Christie sued York Tavern, but the Supreme Court of Canada decided in favour of the merchant's right to choose, not Christie's right to be served. Such was the prevailing attitude toward racial minorities that Christie's own lawyer did not even bother to question the assumption that whites did not want to eat and drink alongside blacks.[23] A year later, the British Columbia Court of Appeal used the Christie case to sustain the right of a Vancouver hotel to refuse service to a black man because of his race. Although Chief Justice M.A. Macdonald applied the precedent "regretfully," and Justice Cornelius O'Halloran vigorously dissented and insisted that "all British subjects have the same rights and privileges under the common law," the Supreme Court of Canada's *Christie v. York* decision remained binding until the 1960s.[24]

British Columbia and Ontario were once again key sites of innovation during the post-war period. The British Columbia Social Assistance Act of 1945 banned discrimination on the basis of race, creed, or political affiliation in the provision of social assistance.[25] Ontario prohibited any signs or publications expressing racial or religious discrimination with the 1944 Racial Discrimination Act and, in the same year, passed a regulation under the Community Halls Act to proscribe discrimination in halls that received public funds.[26] In retrospect, however, it was really Saskatchewan that ushered in a new era when its provincial government introduced the country's first bill of rights. Alberta had attempted something similar in 1946, only to have the Alberta Bill of Rights struck down in the courts. The Alberta legislation had promised, among other things, a right to work and to pensions, and it empowered the provincial government to regulate banks. It was a clear violation of federal jurisdiction over banking, and the Judicial Committee of the Privy Council swiftly declared the entire statute ultra vires.[27] None of these initiatives proposed to disallow discrimination against women.

In many ways, the 1947 Saskatchewan Bill of Rights was a remarkable document. It was the first of its kind in Canada. It recognized a broad range of human rights, including rights to speech, religion, association, and assembly; to due process of law; and to freedom from arbitrary arrest. It prohibited discrimination on the basis of race, religion, or national origin in employment, professional associations and unions, property, services, and educational institutions. It did not ban sex discrimination.

The statute received unanimous support in the Saskatchewan legislature. Without the determined efforts of Jewish activists and the CCF in Saskatchewan, however, it would never have been enacted.[28] Over time, social movements would become central in almost every innovation in Canada's human rights law.

To be sure, these were important first steps. Still, a major flaw of the Saskatchewan Bill of Rights and of the Ontario Racial Discrimination Act was that they were quasi-criminal statutes. In other words, enforcement was left to the traditional machinery of the courts. However, as legal scholar Walter Tarnopolsky once noted, the courts were simply not up to the task: victims were reluctant to initiate criminal action; proving that someone had been denied work or access due to discrimination was extraordinarily difficult; the judiciary was disinclined to convict, probably because it did not feel that discrimination was a criminal act; many people, including employers, were unaware of the legislation; members of minority groups were legitimately skeptical of it, fearing that it might simply be a symbolic gesture; and punishments in the form of fines did little to assist victims in finding work or receiving service in restaurants or shops.[29]

Criminal procedures also require a far more demanding burden of proof – beyond a reasonable doubt – in contrast to civil trials, in which accusers need to demonstrate only a balance of probabilities. Since discrimination is always difficult to prove, the legislation was hampered from the beginning because of its dependence on the courts. Ultimately, the Ontario and Saskatchewan initiatives were largely symbolic and did little to eliminate discrimination. Even Saskatchewan premier Tommy Douglas, who vigorously supported the Bill of Rights, acknowledged that it was little more than an educational tool to promote tolerance.[30] Even so, education could matter. As Carmela Patrias recounts in the following experience involving a group of black men in Saskatchewan in 1947, there was reason to hope that the symbolism of the law could have tangible results:

> Charles Blair, an African-Canadian porter working for the CNR, and a group of his friends were refused admittance to a dance hall named Uncle Tom's Cabin (after its owner's name Tom Coburn), in North Battleford, SK. There was nothing 'Uncle Tom'-like about the reaction of Blair and his friends. They refused to leave, forcing Coburn to call the RCMP. Blair informed Officer Bradley, who responded to Coburn's call, that barring African Canadians from the dance hall contravened the provisions of the Saskatchewan Bill of Rights. Coburn insisted that he refused them entry because he had always done so. The policeman, unfamiliar with the Bill of

Rights, asked Blair and his friends to leave and to launch a formal complaint with the RCMP the following morning. The African Canadians did not show up next day, probably because their train had left town. But Blair, a Winnipeg resident, wrote Premier Douglas to complain about the incident. Douglas instructed the RCMP to investigate, and Bradley, after studying the Bill of Rights, warned Coburn that denying entry to African Canadians was against the law. Coburn promised that he would refrain from doing so in the future. This satisfied Premier Douglas. Coburn was not prosecuted.[31]

Soon afterward, in 1950, the Ontario government amended the Labour Relations Act to withhold legal recognition of collective agreements that discriminated on the basis of race or creed. In the same year, the legislature unanimously passed the Conveyancing and Law of Property Amendment Act, which prohibited the enforcement of restrictive covenants (contracts among homeowners to restrict sales of homes to minorities, like the one quoted at the beginning of this chapter).[32] But the province's most important innovation in the 1950s was fair employment and fair accommodation practices legislation to proscribe discrimination in employment and housing.[33] By the end of the decade, most Canadian provinces had introduced similar legislation to ban discrimination on the basis of race, religion, and ethnicity.[34] Parliament enacted the Canada Fair Employment Practices Act in 1953 and the Female Employees' Equal Pay Act in 1956. Between 1953 and 1954, through a series of declarations and regulations (including the Fair Wages and Hours of Labour Act), Ottawa also disallowed discrimination in federal contracts on the basis of national origin, marital status, colour, age, race, and – for the first time – sex.[35]

These initial forays faced intense opposition. R. Brian Howe and David Johnson attribute its persistence among 1940s politicians to a widespread belief in social laissez-faire and volunteerism: "While prejudice and discrimination might be morally wrong or socially undesirable, human rights legislation or legal action against discrimination would do more harm than good. It would involve unwanted state interference with individual freedom, property rights, and the right of contract."[36] Even when George Drew, the premier of Ontario, stood in the legislature to support the 1944 Racial Discrimination Act, he expressed hesitation with the principle embodied in the act: "The best way to avoid racial and religious strife is not by imposing a method of thinking, but by teaching our children that we are all members of a great human family."[37] Maurice Duplessis, the powerful premier of Quebec, a man with an almost visceral hatred of communists and minorities such as Jehovah's Witnesses, declared bluntly that the only protection people needed against discrimination was the Bible.[38] The *Toronto Globe and Mail*, *Toronto Telegram*, and *Toronto Financial Post* condemned Ontario's Racial Discrimination Act as unwarranted state interference in business.[39] "The ultimate cure to discrimination," explained the *Globe and Mail* editors in 1947, "lies in the people themselves."[40]

Many political leaders had simply convinced themselves that discrimination did not exist in their province.[41] In reaction to the Saskatchewan Bill of Rights, critics

> argued that the bill was meaningless, a matter of window dressing, an act of political opportunism. Some of them maintained that no racial discrimination occurred in Saskatchewan, while others, who acknowledged that prejudice and discrimination did exist in the province, held either that it was impossible to legislate an end to such attitudes and practices, or that legislation already existed to safeguard the rights that the new bill was designed to protect.[42]

The social movement coalitions campaigning for anti-discrimination legislation in Ontario faced a similar challenge. Many politicians were confident that discrimination was not a problem or that, if it did exist, legislation was not the solution. Premier Frost

> maintained that the government and people of Ontario were basically opposed to discrimination, and that there was no serious racial problem in the province. On those occasional instances where it did occur, it was best handled through voluntary compliance rather than legal coercion; legislation, he warned, could undermine Ontario's tradition of tolerance and might produce a backlash among the majority population.[43]

Others asserted that traditional British rights and freedoms, protected through common law, were sufficient. Any legislation would be construed as special treatment for a particular group.[44] Alberta premier Ernest Manning's skepticism, as Maureen Riddell explains, reflected the prevailing attitudes of the time:

> Manning apparently endorsed the customary British practice of refraining from committing accepted rights and freedoms to law. The Alberta Premier

agreed with the comment by Sir Winston Churchill to the effect that the freedoms held by subjects under the British flag were too broad to be condensed into legislation. Premier Manning believed that emphasis on individual rights without comparable attention to the responsibilities of persons in society was potentially damaging to the social, cultural and economic fabric of society. Some of the rights which people claimed to possess naturally, he pointed out, were actually privileges and opportunities, to be appreciated, but not demanded or expected.[45]

Employers were also skeptical of the viability of anti-discrimination legislation. A University of Toronto study conducted in 1961 found that "twenty-five out of forty-four employers believed fair practices legislation could not work. They claimed that: (i) discrimination cannot be changed by legislation; (ii) human nature cannot be changed; (iii) discrimination legislation is unenforceable, and (iv) discrimination cannot be proved."[46] In the Ontario case, as Shirley Tillotson has shown, even Louis Fine, the director of the Fair Employment Services Branch, was reluctant to enforce the province's equal pay laws. Fine narrowly interpreted the legislation and even discouraged victims from submitting complaints.[47]

Social movements, and organized labour in particular, played a crucial role in changing attitudes and rallying support for anti-discrimination legislation. By the 1950s, groups as diverse as the Canadian Association for Adult Education, Canadian Association of Social Workers, Canadian Council of Christians and Jews, Fellowship of Reconciliation, Japanese Canadian Citizens' Association, Toronto Social Planning Council, United Nations Association, University of Toronto Faculty of Social Work, and the YMCA/YWCA were engaging in public education campaigns and advocating for fair practices legislation.[48] Thirteen associations, mostly representing organized labour, women, and Jews, presented briefs before the parliamentary committee debating Ottawa's 1953 Fair Employment Practices Act.[49] The Ontario Federation of Labour's annual briefs to government placed a heavy emphasis on human rights legislation, beginning in 1956.[50] Premier Leslie Frost was especially impressed with the presentations of several large delegations, including one that drew hundreds of people and 104 representatives from unions, churches, and civil liberties groups, as well as organizations representing Jews, ethnic minorities, and students. Women figured prominently in the delegations: the National Council of Women as well as women's missionary societies and unions threw their support behind the campaign.[51] An early delegation submitted a brief with Gallup poll data, showing that 64 percent would support an anti-discrimination law and that 68 percent would refuse to sign a restrictive covenant. The delegation also brought a list of resolutions from organizations, including several churches, supporting anti-discrimination legislation.[52] The delegations proved decisive in convincing the premier to introduce fair employment and fair practices legislation.

One of Kalmen Kaplansky's most effective strategies was to focus public attention on blatant examples of discrimination to counter the illusion that it was not a social problem. And few places were as bitterly divided along racial lines as Dresden, Ontario. A small city with a substantial black population, Dresden was notorious for racial prejudice. Blacks could not eat at any of the town's three restaurants or get a haircut at its four barbershops or the beauty parlour; they were banned from all but one pool hall, denied entry to the Canadian Legion except at stag parties, and could not attend the white church. Sidney Katz, who visited Dresden in October 1949 for *Maclean's Magazine,* later wrote that "the chances of a trained young Negro getting a good nonmanual job are almost nil. I did not find a single Negro in Dresden working in an office or waiting on customers."[53] Ironically, the town's primary tourist attraction was Uncle Tom's grave, as Dresden had once been a terminus for an underground railway that helped black slaves escape the United States. In a 1949 municipal referendum, local citizens voted by a margin of five to one *against* a proposed bylaw banning discrimination (the only vote of its kind in Canadian history).[54] Morley McKay, the owner of Kay's Café, was especially infamous in Dresden. A burly black-haired Scot with a short temper, McKay refused to serve blacks at his establishment, so the JLC arranged several "tests" of Kay's Café. Two black volunteers entered it, McKay refused to serve them, and the JLC documented the episode and shared its information with the media and politicians. The strategy infuriated McKay, who at one point was wielding a large meat cleaver and appeared to be controlling his temper only with difficulty.[55] When he was interviewed by Katz, McKay said, "Do you know that for three days after I get raging mad every time I see a Negro. Maybe it's like an animal who's had a smell of blood."[56] Every time Dresden appeared in newspaper headlines, politicians' insistence that anti-discrimination legislation was unnecessary became increasingly difficult to maintain. Dresden provided Sid Blum, secretary for the JLC Toronto committee, with the ammunition he desperately needed to challenge popular perceptions about prejudice in Ontario.

Social movement organizations' determination to combat discrimination was not limited to lobbying politicians.[57] Blum undertook fact-finding

Jewish Labour Committee anti-discrimination poster

trips to Dresden to confirm that the fair employment/practices legislation was not being enforced, and he lobbied for formal inquiries while at the same time persuading trade councils to pressure the government. And he cultivated close relationships with reporters, who would witness the test cases and use their newspapers to draw attention to the law's inadequacies.[58] In this way, the JLC was engaged in enforcing the law. For its part, the Canadian Jewish Congress trained volunteers who approached local businesses and asked them not to discriminate in their hiring practices. During these encounters, volunteers sought to spread awareness about discrimination's negative effect on the economy, while appealing to individuals' beliefs in democracy, equality, and rewarding merit.[59] Several unions also negotiated anti-discrimination clauses in their collective agreements. In October 1952, for instance, a conciliation board in Vancouver endorsed an anti-discrimination clause (regarding race, colour, religion, and national origin) in a collective agreement between the Vancouver Building Exchange and the International Brotherhood of Electrical Workers. In another example of organized labour's assertiveness, Local 717 of the International Association of Machinists cancelled a golf tournament after one of its African Canadian members was denied entry to the course.[60]

The impact of the JLC's efforts (and those of organized labour generally) was felt across Canada. Kaplansky was adept at raising funds and overcoming divisions within the labour movement. It is likely that "without Kaplansky's leadership, and the support of the JLC, the labour committees would probably have ceased to exist."[61] By the 1950s, a coordinated national strategy was in place, and it produced tangible results (Figure 1). The federal government introduced a fair employment practices law in 1953 and added an anti-discrimination provision to the National Housing Act in 1960, largely in response to labour movement lobbying.[62] The New Brunswick government enacted fair employment practices legislation in 1959, less than a year after the provincial federation of labour began to lobby for anti-discrimination legislation.[63] Successive Quebec governments had resisted implementing anti-discrimination laws, but thanks to the efforts of the JLC's Montreal affiliate (the United Council for Human Rights) and the Quebec Federation of Labour, the provincial government enacted An Act Respecting Discrimination in Employment in 1964.[64] In a brief to the Quebec premier, the JLC claimed the support of forty social movement organizations representing unions, churches, Jews, students, ethnic minorities, women, and prisoners.[65] Ottawa's first anti-discrimination legislation, in 1952, was largely the product of a campaign by organized labour and allies in Parliament.[66] In Nova Scotia and Saskatchewan, municipal labour councils, provincial labour federations, and the JLC worked closely to secure anti-discrimination legislation and to improve existing legislation (the Halifax Human Rights Advisory Committee and the Nova Scotia Association for the Advancement of Coloured People were also part of the campaign).[67] If fair employment practices legislation already existed, organizations such as the British Columbia Federation of Labour or the Toronto Labour Committee for Human Rights lobbied for fair *accommodations* practices legislation.[68] As the federal Department of Labour acknowledged, "it can be stated without qualification that the history of

FIGURE 1 **Anti-discrimination legislation**

1944	Ontario Racial Discrimination Act
1947	Saskatchewan Bill of Rights
1951	Ontario Fair Employment Practices Act
1953	Canada Fair Employment Practices Act
1953	Manitoba Fair Employment Practices Act
1954	Ontario Fair Accommodation Practices Act
1955	Nova Scotia Fair Employment Practices Act
1956	British Columbia Fair Employment Practices Act
1956	New Brunswick Fair Employment Practices Act
1956	Saskatchewan Fair Accommodation Practices Act
1959	New Brunswick Fair Accommodation Practices Act
1959	Nova Scotia Fair Accommodation Practices Act
1960	Manitoba Fair Accommodation Practices Act
1961	British Columbia Public Accommodation Practices Act
1964	Quebec Act Respecting Discrimination in Employment
1966	Northwest Territories Fair Practices Ordinance

fair employment practices legislation in Canada testifies to the effectiveness of the fundamental educational groundwork carried on by labour."[69]

ANTI-DISCRIMINATION LAW IN PRACTICE

Unlike the Saskatchewan Bill of Rights, fair employment and practices statutes were based on an administrative (not criminal) model. They empowered a minister (usually the minister of labour) to appoint an investigator, and if necessary, the minister could appoint an independent ad hoc commission to consider the case and recommend a remedy (such as a fine or an offer of employment). Complainants did not have to resort to the courts, and the administrative apparatus favoured an initial attempt at conciliation rather than direct confrontation. For the complainants, this model had the added benefit of placing the burden of investigation on state officials, rather than requiring that they themselves hire (and pay) their own lawyers and investigators, as most did not have the resources to pursue complaints on their own. The administrative model required them to prove a balance of probabilities of guilt, not guilt beyond a reasonable doubt, the more demanding standard of criminal proceedings. If, however, the complainant continued to face discrimination, the case would be referred to the courts. In this instance, the burden of proof was more stringent, and the complainant would receive no remedy (court-imposed fines were collected by the government).

For these reasons, anti-discrimination laws were ineffective. Of the 502 complaints received between 1951 and 1962, only 1 was successfully prosecuted under Ontario's Fair Accommodation Practices Act (Morley McKay was fined $25 and an additional $155 for costs in 1955).[70] The number of complaints investigated in other jurisdictions from the mid-1950s to the late 1960s was a fraction of those received in Ontario: Manitoba (2), New Brunswick (15), Quebec (24), and Saskatchewan (30).[71] The federal legislation also went largely unused: only thirty people sought relief under the law between 1953 and 1960.[72]

The failure of early anti-discrimination measures is not difficult to explain. The legislation was unwieldy and difficult to enforce. Discrimination was notoriously hard to prove. Responsibility for enforcing the law was hoisted onto the shoulders of civil servants with no expertise, and often little interest, in the issue. "Since these administrative officials," as Howe and Johnson argue,

> were civil servants in regular government departments performing a wide variety of duties, the handling and prosecution of equal rights cases, only one task among many, was done on a part-time basis under the constraints of time and bureaucratic hierarchy. Having little education about the law and knowing that the procedure was ad hoc and administered only grudgingly by part-time officials, victims of discrimination were still reluctant to come forward.[73]

Bill Black offered a similar critique of British Columbia's early anti-discrimination legislation:

> One notable feature of these statutes is that they each dealt with a separate area of activity, such as public accommodation or employment. They did not reflect a recognition that discrimination in different areas of activity has common causes. Moreover, responsibility for enforcement was divided between different officials. Often, these officials were responsible for enforcing the statute along with other unrelated duties. The result was that the legislation was not widely known and enforcement efforts were often meagre. Certainly, they cannot be credited with significant change in the situation

of those allegedly protected by the legislation. Though these features of the legislation do not distinguish British Columbia from most other Canadian jurisdictions at that time, it is also fair to say that it was far from the forefront of new developments.[74]

Governments were unwilling to dedicate the necessary resources to enforce the legislation. When the federal minister of labour introduced the 1953 Fair Employment Practices Act, he insisted that "it is not anticipated that additional costs for administration will be great."[75] Moreover, with no budget for education or promotion, it is likely that, as the British Columbia Federation of Labour suggested, few people were even aware that the law existed.

The 1960 case of Gerri Sylvia, a young black woman living in Winnipeg, exemplified the failure of such laws. After a year of struggling to find work as a waitress, she picked up the phone and called David Orlikow. He was an NDP member of the Manitoba Legislative Assembly and the secretary for the local Joint Labour Committee to Combat Racial Discrimination (and, later, national director of the JLC). Orlikow drove around the city with Sylvia, and as he waited in the car, she walked into Hilton Restaurant, Raphael's Restaurant, South Seas Restaurant, and Zoratti's Restaurant to apply for jobs that had been advertised in the newspaper. Her applications were quickly rejected, and in some instances, no one even bothered to ask about her qualifications. The next day, Orlikow sent two white women to the same restaurants to apply for the same jobs. They were promptly offered the positions. Orlikow brought the case to the provincial minister of labour, who appointed a commission under the Fair Employment Practices Act. After numerous delays, the commission dismissed the case on a technicality. In addition to citing lack of evidence, the inquiry's chairman, G.F.D. Bond, insisted that Sylvia was not looking for work, only investigating whether the restaurants practised discrimination, and thus was not genuinely denied employment (Sylvia had filed a complaint in the previous year after ten cafes refused to hire her, but that complaint was dismissed without an inquiry due to lack of evidence).[76]

In Halifax, Montreal, Toronto, Vancouver, and Winnipeg, the JLC sought to highlight the failure of existing legislation.[77] The Montreal JLC committee, for example, lobbied for the creation of a human rights commission to enforce the 1964 law banning discrimination in employment.[78] Its objective was, first, to secure a commission and, second, to lobby for more expansive legislation. Similarly, in Nova Scotia, the JLC organized a series of test cases soon after the Fair Employment and

Accommodations Practices legislation were introduced. As in the *Sylvia* case, the local JLC secretary recruited black and white individuals to apply for the same service or employment and, in situations when the former were denied, documented the incident and submitted a formal complaint of discrimination. The complaint was usually dismissed. The purpose of the exercise was to demonstrate the many limitations (such as delays, costs, and restricted scope) of the legislation and to set the stage for a campaign to lobby for a proper human rights law.[79]

The JLC was hardly alone in recognizing the law's inadequacies. There were many critics. Eamon Park, an Ontario CCF MLA (and publicity director for the United Steelworkers of America), criticized Ontario's equal pay legislation for containing so many loopholes that probably only a hundred women in the entire province would qualify. E.B. Joliffe, Ontario CCF leader, derided the province's equal pay and fair employment laws for not protecting complainants from being fired for submitting a complaint. The CCF's research director described the two laws as "unworkable and unenforceable frauds." Reverend W.C. Perry, the presiding elder of the African Methodist Episcopal Church in Canada, wondered whether or not the low fines in Ontario's fair employment legislation would deter violators.[80] Bora Laskin, recently elevated to the Ontario Court of Appeal (and soon to be appointed to the Supreme Court of Canada), was concerned with the failure to adequately enforce the legislation: "Since one of the underpinnings of anti-discrimination legislation is its educative value, the failure to provide full-time administration undercuts enforcement at large as well as individual complaint cases. Tokenism expressed in part-time administration is not a very warming assurance that the implications of a public policy of anti-discrimination are fully understood or fully endorsed."[81] The pressure to introduce more effective laws mounted as critics grew more numerous each year.

Meanwhile, Canada's workforce was undergoing dramatic changes.[82] The visible minority population in Canada increased from 264,000 in 1941 to 584,000 in 1961, and to 1,505,000 in 1981 (it was also concentrated in urban areas).[83] The number of women in the workforce climbed from 20 percent in 1941 to almost 40 percent of the total Canadian labour force in 1980.[84] The influx of non-white and non-male workers invariably produced more complaints and created pressure to establish a more responsive system. Discrimination in services, accommodation, and employment remained pervasive throughout Canada despite the proliferation of anti-discrimination statutes. Blacks in Nova Scotia, for example, faced an array of abuses:

In 1962, Calvin Ruck, a black civil servant, was refused a haircut by a white barber. The barber told Ruck, "You'll not get a haircut here." Two years earlier, a white landlord refused to rent an apartment to Mrs. Mildred Haley upon the landlord's realization that Mrs. Haley, a widow with two young children, was black. In 1964, a black Beechville man tried to enroll his daughter at a school in Lakeside in hopes the young girl would receive a better education in a predominantly white community. The father was told, first by the Lakeside principal and then by the school board, that he would have to register his daughter in their home community of Beechville. At the same time, however, a white Beechville woman with the same intentions was successful in enrolling her child at the Lakeside school.[85]

A more sophisticated human rights system was needed to address such a fundamental social problem. Reality did not reflect rhetoric. In any case, most political leaders continued to oppose expansive human rights legislation. Even when policy-makers agreed that the state had a responsibility to advance human rights, in practice the law often failed to achieve its own limited mandate. Certainly, the failure to include sex discrimination suggested a narrow vision for the human rights state in the late 1950s.

3
Gender and Canada's Human Rights State

Anti-discrimination legislation was, to be sure, an important legal innovation. It challenged over a century of inequitable practices, especially in employment. Nevertheless, it contained an obvious flaw: a narrow focus on race, religion, and ethnicity. Why is it that, during an era of numerous milestones in anti-discrimination law, not a single statute prohibited discrimination against women?

It was not as if sex discrimination was invisible. Consider, for example, Doris Anderson, who was editor of the leading women's magazine from 1957 to 1977 and instrumental in turning *Chatelaine* into the most successful magazine in the country. She was a highly visible public figure and in some ways an icon of liberal feminism. Even she faced many of the same obstacles and frustrations most women encountered at work every day. She was never promoted above editor, earned 20 percent less than other editors in the company, and was almost fired when she became pregnant. As an associate editor, she also had to endure weekly lunch meetings with her male editor:

> He insisted I match him drink for drink, although he must have weighed a good hundred pounds more than I. In those days I could hold my own – as most women in my business had to learn to do. After lunches with Clare, though, I always took a trip to the washroom, put my finger down my throat, and threw up; otherwise I would never have been able to go back to the office and function with any degree of efficacy.[1]

Employers often justified lower wages for women on the basis of stereotypes or unsubstantiated beliefs: women were financially supported by men or they needed only to support themselves; they had a lower standard of living; they ate less; they did not spend money on luxuries such as alcohol or tobacco.[2] Workers' organizations were also exclusionary. In the 1910s, the Moulders' Union, with the support of the Vancouver Trades and Labour Council, wanted to prohibit female labour in foundries because the work was unsuitable for women. The Barbers' Union also banned women for reasons it explained during the 1914 hearings of the Royal Commission on Labour Conditions in British Columbia: "When women come slopping around over some of these dirty old bums the way they sometimes have to do we don't consider that they ought out be in that kind of business. It does them no good as a general rule. I don't think you would choose a lady barber for a wife."[3]

Employers refused to hire women in certain professions, and they published advertisements for "male only" positions; women were ghettoized in low-paying jobs or refused promotion; unions often endorsed separate wage scales; employers imposed job requirements such as height and weight minimums; and women were fired when they became pregnant or married or divorced. And these were just some of the most common and visible examples. Before she became editor of *Chatelaine*, Doris Anderson struggled every day in a male-oriented work culture. Newspaper editors treated female copywriters differently: "The head of the millinery department would often just slash through my heading and blurb with a black pencil and send it back. Later that day, looking over my revised copy, he would compliment me on a 'vastly improved' effort. Usually I had given him almost identical copy, knowing his mood 'improved vastly' by the afternoon."[4] Working-class women who were the first to be employed in male-dominated mines faced employers who were openly hostile to their presence. Several companies, such as Lornex in British Columbia and Stelco in Ontario, simply refused to build washrooms for women. Debbie Field was twenty-eight when she and 180 others were the first women to work for Stelco in Hamilton. According to Field, Stelco was determined that they would fail:

> Washrooms and showers were a huge issue. The women had a trailer in which to change their clothes and take a shower, and we had to walk huge distances to it. We had to share a washroom with the men. They put up dividers so we couldn't see the urinals. So you would walk into a washroom

and there would be an older immigrant man who was totally mortified because he has just finished peeing.[5]

Sexual harassment, which Anderson describes as "so common that it was rarely even talked about," usually appeared in the form of pin-ups or graffiti if not outright groping or propositions from male staff.[6]

According to Frager and Patrias, Ontario's failure to recognize sex discrimination in its legislation reflected "conventional beliefs about women's fundamental nature, and, with few exceptions, [politicians] were therefore blind to much of the discrimination women faced."[7] Dean Beeby explains that the Co-operative Commonwealth Federation (CCF) hesitated to criticize the Ontario Conservative government's proposed bill of rights in 1947 for not including sex discrimination because the party did not have sufficient evidence to argue the social implications of discrimination against women: "CCFers, as well as many social critics, were aware of instances of injustices against women in the labour force, but something more comprehensive was required to bring such questions into legislative form."[8] Four years later, the CCF recommended in committee that the Conservative government amend its proposed Fair Employment Practices Act to include sex, but the proposal was soundly rejected.[9] In the case of the Saskatchewan Bill of Rights,

> much to the chagrin of key female CCF activists such as Marjory Mann and Barbara Cass-Beggs, the prohibition of discrimination based on sex, originally included by [Morris] Shumiatcher, was dropped from the bill's final draft. The desire to maintain protective labour legislation for women, as well as a more general paternalistic attitude toward them, was probably responsible for this omission.[10]

The potential threat to protective labour legislation, or the belief that equal pay was an economic issue, whereas anti-discrimination was a social issue (or that equal pay would backfire and create unemployment for women), led some women's rights advocates to accept the divide between equal pay and anti-discrimination legislation.[11]

Only three people, Stanley Knowles and Alistair Stewart of the CCF, and Social Credit MP C.E. Johnston, raised concerns in Parliament about the failure to include sex discrimination in the federal Fair Employment Practices bill. Not even Ellen Fairclough, one of the few female MPs in the country, raised the issue or included sex in her own private member's bill (she did sponsor a bill for equal pay). When confronted with this omission, Minister of Justice Milton Gregg responded that including sex would be too complicated and that the government wanted to begin with the "basics."[12]

Advocates for women's rights were not silent. Johnston, for instance, indicated in Parliament that MPs had received numerous letters from women's organizations throughout Canada protesting the bill's failure to prohibit sex discrimination.[13] Agnes Macphail expressed her own exasperation with the failure of the Ontario legislation to include sex:

> What are women to think? ... Anybody of any creed, anybody of any colour, anybody of any nationality, anybody of any ancestry or anybody of any religion, so long as they are male will get equal treatment, but, if it is a woman involved, even if her ancestry is strictly Canadian, she has been here all her life and her family for generations, she can be discriminated against.[14]

In an interview with historians Ruth Frager and Carmela Patrias, Kalmen Kaplansky admitted that he and other advocates failed to fully acknowledge sex discrimination. According to Frager and Patrias,

> Kaplansky, a leader of the human rights campaigns in the 1940s and early 1950s, declared that the reason was straightforward: women were just not considered equal at that time, for they were expected to be mothers and to concentrate on looking after their families. Most human rights activists apparently believed that women were so fundamentally different from men that issues of sex discrimination could be dismissed on that basis. Many activists held deep convictions concerning the injustice of racist, ethnic and religious discrimination, while remaining blind to sex discrimination. In short, they reflected the sexism that was so widespread in Canadian society at that time.[15]

Organized labour, which was in the vanguard of campaigns for anti-discrimination legislation, was similarly blind to sex discrimination. Sexism was prevalent within its ranks. Unions had a long history of supporting lower wages for women (including for paid staff working for unions), weak support for unionizing female workers, ignoring issues of special concern to women, and portraying female employment as a threat to male wages and job security. Men dominated union leadership. Many unions negotiated separate salary scales for men and women until the advent of equal pay legislation.[16] Not until 1968 did the Canadian Labour Congress, which had been a leading advocate for anti-discrimination legislation since the 1940s, include sex discrimination in its official agenda.[17]

Another possible explanation for the lack of legislation dealing with sex discrimination in 1950s Canada is that women did not have the political influence or organizational strength to force the issue onto the political agenda. Certainly, the leading feminist groups of the period, including the Canadian Federation of Business and Professional Women's Clubs, National Council of Women, and the Young Women's Christian Association (among others), were calling for the inclusion of sex in anti-discrimination laws. In 1953, for instance, a delegation from the Canadian Federation of Business and Professional Women's Clubs and the National Council of Women lobbied for a federal ban on sex discrimination as well as for equal pay legislation.[18] The federation complained that the legislation would "afford protection in matters of employment – hiring, promotion and pay – for Jews, Chinamen and Negros, but not for women."[19] But few women held elected office before the late 1960s. In British Columbia, for example, no woman held a cabinet portfolio until Tilly Rolston was appointed in 1952, and her death soon afterward left a male-dominated cabinet. Grace McInnis, the province's first female MP, was elected in 1965 and was the only woman in Parliament from 1968 to 1972.

During the first successful campaigns for anti-discrimination legislation in Ontario, male activists and reformers advanced their cause by exploiting their close ties to the political elite.[20] Women did not have equal access. The early delegations to Premier Frost did represent women's organizations, but they were a minority voice among the male lawyers, clergymen, and union leaders who dominated the proceedings. True, women's groups successfully fought for equal pay legislation, but most of them lamented its weakness. And unlike fair employment or accommodation practices legislation, equal pay legislation reinforced a gendered division of labour rather than the principle of equal treatment.[21]

Perhaps the most fascinating and telling evidence regarding the failure to ban sex discrimination came from the women's movement itself. In 1912, for example, several unions recommended to the Royal Commission on Labour Conditions that the government establish a minimum weekly wage of $6.50 for female workers. However, the Vancouver Local Council of Women suggested that the wage should be set at $5.00 "to be fair to employers as well as employees."[22] In the 1930s, the Canadian Federation of Business and Professional Women's Clubs had emerged as a vocal advocate for women's right to work. It condemned low salaries and passed resolutions against workplace discrimination based on marital status. And yet, by the late 1930s, "even the federation's president used the language of need rather than rights to justify her organization's defence of employed women. In a similar vein, most spokespersons for the National Council of Women (an umbrella organization for various women's groups) steered clear of the language of rights and argued that only financial need could justify married women's work."[23]

This was no longer the case in the 1950s. Several women's organizations, including the Canadian Federation of Business and Professional Women's Clubs, Imperial Order Daughters of the Empire, and the University Women's Club (St. Catherine's), protested Ottawa's failure to include sex in the 1953 Fair Employment Practices Act. However, the Toronto branch of the National Council of Jewish Women commended the government and made no mention of the omission.[24] Margaret Hyndman, president of the Business and Professional Women's Clubs, lobbied Ontario premier Leslie Frost for equal pay legislation while at the same time endorsing sex stereotyping of jobs. She assured Frost that large sectors of the economy were male-dominated and that equal pay would not affect them. The federation also showed no awareness of the situation facing minority women, although by the 1940s the National Council of Women and the YWCA were committed to fighting sex and racial discrimination.[25] Even then, it is unclear whether their position found much support among local chapters. It is noteworthy that the Vancouver Council of Women's 1959 resolution calling for fair practices legislation *did not include sex*. Instead, it recommended a ban against discrimination on the basis of race, colour, religion, and national origin.[26] And when the National Council of Jewish Women's Toronto branch sent a letter to the premier of Ontario, calling for an end to discrimination in employment, it asked for legislation dealing with race, colour, or creed – not sex.

Equal Pay

Without a doubt, sex discrimination was a perplexing omission in early anti-discrimination legislation. However, most jurisdictions did introduce a series of equal pay laws during the 1950s (the National War Labour Board had implemented "equal pay for equal work" in 1942, which lasted throughout the Second World War).[27] Unequal pay was perhaps the most common form of sex discrimination in employment, and it affected all women. The impetus for legislation was undoubtedly a response to women's expanding role in the labour force. As Ruth Frager and Carmela Patrias note, women as a percentage of the paid workforce "climbed slowly in the first four decades of the twentieth century, from 13 percent in 1901 to 17 percent in 1931 and almost 20 percent in 1941. More dramatic changes have taken place in the last half century, from 22 percent in 1951 to 34 percent in 1971 and almost 45 percent in 1991."[28] And yet, differential minimum wage laws for men and women were enforced in most provinces. As late as 1971, according to Statistics Canada, women working full-time jobs earned less than 60 percent of a male wage: "In every occupational category, in every age group, and at every level of education, women on average, still earned less than men."[29]

Social movements also played a crucial role in securing the first equal pay laws.[30] The National Council of Women had been advocating for equal pay since the 1920s.[31] During the war, women's organizations successfully lobbied to raise the basic pay for servicewomen to 90 percent of the male rate. In 1950, twenty-one affiliates of the YWCA established public affairs committees in Ontario to advocate for laws to ban sex discrimination. Margaret Hyndman, president of the Business and Professional Women's Clubs, led a delegation to Premier Leslie Frost in 1951 to demand equal pay legislation and a prohibition on sex discrimination in employment. Hyndman, a lawyer, helped draft the Ontario Female Employees Fair Remuneration Act (1951), which was the first equal pay statute in Canada. Business and Professional Women's Clubs committees outside Ontario also lobbied for equal pay laws.[32] Meanwhile, in Ottawa, the Business and Professional Women's Clubs and the National Council of Women convinced the federal Liberal government to implement equal pay legislation covering seventy thousand women working in federal jurisdiction.[33] Women's Institutes were also active in lobbying for equal pay.[34]

The CCF's influence was especially notable in Ontario. Because of its close ties to organized labour, the party had a natural interest in equal pay, especially as many male workers believed that hiring women depressed wages.[35] The Women's Committee of the Ontario CCF convinced the party leadership to submit an equal pay law to the legislature in 1949 (the bill was defeated).[36] Although the CCF failed to form a government, this did not prevent other parties, concerned about the threat of a party with a strong base of support among women and workers, from borrowing its policies. Ontario's 1951 Female Employees Fair Remuneration Act was replicated in many other jurisdictions by 1960 (Figure 2).

FIGURE 2 **Equal pay legislation**

1951	Ontario Female Employees Fair Remuneration Act
1952	Saskatchewan Equal Pay Act
1953	British Columbia Equal Pay Act
1956	Canada Female Employees Equal Pay Act
1956	Manitoba Equal Pay Act
1956	Nova Scotia Equal Pay Act
1957	Alberta Act to amend The Alberta Labour Act (equal pay amendment)
1959	PEI Equal Pay Act
1960	New Brunswick Female Employees Fair Remuneration Act
1969	Newfoundland Human Rights Code
1970	Ontario Women's Equal Employment Opportunity Act
1975	Quebec Charter of Human Rights and Freedoms

But equal pay laws were largely symbolic. They did little to advance equal pay for women, because they were not adequately enforced and because women feared retribution from their employers. As the authors of the leading textbook on women's history in Canada point out, the laws were fundamentally flawed:

> The wage differential continued to exist despite the enactment between 1951 and 1973 of equal pay for equal work legislation by the federal government and all the provincial governments except Quebec. The primary weakness of these laws was that they applied only when women performed the same or very similar work to men in the same establishment, a situation that the existence of female work ghettos precluded. Equal pay laws sometimes actually reinforced the sexual division of labour, since employers in industries highly reliant on female labour could benefit from employing only women and paying them low wages.[37]

Ontario's Female Employees Fair Remuneration Act (1951-60) was equally dismal. Only twelve employers (involving 124 women) faced charges under the legislation, and in virtually every case nothing resulted from the complaint despite an obvious gap in wages.[38] The CCF's Status of Women Committee described the act as "a toothless ghost of a real equal-pay bill."[39] Maureen Richardson's 1954 equal pay complaint in Ontario is a perfect example of how the law was ineffective, not only in and of itself, but also because of the people who were responsible for enforcing it:

FIGURE 3 Sex discrimination amendments to human rights legislation

1969	British Columbia	Human Rights Act
1969	Newfoundland	Human Rights Code
1970	Manitoba	Human Rights Act
1971	Alberta	An Act to Amend the Human Rights Act
1971	New Brunswick	Human Rights Code
1972	Nova Scotia	An Act to Amend Chapter 11 of the Human Rights Act
1972	Ontario	An Act to amend The Ontario Human Rights Code
1972	Saskatchewan	An Act to amend the Saskatchewan Bill of Rights Act (with similar amendments to Fair Employment and Practices statutes)
1975	Prince Edward Island	Human Rights Act
1975	Quebec	Charter of Human Rights and Freedoms
1977	Canada	Canadian Human Rights Act

Richardson's contention was that she had replaced a man who worked on a particular machine but that her pay was significantly less than his had been. [Louis Fine, director of the Fair Employment Services Branch] responded curtly that "a female employee must compare the work she is now doing with the work that a male is now doing." Richardson's union representative charged that Fine's narrow interpretations of the act was "not consistent with the actual wording." However, Fine refused to budge, and Fine's notes in the file indicate that his rigid interpretation was later confirmed by the minister of labour.[40]

The federal Bill of Rights (1960) banned sex discrimination in employment; however, as Beverley Baines explains, in practice it "never guaranteed sex equality to women."[41] Ontario's Human Rights Code (1962) did not include sex. Not until British Columbia's 1969 Human Rights Act (and Newfoundland's Human Rights Code of the same year) did a human rights statute contain an enforceable prohibition on sex discrimination. Within eight years, though, every other jurisdiction would follow suit (Figure 3). Recognizing this form of discrimination became part of the process of shifting from fair employment and accommodation practices legislation to expansive human rights law.

Human Rights Legislation

The emergence of a more sophisticated human rights state in the 1960s was partly attributable to the popularization of human rights around the world. The European Convention on Human Rights (1950), one of the first regional human rights treaties, included an enforcement mechanism in the form of the European Court of Human Rights. In the United States, Washington passed civil rights legislation in 1959 and 1964, and many US states implemented anti-discrimination laws in the 1940s and 1950s.[42] The Australian government cited international obligations when it introduced its own legislation during the 1970s.[43] The United Kingdom established Racial Equality and Equal Opportunities Commissions in 1971 and 1975, respectively. By the 1970s, national human rights institutions had begun to proliferate across the globe.[44] Thomas Pegram describes their diffusion as a "contagion effect": a process arising from a "complex domestic, regional, and international interaction of actors, arenas, and modalities of diffusion" that resulted in a "wave phoenomenon of varying intensity across regions," beginning in Europe and North America.[45]

In Canada, international developments were often cited to justify legal reform. During the 1940s, as Eric Adams points out,

> civil liberties groups called for the entrenchment of constitutional rights, as did the Jehovah's Witnesses, the Canadian Jewish Congress, the National Council of Women of Canada, representatives of the Chinese Canadian community, and a number of other churches, unions, and social organizations. Virtually all cited the United Nations Charter or UDHR [Universal Declaration of Human Rights] as a touchstone for Canada to emulate.[46]

Premier Leslie Frost of Ontario often invoked the international context to justify the first anti-discrimination laws.[47] When Prime Minister John Diefenbaker introduced a bill that would ultimately result in the 1960 Canadian Bill of Rights (statutory, not constitutional), he declared that the "measure that I introduce is the first step on the part of Canada to carry out the acceptance either of the [UDHR] or the principles that activated those who produced that noble document."[48] Direct reference to the UDHR was made in the Ontario Human Rights Code (1962), and it was the model for the Quebec Charter of Human Rights and Freedoms (1975). Alberta, Manitoba, New Brunswick, Newfoundland, Prince Edward Island, and Quebec also introduced their human rights laws partly in response to international human rights treaties or events such as the International Year for Human Rights.[49] In the case of New Brunswick, the "*Human Rights Act* was deeply influenced by the human rights initiatives drafted by the United Nations, and was an important step in the promoting of a human rights culture."[50] Social movements in each of these provinces, which were at the forefront of lobbying for human rights legislation, all referred to the UDHR in their foundation constitutions.[51]

Ontario began Canada's process of human rights legal reform in 1962. The province boasted a racially and ethnically diverse population, and its rapid economic growth attracted many post-war immigrants to Canada. Discrimination was a greater problem in a province undergoing a significant demographic change than in, for instance, Newfoundland, where whites of European ancestry vastly dominated the region. (By the 1930s, 95 percent of Newfoundland's population was native-born, mainly of English and Irish descent. Between 1946 and 1961, only 4,236 people immigrated to Newfoundland, which in 1961 had a population of 457,853.)[52] Ontario politicians thus found it increasingly difficult to refute claims that discrimination was a social problem. And given the central role that social movements have historically played in securing human rights legislation, it is not surprising that the province consistently led the way in introducing progressive laws. Toronto alone possessed a vibrant social movement sector, including organized labour, civil libertarians, churches, associations representing minorities and women, and an influential Jewish community.[53]

The Ontario Human Rights Code (1962) incorporated existing provincial anti-discrimination laws into a single statute that was enforced through the Human Rights Commission.[54] The code prohibited discrimination on the basis of religion, race, and ethnicity in accommodation, employment, and services (Ontario banned sex discrimination in employment in 1970). Full-time human rights officers – civil servants working for the government – staffed the commission and were responsible for receiving and investigating complaints. If an individual had a legitimate complaint within the scope of the code, the officer would first attempt conciliation between the two parties. If this failed, the commission could recommend that the case be sent to an independent board of inquiry appointed by the minister of labour to force a settlement. Perhaps the most important innovation contained in the Ontario legislation, in addition to having the government absorb the entire cost of investigating the complaint, was that the commission would represent the complainant before the board of inquiry. As a result, complainants did not shoulder the burden of investigating and litigating the complaint, which was a major obstacle to seeking remedy through the courts.[55] Offenders might pay a fine, offer an apology, reinstate an employee, or agree to a negotiated settlement. The commission was further mandated to educate the public about human rights.

The Ontario Human Rights Code was amended numerous times in the following decade. In 1965, it was extended to cover the government and all its agencies, as well as the occupancy of commercial space. The housing section was revised to apply to three or more self-contained units in apartment buildings (from six). In 1967, an amendment extended coverage to all housing and eliminated the exemption for employers with fewer than five employees. The government passed the Age Discrimination Act in 1966 to protect workers between the ages of forty and sixty-five, and the law was further amended in 1968 to prohibit age discrimination in advertising. Additional amendments in 1969 included replacing the exemption for religious, philanthropic, educational, social, and fraternal organizations with a "bona fide occupation requirement" clause; a section was added to protect individuals from reprisals for submitting complaints; and the fines for violations of the code were increased from $100 to $500 for individuals. A year later, the law was changed to enhance the commission's power to investigate complaints (it could now obtain warrants) and to receive complaints from third parties. Without going to court, boards of inquiry could now award damages and order individuals to comply with the law. Finally, in 1972, potential fines were increased to $1,000 for individuals and $5,000 for organizations; age and sex discrimination were incorporated into all aspects of the code; and self-governing professions were added to it. The Human Rights Commission was also given the authority to initiate complaints and to approve affirmative action programs.[56]

These reforms were not without opposition, but criticisms were far more muted by this time. In 1966, the *Toronto Globe and Mail* described the Ontario Age Discrimination Act as "another unworkable law." Although the legislation was laudable in principle, the editors suggested, the commission could not possibly navigate the complexities of determining whether someone had been denied employment due to age or an inability to do the work. Two years later, when the first case was brought before a board of inquiry, the *Globe and Mail* editors were again critical. But their reservations reflected the same tired rhetoric from the 1940s. After an inquiry fined an employment agency five hundred dollars for advertising a secretarial position limited to a specific age range, the newspaper lamented the government's interference in business practices and raised concerns about the implications of administrative boards with judicial powers.[57]

FIGURE 4 **Human rights legislation**

Year	Legislation	Commission or tribunal
1962	Ontario Human Rights Code	1961
1963	Nova Scotia Human Rights Act	1967
1966	Alberta Human Rights Act	1972
1967	New Brunswick Human Rights Act	1967
1968	PEI Human Rights Code	1975
1969	BC Human Rights Act	1969
1969	Newfoundland Human Rights Code	1971
1970	Manitoba Human Rights Act	1970
1971	Alberta Bill of Rights & Individual Rights Protection Act	1972
1972	British Columbia Human Rights Code	1972
1975	Quebec Charter of Human Rights and Freedoms	1975
1977	Canada Human Rights Act	1977
1979	Saskatchewan Human Rights Code	1972
1987	Yukon Human Rights Act	1987
2002	Northwest Territories Human Rights Act	2002
2003	Nunavut Human Rights Act	2003

NOTE: Ontario and Saskatchewan established commissions to enforce existing legislation before they enacted human rights legislation.

Concerns surrounding the implications of this new form of state regulation did not hinder the spread of reforms to the human rights state. Human rights laws and commissions were introduced throughout Canada in the fifteen years following the Ontario Human Rights Code (Figure 4).[58] Ontario's statute became the model that was replicated in other jurisdictions, which resulted in a remarkably uniform system across the country. Political leaders gave various reasons for implementing human rights legislation, including international obligations. Discrimination against black citizens in Nova Scotia was a key factor in that province.[59] Quebec's human rights law was delayed until 1975 as the government struggled to address the contentious issue of language rights in separate legislation.

Human rights legislation was vastly more effective than its antidiscrimination counterpart. Jane Gawne's case was a typical example of how it functioned in practice. On 30 November 1976, responding to a Canadian Manpower posting from an engineering firm for a job on a survey crew, Gawne and her husband visited the company's offices in Penticton, British Columbia. After waiting in the outer office for a few minutes, they were called into Richard Chapman's private office to discuss the position. Chapman made it clear that he did not think the work was appropriate for a woman. The investigator assigned to the case stated that

> Mr. Chapman did not pursue [Gawne's] experience. According to her, he stated that he had hired a woman before and that there had been problems – it hadn't worked out. He felt that hiring a woman would create two problems: first, the extra cost to the company of obtaining an extra room for out of town trips and, second, the fact that hiring a woman might upset the wives of other crew members. He asked her husband whether he would object to her going out of town with other men for periods of time and was advised by him that that would not be a problem.[60]

After the interview, as Chapman was walking Gawne and her husband out, he asked another man in the office about her application. His colleague agreed that hiring a woman to work on a crew out of town would be impractical. Chapman promised that, if any jobs came up in the city, he would contact her. He never did.

The British Columbia Human Rights Branch dispatched a human rights investigator to speak with Gawne and Chapman several times over the next year. The officer hoped that Chapman would reconsider his decision, but Chapman refused to listen and later conceded that he did not take the officer's attempts very seriously. Unable to effectuate a settlement, the officer recommended to the director of the Human Rights Branch that the case be sent to a board of inquiry. The director agreed and submitted a request to the minister of labour, who then appointed University of British Columbia law professor Beverley M. McLachlin (a future chief justice of the Supreme Court of Canada) to hold a board of inquiry. The hearing took place in an office (not a courtroom) of the Penticton Court House on 8 December 1978. McLachlin, Chapman, Gawne, and a lawyer appointed by the Human Rights Commission to represent Gawne sat around a desk to hear Chapman defend his actions. He spoke in detail about how he had acted with the best of intentions and as a fair-minded person. He admitted that he had considered the suitability of a woman to work on a survey crew but insisted that this had not affected his decision. McLachlin was not convinced. Everyone agreed that Gawne was fully qualified for the job, and nothing except sex discrimination could explain Chapman's refusal to hire her. Under normal circumstances, McLachlin would have ordered Chapman to employ Gawne, but Gawne was no longer interested in the position. Instead,

McLachlin ordered Chapman to cease acting in a discriminatory manner, pay Gawne damages in the amount of $280 (ten days' earnings), and pay $500 for having delayed the investigation over two years.[61]

Although Gawne's case went to a board of inquiry, it is important to note that the human rights officer had initially attempted an informal resolution. Conciliation, not confrontation, was an emerging feature of the human rights state. Daniel G. Hill, the first chair of the Ontario Human Rights Commission, emphasized the importance of this aspect of the commission's work: "The conciliation process is highly flexible and, as a policy, the investigator concentrates rather less on the issue of legal guilt than on the issue of effectuating a satisfactory settlement. Such procedure is predicated on the thesis that confrontation and accusation tend to reinforce the discriminatory attitude."[62] He described the process of conciliating a complaint as follows:

> The investigator, who detects discrimination, seeks not only to settle the case, but to start a process of reeducation with the respondent. In this regard, he listens patiently to all the anxieties and reasons for practicing discrimination expressed by the respondent. During such discussions, the respondent is generally assured that, based on Canadian experience, he will lose neither money nor status if he accepts minority group members in his establishment. He is also reminded, throughout, of his responsibilities as a citizen to abide by the legislation of this province.[63]

Conciliation became a common feature of Canadian human rights law. Hill and Thomas Eberlee, another official with the Ontario Human Rights Commission, described how it worked during these early years:

> A typical example of an informal complaint occurred not long ago when a landlord in Toronto decided to evict a Negro family from a house which he had let to them. He was, presumably, acting under pressure from persons in the area who objected to the presence of Negroes in their neighbourhood. A labour organization acting for the complainants had tried, in vain, to obtain revocation of the notice but finally appealed to the commission to assist in the case. The matter was negotiated successfully and the eviction notice withdrawn.[64]

Another pillar of the emerging human rights state was education. The goal of favouring conciliation rather than confrontation was the promotion of tolerance. The new focus of the human rights state, therefore, was *prevention;* punishment was a last resort. The education mandate was an enduring legacy of the human rights state.[65] As law professor Bill Black noted in a review of BC human rights legislation, "If a central goal of the Code is prevention, education and information must be a key part of the strategy."[66]

Some provinces lagged in this area. Newfoundland and Prince Edward Island, for example, had no human rights education program whatsoever until the mid-1980s.[67] The BC Social Credit government, as we will see later, disdained human rights legislation and provided no resources for education. Other provinces set aside modest resources, and over time education became a mainstay of the human rights state. In New Brunswick, for instance, the Human Rights Commission engaged in "the production of educational materials including printed material and videos; the presentation of public workshops; involvement in community development activities; assisting employers with policy development; and the annual presentation of the Human Rights Award recognizing individuals who have promoted human rights in New Brunswick."[68] It also actively sought to make people aware of the commission and the legislation through seminars, newspaper, television, and radio interviews, television advertisements, pamphlets, and conferences. This type of educational outreach was typical of other commissions in Canada by the late 1970s. By 1968, almost 90 percent of the New Brunswick Human Rights Commission budget was devoted to promotional efforts.[69]

Social movements continued to play a central role in securing legal reform. Campaigns for more expansive human rights legislation were buoyed with the emergence of large numbers of human rights organizations. Whereas only a few civil liberties groups were active in the 1940s and 1950s, dozens of new ones were born in the 1960s and 1970s (at least one in each province). Many were self-identified "human rights" associations dedicated to the more expansive principles of the Universal Declaration of Human Rights.[70] All became powerful advocates for reform. In Alberta, Newfoundland, and Saskatchewan, human rights associations were created in the wake of the International Year for Human Rights in 1968, and a primary mandate for each was the creation of a human rights regime similar to the Ontario model. The Newfoundland Human Rights Association was the leading advocate for implementing, and later reforming, human rights law in that province.[71] Saskatchewan's Human Rights Association spent years working with the provincial government to introduce stronger human rights legislation.[72] Immediately after its creation, the Alberta Human Rights and Civil Liberties Association struck a working group to lobby for amendments to the province's proposed human rights legislation.[73] Similar reform campaigns were launched by the British Columbia Civil Liberties Association, Canadian Civil Liberties Association (Toronto), Manitoba Association for Rights and Liberties, Nova Scotia Human Rights Association, and the Prince Edward Island Civil Liberties Association. Of all these groups, though, none was more important in the creation of an expansive human rights regime than Quebec's Ligue des droits de l'homme. It advocated tirelessly for provincial human rights legislation and is generally credited as the primary influence in the final draft of the 1975 Quebec Charter of Human Rights and Freedoms.[74]

Organized labour could often be counted upon during this period to support human rights legislation. The Canadian Labour Congress participated in consultations in the creation of the 1977 Canadian Human Rights Act, and its provincial affiliates were at the forefront of campaigns for provincial legislation.[75] In Nova Scotia, the government consulted with the labour congress's Human Rights Committee in drafting the Human Rights Code. The Jewish Labour Committee (JLC) remained active throughout the 1970s, although rights associations had largely eclipsed its activities by this time. The Montreal JLC affiliate organized several delegations to the provincial government in the early 1970s for a human rights law.[76] In Ontario, the provincial labour federation kept a close watch on the enforcement of human rights legislation and regularly lobbied for reform.[77] But there were limits to labour movement advocacy. For instance, although the Saskatchewan Federation of Labour generated a 1976 policy that disallowed discrimination on the basis of sexual orientation, other Canadian labour federations did not follow its lead for many years to come.[78]

The labour movement and human rights associations were only a few among many social movement organizations lobbying for the creation of human rights legislation to replace ineffective anti-discrimination laws. Groups as diverse as the Conseil du Patronat du Québec, the Newfoundland Status of Women Council, the Nova Scotia Association for the Advancement of Coloured People, and Vancouver's Civic Unity Association added their support to campaigns for legal reform.[79] In fact, as we will see, social movements were not only a key factor in the creation of the human rights state, but were also essential to the enforcement of human rights law.

In 1979, Saskatchewan became the final jurisdiction to move beyond fair employment and accommodations practices legislation to enter a new era of human rights law. Despite having a separate legal regime in each jurisdiction, the human rights state was surprisingly uniform across Canada: it entailed a comprehensive human rights law that encompassed employment, housing, and services; it created an agency with a mandate for enforcement, research, education, and legal reform; it engaged full-time civil servants who specialized in human rights enforcement; it emphasized conciliation rather than litigation; its commissions represented complainants before formal inquiries; it established independent boards of inquiry; and it offered remedies in the form of fines, reinstating an employee, or providing a service or an apology. The person responsible for implementing human rights was always the attorney general or the minister of labour or justice (except in Manitoba and Ottawa, where the minister of municipal affairs and the secretary of state were tasked with the chore). They appointed boards of inquiry, and the commission had carriage of the complaint (in Quebec the legislation was enforced by courts until 1989, when a permanent human rights tribunal was created). Each statute prohibited discrimination on the basis of race, colour, religion, sex, ethnicity, age, and marital status (over time at least thirty grounds for discrimination were recognized in Canada).[80]

Human rights legislation was far from perfect, however. Discrimination against people with disabilities was not banned until the 1980s, and many provinces refused to recognize sexual orientation until the late 1990s. Whether or not Aboriginal people were adequately protected under human rights law was another complication. Under the federal Human Rights Act, Aboriginal people on reserves were not permitted to submit complaints to the Canadian Human Rights Commission. They could, and did, submit complaints under provincial statutes for racial discrimination.[81] For example, the first BC board of inquiry involving an Aboriginal was held in 1975. Jean Sam, an Aboriginal resident of Houston who was commuting to Burns Lake to take courses at the Regional College, attempted to rent a room at the Tweedsmuir Hotel. When Sam asked the hotel desk clerk about renting a room for three weeks, she was told to speak to the manager. As she walked toward the bar, she encountered the owner, Paul Tymchischin, and asked him about renting a room. Tymchischin promptly refused her request, saying that renting to "Indians" was bad business: they caused damages, never had money to pay rent, brought undesirable people into the hotel, and partied too much. When she asked him bluntly,

"So you won't rent a room to an Indian?" Tymchischin responded "No." Witnesses later testified that Tymchischin told them that Indians did not live like white people and that 95 percent of them were "no good," that they treated white people like animals, that they did not look respectable, and that their presence would force others out of the Tweedsmuir. An investigation later uncovered that the hotel had posted a notice behind the desk, which informed employees of its policy:

> Notice to All Desk Clerks – Do not rent any rooms to any Indians, no matter who unless checked out first with Paul. Also, do not rent to anyone that is intoxicated in any way or is abusive in any way – Excuse – we are all full up, sorry, etc. etc. this applies all the time. We are trying to run a decent place so that tourists are not afraid to walk into the lobby. Please see that all desk clerks adhere to this rule. Thank you. Manager.[82]

Maurice Guilbault, a human rights investigator, endeavoured to settle the complaint. But Tymchischin refused to speak with him or provide any documents. He told Guilbault that he "didn't give a damn about the regulations" and that Guilbault could "go to hell." A board of inquiry was appointed. However, when it arrived in Burns Lake to hold the hearing, the board chairman received a letter from Tymchischin, which explained that he was unable to attend because the hearing coincided with Ukrainian Christmas (in fact, Ukrainian Christmas was not for another week, and Guilbault spotted Tymchischin eating at a diner across the street). The board of inquiry awarded Sam $1,250, the largest penalty ever granted at that time.[83]

But the Sam case was rare. Although British Columbia had a substantial Aboriginal population, fewer than 5 percent of boards of inquiry involved Aboriginal people. The New Brunswick Human Rights Commission, which was unique in establishing a "Native Desk" to address Aboriginal issues, received many complaints of rights violations on reserves. Because provincial commissions had no jurisdiction on reserves, they had to rely on informal discussions to attempt conciliation.[84]

Other deficiencies with human rights law were common across Canada. Fines were modest, often between $500 and $1,000. Only Quebec's legislation recognized economic, social, and cultural rights. Quebec was also the only jurisdiction where commissioners were appointed directly by the National Assembly, which assured a greater degree of independence and job security. Other statutes empowered the cabinet to appoint commissioners, and except in Quebec and federally, they held their positions at the discretion of the minister. Moreover, many of the first human rights laws included exemptions for charitable, philanthropic, or religious institutions, as well as major employers and service providers such as educational institutions.[85] These exemptions later became the source of intense controversy. In Newfoundland, for instance, Christian churches monopolized the education system, and their refusal to hire people outside their faith or to allow non-Christians to be elected to local school boards clearly violated the spirit of the law.[86] These exemptions also had a particular impact on women. Kimberly Nixon was refused permission to volunteer as a peer counsellor at Vancouver Rape Relief in 1995 because she was born male. The British Columbia Human Rights Tribunal ruled that Rape Relief's action constituted sex discrimination. But the BC Supreme Court overturned the tribunal's decision and determined that the service was a legitimate exemption to the legislation.[87]

Still, it is difficult to overstate the significance of the human rights state. Human rights commissions were more efficient, faster, and accessible than the courts. They bore the cost of investigating and resolving conflicts. Human rights adjudication was also more accessible than the courts. Specially trained human rights officers investigated complaints, and the staff of human rights commissions were drawn from academia, the media, social activists, churches, and the legal community. By incorporating existing legislation into a single statute, and developing experts in the field of human rights, the state accepted (to a degree) that discrimination was a systemic social problem. As Walter Tarnopolsky suggests, the "consolidation of human rights legislation into a Code to be enforced by Commissions ensures community vindication of the person discriminated against."[88] Significant resources were provided for most human rights adjudication, and each commission had a mandate to educate the public and to recommend future legislative reform to the government. Invariably, with a dedicated bureaucracy and a mandate to educate and promote human rights, the numbers of complaints would have a snowball effect, particularly as citizens became aware of the commission and would not face the financial hardships commonly associated with litigation. A genuine rights revolution had occurred in Canadian law.

4
Women and Anti-Discrimination Law in British Columbia, 1953-69

The BC Equal Pay Act of 1953 was a legal milestone in the province's history. Over the next three decades, the human rights state evolved into one of the most progressive legal regimes in Canada. At the same time, the politics of human rights was nowhere more divisive than in British Columbia. The New Democratic Party (NDP) and the Social Credit Party advanced two competing and dramatically different visions of the human rights state. Both parties were committed to government intervention in the economy, but for different reasons. Whereas the Socreds sought to use the state to enhance the private business sector, the NDP envisioned economic development as a tool for promoting the redistribution of wealth and equality among citizens. Their respective human rights policies reflected their economic philosophies. The NDP wanted to expand the human rights state, whereas the Socreds were determined to restrict its scope. This conflict culminated in 1984, when the Social Credit government introduced new human rights legislation that was so far outside the Canadian standard that it instigated a national debate around the legitimacy of the human rights state.

The evolution of British Columbia's human rights state mirrored that of the rest of Canada. Attempts by the Opposition CCF to introduce resolutions for a provincial bill of rights were defeated by the BC government in 1948, 1950, and 1951.[1] However, the impressive reach of the Jewish Labour Committee (JLC) also extended to Canada's westernmost province. The JLC helped establish the Vancouver Civic Unity Association in 1950 to bring together labour with social movement organizations to campaign for legislation.[2] The JLC also campaigned for a municipal by-law, following several notorious incidents involving interracial couples and groups of friends who were denied services in hotels and bars. The City of Vancouver, in 1952, was one of the first municipalities in Canada to introduce an anti-discrimination bylaw.[3] Similar bylaws had been introduced in Toronto in 1947 and in Windsor, Hamilton, and Oshawa in 1944, 1947, and 1949, respectively.[4] However, Vancouver's bylaw was rarely enforced. Its first test – regarding a black Jamaican man who was refused service at a bar – failed. The court ruled that only the owner of the liquor licence, not the bartender, was liable under the bylaw (but it was the bartender, not the owner, who had discriminated against the customer).[5]

The Equal Pay Act was the first BC statute with the explicit purpose of prohibiting discriminatory practices. The province's female workforce increased from 66,000 in 1953 to 163,000 in 1964. According to the BC Women's Bureau, women constituted a third of the 796,000-strong provincial labour force by 1967.[6] And yet, their opportunities in the labour market were severely restricted. For example, in 1953, of the more than 2,400 British Columbians classified as "Producers of Building Material," only 9 were women; of the 1,700 coal miners, 2 were female; and there were fewer than 200 women among the thousands employed in coastal shipping.[7] In most BC professions, women typically earned less than men. For instance, female clerical staff in 1955 were paid an average weekly salary of $45.84, whereas their male counterparts received $75.36.[8] A veteran female nurse, with far more education than an inexperienced male orderly, earned less than he did.[9]

The systemic underpayment of women's labour had profound personal consequences. Joan Sangster's account of letters to the Royal Commission on the Status of Women offers a window into how women struggled for basic necessities:

> Some of the most painful letters to read are from single working mothers, often deserted, who knew first-hand the injustice of divorce laws, the uselessness of trying to secure spousal support, and the difficulty of supporting their children on a woman's wage. Their budgets – relayed to the last cent – were so tight that a few bus tickets or an extra lunch could make the difference between ending the month in the red or the black.[10]

Women's clerical salaries were so low that few could expect to buy a house or even rent an apartment, and they often relied on bedsits or rented rooms (or depended on their families).[11] Older women, in particular, were often shut out of the job market. Some employers simply replaced them with younger staff. Employment agencies might refuse to hire women over fifty or would use them for cheap labour. The sexual division of labour meant that many women earned half the male wage and would probably be fired when they married or became pregnant. Women in the BC Interior complained about the lack of anything but low-paid seasonal work. Working mothers found themselves stigmatized and accused of neglecting their children: "The charge that working mothers neglected their children was particularly galling, and many women were at pains to point out that they worked *for* their children, so they could have an education, music lessons, even food on the table."[12]

Unequal pay often resulted from the arbitrary decisions of employers. Victoria's school board paid female and male janitors differential wages because the women were assigned different duties: they did not climb ladders. But this decision came from the school board, not the female janitors. In addition, until 1967, employers were not legally required to offer holiday pay for female staff during statutory holidays.[13] Provincial law still recognized a separate minimum wage for men and women until 1971, when the Board of Industrial Relations began to enforce the male minimum wage for female workers.[14] But that did not remedy the sexual division of labour. In 1972, the Status of Women Action Group (SWAG) examined twenty-four retail stores in Victoria and confirmed a long-standing practice that male and female employees were not paid the same, because they were segregated into different departments.[15] Yet, as the Voice of Women and the Victoria Labour Council noted wryly in their submission to the legislature, which cited the SWAG study, "it is difficult to see how selling men's shirts is, in reality, 'substantially' different from selling women's blouses."[16]

The women's movement was not well organized in British Columbia during the 1950s, and there is little evidence to suggest that equal pay legislation was a product of social movement activism. Nonetheless, at least some women's organizations campaigned for equal pay. The Vancouver branch of the Canadian Federation of Business and Professional Women's Clubs castigated Ottawa's failure to include sex in the 1953 Fair Employment Practices Act.[17] As the president of British Columbia's Provincial Council of Women, perhaps the leading women's advocacy group at the time, insisted in 1950, "Equal opportunity and equal pay for men and women, regardless of sex, marital status, race, colour or creed, will not be firmly established unless vigorously promoted by education and legislation."[18]

Certainly, the Equal Pay Act was a far cry from recognizing women's full role in the social, political, and economic life of the province.[19] In fact, according to newspaper coverage, the impetus for its creation was the recent death of the Social Credit minister of education, Tilly Rolston, who had long sought legislation recognizing the equal worth of working women.[20] The act was a symbolic rather than a substantive change in government policy. Laura Jamieson, speaking for the Vancouver Council of Women, grasped its primary weakness in 1953, when she insisted that the provision of equal pay for the "same work as men" was too vague. Her group wanted the legislation to enforce equal pay for work "of comparable nature." According to Jamieson, an employer could simply adjust the duties or classification of female staff to circumvent the act.[21]

Jamieson was right. The Equal Pay Act (1953-69) was a dismal failure. It barred employers from paying lower wages to women who did the same work as men in the same establishment. Only thirty-three women (involving eleven employers) successfully applied for restitution under the act.[22] A *Vancouver Sun* reporter noted in 1953 that there were only twenty-five inspectors across the province who could respond to equal pay complaints, and even then the process did not favour the complainant:

> When a complaint is received, an inspector will move into the plant to check the type of complaint and records and then ask the employers to adjust the female pay scale. Labor department officials say there is "not too much" protection in the act for women who complain. They can protect identity up to a point, but if the issue turns into a dispute a woman worker might find herself revealed to the boss and perhaps fired, unless there is a strong union in the plant.[23]

The Equal Pay Act was soon followed by the Fair Employment Practices Act (1956) and the Public Accommodation Practices Act (1961). A main obstacle faced by the JLC in its campaign, as was the case throughout the country, was the belief that discrimination was not a social problem. One BC MLA insisted during the debates regarding the Fair Employment Practices Act that "discrimination on any grounds contemplated by this bill is virtually non-existent ... Besides, you simply cannot legislate people into the Kingdom of Heaven."[24] And securing the legislation was only the beginning. Because the law was often poorly enforced, social movement groups were required to take up the slack to make it work. In this way, the JLC and organized labour were crucial to the emerging human rights state. Vancouver's JLC committee was typical: it produced educational programs (films, public lectures, literature, an annual race relations institute seminar); wrote briefs to the provincial government; prepared test cases to investigate allegations of discrimination; issued press releases and spoke on local radio; and investigated complaints.[25] It often received complaints on the phone, which it forwarded to the appropriate government department. It also helped victims prepare written complaints and provided someone to assist in conciliation meetings or act as a witness in public hearings.[26] One of its earliest successes came in 1959, when it convinced the Downtown Hotel to stop refusing service to blacks. The hotel owner initially refused but later conceded when the JLC secured a promise from the British Columbia Automobile Association to remove the hotel from its "approved" ranking.[27]

The provincial government did nothing to publicize its anti-discrimination legislation, so it was left to the British Columbia Federation of Labour to produce a *Guide to Employers* and to distribute it across the province. The federation also hired William Giesbrecht as a human rights worker. One of his first projects was a survey of job advertisements and applications in the province. Giesbrecht identified cases of discrimination and forwarded the results to the civil servant responsible for enforcing the legislation (employers routinely included questions on job application forms regarding religious preference, nationality, race, or place of origin).[28] Or, in cases when the government delayed responding to an individual complaint, Giesbrecht lobbied to have the complaint pursued.[29] In several instances, he persuaded large companies to revise their application forms, and he often convinced landlords or cemetery managers to stop discriminating against blacks or Jews.[30] Giesbrecht also worked with the Vancouver Civic Unity Association to arrange test cases for housing discrimination.[31]

The Fair Employment Practices Act and the Public Accommodation Practices Act were no more successful than the Equal Pay Act.[32] A mere six complaints were received under the former and only three under the latter. Four of the six employment complaints and two of the three accommodation complaints were dismissed for falling outside the scope of the legislation (although an unspecified number of infractions were resolved through informal conversations and correspondence with the Department of Labour).[33] The exclusion of charitable, philanthropic, educational, fraternal, religious, and social organizations, as well as the government itself, further hindered the effectiveness of the legislation. And there were several loopholes. In 1967, Giesbrecht helped prepare Lawrence Edgar's complaint under the Public Accommodation Practices Act.[34] Edgar, a carpenter, was an Aboriginal man who had been born and raised near Prince Rupert. In the spring of 1967, he and his wife rented an apartment in North Vancouver that was owned and managed by W.F. Carr and his wife. They moved in on 8 June. The following Sunday, Edgar's sister and niece visited, and as they entered the building, they encountered the managers in the hallway. The next day, Carr and his wife visited the apartment and informed Edgar and his wife that they must vacate the apartment. Carr was quite frank about the reasons: the building had a policy of not renting to coloured people. Edgar was appalled: "I stated that I was an Indian and that I was proud to be an Indian. Mr. and Mrs. Carr indicated that they had not realized from my appearance that I was an Indian and that as far as my wife and I are concerned, they had no complaint against us, but that we would have to move." A few weeks later, Edgar and his wife vacated the apartment. Before leaving, though, Edgar asked Carr for a letter explaining why they had been evicted. He wanted to show it to his wife's cousin to explain why he was no longer allowed to visit. Amazingly, Carr was willing to write a letter explaining that only white people were permitted to rent in the building. That a landlord would provide written evidence of blatant racism was a testament to the pervasive common sense ideas about race at the time. Edgar approached the Federation of Labour and was directed to Giesbrecht, who helped draft the complaint. Giesbrecht wrote to Thomas Berger, a respected Vancouver lawyer, asking for advice. Berger informed him that, although the case was a clear-cut example of discrimination, the law unfortunately did not apply to rental accommodations. Edgar's experience was not, technically, a violation of the law.[35]

As the Edgar case demonstrates, perhaps the greatest failure with these early initiatives was the lack of awareness. In 1972, the British Columbia Federation of Labour's Human Rights Committee warned the government in a brief that far too few employers knew of the law:

> The labour movement and others concerned with eliminating discrimination in our society have fought for strict enforcement of the Act. Very many [businesses] had not known the Act existed ... Year after year briefs submitted by the Federation calling for improvements in Human Rights legislation in British Columbia and, even more important, for improved administration of the legislation, have been ignored by a government that obviously cared little for human rights.[36]

Organizations representing labour, Aboriginal people, and racial, religious, and ethnic minorities routinely reprimanded the government for failing to enforce the law.[37] In a 1964 brief to the minister of labour, a coalition of groups identified dozens of violations of the laws that went unpunished: employment application forms that asked for applicants' racial origin or place of birth (as well as their parents' names and birth place); bus stop posters that advertised accommodation for "whites only"; employment agencies that screened visible minorities; and landlords who refused accommodation to racial minorities or interracial couples. They also lamented the many loopholes in the legislation, such as failing to include age discrimination, not allowing third-party complaints, and exempting apartment buildings.

Moreover, the Fair Employment Practices Act and the Public Accommodation Practices Act, like their counterparts throughout Canada, did not mention sex. This reflected a common bias among activists and policy-makers about gender roles. The British Columbia Federation of Labour was a consistent advocate for anti-discrimination legislation and reform in the 1950s and 1960s. And yet, during the deliberations of its Human Rights Committee, sex discrimination was not a prominent issue. In the early 1960s, the committee was more interested in identifying age discrimination and securing an amendment to the National Housing Act to prevent discrimination on the basis of colour and nationality in addition to race and creed.[38] The federation did not establish a women's committee until the 1970s, when equal pay became a major concern (its Human Rights Committee was established in 1957). A comparable silence pervades the files of the JLC Vancouver committee. Although the JLC was a leading advocate for anti-discrimination legislation in British Columbia, there is no evidence that it lobbied for a ban on sex discrimination. In 1956, when it investigated the case of a woman of Chinese origin who was denied employment as a grocery clerk in a Vancouver store, it "found no evidence which would substantiate advising her to file a complaint."[39] The manager had hired a stockboy of Chinese origin, which would have made it difficult to substantiate a complaint of racial discrimination. Curiously, the JLC did not consider the possibility that the woman was not hired because of her sex, which would have been an ideal opportunity to highlight a deficiency in the law.

International human rights treaties and declarations, which as noted earlier, partly explain the proliferation of human rights legislation in Canada, also had an impact on British Columbia. The International Year for Human Rights in 1968 prompted its political leaders to introduce new legislation.[40] With funding from Ottawa, community groups in every province were mobilized in 1967 to organize a series of events to celebrate the upcoming anniversary of the Universal Declaration of Human Rights.[41]

Preparations for the anniversary led to the introduction of human rights legislation – or significant revisions to existing laws – in Alberta, Manitoba, Newfoundland, and Prince Edward Island.[42] In British Columbia, the Vancouver Civic Unity Association, which had gained prominence in the province for combating discrimination, would take a leading role in preparing a conference for the anniversary. It had been formed in December 1950, with the goal of obtaining community-wide support from ethnic groups, churches, educators, service organizations, community groups, and organized labour to lobby for anti-discrimination legislation. Whereas the provincial government's own programs barely solicited any complaints, the association operated a counselling service that, in 1957 alone, received seventy human rights complaints (the association was renamed the British Columbia Human Rights Council in 1968).[43]

Emily Ostapchuck, executive director of the association, hosted a meeting with Arthur Stinson of the Canadian Citizenship Council on 22 June 1967 to discuss the formation of the British Columbia Commission for the International Year for Human Rights. The commission organized workshops, surveys, and a major conference in December 1968 at the Hotel Vancouver. It brought together a broad spectrum of community groups from around the province.[44] Among the key recommendations arising from its deliberations was expanding the scope of the current anti-discrimination laws and merging them into a single human rights statute.[45] In 1969, Victoria consolidated all anti-discrimination statutes into the Human Rights Act. Although British Columbia was the first province to ban sex discrimination, it remained to be seen whether the legislation would prove effective, or if the government was serious about the issue. A year later, the Royal Commission on the Status of Women published its report, calling on all governments to implement widespread legal reform to advance women's equality. The Social Credit minister of labour confidently announced that the report was written for the rest of Canada and would have no bearing in British Columbia. Sex discrimination, according to him, was not a problem in his province.[46]

5
Jack Sherlock and the Failed Human Rights Act, 1969-73

Despite the Socred minister's claim in 1970, sex discrimination was indeed a problem in British Columbia. In many ways, Canadian women born during the 1940s belonged to a generation in transition. As post-war baby boomers, they joined the thousands who flooded universities. If they were not the first members of their family to attend university, in many cases they were certainly the first *woman* in their family to earn a post-secondary degree.[1] As a result, the 1960s saw BC women entering the labour force in greater numbers than ever before. The female workforce increased 83.9 percent between 1959 and 1968 (the male workforce increased 30.0 percent). Between 1971 and 1981, the number of women in the provincial labour force increased 22.0 percent and the number of working mothers increased from 36.2 percent to 50.7 percent. Women represented 42.1 percent of the total workforce in 1981.[2] But they quickly experienced the contradiction between the promise of education and the reality of the workplace.

A recently published collection of autobiographical essays offers a stark portrait of how women dealt with discrimination at every stage of life.[3] As a teenager in high school, Gail Campbell first encountered it through her sisters, who were schoolteachers: "Male teachers received an allowance for coaching extramural sports teams while women did not; Eileen, an outstanding athlete, refused to become involved in coaching unless she received an equivalent allowance. More significantly, though, women were not eligible for the same insurance benefits as their male colleagues."[4] After graduation,

Campbell decided to pursue post-secondary education at the University of Western Ontario, where she did not have a single female professor.

University life, as Margaret Conrad recalls, was rife with discrimination. She lived in residence during her undergraduate degree at Acadia University between 1963 and 1967. Women, but not men, were confined to residence three nights a week. Like the other female students, she cleaned her own room, whereas the male students had maids. Men, but not women, were allowed to have cars. After completing her degree at Acadia, Conrad moved to Toronto for graduate studies, where she continued to be singled out because of her gender: "I was deeply offended when one of my professors suggested that, since I was the only woman among fifteen men, my presence threatened the male bonding that he promoted in his class. He suggested that I might be 'happier' in another seminar."[5]

While Conrad was taking classes, the University of Toronto was firing female staff for getting married. Audrey Hozak was forced to quit her job in the Personnel Department. However, as Hozak happily discovered, the regulation did not apply to part-time work:

> So, once married, I left the Students' Administrative Council accepting a beautiful, engraved, silver-plated tray as my farewell gift. Immediately I followed up on the idea of part-time work at the university and, lo and behold, there was a part-time position available in Hart House as secretary to the Graduate Secretary. I had found my opening, and shortly thereafter I was back at work at the university.[6]

Because many 1960s employers assumed that women would eventually marry and abandon work, or make it a secondary priority to family, discrimination in pay and responsibilities was explicit, if not widely accepted. Joan Gilroy joined the Maritimes School of Social Work in the early 1960s as a field instructor and adviser. Although she was fully qualified, only men were allowed to teach. And pay discrimination was common:

> The Director told me that two men and one woman were being hired, and that the men, because they were married and had children, would be paid more than the woman was being offered and more than I was earning – even though the Director recognized that our qualifications and experience were roughly the same. This was common practice at the time ... My women colleagues and I talked among ourselves about the differences in salary and work assignments, but we more or less accepted them as normal.[7]

Others, such as Shari Graydon, encountered a segregated job market. While waiting tables to pay for university, she

> was stunned to discover that some restaurant jobs were closed to me by virtue of my gender ... The ritziest eating establishments – while they may have hired women at lunchtime – reserved the more lucrative evening hours for male servers. (I believe this was due to the voice of authority that naturally issues forth from men's throats when they're asked what kind of wine one should consider pairing with the pureed livers of force-fed geese.)[8]

If a married woman kept her job and received a decent salary, she still faced discrimination outside work. Margaret McCrae felt like a second-class citizen when the bank denied her a mortgage:

> In 1970, my husband, Nick, and I wanted to buy our first house. It was such an expense! It cost $33,000 to buy a house in Don Mills, Ontario ... Imagine my disbelief when I was told by my bank manager that indeed we couldn't afford it! The bank would not count my salary in their assessment of our income.[9]

The first anti-discrimination laws in Canada appeared when Campbell, Conrad, Hozak, Gilroy, Graydon, and McCrae were growing up. By the time they reached university in the 1960s, there were still no laws prohibiting sex discrimination, except equal pay legislation, which was clearly ineffective. It was, in many ways, a testament to common sense notions about gender in the mid-twentieth century that, twenty-five years after the first anti-discrimination statute was passed in Canada, only the ineffective federal Bill of Rights purported to ban sex discrimination. This time, it was British Columbia, not Ontario, which set a new standard.

British Columbia's 1969 Human Rights Act was similar to the Ontario model established in 1962.[10] It merged the Equal Pay Act, Fair Employment Practices Act, and the Public Accommodations Act into a single statute. Discrimination on the basis of race, religion, colour, nationality, ancestry, or place of origin was prohibited in employment, accommodation, services, and signs or advertisements. Otherwise, the act did little more than add sex as a prohibited ground for discrimination in employment only. All the weaknesses that typified its precursors, notably the vague language of the Equal Pay Act, which restricted the law to the "same work in the same establishment," were incorporated into the Human Rights Act.

Jack Sherlock and the Failed Human Rights Act

Jack Sherlock, 1972 | George Diack, *Vancouver Province*

Jack Sherlock was the only civil servant assigned to administer the 1969 Human Rights Act. A large, soft-spoken man who was a career bureaucrat, Sherlock had worked for Social Credit governments throughout his entire career. Since 1952, he had been employed as a Labour Department conciliation officer and an industrial relations officer (IRO).[11] He had no ties to community groups and little knowledge of the issues facing women in the workforce. His expertise was in labour relations, and he had no experience dealing with discrimination in employment, much less in services or accommodation. And as a white male living in Victoria, he probably did not encounter discrimination first-hand. By the time Sherlock was appointed director responsible for administering the Human Rights Act, he was nearing retirement. Bill Black, a future member of the Human Rights Commission who interviewed Sherlock in the 1990s, concluded that he "was a labour mediator with very little background in human rights. The entire staff consisted of one secretary, though the Director [Sherlock] was allowed to appoint officials from other branches of the ministry to conduct investigations. Very little was done in the way of education due at least in part to a lack of resources."[12] Sherlock was paid $13,000 a year (a $3,000 raise from his previous salary) to do little more than respond to a trickle of complaints filed between 1969 and 1973.[13] He personally initiated only a handful of complaints annually, which usually involved writing to newspapers at the end of the year to warn them about discriminatory job advertisements (he probably did this to get his statistics up before his annual report was due).[14]

The Socreds' decision to prohibit discrimination against women in employment – making British Columbia the first Canadian jurisdiction to do so – raises an interesting question. Theirs was hardly a women-friendly administration. In fact, as Jean Barman notes, the Social Credit government "was also male government." The proportion of female candidacies in provincial elections fell to 6 percent from a high of 10 percent before Social Credit took power, and less than 20 percent of the women who ran for office in British Columbia during this period did so under the Socred banner.[15] The party's success rested largely on rural votes and close links with small- and large-business owners, hardly a constituency sympathetic to human rights legislation (particularly equal pay). In many respects, Social Credit was ill suited to administer human rights legislation in which the majority of complaints dealt with sex discrimination. To make matters worse, some of the leading figures in the Socred government simply did not believe that sex discrimination was a problem in their province.

One possible explanation – the existence of an influential lobby of women's groups, as was the case in Ontario – is unlikely. As noted earlier, there is no evidence that BC women's rights activists or organized labour conducted a sustained drive to ban sex discrimination.[16] However, the Vancouver Civic Unity Association, which organized local events for the International Year for Human Rights, led a visible campaign to lobby for human rights legislation. In this way, social movements did contribute to the reforms of 1969.[17]

Perhaps the Socreds were conscious of their weakness among the female electorate and hoped to draw more votes from women in the upcoming election of that year. They did manage to stay in office, but they struggled to maintain their support (in 1972, the NDP would finally end their twenty-year reign). Although the Human Rights Act, which did little more than incorporate existing legislation, was hastily passed before the 1969 election, the government trumpeted it as a major advancement in human rights. Pictures of the labour minister sitting on his desk and holding his phone to his ear appeared in all the major newspapers, accompanied by captions that he waited to respond to complaints about discrimination. The government also spent more than $42,000 in public monies to promote the new act in the midst of the election.[18]

Whatever the Socreds' motivation, any attempt to ban sex discrimination at this time was a bold step. The legacy of a sexual division of labour continued to inform employment practices. A representative of the Scott Paper Company told a group of commerce students at the University of British Columbia in 1972 that "the company's policy explicitly prohibits hiring women for managerial positions." According to Charles Faulkes, the regional manager for London Life, "our qualifications are high and we rarely find women who fulfil them." Female employees at London Life did not last long, because "it was too rough for them. Girls are too emotional." Tel Ranel, an Israeli bank teller who had recently immigrated to Canada, could not secure employment as a teller in Vancouver, because he was a man. He was rejected by all five big banks, which claimed that they did not discriminate, although a Bank of Montreal spokesman insisted that he "would not be at all impressed with a man who wanted to be a teller." In Vancouver, the Non-Partisan Association continued to run all-male slates for municipal government, although a new party, TEAM, recruited women to run for city council.[19] But Floyd Rowell, a retiring school board trustee in Vancouver, thought that TEAM had made a mistake in having eight women run for the school board: "It wasn't a broad enough representation, there were too many women. Despite women's lib I don't think women are so emancipated that they don't exhibit certain maternal instincts. I have served on the board when it had four women. It wasn't too satisfactory. Women are too maternal, too soft-hearted." Jerome Smitz, assistant director of the Construction Labour Relations Association, appearing before the British Columbia Mediation Commission in July 1972, explained that his association and the International Brotherhood of Electrical Workers wanted to remove the clause banning sex discrimination in the collective agreement because it reflected badly on the employer and the union.[20]

Whether the Human Rights Act would do much to address such discrimination was doubtful. Certainly, none of the social movement organizations that were deeply involved in the human rights movement saw it as much of an accomplishment. The reaction of the British Columbia Civil Liberties Association perhaps best captures the fundamental weakness of the law:

> The new legislation does little to foster or safeguard basic civil rights of British Columbia. It was appropriate that the Hon. Leslie Peterson introduced the bill in his capacity as labour minister rather than in his other

cabinet role of attorney-general. For the bill is hardly more than a consolidation and updating of existing fair employment and accommodation statutes, and appears weak even within this narrow scope ... The government deliberately intends to restrict severely the scope of the Human Rights Act.[21]

The British Columbia Federation of Labour insisted that the "legislation is not a human rights bill and is only designed to catch votes rather than protect the human rights of the citizens of the province."[22] Even Joseph Katz, a future human rights commissioner, would later attack the legislation for its narrow focus and insufficient penalties.[23]

The first formal hearing held under the legislation demonstrated its ineffectiveness. Hanne Jensen had left Denmark to join thousands of other international visitors flocking to Expo 67 in Montreal. She was twenty years old. Jensen decided to stay in Canada and was soon married and living in Vancouver. She began working for Office Assistance Limited in 1970, helping companies find temporary staff.[24] Jensen enjoyed her job and was especially proud of working in a business started by women and employing mostly women. Two years later, she discovered that, ironically, the company paid one of its few male employees (the male division was called "key personnel") $600 per month, whereas she herself received $450 for exactly the same work (she was also more senior, having trained one of the male staff). Jensen stated that "the sales manager (a man) told me that I should be grateful that I had a job that would get me outside and there was a line-up of girls (as he put it) who would gladly take my job at $100 less."[25] During a lunch break, she visited the office of the Vancouver Status of Women, where the volunteers helped her draft a complaint under the Human Rights Act.

Jensen was fortunate that her case fell under the scope of the legislation. The Socred vision for the human rights state was fundamentally flawed. Had she been a domestic servant working for a private employer or renting a room in a house, for instance, she would not have been covered under the act.[26] In addition, the provisions prohibiting sex discrimination did not apply to accommodation or employment application forms and advertising. So if landlords stated openly that they did not rent rooms in a house to women, or a taxi company advertised for men only, they would not be in violation of the Human Rights Act. Nor was the law binding on the government. The latter was a major loophole, given that sex discrimination was rampant in the public service, as Marcy Cohen pointed out in a brief to the Human Rights Commission on behalf of the Vancouver Women's Caucus. In the attorney general's office, for instance, women were paid less than men. And only a few months earlier, according to Cohen, the Liquor Control Board had demoted a woman who was about to receive a salary similar to that of male staff.[27] In fact, the Liquor Control Board employed only 35 women, compared with 764 men. The board had a long-time regulation (the reasons for its creation long since forgotten) that banned women from serving liquor in a lounge or public house, and because the board was a government agency, the Human Rights Act did not apply to it. In sum, women were not allowed to be barmaids.[28]

In Jensen's case, the salary system of Office Assistance Limited obviously violated the legislation's equal pay provisions. Jensen mailed her complaint to Jack Sherlock and was assigned an industrial relations officer (IRO). Under the legislation, if Sherlock determined that a complaint was valid, he could request that an IRO investigate. IROs were not good case officers: they had no training in human rights, and their main job was mediating between unions and employers. When Jensen first spoke with an IRO, he was not convinced that she had a valid case. Eventually, however, he agreed to investigate, albeit after several attempts to discourage both her and her co-worker Aileen Cassidy (who joined her in the complaint) from pursuing their case. Very soon, the atmosphere at work became toxic (in an open-concept office), and the company ignored the IRO's attempts at conciliation.

Since Office Assistance refused to cooperate, the IRO sent the case back to Sherlock. The legislation had also created a Human Rights Commission, so Sherlock sent Jensen's complaint to the commission to force a resolution. The commission could hold a formal hearing and issue an order for an individual or company to offer a service, provide accommodations or employment, apologize, pay lost wages, or post a sign assuring the public that they would henceforth follow the provisions of the Human Rights Act. The commission could also ask a Supreme Court judge to issue an order to force the respondent to comply with its order.

In actual fact, however, there never was a real, separate commission. Because the legislation indicated only that the government *may* create a human rights commission, it was able to foist responsibility for enforcing the act onto the Board of Industrial Relations. In other words, the board (whose members also constituted the Labour Relations Board) acted as the de facto Human Rights Commission. In contrast, other provinces, drawing on the Ontario precedent, established a separate human rights commission. The BC Board of Industrial Relations, already occupied with its current responsibilities, was poorly situated to deal with human rights complaints. (Attempts by the Opposition NDP to amend the legislation

Hanne Jensen *(left)* and Aileen Cassidy, 1972 | Ray Allan, *Vancouver Sun*

to include an independent enforcement agency and a broader definition of sex discrimination were defeated in the legislature.)[29] Eight of the nine members of the board/commission (almost all men) came from Vancouver; the ninth was from Kelowna.[30] Moreover, in at least one case, the chairman, William H. Sands, demonstrated a complete lack of regard for sex discrimination. He dismissed the Vancouver Women's Caucus brief and told Marcy Cohen that "he felt sorry for her and suggested she look at the legislation to see what is going on."[31] The British Columbia Human Rights Commission was, in essence, a poor shadow of its Ontario counterpart.

A formal hearing to decide Jensen's case was scheduled before the Human Rights Commission. Once again, the IRO was obstructionist. He assured Jensen and Cassidy that they did not need a lawyer, even though the company had hired legal counsel. Fortunately, the two women realized that the IRO was at best uninterested in their case, and they secured a lawyer (working pro bono) with the help of the Vancouver Status of Women. The hearing was to take place in Victoria. As vice-chairman of

Jack Sherlock and the Failed Human Rights Act

Human Rights Commission, 1969 | *Vancouver Province*

the Board of Industrial Relations/Human Rights Commission, Jim Edgett was responsible for chairing it. If there were any question that the Socreds were not serious about human rights when they appointed Sherlock as director, there was no doubting their disregard when they tasked Edgett with the responsibility for the hearings. He had graduated from the University of British Columbia in 1948 and served on the Board of Industrial Relations between 1961 and 1972. He had no experience or training whatsoever in human rights or discrimination. In fact, Edgett would distinguish himself years later for rejecting sexual harassment as a human rights issue. Several people described him as a "letch" and suggested that women should avoid being alone with him in an elevator.

The 1972 hearing, the first one held under the law, even though it had been passed in 1969, was a sham. Jensen and Cassidy found themselves in an office at the Department of Labour, facing the entire nine-person Human Rights Commission, their bosses, and the company lawyer. As Jensen would later recall, the hearing was unprofessional, disorganized, and intimidating. The lawyer, the same man who would represent Lornex Mining Company in a later complaint, compared a woman who demanded equal pay to a prostitute. The IRO, acting as a labour mediator rather than an advocate for the complainants, did nothing to defend Jensen and Cassidy.

Jensen and Cassidy's experience in the hearing was typical. The following account – given by Kathleen Ruff (the future director of the Human Rights Branch) of another case before the Human Rights Commission – demonstrates the problem of using labour mediators to adjudicate human rights complaints:

One complainant – I'm not going to remember the details – she had agreed to drop it or settle it. Most people are persuaded to drop it. But she refused. She asked if I could go with her to the settlement meeting and they [the IRO] agreed on condition I not say anything. It was interesting because it was an example of how the system worked. And it is not to say that these are bad people, but the system was set up to fail ... The entire process was set up to settle, settle, settle. It was mediation – that was their skill. That's OK if you've got a union on one side and an employer on another. More of a chance of a balance. But when you have some individual, a woman on her own, especially a minority, and usually the company or the owner, it is not a fair match at all. And this was the case when I went to this settlement meeting. It was this company – I can't remember who it was – it was an unusually big company. There was the president, executive officer ... a couple of top people, perhaps more. And then this woman on her own. And then there was the IRO. Basically, he doesn't do anything. He's there to let them mediate. And this woman on her own! What is she going to do! She just got wiped off the floor. I mean, what was she going to do? She didn't have a chance ... And in other cases, there was the same thing. Take, for example, an equal pay case of a woman who had the same qualifications of a man. The company would say that, yes, the qualifications you have on paper are better and stronger, but what we are interested in is experience or a certain experience. Whatever his experience was would be better. So they would interpret it that way. If you had better qualifications as a woman, then you lost the case. But if the man had better qualifications, and you had more experience, they would say ... that they were not interested in experience but qualifications. You could never win.

[The settlement meeting took place] at a government office. People there would be myself, the woman, the executives, and the IRO – that was it. The [IRO] didn't play any role. He thought he was doing a great job! The issue was settled/mediated. But that is what they do in a labour dispute. Usually, they play a mediating role, with employer and union working it out. It wouldn't matter if it was unjust or not; their role was to secure the settlement. Labour relations settlement is everything ... All the focus was on her to back down. I wasn't allowed to say anything or to speak. If I could be allowed to speak, I would have disagreed. I would have argued that the law says different. But she doesn't have any background. [Later in the interview, Ruff recounted that IROs had often endorsed union contracts in the past that explicitly discriminated against women through, for example, separate wage scales.][32]

Jensen and Cassidy were more fortunate: the commission decided in their favour and ordered the company to adjust their salaries. But their "victory" was short-lived. On the day of the decision, both were fired. Office Assistance asserted that they were fired for theft, but following a second hearing, the commission ordered the company to reinstate both women and to pay them each $205.80 for lost wages. Undeterred, the company made their lives miserable at work, at one point insisting that Jensen sit at a desk beside her supervisor, who watched over her shoulder the entire day. Jensen and Cassidy were also banned from going to the washroom or taking breaks together. Jensen contacted Sherlock, but he insisted that, as long as they were being paid, there was nothing he could do. Discouraged and exhausted, Jensen and Cassidy quit two days later. In an ironic twist, given that the purpose of the Human Rights Act was to provide a forum for victims to seek restitution outside the courts, Jensen and Cassidy successfully sued Office Assistance in civil court.

Obviously, the system was significantly flawed. Hearings were rare, and when they did occur, the odds were stacked against the complainants. The people responsible for administering the legislation were largely uninformed, uninterested, and unsympathetic. Employers could quickly find ways to circumvent the act and to pressure their employees to quit (the law did not allow for damages). After Jensen and Cassidy's case concluded, the Vancouver Status of Women decided that one of its main priorities must be lobbying for a new human rights statute. In addition to the failure to protect complainants, Jensen and Cassidy's case revealed extensive inadequacies with the legislation as it applied to women: an order by the commission could not be extended to other employees; complainants were not provided with representation during the investigation process; the thousands of women who worked in government, education, or non-profits were not covered under the act; and it did not address marital status, which was often the source of discrimination in hiring, wages, and promotion.[33]

Jensen's case was one of only four orders issued by the Human Rights Commission between 1969 and 1973.[34] Overall, Sherlock received an average of 700 inquiries and complaints each year, only 30 to 80 of which were assigned to IROs (and there were only forty to fifty IROs scattered throughout the entire province). Of the 2,092 inquiries or complaints received between 1969 and 1973, approximately 208 fell within the scope of the legislation. The 174 cases that were eventually investigated resulted in the following: IROs informally settled 92 cases; 6 complaints were withdrawn; 53 were found to be without merit; and 23 were recommended for a formal hearing with the commission (most of which were delayed/pending by 1973). Investigations would last at least a week, and in some cases the IRO could take as long as three months; 8 cases took between three and six months to investigate. IROs were far more likely to find a complaint without merit (especially in long investigations). Sherlock was expected to supervise their work, but in practice he rarely challenged their findings. He rejected an IRO's findings twice, and concluded in only 23 instances that further investigation was warranted. On the whole, those who filed a complaint under the Human Rights Act may have hoped for an informal settlement (although there was no guarantee that it would favour them), but they ran a significant risk of having it dismissed or simply withdrawn.

Despite the law's obvious failings, these 208 complaints represented a broad sample (Figure 5). Granted, most involved sex discrimination at work. Only 18 investigations focused on accommodation, and only a handful of complaints involved services to the public. However, IROs also dealt with cases involving race (or colour), nationality (or place of origin), religion, and age (in 8 complaints, people had been fired for having long hair). The Civil Service Commission, the provincial government, and the *Vancouver Sun* were the targets of multiple complaints. Otherwise, the 208 complaints focused on a wide range of employers, including retail (A&W Food Services, Best Cleaning Services, Ocean Beach Hotel); resource companies (Gold River Pulp Mill, Northwood Pulp and Timber, Standard Oil); and public agencies (BC Correctional Institute, City of Victoria, Delta School Board). The vast majority came from the Lower Mainland (132), with a few from cities such as Kamloops (5), Nanaimo (5), Prince George (6), and Victoria (30). This was unsurprising, given that complaints often involved the retail sector and because the Department of Labour's offices were located in major cities. Still, at least 1 complaint came from remote or small towns throughout the province, such as Campbell River, Dawson Creek, Fort St. John, Prince Rupert, Terrace, Williams Lake, Youbou, and more than twenty others.[35]

There were also some notable victories between 1969 and 1973. At times, an order from the Human Rights Commission was required, but informal resolutions could also be highly effective. In 1971, the commission ordered Vancouver General Hospital to pay $20,000 and adjust salary scales in a department that paid women less than men for the same work. By far the most successful case was an informal settlement between 324 nurses and the minister of health that resulted in a significant wage adjustment and

FIGURE 5 Human rights complaints, 1969-73

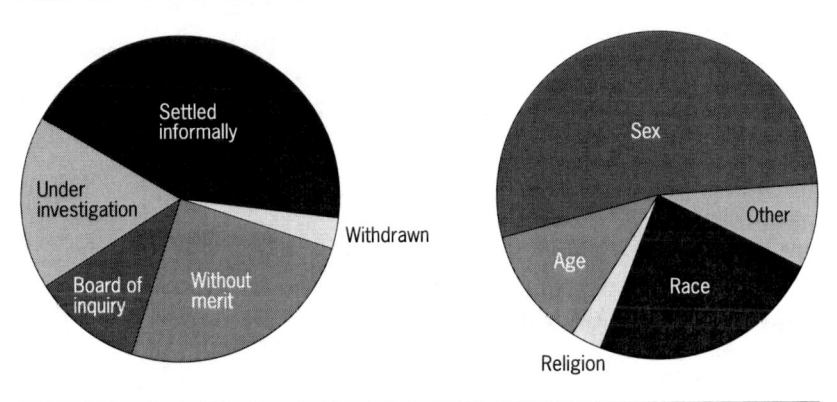

NOTE: The figure does not include 342 equal pay complaints in the hospital industry that led to a voluntary raise in salary for women.
SOURCE: British Columbia, Department of Labour, Annual Reports, 1970-73.

$5 million in retroactive pay. IROs managed to negotiate two dozen settlements without having to resort to the commission. Settlements included reinstating an individual in a job (or offering to do so), writing a letter of apology, withdrawing an eviction notice (in a case where a black person had visited the complainant's apartment), or posting a sign in a workplace, indicating the employer's commitment to no longer discriminate. In a few cases, there was a cash payment.

These were hard-won battles. No less than the minister of health, Ralph R. Loffmark, fought against the equal pay order for Vancouver General Hospital. He entreated Premier Bennett to prevent Sherlock from pursuing the complaint. Better to revise employee classification systems and reassign duties, he insisted, than pay female nurses the same as male orderlies. In his view, the cost of equal pay was simply "not realistic."[36] A year later, the Vancouver Status of Women assisted sixty-three dietary aides at Riverview Hospital in pursuing an equal pay complaint because their salaries were lower than those of male cook helpers. Although the union and hospital administrators acknowledged that the pay was discriminatory, the British Columbia Government Employees' Union proceeded to negotiate higher salaries for the male workers, and the Civil Service Commission recommended reclassification in such a way as to ensure that women would continue to earn lower wages.[37]

The shortcomings of the legislation reflected its (male) framers' attitudes toward sex discrimination. When the Voice of Women confronted the minister of labour with a position paper outlining pay discrimination in the public service, he refused to see the problem as systemic or requiring state intervention. For him, the problem was the high turnover rate among female employees and their disproportionate representation as low-paid clerical workers, a situation that the state was in no position to resolve.[38] The refusal of many policy-makers to acknowledge sex discrimination as a systemic social problem had a direct impact on the operations of the human rights state. Human rights legislation in British Columbia was narrow and poorly enforced and promoted. It rarely required legislators to meaningfully engage with human rights issues. Given this, it is not surprising that the Human Rights Act had little effect.

The Human Rights Act was a bitter disappointment for social movements with a broader vision for the human rights state. It depended on untrained IROs and a single administrator in Victoria; it operated with almost no resources, including no money for education; and it generated only a few complaints. The Socreds never envisioned a genuine human rights agency. They did not bother to have a budget line for human rights in the public finances. Even Sherlock had little experience or motivation to proactively address discrimination. Years later, when the NDP was preparing to scrap the act, NDP MLA Emery Barnes pointed out that the director responsible for enforcing it had found it a challenge: "I think the whole problem was put forth by Mr. Jack Sherlock, who is now retired, when he said himself that we had to get proof and when we got proof we couldn't substantiate it in court because of the nebulousness of the sections and the ambiguity of the sections, and so forth. He himself was often frustrated."[39]

6
Kathleen Ruff and the Human Rights Code, 1973-79

LINDA SPROULE-JONES: *One of my big cases was a gay man who had applied for a government position and didn't get it. He thought he was the most qualified, and he asked for his resumé back. And the idiotic interviewer has written "gay" across the back! So this fella came running to the Human Rights Branch ... He [the interviewer] probably did not realize this. And this fella turned it over, and there it was.*

QUESTION: *What ended up happening with the case?*

LINDA: *Well, I investigated it. I didn't tell the interviewer that I had the resumé. I asked, "What was the criteria? How did you choose? Show me the resumés of the two people. How come you chose this one? Why did you choose this one? Did you know he was gay?" "Oh, that didn't make a difference," he insisted. Anyway, I guess he wasn't going to settle. David Vickers was our branch lawyer before he became deputy minister. We were going to take the case to a board of inquiry, and we took it to David Vickers. And he said, "This is ridiculous." He got on the phone over to the employer and said, "You're gonna get killed," or words to that effect. And so they settled.*

– *Linda Sproule-Jones (former human rights investigator), author interview*

Jack Sherlock retired in 1973 and was replaced with Kathleen Ruff. Born in 1940, Ruff moved to Victoria during the 1960s, after completing undergraduate and master's degrees abroad. She married Norman Ruff, a political science professor at the University of Victoria, and by 1973 they had a son and a daughter. A young, charismatic, and energetic anti-war activist, Ruff had been involved in the women's movement for many years, first in the Voice of Women and then as president of the Status of Women Action Group. In the 1972 provincial election, she ran for office but was defeated in her Victoria riding. Fortunately, the new NDP government was looking to replace Sherlock, and it offered her the job. She was responsible for administering the Human Rights Act for a few months until the Human Rights Code (passed in 1973) came into effect in 1974. She was appointed under the new legislation as executive director of the Human Rights Commission but quickly decided to create a separate Human Rights Branch and divide responsibilities: the Branch would be the primary agency and would investigate complaints, whereas the commission would have a secondary role focusing mainly on education. Ruff therefore became the first director of the Human Rights Branch, where she remained until 1979. She later became the host of CBC TV's *Ombudswoman,* a founding editor of the *Canadian Human Rights Reporter,* and director of the federal government's Court Challenges Program.

In the summer of 1973, only a few weeks after replacing Sherlock, Ruff walked into a coffee shop on Broadway Street in Vancouver to meet Shelagh Day. Day did not know it yet but she was about to be offered a job as the province's first human rights investigator. After earning an undergraduate degree in Minnesota in 1963, Day was awarded a master's degree at Harvard University in 1964. She began teaching at the University of British Columbia soon afterward and quickly realized that, although the university was happy to have someone with a Harvard degree, it was less eager to offer a tenure-track job to a woman. In fact, it had little regard for female professors, and Day became involved with a group of female academics who were determined to address the university's attitude toward women. After helping organize the country's first women's studies courses (open gatherings that drew hundreds of people to large lecture halls every week), Day authored a report on the status of women at the university. A year later, she was working for Ruff. After leaving the Human Rights Branch in 1978, Day had a distinguished career in promoting human rights across Canada, including as chair of the Saskatchewan Human Rights Commission.[1]

Ruff and Day faced enormous challenges in developing British Columbia's human rights state. The editors of the *Vancouver Sun* had hailed

Kathleen Ruff, 1975 | *Vancouver Sun*

the 1969 Human Rights Act as a "Charter of Women's Rights."[2] Skeptics, however, including the editors of the *Vancouver Province,* were convinced that there was "no way to eliminate such discrimination, outside of blindfolding employers or requiring that female applicants wear veils and walk around in barrels while being interviewed ... [Matrimony] is the most important career of all for a woman – the most vital and, hopefully, long-lasting."[3] Creating a government agency from scratch would be the easy part! Convincing employers to abide by the expansive Human Rights Code would be far more onerous.

That Ruff and Day had chosen the women's movement as a focus of their activism was not unusual. By the 1970s, newly emerging social movement organizations had largely displaced labour and the Jewish Labour Committee in campaigning for human rights legislation. Three groups in particular – the British Columbia Civil Liberties Association (BCCLA), Vancouver Status of Women (VSW), and the Status of Women Action Group (SWAG) – would play a prominent role over the next decade in building the human rights state. The BCCLA was a leading civil liberties group in Canada. In 1962, the attorney general charged the Sons of

Freedom – a small sect of Doukhobours in rural British Columbia who were blowing up telephone poles and burning buildings to protest modern ways of life – with "conspiracy to intimidate the legislature." A group of citizens, mainly lawyers and professors, reacted to this blatantly excessive charge by forming the BCCLA. Its first president was a Vancouver Anglican minister, Philip Hewett, who was later replaced by James Foulks, founding head of the Department of Pharmacology at the University of British Columbia. Over the next decade, the BCCLA fought a string of campaigns around censorship, most notably against attempts to shut down the highly controversial *Georgia Straight,* challenged provincial legislation to forcibly treat heroin addicts, and came to the defence of youth caught up in the 1971 Gastown Riot.[4] With the help of a young law professor, Bill Black, and his students at the University of British Columbia, the BCCLA also made a significant contribution in drafting the 1973 Human Rights Code.

Perhaps the most vocal proponent of human rights legislation in the 1970s was the Vancouver Status of Women (VSW), which was created in 1971 in response to the Royal Commission on the Status of Women. The VSW "dealt only in women's rights," and its key objective was to "foster public knowledge of the rights and status of women in Canada."[5] The VSW wrote briefs and lobbied the government; assigned people to attend all-candidates meetings during elections to raise the issue of human rights legal reform; and flooded the media with material on human rights policy. One of its most innovative measures was creating the position of ombudswoman, whose job was to provide free advocacy and support for women in need (e.g., drafting human rights complaints). By 1978, the VSW had 780 members (as well as 53 group members and twenty-three libraries), six full-time staff, and a budget of over $90,000.[6] It was the leading women's group in the province in terms of name recognition, membership, and resources.

The Status of Women Action Group (SWAG) was established in Victoria in 1978 for the purpose of "promoting the full participation of women in the social, economic, and political life of this country."[7] It elected Ruff as its first president and began meeting once a month in a junior high school classroom, with membership fees of a dollar. One of SWAG's first priorities was reforming human rights legislation. Its members fanned out across Victoria to speak to the female staff in retail stores about unequal pay, and they interviewed school officials to document sex discrimination in employment. Over the next decade, SWAG became one of the most prominent women's rights groups in the province. It organized conferences, letter-writing campaigns, and public lectures, it established a phone crisis line, and it hosted social events such as Gal's Night Out or Hot Flashes Coffee House.[8]

These three organizations appeared during a period of human rights innovation in Canada. Several provinces experimented with their respective human rights statutes, adding new prohibited grounds for discrimination, expanding the powers and funding of human rights commissions, and incorporating a mandate to investigate systemic discrimination.[9] Quebec's Charter of Human Rights and Freedoms included economic, social, and cultural rights. It banned discrimination on the basis of social condition, and it took precedence over all laws in the province. And in Quebec, the legislature (not a minister) appointed members of the Human Rights Commission.[10] The federal Human Rights Act (1977) banned discrimination on the basis of pardoned conviction and disability while requiring equal pay for work of equal value (rather than the same work). British Columbia was at the forefront of these developments. It was the first jurisdiction to introduce widespread amendments to human rights legislation since Ontario's pioneering statute in 1962. The NDP's Human Rights Code was, without a doubt, the most progressive human rights legislation in Canada.

Many of these innovations involved discrimination against women. Feminists organized to campaign for legislative reform. Activists promoted a broader vision of the human rights state that encompassed a wide range of issues specific to women, such as sexual harassment and pregnancy. Women also worked from within the government to create a more effective enforcement mechanism and to hold employers, landlords, and service providers accountable for discrimination. Meanwhile, individual women throughout the province defied their employers by mounting challenges that eventually led to a more generous interpretation of the provisions in human rights law.

The Human Rights Code

The NDP passed the Human Rights Code in 1973, which came into effect in 1974. A certain symbolism marked the occasion: 1973 was the twenty-fifth anniversary of the Universal Declaration of Human Rights. Minister of Labour Bill King introduced the code, which was part of an ambitious legislative agenda during the brief NDP interregnum from 1972 to 1975. Under W.A.C. Bennett, the Social Credit Party introduced an average of forty bills during a legislative session; the NDP introduced four hundred bills in four years! Some of these initiatives included establishing a monopoly in auto insurance; creating rent controls and a rentalsman office; generating a new labour code; funding rape crisis centres and transition houses; and forming new Crown corporations such as the BC Petroleum Corporation and the BC Land Commission. Government expenditures nearly doubled between 1970 and 1974.[11] With the Human Rights Code, King hoped to address numerous deficiencies in the Human Rights Act: too few prohibited grounds for discrimination; a poor enforcement mechanism; weak penalties; no mandate to educate the public; limited resources and staff; and lack of independence from the Department of Labour.[12] Soon after the election, King formed a committee to create new legislation, and one of its members worked with the BCCLA and Professor Bill Black at the UBC Faculty of Law to draft it.[13]

Social movements supported NDP efforts to revitalize the human rights state. Fourteen social movement organizations attended a workshop hosted by the BCCLA and produced several recommendations for new legislation. These recommendations, as well as briefs from various groups, provided the foundation for the Human Rights Code. Women's associations had lobbied extensively since 1970 for new legislation. Rosemary Brown, a former ombudswoman for the VSW and an NDP MLA, was an influential proponent of the new code.[14] The British Columbia Federation of Women, the NDP Women's Rights Committee, SWAG, Vancouver Women's Caucus, and the YWCA also lobbied for human rights legislation.[15]

The code was a significant departure from the Human Rights Act. The latter provided few options for redress, and it focused on punishment; people who were found guilty of violating the law could be fined or forced to employ an individual (the statute prescribed no explicit penalties for violating the sections on signs or accommodation). In contrast, the code was more consistent with the principles of Canada's evolving human rights state in that it placed a priority on conciliation and negotiation. Whereas other provinces established a commission that administered every aspect of the legislation, the code allowed Ruff to create a separate Human Rights *Branch* to process and investigate complaints, whereas a new Human Rights *Commission* focus on education. The NDP dispensed with the Socred practice of using industrial relations officers, hiring full-time human rights investigators instead. The code also contained a unique requirement that the branch was to investigate *all* complaints – it could not arbitrarily dismiss them. The law was also binding on the Crown. Once a complaint was received, the branch would dispatch a human rights officer to speak to the complainant and the alleged perpetrator. Investigators who found merit in a complaint would initially attempt an informal conciliation. Hundreds of complaints were handled in this fashion.[16]

If conciliation failed, the branch could ask the minister of labour to appoint a board of inquiry. This held a quasi-judicial proceeding, where one or a few individuals appointed by the minister would meet with the complainant and the accused (often in a county courthouse or a hotel), hear their arguments, and render a decision in favour of one of the parties. The branch was responsible for representing complainants during the proceedings, therefore guaranteeing that people of limited resources would be adequately represented.[17] If the board of inquiry ruled in favour of the complainant, it was empowered to force the respondent to remedy the situation (for example, by offering a job or service) and to assess monetary damages. The board's decision had the full force of law, although the respondent could appeal in court. Finally, both the Human Rights Commission and the branch could initiate complaints. This provision, as King explained to the legislature, represented a new vision for the human rights state in British Columbia:

> In other words, they [the commission] are not restrained to a strictly responding role now; they have the authority and they will have the wherewithal to make themselves a vital force in the community, not only in terms of educating the public, employers and trade unions on what their obligations are under the concept of equality and human rights, but also in terms of coming to grips with violations, rather than sitting and waiting until a complaint is received from some individual who feels he has suffered as a result of discrimination.[18]

Surprisingly, the NDP had not campaigned on a platform for major human rights reform, and perhaps for this reason the new government did not have an explicit position on equal pay. Unwilling to go as far as legislating equal pay for work of equal value, but cognizant of the failure of the Human Rights Act's equal pay provisions, King chose a compromise position. Equal pay for the "same or substantially same work" was replaced with "similar or substantially similar work" (the change was not in the original bill, but King agreed to the amendment in committee).

Third parties (such as a trade union or a social movement organization) could now lay complaints on behalf of others, and the government was bound by the legislation. In addition to expanding discrimination prohibitions to marital status, criminal conviction, and political belief, the code also applied to any space offered for occupancy (rather than being restricted to a commercial or self-contained dwelling unit). Most importantly, whereas the Human Rights Act prohibited sex discrimination only in employment, the Human Rights Code banned it in all forms. Norene Warren was one of the first women to take advantage of this change in the law. Separated from her husband, she and her three children, two daughters aged sixteen and twelve, and an eleven-year-old son, lived with her mother. While walking along East Forty-first Avenue in Vancouver in the summer of 1974, she spotted a rental sign outside a house. It was an older home with a fireplace, four bedrooms, and a modest garden in the back. She called the number on the sign and met with one of the owners, Frank Cleland, to visit the house. As they walked through it, Cleland told Warren that she was first in line and that he was hoping to rent to a family. When she informed him that she was a single mother, Cleland seemed concerned about whether she could pay the $350 in rent and did not bother to ask for her references. Two days later, Cleland called Warren to tell her that he had decided to rent to another family. He was worried that she could not afford the rent and could not, as a single mother with a job, properly maintain the house. Warren was so upset that she simply thanked him and hung up. But her frustration turned to anger, and she submitted a human rights complaint the next day on the basis that Cleland had refused her because of her marital status. A board of inquiry sustained her complaint, and although she was not asking for financial compensation and had found another place to rent, the board awarded her a symbolic twenty-five dollars (ironically, the people who rented Cleland's property later caused extensive damage to it).[19]

The code also included a blanket prohibition on all forms of discrimination unless the accused could demonstrate "reasonable cause."[20] Without a doubt, this was the NDP's most significant innovation. All other anti-discrimination laws in Canada were limited to specific grounds, such as race or religion.[21] In contrast, the reasonable cause section allowed women to establish a host of new precedents in human rights law. H.W. – who is known only by her initials – launched the first successful human rights complaint in Canada for discrimination on the basis of pregnancy.[22] She began working for Riviera Reservations, a travel agency, on 21 March 1975, earning six hundred dollars a month. She and her boss, Jack Kroff, were the only ones working in the office, and most of her duties involved answering the phones and booking reservations. When she was hired, H.W. had no idea that she was pregnant. Three months later, her doctor confirmed the pregnancy, and on the same day, Kroff confronted her in the office. She indicated that, yes, she was pregnant but that it would not interfere with her work. The next day, Kroff fired her. A board of inquiry rejected his contention that she was fired for incompetence and concluded that pregnancy fell under the reasonable cause section. H.W. was awarded forty dollars in lost wages.[23] Within a few years, the Human Rights Branch was receiving a flood of complaints for pregnancy-related dismissals. In 1978 alone, at least forty women complained of being fired because they were pregnant. Most were stenographers or clerks who worked in non-union offices.[24]

The code also set a precedent in the area of sexual harassment, which profoundly challenged the entrenched male culture of many workplaces. The term "sexual harassment" was first coined at a "speak-out" rally in Ithaca, New York, where women were protesting the intimidation they encountered at work. The first American study of the subject appeared in 1978, followed by the first Canadian study in 1979.[25] As Doris Anderson suggested in her memoirs, many men viewed sexual harassment as "a perk of being boss – whether it involved gross and demeaning comments, nude pictures on the wall, or sleeping privileges ... Every single woman I knew had been propositioned at some time, mostly by married men."[26] Perhaps because sexual harassment was commonplace at work, because victims feared reprisals for speaking out, because they were humiliated, or because they did not want their families to know, a code of silence surrounded sexual harassment in the workplace.[27] Renee Carignan challenged this silence. Soon after she began working at Mastercraft Publications, mainly handling clerical duties and promoting the publications over the phone, her boss, Bhan Sharma, began making unwanted advances. According to the inquiry transcript,

> things began to go sour almost immediately. She had lunch with Mr. Sharma on the first day, ostensibly to discuss the job. He asked if she liked strippers or enjoyed sex with different people. She tried to steer the conversation back to work-related topics. During the first few days at work, he brushed by the complainant very closely and may have run his hand across her bottom.[28]

Sharma routinely embraced her, touched her, and invited her out to drink with him. The harassment became more frequent over time: "After she had made a good advertising sale, he came out of his office and embraced her in a bear hug. He feigned innocence when she complained, stating that he was merely congratulating her ... She recalled yet another incident when he sneaked up behind her and put his arms around her waist for no apparent, work-related reason." Carignan rejected his advances and insisted that he stop, but as his behaviour continued, she was forced to quit her job:

> It was taking all the energy I had just to be on my guard, and I couldn't even do my work properly ... If he came into the room, I got far, you know, anything like that, if he came in, I was out for stamps, if he came into my office, I was in the washroom. I was really frightened.

A board of inquiry determined that sexual harassment fell under the reasonable cause section. It awarded Carignan $1,600 for lost wages and compensation for humiliation.[29]

People were able to use the reasonable cause section to set new precedents in other areas such as physical appearance, disability, criminal record, age, language fluency, sexual orientation, and immigrant status.[30] Several boards of inquiry also recognized the existence of systemic discrimination, and that actions could be discriminatory even if there was no evidence of intent. Most importantly, the reasonable cause section closed potential loopholes in the legislation. A year before it came into effect, a woman submitted a complaint after she was evicted from her apartment. She was white, but her boyfriend was black. When the owner saw a black man visiting her suite, he demanded that she vacate the premises (he claimed that the reason was excessive noise, but the subsequent investigation suggested otherwise). Unfortunately, the Human Rights Act did not cover a situation where someone was discriminated against because of the race of a friend or partner. Under the Human Rights Code, however, the eviction would not have constituted reasonable cause.[31]

Finally, the code provided a broader range of possible remedies, which was consistent with other jurisdictions: these included a payment to cover lost wages; instatement or reinstatement in a job; offering tenancy in an apartment; a payment of damages or expenses; an agreement with the branch to discontinue discriminatory practices; an agreement to inform and educate the pertinent company official of the code's provisions; or an apology to the complainant.[32] Sometimes, the guilty party was asked to publish an apology in a local newspaper, especially if the complaint originated in a small town. In March 1975, for example, Linda Ward telephoned Pilgrim House Motel about applying for a night-shift desk clerk position that had been advertised in the *Penticton Herald*. The owner, Harley McCord, politely informed her that, for safety reasons, he did not hire women to work at night. Ward's next phone call was to the Human Rights Branch, and within a few days she filed a written complaint. After a human rights officer investigated and substantiated the accusation, and McCord refused conciliation, the minister appointed a board of inquiry. Perhaps realizing that his case was a lost cause, or preferring to pay a fine rather than a lawyer, McCord agreed to settle the case before the hearing. As he told a local reporter, "I am going to give her $400 and tell her to go to hell." Instead, the branch negotiated a $500 payment and insisted that McCord publish the following notice in the *Penticton Herald:* "Pilgrim House Penticton Limited has apologized to Linda Ward for refusing to consider her for employment as a desk clerk because of her sex and announces that all jobs at the Pilgrim House are open to both men and women on the basis of ability."[33]

The code dramatically expanded the human rights state in British Columbia. The number of inquiries (and informal complaints that were never investigated) increased from 660 in 1973 to 3,500 in 1976 and 10,391 in 1982.[34] Between 1969 and 1973, Sherlock received 2,092 complaints but investigated only 208. The Human Rights Code, however, required the branch to investigate every complaint. It scrutinized 709 complaints in 1978 (184 carried over from 1977) and closed 379 cases.[35] Human rights officers conducted almost 600 investigations per year. Overall, between 1974 and 1982, the branch received nearly 50,000 inquiries and investigated 4,630 complaints. Whereas in Ontario the per capita increase in cases from 1973 to 1975 was 38 percent, the number of cases investigated per capita in British Columbia rose 143 percent.[36]

The Human Rights Code received unanimous support in the legislature (in light of its future actions, it is surprising that the Social Credit Party raised so few objections to the bill). In 1974, in an appropriate demonstration of both the importance of the new code in a national context and the NDP's break from the past, British Columbia hosted the first national conference of human rights ministers in Canada.[37] The province also joined the Canadian Association of Statutory Human Rights Agencies in 1973 (the Socreds had rejected membership). Ruff became its first president.

The Human Rights Branch

British Columbia's Human Rights Code was the most progressive human rights law in the country. In many ways, its content was unlike anything else in Canada. But the success of the human rights state in British Columbia was founded as much – if not more – on the individuals who were responsible for administering the law. Kathleen Ruff was a critical figure during this early period. Her first innovation, unique in Canada, was to create a Human Rights Branch and to divide responsibilities for the human rights program: the branch investigated complaints, and the Human Rights Commission was responsible for education. Ruff spent years nurturing the growth of the Human Rights Branch. Unlike Sherlock, who was a bureaucrat at heart, she was an activist dedicated to aggressively advancing human rights in British Columbia. The investigations carried out by her human rights officers revealed the myriad forms of discrimination, especially in employment, which were pervasive throughout the province.

Ruff faced an unusual dilemma from the outset. There had never been such a thing as a human rights investigator in British Columbia. How, then, could she find qualified people? Her solution was inspired. She began by recruiting women who had been active in feminist organizations. This was a conscious strategy to staff the branch with individuals who, unlike Sherlock and the IROs, were dedicated to pursuing social equality. In particular, as a former activist herself, Ruff believed that sex discrimination was a paramount issue. She hired women who were uniquely qualified to investigate grievances of sex discrimination, which soon comprised the largest number of complaints submitted to the branch. This was what led her to invite Shelagh Day for lunch in the summer of 1973. Ruff had never met Day, but she was impressed with her report on sex discrimination at UBC. She offered her a job on the spot.[38]

On her first day, Day found herself walking alone into a small, empty office in a Department of Labour building on Dunsmuir Street in Vancouver. Although she would eventually become one of the country's leading human rights experts, at that time she was a twenty-nine-year-old former lecturer starting a new job. And neither she nor her colleagues had any idea of what they were supposed to do. As Day later suggested, "We were very young and new at it. We figured out techniques eventually for dealing with people's response."[39] Her first task was to contact the IROs who were handling the existing cases.[40] IROs, Day soon discovered, had "absolutely no sympathy for human rights." Their training did not prepare them for human rights investigations. Day commented:

> What is this? We go around and talk to people about hours of work and wages, but we don't talk about what questions they ask when they hire people. This was a general attitude among IROs with maybe a few exceptions. They didn't like to have this as part of their job, they didn't like us,

and they didn't like the new ones who would come along because we knew more about how to do this than they did.[41]

No policies or procedures for investigations were in place when Day arrived. IROs usually made no more than one visit to follow up a complaint, which led to extensive delays. When a human rights officer was assigned to the Kelowna region in 1976, she found a backlog of cases dating back more than a year.[42]

Ruff was busy establishing the Victoria office. The next person she hired was Maurice Guilbault, whose initial job was to travel around the province and speak to people about the law. Guilbault, an affable French Canadian, had a talent for meeting people. He would travel to a town and find ways to spread the message, from meeting with community groups to giving presentations at public libraries. Meanwhile, in Vancouver, Day began taking over some investigations:

> I was doing everything from talking to people on the telephone, giving them advice on whether they had a complaint or not, to going out and investigating all over the place. All kinds of different places. To writing analyses to determine if there was a violation of the law or not, talking to Kathleen [Ruff] whether or not something should go to a hearing, trying to figure out how we should be thinking about these parts of the law and what they meant. I mean, the thing that was most exciting about it was that it was brand new law, not just here, but right across the country. It was just in its formative stages, the thinking about what discrimination means or has it happened in these circumstances, all absolutely brand new. I credit British Columbia and Kathleen, in particular, for a lot of really, really clever thinking in the early days. These were the days when we had to think about whether or not we need to … know, intention … did they mean it or not … did it matter.[43]

For a brief period, the entire human rights program consisted of Kathleen Ruff in Victoria and Shelagh Day in Vancouver. Together, they laid the groundwork for expanding the human rights state. Their first challenge was simply responding to a wide range of inquiries and establishing a guiding vision for the branch. Ruff spent hours answering hundreds of letters. She wrote to one Aboriginal woman in Vancouver to explain that the Kinsman Club policy of not allowing children into the restaurant, because it served liquor, did not constitute racial discrimination. In other cases, Ruff and Day managed to avoid formal complaints and to assist dozens of complainants via a letter or a phone call. After reading a letter from Heather McAuley in Victoria, who was told by the National Trust bank that she could not use her common law husband's surname, Ruff wrote to the bank and the policy was rescinded. Day also spent a great deal of time with IROs, who still did the bulk of the investigations, to push them to aggressively investigate human rights complaints. Among other things, Day insisted that they meet more often with employers and complainants.

Another of Ruff's initial recruits was Linda Sproule-Jones, who agreed to work part-time in the Victoria office. There was little training. After shadowing Shelagh Day in Vancouver for a few days, Sproule-Jones was quickly handed her first case. It was a typically difficult one. Victoria's city clerk had retired and his assistant, a woman who had worked in the office for many years, was refused the position. She filed a claim of sex discrimination. But the city insisted that she was rejected because, during the interview, she stated that she would not change office procedures, which did not suit city officials, who were keen to revitalize the office and implement new ones. The union and the complainant were furious with Sproule-Jones for recommending against proceeding with the case. That was her first lesson in the hostility that human rights investigators faced on an almost daily basis.[44]

Within a couple of years, twelve people were working for the branch. The Victoria office was primarily responsible for administration, whereas the Vancouver office was staffed mainly with investigators.[45] Small offices with one or two investigators were later opened in Kamloops, Nelson, Prince George, and Terrace (usually housed in the Ministry of Labour offices). Ruff's choice of staff reflected her vision for the human rights state: proactively addressing discrimination throughout the province in a way that would have a systemic impact rather than simply responding to individual situations. Creating the human rights state, in her view, was part of a much larger mission for social justice that involved governments and social movements working together. To fulfill this vision, Ruff hired people who were dedicated to the issues: "It was difficult work and if you were not committed to the legislation you would not be very effective." Most were in their late twenties or early thirties. Unlike the IROs, they were not drawn from the ranks of the civil service. In addition to hiring women, Ruff sought out people from the communities that faced discrimination, including Chinese Canadians, Aboriginal people, Indo-Canadians, and African Canadians. As she put it, "They also had to know the arguments of the other side better than the other side knew themselves. And if they didn't they would be in trouble. There must be no arrogance. They must listen to everything the other side said. Because they could be right."[46]

The inexperienced staff quickly discovered that the process of investigating human rights complaints was strenuous and difficult. According to Day,

> Most of the intake we did was over the telephone. People would call and say "This just happened to me" or "I'm concerned about this and that" and so on. If it sounded like it was really a serious complaint, usually we would make an appointment with these people, either going to see them in person or get them to come to the office and meet with us and take down a whole lot more details. And then we notified the employer (respondent, whoever it was) and said, "We have a complaint here, we need to talk to you about it," make an appointment, go to see them, explain to them what the legislation was about, what the authority I had, and say what the nature of the complaint was, and ask them for any information that they might have ... Then there were other people to follow up with. Usually, I would go back to the complainant to talk to him or her, or I would need to talk to who he/she had named as witnesses. I needed to talk to whoever the respondent had named as witnesses or other people who had dealt with this problem. And then we would try to put this together, write an investigation report on the whole situation, and make recommendations on what we thought should happen and whether or not I thought it was discriminating. If it went to a board of inquiry, then it was also my job to work with counsel to get them information because I was the one who had the best sense of the file and what the information was and who were the most important people ... It is not a nice process. It is not an easy thing to do. You have to deal with a lot of conflict and people who don't want to deal with you and who are defensive and aggressive.[47]

Ruff hired investigators who were far more proactive at responding to complaints than the IROs were. Most complaints were resolved informally thanks to some creative detective work. For example, Gail Jewsbury, a young woman living in Victoria in 1976, applied for a position as a waste water technician at the Capital Regional District. She had recently completed an oceanography degree at the University of Victoria and was clearly qualified for the job. But her application was quickly rejected. Jewsbury suspected that Frank Remondo, the senior engineer assistant, had rejected her application because she was a woman. When Remondo denied the allegation, Jewsbury filed a complaint, and her case was assigned to Sproule-Jones, who decided to do some investigating before confronting Remondo:

> Before I went to see [Remondo], I went to the central personnel office, and I said I would like to see all of the resumés. I looked and I said I would like copies, and I got copies of everything and everyone who applied. And then I went to see [Remondo], and he was a nice enough fellow but just very old fashioned. "I wouldn't want my wife doing a job like that. It's a dirty job." I said, "Y'know what, she's not your wife. She's studied this. This is her area. This is what she wants to do." And it looked like she was qualified. [He] hesitated, unsure what to do. I went back to talk to the head of the Capital Regional District, but first I went back to personnel, and they had changed some of the stuff. I said, "Can I have a copy of this, please?" I had two documents, before the hiring and one where it had clearly been altered. Again, I gave that to David Vickers [Human Rights Branch legal counsel] and he called [Remondo] and she got the job.[48]

Employers were not necessarily hostile to claims of sex discrimination, and sometimes no more was required than pointing out the contradictions in their hiring practices. One of Sproule-Jones's most memorable cases involved women seeking work at a dynamite factory:

> They did not hire women, because it was a dynamite factory and they didn't have washrooms. For my prep, I went to the *Times-Colonist* library ... went back to the war (World War Two), because I figured there's bound to be stuff. And to help me out, there was a photo because they had won a safety award ... So I made a copy of this photo of practically all female staff and went over and started talking with this guy [the employer]. He said, "Well, it's very dangerous work," and I pulled out this photo and I said, "Well, I see that these female employees won a safety award." He bowed his head and said "OK, what do I have to do?" I told him to build a washroom and stop refusing to hire women.[49]

At times the branch would adopt a more proactive strategy and approach employers without waiting for an individual to submit a complaint. Before the Human Rights Code came into effect, Ruff approached the *Vancouver Sun* about eliminating its policy of dividing job advertisements between male and female employment:

I met with Stewart [the editor], and I had already contacted his person at the *Vancouver Sun* who was in charge of advertising. And his name, believe it or not, was Colonel Toogood. [laughter] He was exactly as he sounds! He just thought it was the most ridiculous thing he had ever heard of. Y'know, this is what many people don't understand. There was so much ridicule against women and equality, and they thought it was idiotic. So he was completely hostile. There was no way they were going to change their system because, y'know, it was a lot of work. So I met with Stewart. I knew his daughter. She was a reporter with the *Victoria Times-Colonist*. She was a young woman and was certainly aware [of the issues], and was feeling that she was a woman and she should be treated equally. So I knew that, although I didn't mention that to him. But I appealed to him that he had an opportunity. And the *Vancouver Sun* and the *Province* had an opportunity: to show leadership. That instead of being dragged, kicking and screaming and being forced to change their system, what would it be like if they themselves voluntarily chose because they supported or recognized that justice and equality for women is something they are not opposed to? In fact, that it was something they supported. And to think of young women looking for jobs, young women looking for work. What a message it would be if the *Vancouver Sun* felt that they should be treated on the basis of their qualifications. And he agreed. So they voluntarily changed their system.[50]

Shelagh Day, Linda Sproule-Jones, and other human rights officers became adept at resolving complaints. Most of their investigations in the early years involved women at work. For instance, of a sample of 264 complaints between 1976 and 1978 that never went to a board of inquiry, the vast majority fell within three categories: sex (151), including marital status (26) and pregnancy (13); reasonable cause (46), predominantly disability and criminal conviction; and race (42). A few complaints alleged discrimination on the basis of age (16), place of origin (7), religion (1), and sexual orientation (1).[51] Of the 264 complaints, 200 dealt with employment, 36 with services, and 28 with accommodations. When Day or Sproule-Jones were called in to investigate, they were usually dealing with a landlord refusing to rent, an employer refusing to hire, or someone who had been denied a service (for instance, a pub or restaurant refusing to serve or an employment agency unwilling to refer to a job). In several instances, investigators concluded that complaints were unsubstantiated (76), usually because of an absence of evidence or because other reasons explained why someone had been fired (such as incompetence or lack of qualifications).

In many cases, complainants decided to withdraw (29) or not to pursue the investigation (35). In these situations, they had left town, lost interest, become frustrated with delays, or found other employment; sometimes the investigator was unable to communicate with them. Day, Sproule-Jones, and the other officers were especially skilled at negotiating settlements. From this sample of 264 complaints, in situations where the complainant stayed the course and the investigator felt that the case was legitimate, only 4 had to be recommended for a board of inquiry, whereas 118 reached a settlement. This was an extraordinary success rate. Most settlements involved nothing more than a letter of apology, although they might also include offering employment, changing company policies and practices, providing a service, or paying financial compensation.

Still, some businesses went to surprising lengths to resist conforming with the new human rights regime and had to be forced to comply with the law. Lornex Mining Company, which operated a mine in northern British Columbia, was a perfect example. Since the mine was geographically isolated, employees were given free accommodation. Working conditions for many women at the mine, though, were intolerable. Bonnie Bukwa, one of its technical specialists, submitted a complaint under the Human Rights Act in 1973 because Lornex refused to provide her with accommodation. An IRO investigated and was unable to secure a settlement, so Jack Sherlock forwarded the case to the Human Rights Commission. In August 1974, after hearing the complaint, the commission ordered Lornex to make its campsite "available to female employees on the same terms and conditions as male employees." It also ordered Lornex to pay Bukwa $2,713 to cover her expenses relating to the complaint.[52]

Defiantly, Lornex appealed the case in court. But in June 1976, the British Columbia Supreme Court sustained the commission's ruling. Unfortunately, the judge concluded that the commission was empowered only to demand money for lost wages, not for damages, which was not the case here. Bukwa won, but it was a pyrrhic victory, and she was no longer working for Lornex.

While the case was pending in court, Lornex had grudgingly agreed to comply with the commission's order to make its worksite accommodations accessible to female employees. Jean Tharpe, a twenty-four-year-old laboratory technologist, moved into the company bunkhouse in 1974. She was shocked to discover, though, that Lornex had adhered to the order by the simple expedient of allowing women to shower and sleep in the same facilities as men. Tharpe submitted a complaint against Lornex in 1974 under the new Human Rights Code, and Shelagh Day was assigned the case. Day secured an agreement from Lornex to accommodate female workers, but once again, it proved evasive. It added a partition in the bunkhouse to separate Tharpe from the other staff, which her male co-workers promptly ignored because her section offered a faster route to the dining area. Tharpe solved her problem by sleeping and showering in a nearby town and commuting to work.

Day recommended a board of inquiry, which was held in 1975. Tharpe "won" her case. After more than a year of consistent conflict with her employer, driving to town to shower, and working in a tense environment, Tharpe was awarded a meagre $250 for her troubles.[53] Neither Tharpe nor Bukwa continued to work for Lornex after their complaint was resolved. The Lornex case demonstrated how far businesses would go to avoid conforming to the new human rights regime, as well as the delays and costs associated with human rights adjudication. For Day, the case was among the most frustrating investigations of her career:

> They were incredibly belligerent. This was new stuff and they did really believe ... I mean, what was this stuff? Come on. These were men's jobs. What are you talking about, silly women and feminism and women's movement nonsense. Men did this. We all knew it. Why don't we? Well, fine. She wants to do the job, she can live with the guys. It was just a real, fundamental refusal to deal with it. Until, y'know ... there was just a huge shift in how people have decided that there is a law, and there really is something there that needs to be paid attention to ... I didn't care about their attitudes. It just had to be clear. It was discrimination. This was the law. They had to behave. They could complain in private ... I wasn't the least bit interested in changing their hearts and minds. I just wanted them to change their behaviour.[54]

Common sense notions about gender were perhaps the greatest challenge for the human rights state. The primary responsibility of human rights investigators was to find an informal resolution that was consistent with the principle of non-discrimination. Punishment was a last resort, which is why officers such as Day and Sproule-Jones went to such lengths to convince employers to voluntarily change their practices. But it was a struggle. They often faced the impossible task of confronting profoundly personal and deeply held beliefs about gender and women's roles. For example, after Linda Ward won her case against Harley McCord and the

Penticton House Motel for refusing to hire a woman as a night shift desk clerk, a *Penticton Herald* editorial attacked the Human Rights Branch and supported McCord's stance:

> Surely here is an instance in which both the law and justice offend ... Granted, women have made many breakthroughs in taking over jobs that have been traditionally considered to be within the exclusive male domain. But common sense suggests there have to be some exceptions. The motel, it would seem, had a valid argument that it was acting in the interests of the safety of the business as well as the employee in deciding that the demands of a night clerk's job were unsuitable or too dangerous for a woman to handle. It follows, then, that it was a bonafide requirement of the job that it should be restricted to male employees ... The case holds out a gold-plated invitation for businesses to be victimized by all kinds of frivolous complaints, the result of which is easy money.[55]

No less than the minister of labour, who was responsible for authorizing boards of inquiry, viewed the case of a golf course that refused to allow women to play as an example of "frivolous" complaints. In a 1975 letter to the Human Rights Branch, Dutchie Mathison described her experience of being denied access to a golf course:

> Easter Monday my daughter, husband, male friend and I arrived to play golf at 9:00am. My daughter and I were told we could *not* play until after 11:00am. My husband and his friend could play if they wished. On questioning this rule I was told that a 6 yr old male child could play but females of any age definitely could not. It was suggested that the two male members of our party play nine holes and that after waiting 2-3 hours my daughter and I could join them for the last 9 holes as it would be past 11:00am.

Mathison went on to quote the responses she received from Terry King, the golf course manager, and his employee Mrs. S. Chappell:

- Present times are fair because men work all week and deserve to have the opportunity to play without being bothered.
- When do you do your housework if you work?
- If you like golfing so much organize your time better so you can play when women are allowed.
- If women are allowed to play before 11:00 am all the male members will quit and go play someplace else.

- If the men quit it will be your fault and you will be taking Terry King's livelihood away from him and causing hardship for his family ... Just because you want to play golf should Terry's family go hungry?
- You are a selfish woman who doesn't respect her husband or you would be delighted that he has time to play with men.[56]

Despite repeated attempts at conciliation, the investigator was unable to convince the golf course to amend its policy. A board of inquiry later decided in favour of Mathison, and soon afterward the golf course stopped banning women from playing before 11:00 a.m. It agreed to publish an ad in the local newspaper to explain the new policy, apologized to Mathison, and amended its lease with the district of Maple Ridge to include a non-discrimination clause.

Sexual harassment was one of the toughest cases for a human rights officer. There were no established techniques for dealing with these complaints, and the concept had yet to gain popular currency in most workplaces. And yet, by 1980, no sexual harassment complaint had reached a board of inquiry, because investigators had managed to settle them informally. The branch had produced a strategy for handling these complaints that, though not ideal, was largely successful. Investigators were warned about the necessity of approaching complaints diplomatically and in the strictest confidence. A false allegation could have serious consequences for a business or an individual's personal life. The branch's procedures emphasized the need to meet in person and talk at length with the complainant and to document, as much as possible, every aspect of the harassment. An officer would then meet with the accused, usually in the workplace, to let him know that a complaint had been filed and to hear his side of the story. If possible, the officer would examine personnel records and interview other employees, former employees, or other witnesses as suggested by both the complainant and the accused. After completing the investigation, the officer then had to make a judgment call on whether the complaint was valid. If it was, the next step focused on negotiating a fair settlement.[57] The goal was rarely to impose any kind of hardship or penalty on the accused. Settlements usually included a letter of apology, an agreement to abide by the Human Rights Code in the future, and an offer to rehire the former employee or to write a positive reference letter. Financial settlements were common, usually in the amount of $1,000. In a few cases, the respondent agreed to seek counselling; another paid for staff assertiveness training; and another gave a symbolic donation to an organization promoting awareness of sexual harassment.

Social Movements and the Law

Despite the proliferation of investigators and an expanding Human Rights Branch, handling the burgeoning caseloads was always a struggle. But the officers were not alone in their efforts. Social movement organizations not only played a crucial role in lobbying and shaping human rights legislation, but were also an integral part of enforcing the legislation. SWAG, for example, had initiated at least two equal pay cases before 1973. The VSW ombudswoman helped many women draft complaints, and the association itself lobbied for legal reform. During the 1975 election, candidates were called upon to support more funding for the Human Rights Branch, to remove any exemptions for government agencies and educational institutions, to provide legal aid for complainants, and to ban discrimination on the basis of pregnancy and marital status.[58] Among the organizations cited in the branch's annual reports between 1974 and 1984 were the BCCLA, British Columbia Federation of Labour Women's Committee, British Columbia Federation of Women, Business and Professional Women's Clubs of British Columbia, National Action Committee on the Status of Women in British Columbia, Provincial Council of Women, SWAG, and the VSW. Clearly, women's rights organizations were prominent in the operation of the human rights state.

At times the VSW was more effective than the branch in enforcing the law. Soon after its creation, the VSW established the position of ombudswoman and hired Rosemary Brown to fill the post. Within two years, however, Brown was elected as an NDP MLA, and the VSW replaced her with Gene Errington. One of her responsibilities was to help women prepare human rights complaints. In this capacity, Brown and Errington often informally adopted the role of a government official. For example, in 1972, Brown met with managers of the Hudson's Bay Company and convinced them to voluntarily raise the salaries of female sales clerks to comply with the legislation.[59] Brown and Errington also provided invaluable support to complainants, in preparing their cases and then providing free legal counsel for the hearing. The VSW was also responsible for initiating the largest equal pay case in the province's history.

The VSW was persistent in its attempts to seek restitution through human rights legislation despite several notable failures. In February 1980, for example, five organizations – the British Columbia Federation of Women, Business and Professional Women's Clubs, Canadian Advisory Council on the Status of Women, Provincial Council of Women, and the VSW – filed a human rights complaint against University of British

Columbia president Doug Kenny, Dean of Science Martin Wedepohl, and Engineering Undergraduate Society president Russ Kinghorn.[60] The complaint was a response to content in the UBC engineering newspaper, *Red Rag*. Nadine Allen of the VSW described the paper as a "pornographic, racist and sexist publication." Its first issue of 1979 depicted young men mockingly raping a woman; three years later, the paper provided a guide to men who were "pussy whipped" on how to sexually harass and abuse women.[61] The complaint was also a response to the notorious Lady Godiva ride, an annual event featuring a naked woman (a stripper hired by the Engineering Undergraduate Society) astride a horse parading around the UBC campus.[62] These practices contributed to an atmosphere of sexual harassment on campus and discouraged women from entering the engineering program. Ellen Woodsworth of the Vancouver Women's Caucus characterized the Lady Godiva ride as the sexual objectification of women.[63] For its part, the administration refused to discipline the engineers.

Lady Godiva ride, UBC, 1981. | Jim Banham photo, University of British Columbia Archives, 41.1/757-2

Student protests at the Lady Godiva ride, UBC, 1981 | Jim Banham photo, University of British Columbia Archives, 41.1/921-1

Such behaviour was commonplace among campus engineering societies in Canada. The University of Saskatchewan's Lady Godiva ride, as well as the engineers' newspaper *Red Eye,* was symptomatic of sexual harassment and male privilege on campuses. The Saskatchewan Action Committee on the Status of Women filed a human rights complaint in 1979 that was later sustained by a board of inquiry. But the case dragged on for years and was overturned in court.[64] The 1980 complaint against the UBC engineers also dragged on for years with no resolution. Only after several organizations filed a complaint with the provincial ombudsman did the UBC president shut down the engineering newspaper and padlock its offices. The Lady Godiva ride, however, continued amidst intense controversy until 1987, when the woman stopped riding naked.[65] Despite such setbacks, the VSW continued to seek restitution through human rights legislation. A review of its annual reports, correspondence, and minutes between 1971 and 1984 reveals an organization deeply implicated in the human rights state.

Social movement groups such as the BCCLA, SWAG, and the VSW engaged in a wide array of activities to enforce the legislation: they documented cases of discrimination; produced surveys or conducted research on issues such as equal pay (e.g., listing the pay scales of specific employers) to initiate inquiries; identified large employers who were violating the legislation; mailed letters with a copy of the statute; sent volunteers to individual employers to discuss hiring and management practices (e.g., department stores that rarely hired women, or factories with segregated job assignments); drew media attention to deficiencies in the legislation, including delays or poorly trained investigators; organized human rights conferences, to which they invited investigators; lobbied government departments on policy issues (such as gender stereotyping in textbooks); promoted awareness of board of inquiry decisions through press releases and newsletters (a common critique was that the government did not publicize rulings); secured federal government funding to promote human rights in the province; and wrote to the branch to support specific cases and to prod officers to advance an inquiry.[66]

Ruff, who had been highly active in the women's movement before she joined the branch, welcomed the support from the VSW and other social movement organizations. She deliberately courted their help, usually by giving a speech or speaking at a meeting. The human rights state in British Columbia expanded dramatically during her tenure as director. In 1970, Sherlock investigated 27 complaints; five years later, under Ruff, the branch investigated 714 complaints.[67] The number of people who worked for the branch had increased to fifteen by 1975. Garry Carson, a former lawyer from Toronto, was appointed assistant director, but he soon quit and was replaced by Reginald Newkirk; Gillian MacGregor was hired as an intake officer (to process complaints for investigators) in Vancouver during 1974; Graham Hope, the education officer, was also headquartered in Vancouver; and the Victoria office hired Helen Austin in 1978 to act as a special consultant for the handicapped. More cases were shifted from IROs to human rights officers. By the time Ruff left the branch in 1979, she had established offices in six cities, hired a dozen human rights investigators, and managed a half dozen support staff.

7
Struggling to Innovate, 1979-83

On 30 April 1978, Kathleen Grafe was visiting the Canada Manpower Office in Sechelt, a small town sixty-six kilometres northwest of Vancouver, to check for any new job advertisements. The only new posting that day was for general employment at Sechelt Building Supplies. Grafe, who was a single woman in her twenties, had been looking for work for several weeks. She visited the company's office the next day. As she approached the man at the front counter, Grafe noticed that there were "quite a few men around." When she informed the man behind the counter that she wished to apply for a job, he appeared "very surprised and shocked ... It was as if he didn't know what to do." Grafe patiently repeated that she had come to apply for work and asked if she should leave her name or fill out an application. The man "yelled to the back to someone behind another office and asked what they had done with the girl that had come yesterday." The voice in the back responded, "Oh, just take her name and number." Within a few minutes, however, Grafe was escorted to an office for an interview with Hayden Killam. He did not ask about her experience and qualifications. At one point, he said, "I wouldn't hold my breath about getting a job here." He wanted to know how much she weighed and to see her muscles. He also asked if she could carry specific weights and lift gyproc off the back of trucks. That was the end of the interview. Grafe never received a call from Sechelt Building Supplies. Instead, the company filled the position with a man later that day.

Grafe filed a human rights complaint a few days later, and Reginald Newkirk was assigned the case. Killam, who was belligerent when Newkirk asked him about the complaint, explained that he had visually assessed Grafe's physical ability and concluded that a 135-pound woman could not do the work. He later told Newkirk on the phone that he felt "only a woman of Herculean size could handle the job." A board of inquiry was held at the Vancouver offices of the Labour Relations Board in 1979, which Killam refused to attend. The chair, Beverley McLachlin, decided to hear the case anyway and concluded that Grafe had been discriminated against on the basis of arbitrary height and weight requirements. One piece of evidence was a copy of Grafe's application form, which Newkirk found during his investigation. On the application, Killam had scrawled "Bitch reported us to human rights." He was later quoted as saying "I am against fucking human rights. I don't want to have anything to do with this human rights bullshit." McLachlin awarded Grafe $280 in lost wages.[1]

Grafe's case was possible only under the Human Rights Code. The human rights state had expanded under Kathleen Ruff's leadership between 1974 and 1979. Ruff recognized, however, that investigating individual complaints was, at best, a stopgap approach. Sex discrimination was a pervasive social practice. Income disparities between Canadian women and men improved only slightly during the 1970s, from approximately 60 percent of a male wage to 66 percent.[2] The disparity was especially pronounced when education and wage were both taken into account:

> When age and educational levels were held constant for full-time female and male workers, the wage gap persisted. Women workers between the ages of 25 and 54 years with a university degree earned an annual average of $21,000 in 1981; their male counterparts earned over $30,000. In fact, men in the same category with only a high school education also earned an average of $21,000 per annum. Even when differences in education, labour force experience, degree of unionization, and number of hours worked were taken into consideration, women still earned 15 to 20 percent less than men.[3]

This income disparity had long-term implications: small pensions, fewer investment opportunities, and a greater likelihood of poverty, especially among older women. In 1981, 30.6 percent of women – compared to 44.8 percent of men – had pensions.[4] As a result, a large number of elderly women were poor: among those aged sixty-five or older, 57 percent reported pension income of less than $5,000 annually in 1980, and 71 percent reported less than $6,000.[5] Their plight was exacerbated by the refusal of insurance companies to continue coverage for women after a divorce. And because women tended to live longer than men, they were charged higher premiums for life insurance.[6]

Women in rural British Columbia faced their own unique challenges. Inadequate child care facilities, occupational ghettos, limited mobility, declining service-sector jobs as a result of new technologies, family obligations, restricted training opportunities: these and many other factors created obstacles for women who sought work. Opportunities for training were limited outside of Prince George and Terrace, and many women simply did not have the resources to temporarily relocate. A government-sponsored report produced for International Women's Year in 1975 noted that women in the North had limited work opportunities and were most often employed in clerical, sales, waitressing, or cleaning fields.[7] The report's author received "many complaints of job counsellors who lack sensitivity to the capabilities and aspirations of women. They often question why women want to work at all, particularly if those women have children. There is frequently still an assumption that women work for frivolous reasons, for pin money."[8] Alcan (a major employer in the region) commissioned another report in 1982 on the labour force in northern British Columbia for its Kemano hydroelectric plant.[9] According to the report, many obstacles that rural women faced in securing employment arose, not necessarily from the employer, but from home:

> The persons interviewed in the northwest repeatedly cited examples of this barrier. One summed it up with the comment that "husbands don't really mind what jobs their wives have, as long as the job doesn't interfere with her taking care of the home and family." Respondents noted that this attitude made shift work, work requiring long absences from home, and even training which caused similar disruptions, difficult to accept.[10]

Even in those professions where women had a strong presence, discrimination was common. Gene Errington, the provincial coordinator for the status of women, produced a report on employment equity in the provincial civil service in 1975. Of the more than 37,000 public servants, approximately 55 percent were female. None were deputy ministers or associate deputy ministers, and only 8 were employed as senior managers.[11] Among British Columbia's 12,844 female and 10,892 male teachers in 1974, gender segregation was standard practice. There were 87 male (and 2,283 female) primary school teachers and 3,490 male (1,529 female) secondary school teachers. Among school administrators, there were 751 men (81 women) in primary and 288 men (2 women) in secondary schools.

Physical education department heads were almost exclusively male, and they received more funding, facilities, equipment, and scheduling priorities for boys' sports (at the University of British Columbia, all students were charged a five-dollar athletic fee, but only eighty cents went to women's programs). There were no female district superintendents. The British Columbia Teachers' Federation had one woman on its twelve-member executive.[12]

School board hiring practices were explicitly discriminatory. As late as 1975, the Ministry of Education required married female teachers to provide copies of their marriage certificates. Ostensibly, the policy was designed to confirm any changes in their surnames, but according to the British Columbia Teachers' Federation, it was "obsolete" because women had the legal right to retain their name.[13] In addition to requiring marriage certificates, school boards predominantly hired men as secondary school teachers and women as primary school teachers.[14] Female teachers were encouraged to quit if they became pregnant; part-time teachers were often denied full-time employment if their male spouse had a full-time job; women with three or more children sometimes lied about their family size due to fear of being denied employment; and female counsellors were assigned only to female students. One woman was asked why, given that she had young children, she was applying for a teaching position and was told that she could not be hired because her children were too young for her to be away from home.[15] The following figure shows the information that one district required from all its female teachers (it did not require family information from male employees).[16]

Physical examination of employees:

Female: frequency of menstruation _____ duration of menstrual period _____ dysmenorrhea? _____ now pregnant? _____ number of pregnancies _____ number and ages of living children _____

By 1979, the Human Rights Branch had processed thousands of complaints each year, employing dedicated civil servants, reaching out to rural British Columbia, and making new law through boards of inquiry. Women continued to occupy key leadership positions in the human rights apparatus. With the help of community activists, especially women's rights advocates, the scope of the human rights state extended to new spheres.

The Human Rights Commission's mandate was to develop education programs and to promote awareness of the legislation. Prevention, rather than simply responding to individual complaints, was the mandate of the human rights state. British Columbia soon became a veritable laboratory for innovation in human rights policy. But these developments were not without controversy, and human rights law was no panacea. Perhaps unsurprisingly, the issue that most clearly demonstrated the limits of the human rights state at this time was equal pay for women.

The Human Rights Branch

Kathleen Ruff left the Human Rights Branch in 1979. Her temporary replacement was Hanne Jensen. Jensen had been responsible for the first formal inquiry under the Human Rights Act in 1972, when she fought her employer over equal pay. Although she won her case, Jensen ultimately quit her job with Office Assistance Limited in 1973 and went to work with the Vancouver Status of Women (VSW) ombudswoman. During that time, she was also elected president of MOSAIC, a multicultural association. Within a year, she left the VSW to work as a human rights investigator and was asked in 1979 to act as interim director until Ruff's replacement could be found. Nola Landucci, a former manager with the federal Human Rights Commission, accepted the job in 1980. Born and raised in Trail, British Columbia, Landucci was the child of immigrant parents who worked at the local smelting company. She was exposed to the civil rights movement and women's rights activism as a university graduate student in Indiana during the 1960s. Like her predecessors, Landucci was committed to advancing women's rights. She served in the federal Department of Labour's Women's Bureau and as director of the Office of Equal Opportunities for Women. By the time she became director of the Human Rights Branch, Landucci had worked for twelve years in the federal civil service, including a stint as the first director of complaints and compliance for the Canadian Human Rights Commission. After fifteen months, however, she left the branch and returned to the federal commission. Jensen replaced her as director in 1981, remaining in the position until the Socreds fired everyone and eliminated the branch and the Human Rights Commission in 1983.

Jensen, Landucci, and Ruff hired people who shared their convictions, amassing a diverse group of civil servants with close ties to community associations. Shelagh Day, April Katz, and Linda Sproule-Jones had been

Hanne Jensen, 1983 | *Vancouver Province*

◂ Nola Landucci, 1980 |
Ralph Bower, *Vancouver Sun*

active in the women's movement, especially the Status of Women Action Group (SWAG) and the VSW. Ross Fedy and Hugh McLeod were active in the disability rights movement; Maurice Guilbault had been involved with the British Columbia Civil Liberties Association (BCCLA); Ajit Mehat was an Indo-Canadian with close links to the local community; and Reginald Newkirk, an African Canadian, was formerly the executive director of an Indian Friendship Centre in Alberta. The staff were equally diverse in age and life experience. Several of them, including Penny Goldrick, Jensen, Landucci, and Newkirk, had some experience working for human rights commissions elsewhere in Canada. In 1981, the branch conducted an informal review of its staff members' links to community groups, compiling an impressive list. All fourteen employees who were consulted had ties to at least fifty-two organizations as diverse as the Elizabeth Fry Society, Greenpeace, and the National Black Women's Congress.[17] Engagement with community organizations represented a significant evolution in the branch's work. Human rights officers, especially those located outside Vancouver, were expected to dedicate at least 10 percent of their time to this task. It was not uncommon for McLeod or Newkirk, for instance, to participate in symposiums organized by the

BCCLA or VSW that led to resolutions calling for legislative reform. In other cases they organized public events to generate awareness of issues such as manifestations of the Ku Klux Klan in the province during the late 1970s.

Many of the staff could draw on their personal experiences, and in this way they were uniquely qualified to investigate complaints. But even this assessment underplays a genuinely impressive feature of the BC human rights state: most of these people were extraordinarily committed to their work. It was not uncommon for human rights investigators in regional offices to put in long hours, including at night and on weekends. Alan Andison, a human rights officer stationed in Prince George, frequently called the Victoria office and found that people were still working at 6:00 or 7:00 p.m.[18] April Katz, who came to Victoria in 1981 as chief of compliance, had worked for the Canadian Human Rights Commission in several regions. She was quickly impressed with the work produced in British Columbia. Katz later recalled that the quality of investigations and reporting was superior to anything she had seen elsewhere in Canada. The branch was able to attract talented people who had a personal commitment to the work (the average salary for investigators was $23,000 per year, compared with $40,000 or more for the director). However, soon after arriving in Victoria, Katz also discovered that her officers had a strong independent streak. One of the investigators, who was assigned to Prince George, took two months off in 1981, built a log cabin in Terrace, and then informed the branch several months later that he was now operating out of Terrace, an eight-hour drive from Prince George![19]

Landucci and Jensen presided over an exponential growth in the human rights state. In 1977, the branch was fielding thousands of inquiries and producing two hundred educational programs.[20] It employed more than a dozen human rights officers. At its peak in 1983, it had thirty-seven staff, which included investigators in Cranbrook, Kamloops, Kelowna, Nelson, Prince George, Terrace, Victoria, and Vancouver. Except for the Vancouver office, each regional office (often with only a single investigator) was responsible for covering an enormous territory.[21] Collectively, officers in Cranbrook, Kamloops, Prince George, Terrace, and Victoria logged more than twelve thousand kilometres in car travel during 1983.[22] And they could barely keep up, as more complaints were filed every year. Forty case closures per officer in a year was considered a relatively high number for any jurisdiction in Canada. In 1982, for instance, the average annual caseload in Ontario was twenty-two per officer, and the federal commission assigned seventeen per officer; in British Columbia, officers had an average caseload of seventy-six, and they closed an average of fifty each year (a board of inquiry could occupy a single officer for two weeks). Increasingly, cases were delayed. In 1981, the branch received nine thousand calls from the public, up from five thousand in 1979.[23]

The scope of the human rights state was remarkable. Branch officers spread out across the province: between 1981 and 1982, they conducted investigations in at least eighty cities. Most of the major population areas, including the Lower Mainland, Okanagan, Prince George, Vancouver Island, and West Kootenay, were assigned human rights officers. They travelled to remote areas such as Dawson Creek in the northeast and Cassiar near the Yukon border.

If statistics are any indication, human rights officers were very good at their work. A sample of 397 complaints in 1981 shows that only 14 percent were withdrawn and 19 percent unresolved; the remaining 67 percent were resolved or settled (Figure 6).[24] One of the most significant changes between 1969 and 1983 was the increase in complaints for refusal of service or accommodation. Between 1969 and 1973, 99 percent of complaints were based on employment discrimination. Between 1980 and 1982, 75 percent dealt with employment, 16 percent applied to services, and 9 percent to accommodations. Except for an unusually large number of complaints dealing with age between 1969 and 1973 (mainly challenges to mandatory retirement), most focused on sex and race. As Figure 7 demonstrates, sex discrimination continued to dominate the number of complaints. Human rights officers had also become adept at negotiating settlements without

FIGURE 6 Settlements

Cash	55
Amended policy	17
Letter of apology	44
Letter of compliance	49
Offer of employment	16
Verbal apology	5
Offer next vacancy	3
Reconsider application	4
Unsubstantiated	50

NOTE: Based on a sample of 251 complaints submitted between 1981 and 1982.

FIGURE 7 Human rights complaints, 1974-82

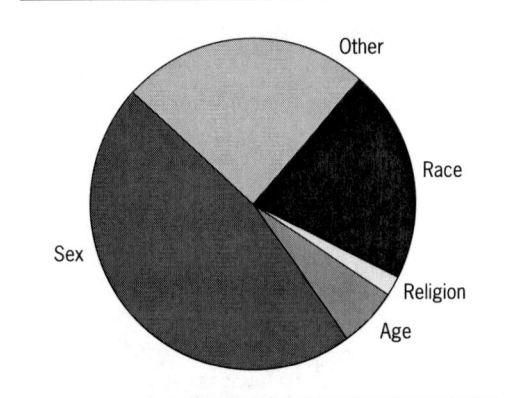

SOURCE: British Columbia, Department of Labour, Annual Reports, 1974-82.

requiring a formal inquiry. These took the form of cash payments, letters of apology or compliance, offering employment, reconsidering an application, or amending an internal policy.

The Human Rights Commission

A BC innovation was the creation of a separate agency with a mandate for education. Under the Human Rights Code, the Human Rights Commission would complement the branch's efforts by working to prevent discrimination rather than responding to complaints. As Kathleen Strenja's case highlights, there was a desperate need to promote awareness of the law.

Strenja, a young mother living in Vancouver whose husband was on welfare following a workplace injury, responded to a notice board advertisement for replacement taxi drivers in May 1980. She was hired on the spot. After driving for a few hours, Strenja returned to the head office and encountered the owner's son as she walked out the door. Shocked that the manager had hired a woman, he explained that he and his father, Bob Bennett, did not like women driving cabs. He insisted that she park the car while he looked for his father. A few minutes later, Bob Bennett, out walking his dog, became irate when he saw Strenja exiting the cab. Insisting that he would never hire a woman, he removed the taxi's municipal licence plate and threw it into the garbage. Undeterred, Strenja jumped into the car and headed off to the nearest RCMP station, with Bennett (and his dog) chasing her in another taxi. At the station, Bennett and Strenja engaged in a heated argument. According to the officer on the scene,

> He [Bennett] said that his policy was not to hire women, that this was Company policy, that he had been with the taxi business since 1954 and that women attracted too much trouble. He also told Corporal Geisser that women drivers just don't work out in this town. He said that he hired women as dispatchers, but not as drivers because they're "just trouble"; he mentioned the risk of rapes.[25]

A board of inquiry fined Bennett $1,880 for damages and lost wages.

Among the many bizarre aspects of the Strenja case was that Bennett appeared to be totally ignorant of the law. His statements to the RCMP officer suggest that he was unaware that his actions obviously violated the Human Rights Code. The case highlights a fundamental objective of the human rights state: education. This was the primary mandate for the

Human Rights Commission. Unfortunately, the commission struggled to define a role for itself. The relationship between it and the branch was always awkward. Other jurisdictions in Canada had a human rights commission that dealt with complaints and managed an education program. In British Columbia, however, Ruff had divided the responsibilities for administering the human rights program between the branch and the commission: the former handled investigations and the latter focused on education. Between 1974 and 1983, there were three Human Rights Commissions. Bishop Remi B. De Roo chaired the first one, which was appointed under the NDP in 1974 for a four-year term. De Roo was the Catholic bishop of Victoria. Widely respected, he held strong liberal views. The other four commissioners were equally well qualified: Bill Black (UBC Faculty of Law professor and the province's leading expert on human rights law); Rose Charlie (president, Indian Homemakers Association); Gene Errington (VSW ombudswoman); and Larry Ryan (secretary-treasurer, Victoria Labour Council). Under the Human Rights Code, the director of the Human Rights Branch was also the executive director of the Human Rights Commission (presumably to facilitate a working relationship between the two agencies). In practice, Jensen, Landucci, and Ruff generally allowed the commission to operate on its own and acted mainly as a liaison between it and the branch.

Under De Roo, the commission functioned primarily as an advisory body for the branch, often providing advice to Ruff in the early days when everything was a new challenge. Otherwise, it did very little and met only a few times a year. Occasionally, De Roo would help with complaints, and he chaired at least one board of inquiry. In 1975, he wrote to the manager of a SuperValu store in Kelowna after receiving correspondence from a woman who had been forced to provide the name of her husband to cash a cheque.[26] The store agreed to discontinue the practice. Sometimes De Roo would castigate the government through press releases and media interviews on issues such as poverty among Aboriginal people or its refusal to support the Gay Alliance Towards Equality's appeal to the Supreme Court of Canada. Overall, however, the first commission never determined a clear role for itself.

As a result of the commission's vague mandate, its relationship with the branch became increasingly strained. After De Roo and the other NDP-appointed commissioners finished their terms in 1978, the Social Credit government replaced them with an ineffectual group of mostly partisan loyalists. Margaret Strongitharm, the commission's chair, was the mother of the attorney general's executive assistant and had no experience or public

Bishop Remi De Roo, 1977 | Steve Bosch, *Vancouver Sun*

profile. Her colleagues on the commission were similarly ill-equipped – one of them had even been twice prosecuted under the Human Rights Code! Kathleen Ruff, the stalwart and dedicated advocate, was disgusted with this group, which quickly embarrassed itself. The instability of this relationship finally came to a head in 1979, when Ruff, a few months away from resigning, openly criticized the government for ignoring branch requests to appoint boards of inquiry. The commission held a secret meeting and passed a motion demanding that Ruff refrain from making statements to the media. This was a pointless exercise, as the commissioners had no authority over the branch director, who in any event was also their own executive director.[27] Their move simply further alienated the branch. Landucci attempted but failed to heal the rift between the two agencies. In truth, most staff at the branch had little respect for the commission. Landucci and Jensen's relationship with it was little better than that of Ruff.[28]

The second commission, led by Strongitharm, was given a small budget to distribute grants to community groups to promote human rights education. Mostly, these grants funded conferences, research on issues such as mandatory retirement, or the production of educational materials.[29] Some of the organizations supplying human rights education services included the Associated Disabled Persons of BC, Canadian Council of Christians and Jews, Committee for Racial Justice, Surrey-Delta Immigrant Services Society, Vancouver Gay Community Centre Society, Vancouver Island Multicultural Association, Vancouver Native Police Liaison Program, and Women Against Violence Against Women.[30] By the early 1980s, social movement organizations across the province were essentially carrying out the commission's education mandate. The commission was also responsible for approving exemptions under the code for affirmative action programs, and it provided several exemptions in the late 1970s. For instance, penitentiaries and rape crisis centres were given exemptions to restrict employment to women or men, and non-profit groups would be permitted to restrict positions to disabled or Aboriginal people. The commission also took a public stand on pornography, hate speech, and other human rights issues, but otherwise it remained largely quiescent.

Strongitharm and her colleagues were dismissed and replaced with a small but more dedicated group of commissioners in 1981. They served until 1983, when the commission was disbanded. Charles Paris, the former regional representative for the Canadian Council of Christians and Jews, chaired the third commission. The other two commissioners were Gloria George, the former president of the Native Council of Canada who had spent many years working with various Aboriginal rights organizations; and Renate Shearer, a former social worker and YWCA director until she was hired by the City of Vancouver as a social planner, where she developed programs for battered women. Under Paris, the commission continued to distribute grants, approve exemptions under the code, write letters and engage with the media on human rights issues, and produce educational materials such as short videos or booklets for teachers. Paris was also a far more vocal critic of the government than Strongitharm had been. He lobbied the minister of labour to provide legal counsel to appeal cases where the courts had overturned a board of inquiry decision, to appoint more boards of inquiry, and to reform the code. In 1981, when the commission held public hearings with the intent of improving the code, Paris led the consultations.

The commission concluded its hearings in 1982 and produced two booklets that contained controversial recommendations for amending the Human Rights Code. The reports, as explored in Chapter 9, were completely at odds with the government's vision for the human rights state. Their recommendations were never implemented, and the commission's efforts accomplished little in the end. In retrospect, having a separate branch and commission was promising in theory, but in practice the Human Rights Commission of 1974-83 left no lasting legacy.

Beyond the Metropolis

The commission and the branch concentrated their work in those major cities where their staff were located. But there was a desperate need to extend the human rights state throughout the province. Discrimination, as in the case of the Alkali Lake Band hockey team in 1980, was no less pervasive in rural British Columbia.

On 2 February 1980, Chief Andy Chelsea of the Alkali Lake Band left Williams Lake with a busload of adult hockey players for a 321-kilometre drive to Merritt, a small town of a few thousand people located 267 kilometres east of Vancouver. The Alkali Braves were participating in a weekend hockey tournament, and the band manager, Charmane Belleau, had booked rooms for them at the Merritt Sportsman's Motel. The bus departed later than anticipated, and they arrived at the motel in the evening. As the team disembarked, Chelsea entered the motel and approached the front desk to speak with the owner, Roger Lecompte. Upon seeing Chelsea, Lecompte yelled, "What the hell do you guys want, we are closed." Chelsea explained that they had a reservation. Lecompte denied any knowledge of the reservation and insisted that the motel was full. Chelsea pointed out that the vacancy sign was illuminated, and all indications were that the motel was empty (there were no cars in the parking lot). Lecompte produced a piece of paper, wrote "No Vacancy" on it, and taped it to the front door. When Chelsea protested and insisted that the team had a reservation, Lecompte explained that he did not accept adult hockey teams, especially "fucking Indian hockey teams."

A board of inquiry was held in Merritt and chaired by a lawyer, Dermod Owen-Flood. One of the witnesses at the inquiry was RCMP corporal Gillespie, who had spoken to Lecompte at the motel after receiving a complaint from Chief Chelsea. According to him, Lecompte repeated that he did not rent to "fucking Indian hockey teams." The human rights officer assigned to the case, Alan McCann, received a similar response when he spoke to Lecompte on the phone. In light of their testimony, Owen-Flood had no difficulty concluding that the case was one of racial discrimination:

> The Sportsman's Motel in Merritt is in an area where, indeed, racial discrimination is of grave and somber significance ... I hold that the Respondent knew that it had made a reservation and deliberately disregarded its obligations and in doing so its conduct, with language that can only be described

as Billingsgate, to say the least. The result was that they were unable to get proper accommodation. They had to stay up most of the night before the tournament, with disastrous and humiliating results. They truly suffered damages.

He awarded $1,600 to the hockey team and $1,500 in costs to the branch.[31]

The Chelsea case, decided in 1980, was possible because of a concerted effort on the part of the Human Rights Branch to extend the enforcement of human rights law across the province. For British Columbians outside Victoria and the Lower Mainland, the human rights state might as well not have existed by the mid-1970s. Although complaints arrived from throughout the province, there were at most one or two investigations beyond major urban areas. Even then, the vast majority took place in the major towns. In a 1975 letter to the minister of labour, Henry Jay, president of the British Columbia Association of Non-Status Indians, complained about the lack of human rights officers in regions such as the Kootenays: "Another problem is that when Human Rights, in Victoria, assigns Industrial Labour Relations men to these cases, very often these men are biased in their views and their work. Also, these workers are tied up with their own work that they do not have time to work any Human Rights problems."[32] One of the most significant accomplishments between 1979 and 1983 was to extend the human rights state beyond Victoria and the Lower Mainland.

Rather than sending human rights officers from Vancouver to investigate cases in Prince George – which had been the practice in the past – the branch stationed them throughout the province. The amount of territory they had to cover was enormous. Bill Parkison in Terrace investigated cases throughout the northwest to Prince Rupert and Stewart, as well as Ocean Falls and east to Vanderhoof. Susan Charlton in Nelson was responsible for the Kootenays north to Golden and east to the Alberta border. Leigh Who-Peng in Kamloops travelled from Chase west to Lillooet and south through the Okanagan and Osoyoos. And Alan Andison in Prince George was expected to handle complaints ranging from Fort Nelson in the northeast to Dawson Creek and the Yukon border, as well as out west to Vanderhoof and south to 100 Mile House and Revelstoke. The few officers stationed in Victoria were also responsible for the entirety of Vancouver Island (460 kilometres long and 80 kilometres wide).[33]

Andison was part of a cohort of human rights officers hired after 1975 and stationed outside Victoria and Vancouver. He was typical of the people drawn to the branch: he had been exposed to radical student activism as an undergraduate at Simon Fraser University in the late 1960s and had spent two years in Malawi with the Canadian University Service Overseas (CUSO). In 1977, when Hanne Jensen interviewed and hired him as a human rights officer for Prince George, he was twenty-five years old. After a brief training period in Vancouver, where he spent four months following other human rights officers to learn the trade, Andison headed north. Prince George was the gateway to northern British Columbia. In this case, literally all roads led to the city. It was the heart of one of the province's most important industries: forestry. Enormous forests, mountains, and numerous pulp mills and sawmills stretching along the railroads surrounded the city. Loggers and mill workers routinely found their way to Prince George to drink, gamble, and shop. More than any other city in the province, Prince George was the conjunction of the rural and the urban. As the only branch representative in the region, Andison worked out of the Department of Labour offices alongside industrial relations officers (IROs).[34] He was responsible for a huge territory of thousands of square kilometres (often inaccessible), and because Terrace had no human rights officer at the time, he had to travel as far west as the Queen Charlotte Islands.[35]

Andison set the framework for what future officers in cities such as Cranbrook, Kamloops, Kelowna, and Terrace would do to establish regional offices. First, he contacted local media and encouraged them to publish stories about the branch, the Human Rights Code, and how to reach his office (the *PG Citizen* produced a full-page story titled "From Africa to Prince George"). Second, he drove throughout the region, meeting with women's associations, Aboriginal friendship centres, church groups, and other social movement organizations. Third, he participated in talk-radio shows in several small cities and accepted numerous speaking engagements. Finally, he developed a close working relationship with the IROs, who would come to play a key role in promoting the branch through word of mouth. Within a few months, Andison had a growing caseload and enough work for two human rights officers.

The work was rewarding, especially when a complaint ended in a positive outcome. Northern British Columbia was highly dependent on resource-based industries, so it was not surprising that Andison's cases often involved women who were seeking work in mines, pulp mills, or similar industries. Andison recalled a typical complaint, of a woman who could not secure employment at a sawmill in Taylor:

I drove to Taylor one morning [a six-hour drive north of Prince George] and met a young lady who had been applying for jobs (and it was cold as hell because it is Peace River country). She said she had been trying to get a job at the mill and had been many times. I went to the mill and met with the mill manager and the owner. Told them that she was applying for jobs. Did the investigation. Asked to see her application, other applications, and then determined how many were men and how many were women. The pattern soon became clear. No female hires, all male. They insisted that they did not discriminate but were only looking for the most talented individual. Working on a green chain requires a big strong guy. I made the case that just because someone was smaller was not that they couldn't do the job. The mill owner said ok, send her down and we'll start her tomorrow. I then met with her and said she could start tomorrow. She started crying, she was so happy. It was real feel-good stuff. That is an example of what would happen.[36]

Until Andison arrived, there were few complaints and hardly any investigations in the region. The branch produced a survey of newspaper articles on human rights issues from the early to mid-1970s, which concluded that "the northern newspapers are quite small in their reporting in comparison to the rest of BC's newspapers."[37] None of the IROs had open human rights case files when Andison moved north. In 1979 alone, though, he processed 410 new contacts and opened 132 new complaint files. This was significantly lower than the number of new cases (2,394) in Vancouver, of course, but surprisingly comparable to Victoria (150 new cases). Especially interesting is that, although sex discrimination complaints consistently predominated in major urban areas throughout this decade, many complaints in the North involved racial discrimination (59 in 1979, compared with 47 for sex discrimination). Andison also dealt with a far larger percentage of cases involving accommodation or services than did his colleagues in the Lower Mainland.[38]

Northern British Columbia was home to a large Aboriginal population as well as several visible minority communities, which probably explains the predominance of racial discrimination complaints. In Prince Rupert (eight hundred kilometres west of Prince George), for instance, the security guard at the local Hudson's Bay Company, the main retail outlet for the town, routinely followed Aboriginal men when they visited the store, often little more than a few feet behind. The leaders of the local Aboriginal Friendship Centre were furious with the company's policy and asked

Andison to investigate. He quickly convinced the store manager to change the policy. Meanwhile, in Quesnel (an hour south of Prince George), "there was a bit of a racial war going on."[39] Andison recalled that a taxi company owned by East Indians refused to transport Aboriginal people:

> I talked to the company and said that I appreciate that you may have had some difficulties with some of the clientele that you have picked up, especially at the bar at 2:00 a.m. and getting sick in your cars. But there is a law that says you can't discriminate. And here are the penalties associated with doing that. You can observe the law, or you can deal with me. I'm not going away, and you probably have better things to do than deal with me. The company agreed to stop the practice.[40]

Andison handled a wide variety of complaints, such as those involving Sikhs who wore turbans despite factory safety policies (or who refused to shave, which meant that their air masks might not seal properly over their mouth); he investigated prisons, where women were routinely denied employment. Because of the unique challenges in dealing with cases that were often hundreds of kilometres distant, a human rights officer in rural areas could not afford the luxury of a drawn-out investigation. As Andison put it, "I could roll into town. Interview the complainant. Interview the company. Interview the human resources manager or whoever I was dealing with at the store. And by the end of the afternoon, it was all over."[41]

Constructing the human rights state in the 1970s, in any context, was never an easy task. Even in the major urban centres, the branch struggled to fulfill its mandate. And in many ways, human rights officers in rural British Columbia dealt with much the same basic issues as their counterparts in the Lower Mainland, whether they involved women who were fired for being pregnant or discriminatory practices in retail stores. The branch's survey of every newspaper in the province found remarkable similarities in each region: the largest number of human rights articles involved women and employment, followed by racial discrimination.[42]

Still, human rights law had to adapt to exceptional circumstances in the North. The same survey found that, in the Interior and northern British Columbia, newspaper articles that discussed human rights often focused on Aboriginal people. Living in the North posed unique challenges. According to a 1982 employment study produced by Alcan, the attitudes of business proprietors and first-line supervisors were a major barrier to employing women: "systemic discrimination was seen as more pervasive in the northwest." In particular, the report cited "unrealistic height and weight requirements imposed by resource sector employers for entry level jobs normally held by males." Young women found it difficult to enter the workforce. Many went directly from school to raising a family, and thus "many of the towns were characterized by large numbers of women with minimal labour market skills or experience. Many did not have the educational background necessary to take advantage of skill training, thereby exacerbating the problems associated with lack of confidence."[43] There was also a correlation between establishing a regional office, as well as promotional programs, and an increase in the number of human rights complaints. But most regional offices had just one human rights officer. Very rarely could the branch reach out to community groups (if there were any) and schools in remote rural areas to promote awareness of the human rights state, especially given that the only way to reach the Far North or the Queen Charlotte Islands was by plane. Overall, urban areas produced a far larger per capita proportion of complaints but not necessarily because discrimination was a more serious issue in Victoria or Vancouver. The branch provided funding only for vehicles and very rarely for plane travel. State policy, it appears, did not always benefit all citizens equally.

Human rights officers, who for all intents and purposes were the cops of the human rights state (they were even assigned badges), faced unique obstacles if they were assigned a large rural constituency. Andison was replaced with two officers in 1981, who still had the largest territory and caseload in the province.[44] In most instances, as in Kamloops, Kelowna, and Terrace, human rights officers were alone, with no one to share the workload or help with difficult cases. They also had to cope with daunting travel distances to investigate complaints, often with few resources for travel or accommodation. When officers did travel, they might find themselves dealing with entire towns dominated by a single company, poor communication networks, a far more dispersed population, which made it difficult to communicate with community groups and spread awareness, and forms of discrimination specific to the demographics and economy of the region. Nonetheless, simply extending the human rights state to these areas was a worthy accomplishment.

Equal Pay

By the early 1980s, it was evident that the Human Rights Code was imperfect. As a result, the Human Rights Commission initiated a province-wide consultation with stakeholders in 1981. SWAG identified several issues: employers were using differing job descriptions to avoid equal pay; restricting age discrimination to individuals between forty-five and sixty-five was arbitrary; the code did not refer explicitly to sexual harassment or to discrimination due to pregnancy (which represented about 25 percent of sex discrimination complaints in 1979), marital status, disability, or sexual orientation; only a few affirmative action programs had been approved; the code should be expanded to include classes of persons, not just individuals; and settlements should receive more publicity.[45] A loophole identified by the BCCLA was that the code did not apply to licences. Individuals were losing jobs because they could not secure, for instance, a driver's licence due to unrelated issues such as a former criminal conviction.[46] Other recommendations included making the code supreme above other laws, creating a more transparent process for appointing boards of inquiry, extending the period for submitting complaints, granting more independence to the Human Rights Commission, prohibiting discrimination against individuals on social assistance, especially single mothers, generating a more proactive education program, including developing non-sexist books for schools, and allowing the branch to dismiss frivolous complaints (the law required that it investigate *all* complaints).

Most stakeholders also endorsed banning discrimination on the basis of disability and sexual orientation.[47] Moreover, almost everyone agreed that the equal pay law was not working, and they were unanimous in calling for equal pay for work of equal value. The Victoria Human Rights Coalition, for instance, suggested that a female salesperson in Victoria earned an average of 39.2 percent less than her male counterpart, and that a female nurse's aide earned only $184 per week, whereas a male uncertified orderly earned $195. The coalition also noted that resolving equal pay complaints could take a year and that a "woman who faces the emotional and financial strain of opposing an employer with large resources will just give up."[48]

Most equal pay complaints failed under the Human Rights Act. Gwen R. Nechiporenko had filed an equal pay complaint under the original human rights statute against her employer, Hickman Tye Hardware. She argued before a board of inquiry that, although the company pay scales were based on job classifications, she did essentially the same work as her male colleagues:

> Ms. Nechiporenko was then employed as a stock records clerk and the complaint alleged that she should have received the same pay as an order filler. Her job required counting all the stock in the warehouse on a rotating

basis, completing an entire count approximately every thirty days. The stock was kept in bins and on shelves in the warehouse and counting it necessitated climbing, moving and lifting stock. The order fillers, shopping carts or a hand-jack, moved from bin to shelf, picking the items required to fill customer orders and delivering them to shippers/receivers for checking and packing.[49]

Her complaint failed. The board concluded that, although it did not see how the differences in work justified a $130 per month pay differential, the distinctions were sufficient to defeat the complaint under the wording of the Human Rights Act.

The Human Rights Code, in contrast, was far more effective. Diane Davies and two other female police clerks filed the first equal pay complaint under its provisions. Most of their work as dispatchers involved receiving calls and relaying them to the appropriate agency (fire, ambulance, police). They also did some clerical work, and when female prisoners were brought in, they conducted the body searches and escorted women to the cells. The male dispatchers had essentially the same duties, except they worked at night (women worked during the day) and attended to male prisoners. A board of inquiry concluded that the work involved similar responsibilities and skills, and awarded Davies and her co-workers back pay and a change in salaries.[50] Another board of inquiry awarded a comparable settlement to Loraine Warren, who discovered in 1976 that her employer, Creditel, offered her male colleagues in the Collection Sales Department an extra $2,000 in starting pay for the same work. Creditel insisted that it negotiated separate salaries for each employee and that Warren simply negotiated poorly. But a board of inquiry, which awarded her back pay, concluded that this rationale was an insufficient justification for paying a woman less than male staff who were doing the same work.[51] Similarly, in 1981, employees in a Burnaby trucking company went on a failed strike to secure higher wages for data processors. All the data processors were women who earned $7.07 an hour, whereas unskilled summer staff received $8.17. But the employer refused to budge, because "it was a matter of principle" (although which principle was unclear), and the company was not responsible for correcting "the ills of society."[52] The data processors decided to seek a resolution under the Human Rights Code. A board of inquiry sided with them and awarded back pay.

Kathleen Ruff was able to secure significant changes to pay scales for practical nurses who worked in hospitals across the province. Fourteen million dollars were paid between 1973 and 1975 to female hospital staff in British Columbia to create a common base salary scale. Between 1973 and 1977, the branch had secured approximately $50,000 through individual equal pay complaints.[53] These successes, however, had to be weighed against the difficulties of enforcing equal pay under the code. Sometimes inquiry boards required an impossible standard of proof. Billie Linton's case was a typical example. The Equal Pay Act had forced her employer, Nabob Foods, to discontinue its differential wage scale for men and women in its Vancouver meat-processing plant in 1953. By replacing the gendered wage scale with separate job classifications (with separate seniority lists), the company avoided making any changes to its payroll. The plant was a food-processing and wholesale distribution centre with 225 employees. When Linton began working there in 1973, all the order-selectors were men. Their job was to retrieve written orders from a peg board, assemble the products on a pallet moved about by a handjack, and deliver the pallet to an office, where it was prepared for loading on a train or truck. Linton was hired as a packer, which meant that she worked alongside dozens of other women, packing meat as it arrived in raw bulk by rail or truck. All the packers were women, and they made less money than order-selectors. Linton was temporarily promoted (due to seniority) to order-selector in 1976, which made her the first woman ever to work in the warehouse in that position. Her new supervisor, Kenneth Sanderson, called her into his office numerous times to question her about her productivity. Linton said little during these encounters. Then, after working for twenty-four days, she was demoted back to her old job. She filed a complaint in 1976, alleging that the company's refusal to allow her to work as an order-selector constituted sex discrimination. Sanderson told the human rights investigator assigned to the case, Shelagh Day, that "the warehouse was no place for a woman as it was too cold and too dusty," and that "a boxcar was no place for a woman."[54] At the hearing, Linton argued that Sanderson's concern with her productivity was no more than camouflage for his belief that a woman shouldn't be doing a man's job. Sanderson routinely treated her differently, assigning her to the dispatch office to file invoices rather than loading and delivering pallets. A board of inquiry, however, sided with the company, placing a burden of proof on Linton that was almost impossible to satisfy: she must produce evidence that the company explicitly banned women as order-selectors. One of the three individuals chairing the inquiry responded to this decision by writing a dissenting opinion: "It is trite to state that discrimination is seldom susceptible of direct proof. Seldom is there an open admission of discrimination by the respondent ... Once a prima facie case of discrimination is established, the onus of proving a non-discriminatory cause as well as the reasonableness of the cause shifts to the respondent."[55]

Equal pay violations often remained unfiled, either due to ignorance of the legislation or fear of repercussions from an employer.[56] Women could easily endanger their promotions and other opportunities if they filed a complaint. Investigations could take a year or two to resolve (Loraine Warren's case against Creditel took eighteen months). Between 1977 and 1982, the branch handled a mere eight to twelve equal pay complaints annually, and since 1975 only five boards of inquiry had addressed equal pay. Of a sample of 346 complaints between 1980 and 1982, only 16 dealt with equal pay. Sometimes the branch did secure a spectacular success, as in the case of two female janitors who were awarded a $50,000 settlement in 1978, but more often than not the complaint was either not pursued or withdrawn, or the settlement involved a few hundred dollars in back pay.[57] Or, as in Hanne Jensen's case, her employer was able to harass her sufficiently that she quit despite winning her case.

The equal pay provisions of the Human Rights Code were limited by a vision of formal rather than substantive equality. The law was concerned with the explicit differential treatment rather than unequal pay that resulted from stereotypes, prejudices, or social disadvantage that was a product of generations of labour segregation. Equal pay applied to "similar or substantially similar work." Defining it in terms of doing the same job was a fundamentally flawed policy. Many jobs were segregated by sex anyway: men were hired to drive taxis or buses, for instance, and as lawyers or doctors; women were employed as clerical workers, nurses, or legal aids. And sex segregation could easily take place within a single workplace. It was a simple matter for employers to create different classifications (unskilled versus skilled) or descriptions for jobs, and to justify salaries based on the work, not gender. The law did not address the root causes of gender inequality or how gender-based stereotypes and prejudices undervalued female labour.[58] Only Quebec in 1976, and the federal government in 1977, had amended their human rights laws to require equal pay for work of equal value. This step was essential to move beyond debates regarding whether men and women were doing the same work, to allow comparisons between different types of employment to challenge common sense notions of work and value.

For this reason, Shelagh Day concluded in 1977 that "equal pay legislation which has been in effect in all the Provinces since the 1950s, is clearly not effective in closing the gap between men's and women's earnings."[59] Between 1971 and 1981, the number of women in the provincial labour force increased 22 percent (in 1981, 52.7 percent of BC women were in the workforce), and the number of working mothers increased from 36.2 percent to 50.7 percent. And yet, in 1981 the average woman barely made 62 percent of a man's wage, a small rise of 5 percent from the 1971 figure. The proportion of total income earned by women in British Columbia barely budged over ten years, increasing from 22.4 percent in 1970 to 29.2 percent in 1980. Women in 1981 continued to cluster disproportionately in low-paying jobs. In 1971, 6.1 percent of physicians, dentists, lawyers, and managers were female, whereas 60.2 percent of clerical and service workers were. By 1981, this gap had hardly shifted; women represented 9.6 percent of the former and 57.7 percent of the latter category.[60] In 1983, thirty years after the Equal Pay Act came into force, none other than the Human Rights Commission concluded that "equal pay legislation simply doesn't work."[61]

Unsurprisingly, many businesses opposed strengthening the equal pay provisions in the code. The president of the Kelowna chapter of the Canadian Businessmen's Association, concerned that the commission's hearings might result in stronger equal pay laws, wrote to the minister of labour in 1981 to emphasize that his organization was "vehemently opposed as a group of businessmen to a bill of this nature ... The last thing in the world we want is a newly hired Government employee coming in to any and every businessman's office and telling them who is going to be paid and how much."[62] The Hospital Employees Union's leadership also expressed reservations regarding the principle of equal pay for work of equal value, suggesting that the process for determining job value was so complicated as to be ineffective.[63] A year later, in a brief to the minister of labour, the Employers Council of British Columbia questioned

> whether or not equal pay for work of equal value can be implemented without causing massive disruption in the existing labour market and in historical collective bargaining relationships ... Until the [Human Rights Commission] or others succeed in developing an evaluation system which can be practically applied across the board, equal pay for work of equal value must remain a desirable objective rather than a universal reality.[64]

The municipality of West Vancouver, in yet another brief to the labour minister regarding the commission's hearings, also entreated the government to reject equal pay for work of equal value until a "uniformly acceptable job evaluation system" could be created.[65]

8
Making New Law under the Human Rights Code

One of the most exciting aspects of building the human rights state was making new law. British Columbia led Canada in expanding the scope of human rights law. It was the only jurisdiction where a board of inquiry alone could determine the merit of a complaint. Other jurisdictions could dismiss a complaint before it reached the stage of a formal inquiry. Boards of inquiry ruled on a host of new issues, from sexual harassment to arbitrary employment policies, and in doing so they developed a corpus of human rights law. They became contested sites where a broad spectrum of people fought over the meaning of rights and equality. Many of the most critical early innovations involved sex discrimination and women challenging practices in the workplace.

The tension between human rights law as innovative public policy and the limits of the law in practice was evident in boards of inquiry. Alan Andison and other human rights officers often encountered employers who insisted that their refusal to hire someone was based on lack of qualifications. BC Forest Products Limited denied Janice Foster employment at its Youbou mill on Vancouver Island in 1977 because of her weight and height. The company informed Foster, who weighed 105 pounds and was barely five feet tall, that she would be incapable of manually removing lumber from a conveyor belt and placing it in a nearby pile. But the height and weight requirements were arbitrary for work that necessitated more dexterity than physical strength.[1] Andison was not convinced that Foster could not do the job:

> Janice was a very nice young woman ... At that time she was working at a place called the "land of the little people" [small puppets for tourism]. Company took a very strident stand. To work on the green chain, you needed to be of a certain stature. We got some ergonomics tests at University of Victoria ... We brought in technical evidence to show how to lift and if it could be done safely. And the conclusion of that evidence was that, yes, you could do that safely.[2]

A board of inquiry concluded that, although the BC Forest Products policy did not explicitly prohibit women from working, this was its indirect effect. It was another form of sex discrimination. The board ordered that the mill offer Foster a full-time position.

Under the Human Rights Code, boards of inquiry were designed to be more efficient, faster, and accessible than the courts, and to absorb the cost of investigating and resolving complaints. Human rights officers would recommend to the Human Rights Branch that a board of inquiry be held if they were unable to conciliate the dispute. If the minister of labour followed the branch's recommendation to appoint an inquiry, the branch would ask a lawyer to work pro bono (or have one assigned from the attorney general's office) to represent the complainant. This was a vast improvement from Hanne Jensen's experience with the Human Rights Act. She was lucky to have a lawyer working pro bono on behalf of the Vancouver Status of Women. She was obliged to travel to Victoria for the hearing, was restricted to one day for arguments, and was faced with the entire Human Rights Commission, which had little experience in human rights adjudication. In contrast, under the Human Rights Code, hearings took place throughout the province, from Lillooet to Penticton to Prince George and Burns Lake. It was not uncommon for the branch to rent a hotel room or borrow space in a courthouse or a Ministry of Labour office to hold an inquiry. The complainant was well prepared when he or she arrived, usually in the company of a lawyer provided by the branch, as well as the human rights officer and the director of the branch. Often the complainant sat across from the respondent and his or her lawyer, with the chairperson at the end of the table. Each person had a chance to summarize his or her case and to question witnesses. The entire hearing could be finished in hours or at most in a few days. Soon afterward, the chairperson would issue a written ruling that was binding on everyone. Only an inquiry could impose a settlement, and its decisions were enforceable in the same way as a judicial ruling in court.

The minister of labour usually appointed just one person to chair an inquiry, often a lawyer from the private sector or a university professor. If the case was complex, addressing important issues, the minister might appoint three chairpersons, some of whom could come from the community. Like appointments to the commission, appointments to chair inquiries demonstrate that social movements were an integral component in every aspect of the human rights state. Over the years, inquiry chairs included Lou Demerais (BC Union of Indian Chiefs), William Giesbrecht (BC Federation of Labour), Carol Lecky (Williams Lake Civil Liberties Association), Jordan Priestman (editor, *Salmon Arm Observer*), and Danny Smith (BC Association of Non-Status Indians). Most chairs, however, were young lawyers who would go on to have successful careers. Josiah Wood chaired a dozen cases (more than anyone else) and was later appointed to the British Columbia Court of Appeal. Beverley McLachlin, who chaired several inquiries in the 1970s, became chief justice of the Supreme Court of Canada.

This practice was one of the great achievements of the human rights state. In the 1970s, lawyers had little experience with human rights law. Law schools might offer a course on constitutional law, but it was the rare university that taught human rights law. (Bill Black, who helped draft the Human Rights Code, began teaching one of Canada's first human rights courses at the University of British Columbia in the mid-1970s.) By the early 1980s, a host of BC lawyers had developed an expertise in human rights law after chairing multiple boards of inquiry. Moreover, the branch often sought to use the same lawyers to represent complainants. J.J. Camp, E.N. Hughes, S.F.D. Kelleher, and David Vickers participated in almost half the inquiries. Their expertise would be a major asset for the branch.

In any given year, less than 1 percent of human rights complaints in British Columbia reached a board of inquiry: human rights officers informally settled 40 to 60 percent of them, and 30 to 40 percent of complaints were withdrawn or found to be without merit (Figure 8). Of the 105 boards of inquiry appointed between 1974 and 1984, documentation has survived for 77 (many of the missing cases were probably settled before or during arguments and did not result in a written decision). Most of these inquiries dealt with sex discrimination (42 cases) and employment (59). Only a handful involved accommodation (7) or services (11). Ten dealt with racial discrimination, and 13 fell under the category of reasonable cause (usually involving someone who had been refused employment due to a criminal conviction or a disability). Perhaps because the task of

FIGURE 8 Disposition of complaints, 1970-82

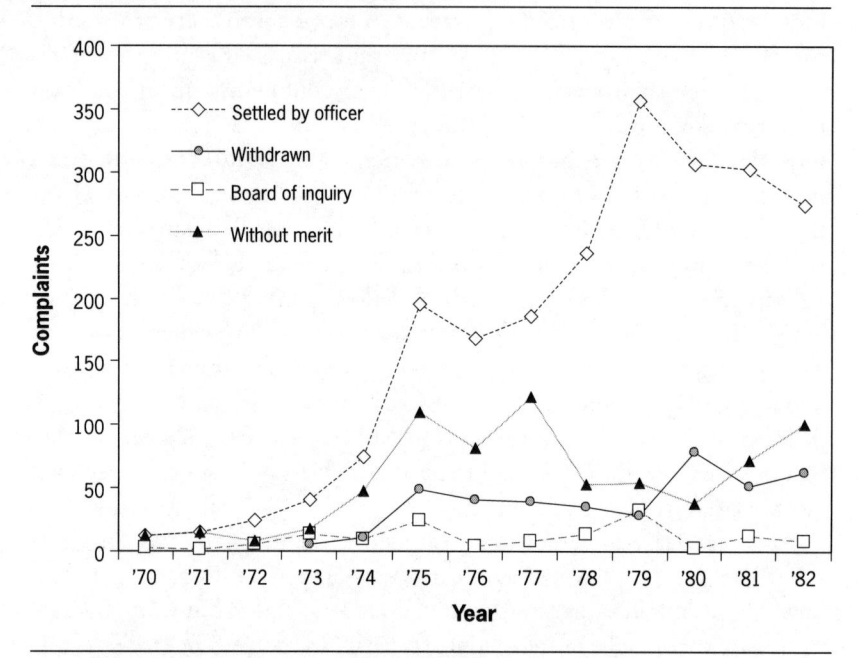

NOTE: The number of complaints withdrawn for 1970-72 was not reported.
SOURCES: British Columbia, Department of Labour, Annual Reports, 1970-82; British Columbia, Human Rights Commission, Annual Reports, 1979-82.

appointing inquiries fell to the minister of labour, the proceedings virtually never targeted the government.

Boards of inquiry favoured the complainant, which suggests that they were tools for forcing recalcitrant employers to accept a settlement. Of the 77 cases for which documentation exists, 58 were upheld and only 15 were dismissed (in 4 the decision is unknown).[3] Between 1978 and 1982, the branch lost only 4 of the 37 cases that went to boards of inquiry. Clearly, it was successful at identifying complaints that would receive a positive response before a formal hearing. But the case files reveal another reality about the human rights state: individuals rarely benefitted materially from pursuing their cases. Of the 58 successful complaints on record, 40 entailed cash settlements (many other settlements included an apology, a promise not to discriminate in future, or a change in company policy). Six settlements involved between $5,000 and $7,000, and 13 offered $1,500 to $3,000. These sums were generous, perhaps, but small consolation for those who had lost their jobs or seen their careers derailed.

Unfortunately, the Human Rights Code offered no guidance on determining damages, and most cash settlements were for a few hundred dollars. Clearly, these awards were symbolic rather than representative of the true damages associated with discrimination. Jean Tharpe, who had spent two years fighting Lornex Mining Company over on-site accommodations and who had been obliged to commute to work, was awarded a meagre $250. Jane Gawne, who was refused a job on a survey crew because the employer worried that hiring a woman would bother the wives of the other crew members, was awarded $280 for lost wages and $500 was awarded to the branch for damages (the code permitted up to $5,000 for damages *in addition* to costs). As chair in the Gawne case, Beverley McLachlin awarded low damages because "previous decisions of Boards appointed under the *Human Rights Code* demonstrate a conservative approach to awarding damages."[4] These decisions raised the ire of some people in the branch. One officer was dismayed after reading the decision in *Driedger v. Peace River Block News,* which involved a woman who had been fired because she had been arrested for possessing marijuana:

> The Board proceeded to whittle away the $2875 in loss of wages due to the complainant for her unlawful termination, taking into account ridiculous factors like the $500.00 she saved in babysitting. The $1722 received in [unemployment insurance] benefits and the $250 knocked off because the respondent did not discriminate vengefully. In the end the woman received $400.00 AND NO COSTS. She may have just broken even.[5]

Boards of inquiry, it appears, were reluctant to impose large fines or awards for damages. This was entirely consistent with a labour relations model designed to avoid excessively punitive measures when resolving conflicts between parties who had a continuing working relationship.[6]

The statistics also hide the reality of what was a cumbersome and exhausting process. Janice Foster, who was denied a job at Youbou sawmill, had to wait two years before her complaint was resolved. Loraine Warren's equal pay case against Creditel was fast compared with some: her hearing took place after only eighteen months. The small amount of financial compensation awarded could not possibly offset the burdens associated with carrying a complaint for such a long time, especially against one's own employer. In most instances, those who pursued complaints did not do so for financial gain.[7] Kathleen Ruff later recalled Tharpe's case as a perfect example of why some women pursued complaints even though they themselves would personally gain very little:

Tharpe stands out because she was all alone in the mine and very much at the mercy of the company, who were mean bastards, vicious, trying to put women in their place. They would not even pay for her meals despite paying for men's food ... Majority of the male workers were very supportive and were appalled by what was going on. They did everything they could to treat her decently ... A gutsy woman. Not doing it for herself, but for paving the way for women in the future and because she felt a sense of injustice ... It was just that beautiful human spirit. Irrepressible. A sense of justice. In her mind, this was wrong and it would never change, it would be the same for the next generation for women unless someone was willing to stand up.[8]

Boards of inquiry were an innovative approach to human rights complaints. Certainly, they were far more accessible to the average person, partly because the proceedings were more informal than a court, but also because the branch helped complainants prepare and present their cases. The branch and many of the individuals who chaired multiple inquiries developed an expertise in human rights adjudication and were therefore adept at dealing with discrimination cases. Moreover, the goal of changing practices and promoting tolerance, which was the mandate of the human rights state, remained the same. Boards of inquiry contributed to altering the behaviour of employers and constructing a culture of rights by raising the level of public debate and awareness. As one inquiry chairman noted, "its [Human Rights Code] aim is to educate the public with respect to the need for tolerance as an essential weave in our social fabric."[9] Boards of inquiry set precedents that human rights officers could use in negotiating informal settlements. In 1981, for example, Clifford Picard submitted a complaint against Dunn Lehman Trucking for refusing to hire him because he was too old. The officer negotiated an agreement that included a letter of apology, a commitment to stop using age as a factor in hiring, and $4,764 for lost income and damages.[10] It seems likely that the precedents set in previous boards of inquiry may have contributed to the company's decision to offer a generous settlement.

Still, boards of inquiry were an imperfect mechanism. Even the few decisions to dismiss cases were often questionable. In several instances, the complaint was upheld but only on the condition that the employer did not have to accept liability. In other words, the potential impact of the decision was limited to the one complaint.[11] One case, involving a man banned from an apprentice program because he was over the age of twenty-five, was dismissed because he had not submitted his complaint within six months of the incident, as required by the statute.[12] But the most dispiriting dismissal was Yvonne Bill's case against J.R. Trailer Sales and Service.

Yvonne Bill, an Aboriginal woman employed with the local band council, attempted to rent accommodation from a Mr. Anderson at a Lillooet trailer park in February 1976. When the on-site supervisor heard that Anderson had agreed to rent to Bill, he called the park's owners, Mr. and Mrs. Young, to warn them that "Anderson rented the trailer to a bunch of drunken Goddamned Indians." (Although the supervisor insisted at the subsequent inquiry that he was not prejudiced, the chair noted wryly that his "sensitivity as to what would constitute a racial slur was somewhat less developed than one would desire.")[13] A few days later, Bill drove to the park to move her possessions into the trailer, but Mrs. Young barred her way and insisted that she needed the Youngs' approval to rent in the park. Not only did they refuse to allow Bill to rent there, but they even forced Anderson to remove his trailer. Bill was convinced that Mrs. Young did not want an Aboriginal living in the park, suspicions that were confirmed when the branch sent two couples, one white and one Aboriginal, to rent trailers (it occasionally used this tactic, especially in cases involving racism in accommodation or services). The Bill case was obviously one of racial discrimination, but the chairman, a lawyer named Alan Hope, dismissed it. In a confusing twist of logic, he concluded that, although Mrs. Young was clearly prejudiced toward Aboriginal people, her decision to evict the trailer was based on Anderson's refusal to seek her approval. Hope even went as far as to draw out a bizarre distinction, arguing that the law "does not prohibit discrimination. It prohibits certain acts that are motivated by discrimination." In reality, the law was evolving in the opposite direction: actions, not motivation, were the basis for proving discrimination. But the distinction mattered little to Yvonne Bill, who lost her year-long case. Kathleen Ruff was furious with the decision:

> It escapes all reasoning how the Board expected Mrs. Young to recognize Native Indians' dignity when they themselves failed to do so. The case is an excellent example of the Board seeing the respondent [Mrs. Young] as persons who are honest, straightforward, prejudiced persons made in the mirror image of the Board members while the complainant whose self-esteem has been stomped on are persons that the Board simply cannot identify with.[14]

Boards of inquiry were, therefore, a mixed bag. Usually, they benefitted the complainant, although the system was hardly immune from bad decisions. Individuals sometimes profited from staying the course, but they typically had to settle for weak awards. Ultimately, the primary significance of the boards lay in developing expertise in human rights adjudication and setting legal precedents. Because British Columbia was the only jurisdiction with an open-ended prohibition on discrimination, its boards of inquiry were among the first in Canada to address a host of emerging human rights issues. The boards quickly came to interpret the reasonable cause section broadly: a violation of the code was defined as the unreasonable treatment of any individual because he or she belonged to a class of people.[15]

The first board of inquiry to hear a case of reasonable cause was in New Denver. Douglas Oram and Joan McLaren had been refused service at the Lucerne Lions Public House because they had long hair. In *Oram and McLaren v. Pho* (1975), the board ruled that denial of services on the basis of physical appearance was unreasonable discrimination. It adopted a definition of reasonable cause that set a standard for others to follow:

> Section 3 of the Code clearly states that no person shall be denied any service customarily available to the public unless there exists reasonable cause for such denial ... It is clear that the very heart and purpose of that section is to protect those persons who for one reason or another find themselves possessed of some differentiating characteristic which attracts to them prejudicial discriminatory conduct.[16]

Subsequent inquiries continued to expand the scope of the law. In *Gay Alliance Towards Equality v. Vancouver Sun* (1975), a board ruled that the *Sun* newspaper discriminated on the basis of sexual orientation when it refused to publish a small ad for the newsletter of Gay Alliance Towards Equality (GATE). This was the first time in Canadian history that sexual orientation had been recognized under human rights law, and the *Sun's* appeal was the first gay rights case to reach the Supreme Court of Canada.[17] In 1976 and 1977, physical disability *(Jefferson v. BC Ferries)*, pregnancy *(H.W. v. Kroff)*, and criminal record *(Heerspink v. ICBC)* were also found to be unreasonable grounds for discrimination. In *Jefferson*, a three-person board of inquiry decided that an employer must have a reasonable basis for believing that a disability would affect an individual's performance at work. And *Heerspink* was a landmark case against the Insurance Corporation of British Columbia, which had refused to provide fire insurance to a man because he had been convicted of possessing marijuana. Two other rulings of the following year held that marital status and political affiliation *(Bremer v. Board of School Trustees)*, as well as age requirements for apprenticeship programs (eighteen to twenty-five years), were also unreasonable. In *Bremer,* the board further clarified the definition of reasonable cause:

> The respondent's reasons for the prohibited conduct are related to the failure of the respondent to make an individual assessment of the person discriminated against ... In every contravention the respondent's reasons for the prohibited conduct involve a consideration by the respondent of the complainant's group factor or characteristic, such as, for example, race or religion. Such group factors are, of course, totally irrelevant and unrelated to the opportunity denied, or in respect of which the complainant is treated unequally. All too frequently, a contravention will be recognizable by a quality of preconceived and unreasonable opinion held by the respondent in relation to the irrelevant and unrelated factor.[18]

In 1978, a board of inquiry found in favour of a woman who had been denied a sick leave benefit because her illness was pregnancy-related *(Gibbs v. Bowman)*. Finally, in 1984, two boards of inquiry confirmed that sexual harassment was unreasonable discrimination.[19] The Supreme Court of Canada would later confirm in two separate 1989 decisions that sexual harassment and denying employment to a woman for being pregnant were forms of sex discrimination.[20]

With some exceptions, human rights law in Canada was largely restricted to race, colour, ethnicity, religion, place of origin, age, and sex. Boards of inquiry in British Columbia challenged these legal boundaries, and over time human rights laws in Canada expanded to include new prohibited grounds. But British Columbia's impact on human rights law went even further. In 1975, the Human Rights Commission (which had the power to initiate complaints, though it rarely did so) successfully argued before a board of inquiry that the College of Physicians and Surgeons policy requiring non-citizens to serve in rural areas was discriminatory (the policy also applied to landed immigrants who were born and trained in Canada). What was significant about the case was that, for the first time, an inquiry ruled that providing evidence of intent to discriminate was unnecessary. In addition, boards of inquiry addressed the issue of systemic discrimination. In *Foster v. British Columbia Forest Products* (1979) and *Grafe v. Sechelt Building Supplies* (1979), the inquiries ruled that arbitrary height and weight requirements had the indirect effect of excluding women from employment. In *Dhaliwal v. British Columbia Timber* (1983), an inquiry board held that language requirements had the effect of excluding certain groups of people. In each case, intent was irrelevant. The effect of the practice was discriminatory and therefore unreasonable.[21] Later cases would take into consideration the indirect effects of ostensibly neutral policies that had the result of restricting entire classes of people from employment. The Heerspink case also had a far more lasting impact than simply expanding the grounds for discrimination to criminal conviction in the provision of public services. In *Heerspink*, the Supreme Court of Canada, on appeal, ruled that human rights legislation was special legislation, which held primacy over other laws. The case set a crucial precedent in defining human rights law as quasi-constitutional.[22]

The very definition of human rights was in flux. The law was evolving, and boards of inquiry in British Columbia played a key role in setting a new direction. The law recognized that discrimination was not necessarily motivated by hatred or fear, but could arise through misunderstandings, discomfort, or confusion. Investigations, and even boards of inquiry, offered an opportunity for people to reassess their opinions and beliefs. Since motivation was not a factor in determining discrimination, the accused need not be labelled a bigot or a sexist to be found guilty. This distinction may have seemed subtle, but it was nonetheless profound and it undoubtedly aided attempts at conciliation in conflicts. And if people refused to change, boards of inquiry could force a settlement. This was a significant shift from earlier anti-discrimination laws that were largely punitive and that perceived discrimination as the fault of prejudiced or biased individuals.

In some instance, a board of inquiry decision was toppled in court. For example, the Supreme Court of Canada overruled *Gay Alliance Towards Equality v. Vancouver Sun* on the basis of freedom of the press, among other things. *Bremer* and the apprenticeship cases were also dismissed, but the written decisions from the inquiry nonetheless added to the growing corpus of case law informing human rights law. Employers also attempted to use the courts to restrict the scope of the law and to limit their own liability. In a few cases, the courts overturned board of inquiry decisions even when discrimination had been incontrovertibly proven. Many employers, for instance, rejected the idea of "vicarious liability." In other words, they argued that they should not be held responsible for the actions of their employees. In *Nelson v. Gubbins,* the court was asked to consider whether or not Byron Price and Associates, which owned a townhouse complex in Victoria, was liable for the actions of its manager, Loretta Gubbins. She had refused to rent accommodation to Alex and Nella Nelson because they were Aboriginal. The judge concluded that the company was not liable: "There is no basis in law for the assertion that the *Human Rights Code* authorizes imposition of vicarious liability on an employer for damages arising out of breach of its terms by his servant."[23] The vicarious liability defence raised serious complications for human rights law. An internal memorandum at the branch explained that "unless employers are, under the Code, responsible for actions of their employees as they are in common law, then the ability to meaningfully remedy injuries suffered by a complainant often disappears, as does the employers' responsibility to ensure their employees abide by the legal obligation imposed by the *Human Rights Code*."[24] The *Gubbins* decision was later sustained on appeal.[25]

Another defence was "honest belief," in which defendants acknowledged that their behaviour was discriminatory but argued that it was founded on an honest belief and was therefore reasonable and not a violation of the law.[26] Janice Foster's case was appealed to the British Columbia Supreme Court, where the judge suggested that "there would be no discrimination which offends against the [Human Rights] Code if the appellant had declined to employ the respondent because of an honest belief that her size or weight made it, in the appellant's judgment unlikely or impossible that she could do the job."[27] The Court of Appeal also addressed the honest belief defence in *Gay Alliance Towards Equality*. In overturning the board of inquiry ruling, Judge Branca essentially justified discrimination on the basis that it was pervasive:

> Many people in our society may well entertain a bias or some predisposition against homosexuals or homosexuality on moral and/or religious grounds. It cannot therefore be justly said that a bias so held has no reasonable foundation ... If one bases a bias against homosexuals because they are persons who engage in unnatural sexual activity which may make them guilty of a serious crime in certain circumstances and because they are forbidden entry into Canada as undesirables, can one say that such a bias, if it is arrived at for those reasons, is unreasonable? I would not think so.[28]

When the case reached the Supreme Court of Canada, Chief Justice Bora Laskin dissented from the majority opinion and rejected the honest belief defence as inconsistent with the spirit of the legislation (*Gay Alliance* was ultimately decided on another issue). Subsequent litigation confirmed that honest belief was not a legitimate defence.

Finally, boards of inquiry were criticized because they failed to expand the definition of sex discrimination. Their rulings on pregnancy (and pregnancy-related benefits), sexual harassment, and arbitrary height and weight requirements were based on the reasonable cause section rather than discrimination on the basis of sex.[29] In the Foster case, for example, the inquiry chair went so far as to conclude that "the fact that Foster is a woman was irrelevant to the hiring decision," even though the effect of the requirement was to ban women from working in the mill. Because British Columbia was the only jurisdiction with a reasonable cause section, the decisions were difficult to apply as precedents in other jurisdictions. Moreover, the reasonable cause section would be repealed in 1984.

By 1983, the human rights state in British Columbia was at its most influential. Admittedly, it was not without flaws. It was inaccessible to many people in rural areas, especially in the North. Victims rarely received fair compensation. Equal pay applied only in a limited context. Boards of inquiry could be unpredictable. The process of investigating complaints was fraught with delays. The system may also have privileged some individuals over others. Although the BC sample is too small to draw conclusions, a survey of inquiry boards in Canada from 1980 to 1989 suggests that racial minority women were underrepresented because they lacked awareness of their rights, clustered in professions that were not covered under the law (such as domestic work), and distrusted the legal system. Some may also have felt, given the pervasive nature of discrimination in their daily lives, that an individual complaint was ineffectual.[30] These were serious limitations of the human rights state. Still, the period was one of human rights innovation, especially in British Columbia. The labour relations model, wherein an industrial relations officer would sit at the head of a table and do little more than facilitate an argument between an employer and an employee, clearly failed Hanne Jensen and others. By the 1980s, the human rights state had moved beyond this model, and individuals were more successful in having their grievances resolved.

British Columbia had a notable impact on human rights law in Canada between 1974 and 1984.[31] No boards of inquiry were held in British Columbia after the Social Credit government passed its Human Rights Act in 1984. The human rights state had many critics, but the greatest threat came from the government itself. The Social Credit Party was suspicious of the branch and its dedicated staff, and it generally disdained the principles of the human rights state. The Socred government did everything in its power to undermine the human rights state during the 1970s and eventually tore it down by 1984.

9

The Politics of (Undermining) Human Rights

The Human Rights Act, 1983-84

Ian Johnstone owned and operated the Wessex Inn in Cowichan Bay, a town of a few thousand people less than an hour's drive north of Victoria. Johnstone, who was in his mid-forties, routinely hired teenage girls to work at the inn, a small and not terribly successful motel on the highway.[1] One of those girls – frustrated and angry at the constant sexual harassment – dragged Johnstone before a board of inquiry in 1984. His surprise at the charge and his futile attempts to justify his behaviour were somewhat understandable: this was one of the first formal inquiries in Canadian history – and the first in British Columbia – to address sexual harassment. The case demonstrated, perhaps better than anything else, the success of the Human Rights Code.

Johnstone had hired Sheri Zarankin, a seventeen-year-old high school student, on 29 August 1981 as a receptionist and chambermaid for the Wessex Inn. This was her first job. She was responsible for checking in customers, answering inquiries, accepting cash, and cleaning rooms. Her shifts usually ran from 10:00 a.m. to 6:00 p.m. on Saturdays and Sundays. Johnstone was often in the motel during her shifts and was always there at the end of the day to collect the cash. In testimony before a board of inquiry, Zarankin described his behaviour: "He didn't have much respect for me. He was always rude and had a vulgar tongue." He frequently tapped her on the head or touched her inappropriately: "If I was sitting down at the desk doing something he'd come in and tap me on the head. He'd just come up behind me and hit me on the bum and laugh and walk away." This type of patting or touching was common: "If I was just standing there, he put his hand around my shoulder." The harassment involved verbal comments as well. In one instance, when Zarankin was closing, Johnstone came in and said, "Let's go in the back room and I'll show you what it's all about" (she didn't respond, just laughed). At other times, "he'd tell me when I was leaving that a couple of hookers were up in the back room. He wanted to make sure that I knew." On 14 March 1982, when Johnstone and two of his friends came across Zarankin cleaning a room, one of the friends asked, "Do you come with the room?" which elicited a great deal of laughter. Zarankin could not recall what she had said, but her response offended Johnstone and embarrassed him in front of his friends. Later that day, he fired her.

The Zarankin case was unusual in many respects. Certainly, not many seventeen-year-olds filed human rights complaints. The case was referred to a board of inquiry in July 1984 after Johnstone refused to consider any form of conciliation. Lynn Smith, a lawyer, was appointed to chair the inquiry. When she asked Zarankin why she had suffered through the harassment for almost a year, Zarankin explained that she was afraid of losing her job. When asked how she felt about her boss's conduct, she replied, "I felt like dirt. I was scared of the man all the time. It always frightened me. I always liked to avoid him when he was coming in. I just didn't say nothing." She wanted to work at the inn because it was good experience for a career in restaurant and hotel management. She tried to discourage the harassment by moving quickly or avoiding Johnstone, but his behaviour remained unchanged. According to staff who were called as witnesses before the inquiry, sexual harassment was common at the Wessex Inn. The "head girl," Donna Young, testified that "he does hit and either you have to put up with it or tell him to get lost." Sheila Burden, an eighteen-year-old high school student, explained that Johnstone "would grab a lot ... He'd grab up top and bottom and he'd make rude comments quite a bit. He would grab my chest, you know, or ass." A couple of times, according to Burden, he had pushed employees onto the waterbed in the back room where he lived. Her response to his touching and lewd comments was to tell him to "get lost" or to "fuck off." He would stop for a while, but only briefly. Another employee, Shelly Parker, provided similar testimony. The human rights officer investigating Zarankin's complaint, Bruce Greenwood, asked Johnstone during their initial meeting about a rumour around town that having sex with him was a condition of employment at the inn (all the staff were female). Johnstone replied that "I've kidded to friends about that, yes."

At the hearing Johnstone refused to testify, asking his friend Jurgen Adelborg (who was not a lawyer) to speak in his place. Their defence was that Zarankin was an incompetent employee who was slow to get the work done and often messy. They did admit, however, that Johnstone routinely touched his staff. Johnstone had admitted to Greenwood that he pinched them on the bottom and patted them on the head, and "that it was all in fun." He did not deny that he conducted himself in the manner described by Zarankin. Smith had no difficulty finding Johnstone guilty of sexual harassment. In her written judgment, she observed that "sexual harassment in the workplace is not a new phenomenon; legal recourse for its victims is new." She concluded that

> there is no doubt the Respondent persistently and frequently touched the Complainant in the manner she described and made the sorts of comments which led her to say he had "a vulgar tongue." Indeed, he did not seem to treat her with much respect, and there is no doubt she was frightened of him ... There was no reasonable basis upon which he could have concluded that she enjoyed or invited this conduct ... I find that he knew or should have known that the fun was one-sided, and was at the expense of his employee's feeling of dignity and self-respect.

The Zarankin case was an important milestone. The term "sexual harassment" appeared nowhere in the Human Rights Code.[2] Instead, Lynn Smith based her ruling on the reasonable cause section and also found Johnstone guilty of discrimination on the basis of sex. Ironically, in the same year the Zarankin case was decided, the Social Credit government achieved its long-sought desire of gutting the human rights state. From the moment it returned to power in 1975, Social Credit used every means at its disposal to undermine the NDP's Human Rights Code. Nine years later, the Socreds would replace the NDP law with a statute premised on a narrow vision of the human rights state. The Socred administration of the NDP's human rights legislation demonstrates that the existence of a law is no assurance that its provisions will be implemented. Laws must be enforced, and not all of them are enforced equally. The history of the human rights state in British Columbia reveals the need to closely examine how laws are received and put into action.

The Human Rights State in Canada

In some ways, the British Columbia experience was typical of developments throughout Canada; in other ways, it was far more progressive.

Funding for human rights programs increased steadily each year in every jurisdiction (Figures 9 and 10). Ontario and Quebec operated the largest human rights programs. The budget for the BC human rights program was comparable to that of Alberta and far more generous than Newfoundland's (Figure 11). Human rights agencies hired more staff and opened regional offices. With the exception of Ontario's fourteen regional offices, British Columbia operated the largest number of offices outside its capital (six).[3] At its peak, the British Columbia Human Rights Branch employed a dozen human rights investigators, compared with thirty-three in Ontario, nine in Manitoba, six in Saskatchewan, and one in Newfoundland.[4]

Caseloads also expanded dramatically. In its first year enforcing the Human Rights Code, the Ontario Human Rights Commission investigated forty-five cases, most of which involved racial discrimination in employment. By the late 1970s, the number of investigations had reached well over a thousand annually. Over time, there was a steady rise in every aspect of the Canadian human rights state, including inquiries, complaints, investigations, boards of inquiry, and educational programs. The number of boards of inquiry increased from 134 reported cases between 1974 and 1979 to 487 between 1980 and 1985 (Figure 12).

FIGURE 9 Combined funding for provincial human rights programs in Canada, 1975-83

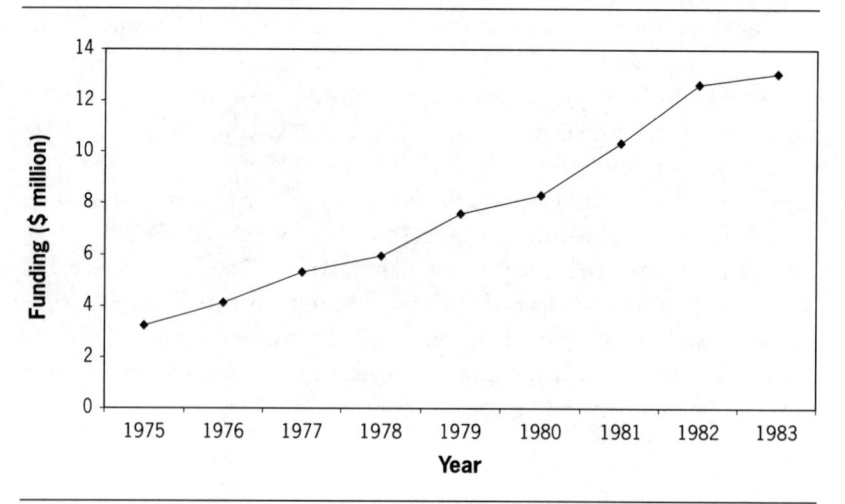

NOTE: The human rights programs of Prince Edward Island and Quebec began in 1975. The budget for the federal commission tripled between 1978 and 1983.

SOURCE: Provincial Public Accounts, 1972-83.

The Human Rights Act   173

FIGURE 10 Provincial funding for human rights programs, 1977, 1981, and 1985

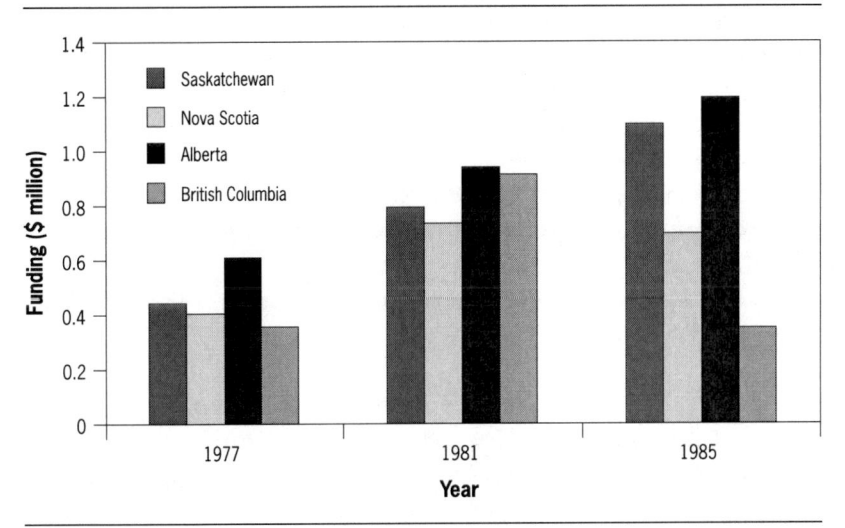

SOURCE: Provincial Public Accounts, 1977, 1981, 1985.

FIGURE 11 Budgets for human rights programs in Canada, 1975-83

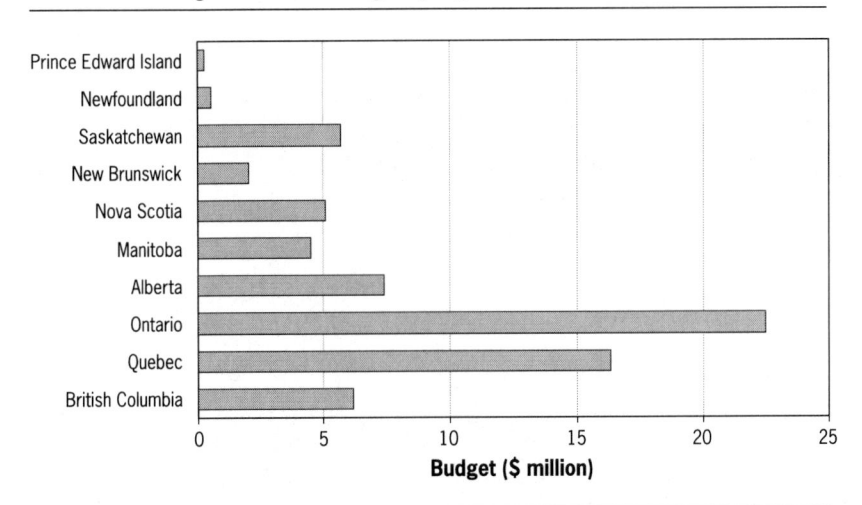

NOTE: The human rights programs of Prince Edward Island and Quebec began in 1975. The federal program is excluded because it did not exist until 1977. The budget for the federal commission was $2,158,917 in 1978 and $6,453,832 in 1983.

SOURCE: Provincial Public Accounts, 1975-83.

Every Canadian jurisdiction had a human rights agency with a mandate for enforcement, research, education, and legal reform. They engaged full-time civil servants who specialized in human rights enforcement, focused on conciliation rather than litigation, represented complainants before formal inquiries, held independent boards of inquiry, and offered remedies that usually involved fines, an apology, a commitment to stop discriminating in the future, or the provision of a service. Cabinet ministers were responsible for appointing boards of inquiry, and human rights agencies had carriage of the complaint. Many jurisdictions, however, experimented with the original model. Commissioners worked part-time or full-time depending on the jurisdiction, and several provinces appointed permanent tribunals to replace ad hoc boards of inquiry. Quebec's legislation recognized economic, social, and cultural rights, and Quebec was also the only jurisdiction whose legislature appointed the commissioners (which assured a greater degree of independence and job security). Other jurisdictions empowered the cabinet to appoint commissioners, and except in the Quebec and federal commissions, they held their positions at the discretion of the minister. Most human rights laws continued to provide exemptions for educational, charitable, philanthropic, or religious institutions (in Newfoundland, because churches held a monopoly over education, the exemption became the source of intense controversy).[5] Legislators amended human rights statutes to include exemptions for affirmative action programs, and by the 1980s several human rights agencies had a mandate to address systemic discrimination (and to initiate their own complaints). Quebec and the federal government also led the way in implementing equal pay for work of equal value.[6]

Otherwise, the British Columbia experience appears to have been typical. The government provided comparable resources throughout the 1970s to fund the activities of both the Human Rights Branch and the Human Rights Commission. The legislative mandate, with some notable exceptions, was the same. The largest number of complaints each year involved sex discrimination. True, Nova Scotia and Ontario faced a slightly larger number of complaints regarding race, but even then sex discrimination cases ran a close second (Figure 13). British Columbia was at the forefront of human rights innovation, but it was also part of a national dialogue on human rights law. Human rights litigation in Canada was not a patchwork – it was an integrated and shared system of evolving human rights ideals. It was perhaps appropriate that Kathleen Ruff played a key role in founding the *Canadian Human Rights Reporter*. This series, which began in 1980, was the first publication in Canada to print board of inquiry decisions across jurisdictions.

Still, the BC human rights state was unique in one key aspect: politics. In no other jurisdiction were human rights subject to such visceral political conflict. Although other governments may have shared the Socred dislike for human rights law, none were as determined or vocal as the Social Credit Party in British Columbia. And no other government dared to go as far as the Socreds in pursuing a radical vision for restructuring the human rights state.

Figure 12 Boards of inquiry appointed, 1974-81

Prince Edward Island (1976-81)	1	Alberta	10
Newfoundland	8	Ontario	173
Saskatchewan	50	Quebec (1976-81)	255
New Brunswick	10	Federal (1977-81)	28
Nova Scotia	32	British Columbia	105
Manitoba	13		

NOTE: Information for Newfoundland is missing for 1978 and 1980.
SOURCE: Provincial Human Rights Commissions' annual reports.

FIGURE 13 Complaints of discrimination on the basis of race and gender as a percentage of all human rights complaints, 1976-81

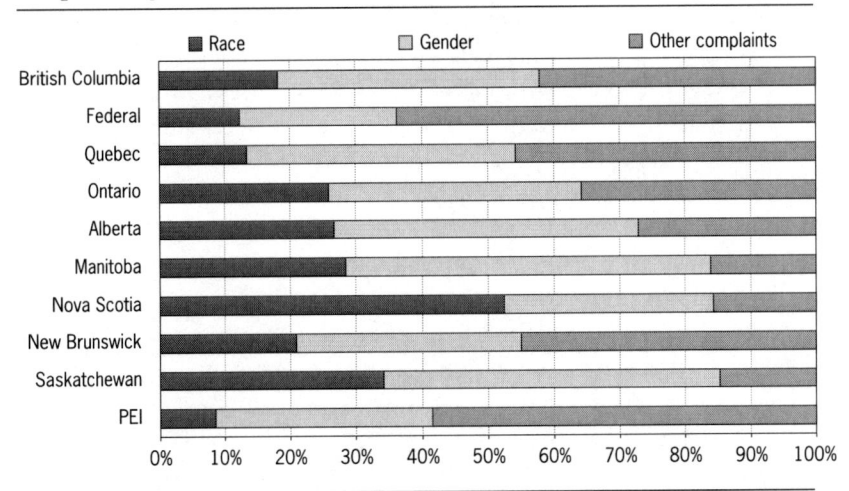

NOTE: Data for Newfoundland are unavailable. The federal program began in 1977.
SOURCE: Provincial Human Rights Commissions' annual reports.

Human Rights State Politics in British Columbia

Between 1975 and 1984, the Social Credit government did what it could to restrict the operations of the Human Rights Branch and the commission. Ministers obfuscated or lied outright; delayed appointments; were recalcitrant in approving boards of inquiry; reduced the number of investigators while resurrecting the practice of using industrial relations officers (IROs); and appointed people who had little or no experience in human rights.[7] The Status of Women Action Group expressed a common grievance with Socred management when it insisted that the "Human Rights Commission is an embarrassment and a bad joke. They have done nothing except show their appalling ignorance and insensitivity to human rights."[8]

The human rights state thrived under the NDP. Offices were opened throughout the province. Human rights officers replaced IROs. Part-time officers were also hired to accommodate skilled individuals who were unable to work full-time. Within a few years, the branch had a growing staff and a budget for human rights education.[9] Boards of inquiry presented their decisions in writing, and the minister of labour did not hesitate to approve formal hearings: eleven inquiries were appointed in 1975 alone. The Socreds, however, did not share the NDP's enthusiasm for the human rights state. Labour minister Robert McClelland, who was responsible for the human rights program, later admitted that he was

> never a fan of the Human Rights Commission or of human rights commissions ... If you look at individual rights and the need for someone to go somewhere if his rights are hampered, that's important, but this commission took on far more than that. They became a force that can intervene; they were really almost a government sort of organization, and they forgot the little people that they were supposed to be serving: I felt that was wrong.[10]

McClelland reduced the number of offices, so that by 1983 only those in Kamloops, Prince George, Vancouver, and Victoria remained (meanwhile, in Manitoba, Ontario, and Quebec, the governments were opening new regional offices). Funding for the human rights program continued to rise after the Socreds returned to power in 1975, but by 1980 the government had begun to restrict funding. The staffs of the branch and the commission were integrated and their numbers reduced. The commission shrank from twelve to six members. Internal committees dedicated to administration, legislative review, and current issues were eliminated.[11] The deputy minister of labour, D.H. Cameron, estimated in 1981 that an

FIGURE 14 British Columbia human rights program budget

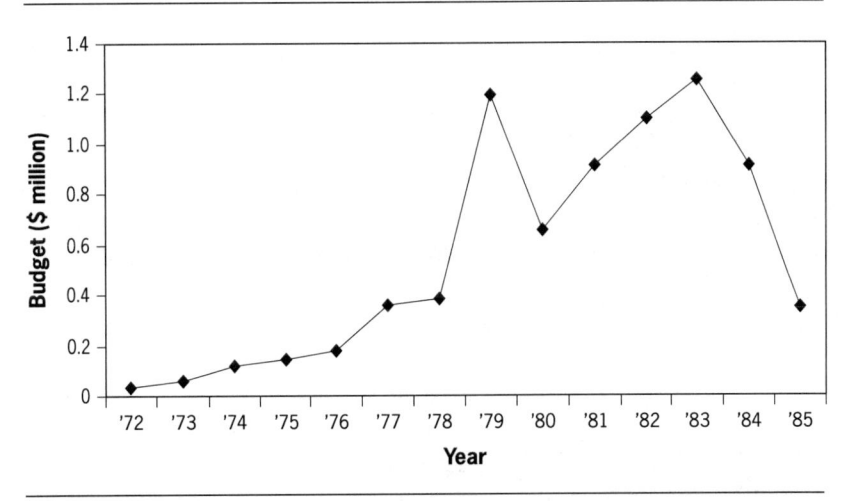

Source: British Columbia, *Public Accounts*, 1972-85.

additional eleven staff (at a cost of $245,000) were needed to maintain the human rights program at its operational minimum. One position was approved but never funded.[12] Funding was pulled from advertising and education programs, staff training and special research projects, and transportation and investigation.[13] Only two representatives (as opposed to five or six from other provinces) were sent to the annual meeting of the Canadian Association of Statutory Human Rights Agencies in 1981.[14] Two years later, the government abandoned the association entirely.[15]

Funding for the human rights program expanded exponentially under the NDP's model for human rights adjudication, a trend that occurred in other provinces (Figure 14). Funding for the BC human rights program was entirely consistent (per capita) with funding levels across the country. By the 1980s, however, it had dropped dramatically, whereas human rights budgets in other jurisdictions remained stable or increased.[16] Compared with the federal Human Rights Commission, for instance, the BC Human Rights Branch was far less active, and it operated with far fewer resources in 1983. The federal commission employed 119 staff (British Columbia had 37); had a budget of $4,267,512 (British Columbia's was $913,023); and referred thirty-six complaints to a board of inquiry (British Columbia referred three; the minister of labour rejected sixteen additional requests by the branch).[17] Even considering the federal commission's larger jurisdiction – it received approximately twice the number of complaints as British Columbia in 1983 – the difference in staff, resources, and inquiries was striking.

Without adequate funding, the branch and commission could not hope to fulfill their mandate, especially when it came to education, which was a crucial component of the human rights state. The human rights state was designed to promote tolerance and to focus on prevention rather than punishment. Small provinces such as Newfoundland and Prince Edward Island lacked the resources to fund expansive education programs.[18] British Columbia, on the other hand, lacked the political will to continue funding a strong human rights education program.[19] The Social Credit government also stymied the work of the branch and commission by delaying appointments and rejecting requests for boards of inquiry. Frustrated at the government's intransigence, the NDP Opposition critic confronted the minister of labour, Allan Williams, in the legislature in June 1978. In response to criticisms that he had not appointed a single board of inquiry since August 1977, or replaced commissioners whose term had expired in December 1977, Williams responded, "So what?"[20] Ten people were eventually appointed to the commission in August 1978, but it continued to diminish. In 1979-80, six expired terms were not renewed, which reduced the commission to only six members. Within a year, the number of commissioners had fallen to four.[21]

The Socreds selected a few new commissioners after the terms of the NDP-appointed incumbents expired in 1978, living up to their reputation for choosing people with dubious qualifications. The new commissioners were a pitiable group of lacklustre individuals who were in no way representative of the community, and their appointment sparked intense criticism of the government. True, some had the potential to be strong members. Joseph Katz (1978-81), for instance, a UBC Faculty of Education professor, had participated in the provincial commission for the International Year for Human Rights, consulted for the federal secretary of state's human rights program, and been active in various human rights organizations. Others, such as Mildred Gottfriedson (president, Native Women's Society and member of the Order of Canada) and Douglas Mowat (executive director, BC Division, Canadian Paraplegic Association), were active in social movements and were deeply familiar with discrimination against minorities.

But other appointments of 1978 were simply embarrassing. As columnist Alan Fotheringham suggested, "the whole range of names on the commission demonstrates Williams' desire to make the commission so bland as to be ineffectual ... There is a well known Socred campaign worker on the list and an almost complete absence of names well known in the civil rights field."[22] One member, Jock Smith, had previously been the target of two complaints for violating the Human Rights Code![23] The chair, Margaret Strongitharm, possessed no relevant experience.[24] It did not take long before the Human Rights Commission lost all credibility. At one point, in 1979, the *Vancouver Express* reported that the commissioners (composed solely of white men and one white woman) exchanged sexist and homophobic comments during a public hearing.[25] To make matters worse, Strongitharm defended their behaviour as an expression of free speech and pointed out that the code did not protect gays anyway.[26] In 1979, Katz joked that female representation was not required on the commission – its members could always obtain a woman's point of view from their wives.[27] Another commissioner, Reverend T. Neil Vant (an Anglican minister from 100 Mile House), opposed hiring homosexuals as teachers and was quoted as saying that prejudice against homosexuals was justified "because when they can't find consenting adults they sometimes prey on others."[28] Unsurprisingly, more than a dozen community groups demanded the resignations of every member of the commission.[29] Even Doris Anderson, writing from Ottawa as the chair of the Canadian Advisory Council on the Status of Women, called on the premier to dismiss them all.[30]

While the commission became increasingly impotent, the branch faced a similar fate. The lifeblood of the modern human rights state, in every jurisdiction, was a professional human rights investigator. Boards of inquiry were the last line of defence. The battle lines of the human rights state were the thousands upon thousands of informal conversations and negotiations carried out by human rights officers. Given the central role of conciliation in human rights law, these individuals were paramount to the successful operation of the human rights state. And yet, once again, the Social Credit government demonstrated its contempt for the law. To be fair, it did continue to employ human rights officers, but the work of the branch was bound to increase as people became more aware of the legislation and their rights. The Socreds, however, refused to hire sufficient experienced staff to handle the enlarged workload. Every human rights agency in Canada complained of lack of staff, but no other jurisdiction at this time used inexperienced and untrained IROs to do the work of human rights officers (a throwback to a similar practice under the 1969 Human Rights Act).

Minister of Labour Allan Williams was unapologetic. British Columbia employed seven investigators in the mid-1970s, compared with Manitoba's eight (in 1979) despite the latter's much smaller population; Ontario *added* six more officers in 1976 alone to deal with burgeoning caseloads.[31] Instead of hiring more officers, Williams found a cheaper solution – the IRO:

> Now with regard to the use of industrial relations officers, yes, they are used ... in the human rights field principally in the outlying areas where the number of complaints which could arise would not really justify maintaining a human rights officer full-time in one of the outlying areas of the province. We do have some who cover significant areas, but principally they're located in the major centres. The industrial relations officers assist.[32]

The government evolved a compromise that appeared harmless on the surface. IROs would conduct routine investigations, and human rights officers would intervene when necessary. But this approach betrayed a fundamental misunderstanding of the nature of human rights adjudication and represented a competing vision of the human rights state. IROs were ill-equipped to investigate and conciliate complaints. Because of their heavy workload, they were unable to speak more than once to the individuals involved in a case.[33] They also lacked proper training. G. Scott Wallace, the leader of the provincial Progressive Conservative Party, vividly articulated a danger of using IROs for front-line human rights work:

> I was made aware as recently as this morning of a case where an industrial relations officer was allocated to investigate a complaint by an individual. This [complainant] discovered that she ended up answering all kinds of questions as to whether she suffered from a neurosis, or if she had ever been considered by her friends to be paranoid, and questions of this nature, which seem to me to be ranging far away and beyond the preliminary kind of discussion that should take place when a man or a woman wants a complaint investigated by the human rights branch.[34]

By 1981, the situation had become dire. Of 881 complaints, only 307 were settled voluntarily, and the minister approved only three boards of inquiry. At least twenty-five branch requests for a board of inquiry were still pending in May 1981; half of them had been sent to the minister in March of that year and several dated from 1980 or 1979. The branch submitted twelve more requests for inquiries to the minister in 1982, and by July more than half had been denied (the others were still pending).[35] Between 1979 and 1982, the branch assigned 2,155 cases to human rights and industrial relations officers throughout the province. Of the 881 complaints in 1981, 379 had been carried over from the previous year because of budget cuts and layoffs, and in 1983 the number of carried-over cases exceeded 500.[36] Investigators were burdened with enormous caseloads, far more than their counterparts in other provinces. Most closed an average of only 50 cases per year, and the number of complaints increased every year even as the number of investigators declined.[37] By 1982, the director of the Human Rights Branch was estimating that her staff received 42 percent more cases than they were capable of handling.

Social movements protested the government's inaction, interference, and cutbacks. Throughout the late 1970s, the Vancouver Status of Women (VSW) campaigned against the Social Credit government's obstinacy in appointing new human rights officers, going so far as to hold a province-wide "day of mourning" on 10 December 1976 (International Human Rights Day).[38] Several groups launched a petition campaign to have the Human Rights Commission dismissed.[39] Two hundred women mobilized in 1975 for a Mother's Day protest in downtown Vancouver, with participation as diverse as the British Columbia Federation of Women, Child Care Federation, Rape Relief, SORWUC (a female labour union), Women's Bookstore, and the Women's Health Collective.[40] The VSW and the Status of Women Action Group (SWAG) played a critical role in organizing the largest mass rally at the Legislative Assembly in the province's history by 1976. "Rally for Action" brought together a host of women from across British Columbia to protest, among other issues, deficiencies in the administration of human rights law.[41] A year later, the British Columbia Civil Liberties Association, the VSW, SWAG, and several other groups successfully lobbied the labour minister to appoint outstanding boards of inquiry.[42]

Few people would have envied the person responsible for leading the branch under the Social Credit government: it went through three directors in nine years. Ruff was an outspoken critic of Socred human rights policies. Her successor, Nola Landucci, initially avoided headlines but soon became an outspoken critic of the government as well. She attacked the minister of labour for constant delays, for declining to appoint boards of inquiry, and for refusing to provide adequate support for the branch. Soon after leaving the branch, Landucci told a reporter that the government obstructed the branch's work through neglect and disinterest, and that it "has demonstrated so well it is not about to be legally or morally bound by the human rights code."[43] Hanne Jensen, who replaced Landucci in 1981, lasted only a few years until the government decided to rid itself of the troublesome branch. Soon after she was fired, Jensen was interviewed about her term as director. She described the government's actions toward the branch as "reckless, senseless and unnecessarily brutal." Senior ministry officials, according to Jensen, undermined the branch's work, and the labour minister, Robert McClelland, resisted her attempts to brief him on human rights issues.[44]

The relationship between the commission and the minister was also strained. Its chair, Margaret Strongitharm, complained to the minister that she had to learn about Landucci's dismissal in the newspaper, and she privately criticized him for his choice of commission members. Her term was not renewed either, and Charles Paris replaced her in 1981.[45] Once again, however, the government found itself under attack from its own Human Rights Commission. Paris insisted on more independence from the ministry: "Fundamentally the Human Rights Commission will not be seen as another arm of the bureaucracy in the Ministry of Labour. The commission must be independent to be effective and enjoy any credibility." In 1983, he criticized the minister for eliminating $25,000 from the commission's budget, reducing staff, and refusing to approve a grant for members of the British Columbia Coalition of the Disabled to attend a conference. He was especially frustrated with delays in appointing boards of inquiry. By 1983, the commission had become another source of aggravation for the government.[46]

The NDP had made a serious miscalculation with the Human Rights Code. By requiring the branch and the commission to report to the minister of labour, rather than to the legislature itself, it created the potential for abuse. Under the NDP, this issue never became serious. For the most part, the NDP preferred to keep the branch and commission at arm's length. The minister of labour even delegated the appointment of inquiry boards to civil servants. However, a government determined to obstruct human rights enforcement could exploit its power. In addition to losing three branch directors, Socred labour ministers refused to follow the NDP practice of delegating responsibility for selecting boards of inquiry. Political interference in the branch's operations was common. After a BC judge quashed a board of inquiry decision requiring the *Vancouver Sun* to publish an advertisement by the Gay Alliance Towards Equality, the branch attempted to appeal the decision in court. But the minister refused to allow any government lawyers to assist it. Only when Kathleen Ruff disregarded his order and found a private lawyer to take the case pro bono did he agree to fund the case (to avoid the embarrassing spectacle of having a private lawyer defend the government's own legislation).[47]

The minister's broad discretionary powers for selecting inquiry boards were another source of strain with the branch. Since political considerations could easily influence cabinet ministers, some jurisdictions laid the responsibility for appointing boards with the Human Rights Commission (Ontario) or mandated Superior Courts to function as boards of inquiry (Quebec). Quebec also had its human rights commission report directly to the legislature. Not so in British Columbia. Shelagh Day recalled several instances in which a Social Credit minister refused to appoint a board of inquiry; there was no apparent reason for this, except perhaps not wanting to antagonize a large employer. "Under the Socreds," according to Day, "we [the Human Rights Branch staff] were all suspect. We had to try and figure out how to get the work done and manoeuvre in a way we did not have to do under the NDP."[48]

The Socreds were not averse to direct political interference. In January 1976, a group of women in Langley booked the municipal curling rink to play during the early evening. Women had never booked ice time at the rink before, and several male teams appealed the decision, insisting that the women play in the afternoon or late at night. Their complaint, of course, was premised on the (false) presumption that none of the women had jobs. The rink acceded and withdrew the booking, an action that clearly constituted discrimination on the basis of sex in the provision of services. Maurice Guilbault, the human rights investigator assigned by the branch, was about to recommend a board of inquiry when he received calls from the mayor of Langley (who was also president of the Social Credit Party) and the deputy minister of labour. Both insisted that Guilbault withdraw from the case and reject the complaint. Not only was the deputy minister furious when Ruff ignored the warning and directed her investigator to submit his report, but to her surprise he sent a memorandum demanding, in writing, that she withdraw the complaint:

> I expect all public servants in our department to carry out their duties and not to allow their own political views to interfere with their own good judgment. In your own case, notwithstanding the fact that you were a candidate of the New Democratic Party for elective office, I am confident that you will perform your job as a public servant under the Social Credit administration with the same vigor and sensitivity that you displayed under the former New Democratic Party administration ... It is my opinion that this complaint does not fall within the jurisdiction of the Human Rights Branch. The complainant should be encouraged to pursue her complaint with the Langley Curling Club executives. She should be told that the scheduling of times for curling is not a proper subject for a human rights complaint. *I require you to cease any further investigation into this complaint.*[49]

Such blatant political interference was rare in Canada. Under the statute, the Human Rights Branch was required to investigate all complaints. The deputy minister was, in effect, ordering Ruff to break the law. She refused to back down, and the rink eventually conceded and allowed the women to book ice time there.[50]

The relationship between the branch and the minister created an awkward dynamic. The case of Charles Wills highlighted the problem. Wills worked at the Victoria Juvenile Detention Home when the government took control of the institution in 1974. Because government policy was to force corrections officers to retire at age sixty, Wills was told to retire in 1979, a decision he challenged. The branch attempted, but failed, to reach a compromise (citing discrimination on the basis of age). Landucci forwarded the case to the minister of labour, Jack Heinrich, in 1980. Heinrich rejected her request for an inquiry board and, in his letter to her, provided no explanation for his decision. The files of the Ministry of Labour for 1980 and 1981 reveal that this commonly occurred. In dozens of cases, Landucci (and Hanne Jensen) recommended the appointment of a board of inquiry, and the minister routinely rejected the request without any explanation (in some instances he included a vague sentence about lack of evidence).[51] Only after a group of social movement organizations lobbied the minister, and the media voiced criticisms, did he consent to several outstanding inquiries in 1979.

These unhealthy circumstances meant that the branch could not predict how the minister would respond to its recommendations for a board of inquiry. For example, in Dr. Jonna Bruh Mou's case against the BC College of Dental Surgeons, the NDP minister of labour, Bill King, had approved a board of inquiry. However, his Socred successor, Allan Williams, reversed the decision.[52] It was not uncommon for months to go by with no answer from the minister. The situation became serious enough to warrant a formal investigation from the provincial ombudsman, Karl Friedman. The labour minister ignored his recommendation to provide greater transparency and even refused to meet with him. Friedman accused the minister of undermining "a fundamental element of administrative fairness."[53]

Jensen's experience as director led her to conclude that "the government was unwilling to undertake human rights programs and the actions of senior ministry officials undermined the branch's work."[54] The branch had limited access to the minister, reporting instead to a deputy minister, and was sometimes virtually ignored by ministry officials. Lack of resources, political interference, delayed and weak appointments, the use of IROs, a revolving leadership, and loopholes in the Human Rights Code profoundly harmed the human rights state in British Columbia (Figure 15).

All of this was perhaps unsurprising, given the nature of the Social Credit Party. It formed a patriarchal government dominated by men whose policies demonstrated little understanding of sex discrimination. Immediately following the 1975 election, the Socreds eliminated the position of coordinator for the status of women and fired the consultant on sex discrimination for the Ministry of Education. Several cabinet ministers also showed startling ignorance of the realities facing women in the workforce.[55] During a television interview in 1984, Minister of Education Jack Heinrich contemptuously dismissed a case initiated a few years earlier by a group of women who had filed a complaint against a golf club that refused to allow women to play on weekends. According to Heinrich, the complaint was frivolous: men worked, women did not, and men should be allowed to have the golf course to themselves on certain days. Heinrich, who, ironically, had been minister of labour at the time, did not even acknowledge that 52.7 percent of BC women worked. Three years later, in the midst of a national debate regarding the Socred plan to eliminate the Human Rights

FIGURE 15 Determination of human rights complaints under the NDP (1972-75) and Social Credit (1970-72, 1975-85) governments

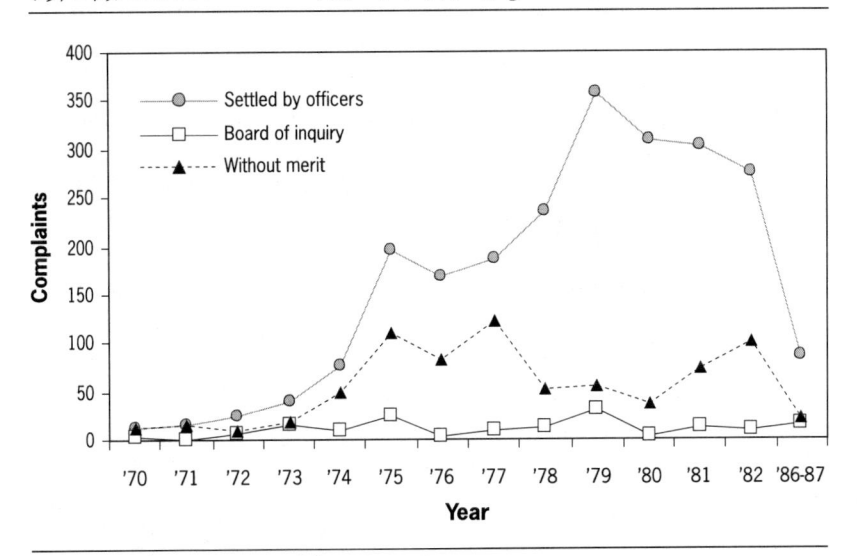

NOTE: No information reported for 1983 to 1985.
SOURCE: British Columbia, Department of Labour, Annual Reports, 1970-86.

Code, the provincial government and the media cited the golf course case as an example of the "trivial" complaints that monopolized the branch.[56] The full extent of the Socreds' determination to weaken the human rights state soon became apparent when they introduced new human rights legislation in the 1980s.

The Human Rights Act, 1984

British Columbia made national headlines with the Social Credit government's plans to radically reform its human rights legislation in the 1980s. But whereas the Human Rights Code was hailed as progressive, the new Human Rights Act was almost universally vilified as a regressive step.

Under Charles Paris the Human Rights Commission produced a series of reports, based on widespread public consultations, that recommended ambitious revisions to the Human Rights Code. The commission suggested adding new prohibited grounds of discrimination: sexual orientation, disability, sexual harassment, poverty, family status, and hate propaganda. The code would be given primacy over all other provincial legislation. In addition, the branch would be empowered to dismiss frivolous complaints (rather than having to investigate every one) and to appoint boards of inquiry (rather than asking the labour minister). The wording of the code's equal pay section would also be amended to "equal pay for work of equal value." Finally, the commission suggested a series of administrative reforms including longer terms for commissioners, greater openness in appointments, and reporting directly to the legislature.[57] One can only imagine the reaction in the Socred inner circle. The government had spent years undermining the work of the branch and commission, and now the latter was proposing a dramatic expansion to the powers and scope of the human rights state. None of the recommendations were implemented.

The Social Credit government did introduce a major overhaul of human rights legislation. The commissioners, however, would have recognized nothing in its vision for the human rights state. The incident that finally provoked the government to introduce new legislation was the Hunky Bill case. William Konyk used the trade name Hunky Bill for his sausage-marketing business and named his booth at the Pacific National Exhibition Hunky Bill's House of Perogies. Because the branch was required to investigate every complaint, it was forced to process the Ukrainian Canadian Association's complaint that the name was offensive.[58] For many, the Hunky

Bill incident typified the frivolous complaints common to the human rights regime (ironically, the commission had sought to amend the legislation to provide the branch with more leeway in dismissing trivial complaints, but the Socreds refused to enact the reform). The case garnered extensive media coverage. Either the Socreds saw it as an opportunity to rid themselves of a troublesome agency or they too were caught up in the reaction to it. In any event, the controversy was little more than a pretext. The Socreds had long opposed the principles that underlay the Human Rights Code.

The Socreds introduced Bill 27 in July 1983, but it immediately stirred intense opposition in the media and among advocacy groups, especially when it was revealed that the government had fired all the human rights staff before the bill had even been passed![59] From Victoria to Vancouver, Prince George, and Terrace, government agents covered the province, handing out dismissal notices to unsuspecting human rights officers, some of whom had been civil servants for years. As one person described it,

> A human rights officer got a knock on the door while opening his birthday gifts – I think this may be the one we read about in the paper, the one the Labour minister knows so much about – and was told to hand over keys, car and credit cards; he was permitted to clean the personal effects from his office under the watchful eye of a government agent.[60]

Meanwhile, members of the Human Rights Commission were summarily dismissed by Order-in-Council, regional offices were shut down, and the director of the branch was fired. Only a few months earlier, the minister of labour had assured Paris "that the government is committed to the Human Rights Commission and we are not considering abolishing it. It is my view that the Commission has a very important role to play in human rights."[61] The Socreds, however, did not anticipate the public backlash to their heavy-handed tactics. They quickly withdrew the bill and promised to introduce new legislation the following year, after consulting with key stakeholders (in the interim, there was no human rights enforcement in the province).

Bill 11, little different from its predecessor, was introduced less than a year later. It was part of the Socreds' infamous "restraint package" of 1983-84: twenty-six statutes that, among other things, directed the government to dismiss thousands of civil servants and cut wages; eliminate services such as the Residential Tenancy Board and the Alcohol and Drug

Commission; and increase taxes.[62] The restraint package, which was passed and became law in 1984, included the Human Rights Act. The Social Credit Party had fully embraced neo-liberal economic and social policies.

True, the Human Rights Act incorporated, for the first time, physical and mental disability.[63] This was its only progressive reform. Under the new act, the maximum possible fine was reduced from $5,000 to $2,000 (the original bill had eliminated fines altogether), and only direct costs could be awarded (no damages). The Human Rights Commission and branch were replaced with the Human Rights Council. There were no more boards of inquiry or human rights investigators: the council was responsible for processing complaints and rendering judgments. The process for submitting complaints was streamlined to allow officials to dismiss them without an investigation.[64] The reasonable cause section, which the federal secretary of state had recently described as placing "British Columbia in the forefront of progressive human rights thinking," was removed.[65] Discrimination was still prohibited in job advertisements but not in employment application forms. British Columbia became the first province to eliminate the education function of its human rights program. There were no more professional human rights investigators. The Human Rights Act was unusual in Canada in that it did not provide for staffing the new Human Rights Council; instead, the council had to depend on other government agencies for its staff. As a result, overworked industrial relations officers were, once again, responsible for following up human rights complaints, and only twenty people were assigned to manage the entire human rights system (staff levels for the Ontario Human Rights Commission, in contrast, rose from thirty-five in 1977 to sixty-eight in 1982).[66] The new regime de-emphasized informal conciliation and concentrated on the quasi-judicial adjudication of complaints.[67] There was no longer carriage of the complaint. Complainants were required to secure witnesses, collect documents, and hire a lawyer or argue the case themselves. The Socred legislation stipulated that a complainant must demonstrate intent, a burden of proof that was often impossible to satisfy and that constituted a departure from the direction of human rights legislation in Canada.

The new Human Rights Council was responsible for administering the legislation. Appointees were chosen at the discretion of the minister of labour, and they served at the cabinet's pleasure. The five individuals appointed to the council included two lawyers, a civil servant, a clergyman, and a person who had experience with helping the disabled find employment. Only one was a woman.[68] Although the council could ask the minister to appoint boards of inquiry to impose a settlement on recalcitrant parties, this never occurred; any adjudication simply involved an informal hearing chaired by a council member. There was no provision for staff to support the council (instead, it borrowed staff from other government departments); nor could the council initiate complaints on behalf of individuals or groups (previously, the commission had done so on behalf of groups to preserve anonymity and avoid retribution). Moreover, trade unions could not submit complaints on behalf of their members; only individuals could submit complaints. And council decisions could not be appealed.

Not a single member of the government defended the bill in the legislature except the minister of labour because one person had to at least table the legislation. The Liberals and the NDP vigorously opposed it.[69] R. Brian Howe and David Johnson suggest that "this was the furthest any Canadian government has ever gone in restructuring its human rights policy."[70] The new system, according to Howe, transferred the burden almost entirely onto the shoulders of victims of discrimination:

> The burden of responsibility in cases was shifted back to complainants, who were given very little administrative support in bringing cases forward. The onus was on complainants to get witnesses, acquire documents, and hire lawyers. Assistance was not entirely ruled out, but when it was provided, it came from part-time rather than full-time, experienced human rights officials. If complainants were able to get enough evidence, they could present their cases before the council. But unlike the role of a commission in other jurisdictions, the council was not a party to the proceedings. Complainants were left on their own, their cases being decided in a summary manner. The system allowed for no appeal other than on procedural grounds of errors in law.[71]

As the editors of the *Vancouver Sun* surmised, the new law would "simply rule out complaints by many of the less fortunate members of society, who almost alone are the victims of discrimination."[72] Bill Black, the UBC law professor who had helped draft the Human Rights Code, offered a similar assessment: "Even well educated and sophisticated persons with legitimate complaints will often find it difficult to obtain a remedy. But human rights legislation is designed to assist people who have been subjected to economic, educational or social disadvantage. It will be almost impossible for many such people to assume the obligations imposed on complainants by the Act."[73]

Minister of Labour Robert McClelland insisted that the previous "system was not working, that justice wasn't being served, that justice delayed was justice denied, and that a totally new system was necessary in order that we could move in a very meaningful way towards the day when we wouldn't have to worry about discrimination in this province."[74] According to him, the new Human Rights Act was necessary to reduce public spending and eliminate groundless complaints. But the cost of maintaining the commission was, at best, a miniscule part of the provincial budget. Moreover, there was already widespread support for deleting the provision of the code that required investigating every complaint. The Socreds had spent years restricting the application of a law that they vehemently opposed. In the Ministry of Labour, the human rights program absorbed an immense amount of the minister's time, who frequently responded to letters and complaints on every aspect of the branch's operations. It was also a constant source of embarrassment, especially surrounding the appointment of boards of inquiry. A confidential cabinet memorandum prepared in May 1982 emphasized the need to protect the minister from negative publicity surrounding human rights complaints: "This public attention is disproportionate to the impact of decisions on individual cases and particularly disproportionate when compared to jurisdictions like Ontario. The Government is perceived as not supportive of women and visible minority rights."[75] The benefits of the new law, as described in the memorandum, had nothing to do with protecting human rights in the province:

> The government of British Columbia will be a prime beneficiary of the implementation of the proposed legislation. The proposed changes will shift the focus of attention and responsibility for "decision" on human rights cases from a Government Minister to an Agency headed by a Commission. The benefit will be that the pressure on the Minister and the Government from media and special interest groups will be relieved.[76]

Many of the stakeholders who supported the code (albeit, insisting that it had limitations) sharply criticized the new legislation. The NDP Women's Rights Committee stated that dismantling the code was "the most serious aspect of the new legislative package [of fiscal restraint]."[77] SWAG accused

Robert McClelland and protesters, 1983 | Canadian Press

the government of pandering to a small but vocal segment of the business community, and it called for the full reinstatement of the code.[78] The Nanaimo Women's Resource Centre feared that the "elimination of the human rights office means that there are little or no protections within provincial jurisdiction."[79] The leading women's groups in the province, including the British Columbia Federation of Women, Rape Relief, and the VSW, energetically opposed the Human Rights Act.[80] Criticism of the reforms was widespread and included organized labour, civil libertarians, anti-racism associations, churches, and seniors' groups.[81] In a joint statement, bodies representing these constituencies described Bill 11 as "a massive fraud" that essentially "legalized discrimination."[82] Even though the act included a new section on disability, associations representing the disabled, such as the British Columbia Association of Social Workers, British Columbia Coalition for the Disabled, British Columbians for Mentally Handicapped, and the Victoria Handicapped Action Committee, all rejected the legislation.[83] COPE, the dynamic municipal party that was changing the landscape in Vancouver city politics, pledged its support for resurrecting progressive human rights policies.[84] Even the *Vancouver Sun* lamented the government's efforts to "trivialize protection of human rights."[85] Opposition to the reforms also became a prominent aspect of the Solidarity Coalition, a campaign led by organized labour alongside a host of other social movements against the Socred restraint package.[86] Renate Shearer, one of the Human Rights Commission members who were dismissed in 1983, was co-chair of the Solidarity Coalition.

Opposition also mobilized outside the province. The reforms sparked a national debate on the future of the human rights state. Gordon Fairweather, the chairman of the federal Human Rights Commission, campaigned against measures that he characterized as "emblematic of a police state."[87] Chief Commissioner Ken Norman of the Saskatchewan Human Rights Commission claimed that "tearing apart the institutional fabric of the human rights commission and human rights branch is a very regressive step."[88] The chairmen of the Manitoba and Alberta Human Rights Commissions and the members of the Canadian Human Rights Commission also expressed their grievances with the radical reform.[89] So did many prominent political figures outside British Columbia, including Manitoba attorney general Roland Penner and the national leader of the NPD (Ed Broadbent).[90] In an uncommon instance of explicit interference in provincial politics, several members of the federal cabinet, including the minister of justice (Mark MacGuigan), minister of labour (Charles Caccia), minister of state for multiculturalism (David Collenette), minister responsible for the status of women (Judy Erola), and secretary of state (Serge Joyal), called on the government to withdraw the legislation.[91] In a letter to McClelland, Joyal warned that the new act could violate Canada's obligations under international human rights treaties. The ministers appealed to the province to retain a reasonable cause section to engage with unforeseen forms of discrimination, as well as systemic discrimination; a commission to represent victims of discrimination before boards of inquiry and to promote human rights education; and full-time human rights officers who could develop an expertise in conciliation.[92]

Some of the leading human rights and law reform agencies in Canada and abroad also joined the resistance. In Ottawa, Ed Ratushney, director of the Human Rights Research and Education Centre, described the government's actions as "savage" and the new law as "a giant step backward from any commitment to advance human rights."[93] The Canadian Association of Statutory Human Rights Agencies (CASHRA) described the Human Rights Act as a "tragic mistake" and insisted that it be reversed.[94] Meeting in Philadelphia, the International Association of Human Rights Agencies passed a resolution expressing opposition to the proposed amendments.[95] The Canadian Advisory Council on the Status of Women, the Canadian Bar Association, and the Canadian Civil Liberties Association were among the many diverse organizations defending the Human Rights Code.[96]

Charles Paris suggested that Bill 11 was not a restraint measure but "a deliberate, philosophical attack on the very concept of human rights legislation."[97] The Socred act represented a sharp break from the NDP vision for the human rights state, which was based on accessibility, conciliation, education, and an expansive interpretation of human rights. The NDP government hired full-time human rights officers, introduced the reasonable cause provision, provided funding for human rights education, and ensured that complainants had representation before boards of inquiry. In contrast, the Socreds balked at aggressive enforcement of a human rights law that favoured complainants: they eliminated the commission, reduced funding, fired the investigators, and placed the onus on victims to pursue complaints. They argued that the code was too cumbersome, created extensive delays that hurt employers, and facilitated frivolous complaints by providing individuals with free representation. The Human Rights Act had no mandate for education and did not provide complainants with representation or counsel before inquiries.

That the Human Rights Act was a regressive turn in the history of British Columbia's human rights state was quickly made apparent when the first decision was handed down. Not long after Sheri Zarankin's sexual harassment case was decided, Andrea Fields, a twenty-year-old waitress at Willie's Rendezvous restaurant in Victoria, submitted a sexual harassment complaint under the new legislation. Fields testified before the Human Rights Council that her boss, Wilhelm Ueffing, attempted to pinch or grab her, wrote harassing notes, and frequently asked her to have sex with him. In the Zarankin case, human rights officers had investigated the complaint, and a lawyer from the branch had represented Zarankin during the inquiry. In contrast, under the Human Rights Act, Fields had to find her own lawyer, secure witnesses, and prepare her own presentation. The person whom the Socreds had appointed to lead the new council, and who was responsible for chairing the hearing, was no less than Jim Edgett. Now well into his sixties, Edgett was the same man who had chaired Hanne Jensen's equal pay complaint in 1971 under the Socreds' first Human Rights Act. Unsurprisingly, Edgett dismissed Fields's complaint, in part because Ueffing "frequently greeted staff and customers with a hug and a kiss" and because there was insufficient evidence to support her testimony.[98] Labour minister McClelland, who a year later was accused of using a government credit card to purchase the services of escorts and exotic dancers, insisted

Andrea Fields, 1984 | John Yanyshyn, *Vancouver Sun*

that the hearing had been fair and that critics "had a skewed idea of justice."[99] As the final insult, Fields learned about the results of her case on the radio. No one at the council had bothered to contact her.

The Fields case was a powerful symbolic defeat for the human rights state.[100] Former human rights officers Reginald Newkirk and Alicia Lawrence decried the decision, the latter suggesting to a reporter that it "set back human rights 50 years."[101] The NDP labour critic described the ruling as "appalling," and Rosemary Brown, a long-time advocate of human rights legislation, insisted that it "serves notice that the government is prepared to condone and encourage sexual harassment."[102] Editors for the *Vancouver Sun* concluded that the case demonstrated the "inadequacy of the legislation under which the council must operate," and the

Victoria Times-Colonist worried that "any female victim of sexual harassment will have a tough time convincing [the council] that anything untoward happened."[103] (The *Vancouver Province,* on the other hand, suggested that an employer who wrote notes to female employees containing the words "looking forward to seeing your sexy body again" and "let's make love" could be perceived as attempting to make them feel good and to start the day bright.)[104] Dozens of community groups, including the British Columbia Federation of Labour, Human Rights Council, and Vancouver Rape Relief, bemoaned the decision. According to the British Columbia Human Rights Coalition, the case revealed "that either Mr. Edgett does not have the competence to hear such cases or that he is carrying out policy decisions for the minister of labour ... This first decision by the Human Rights Council confirms the Coalition's worst fears. Edgett has set back human rights protection for all women."[105]

Appointing Edgett to lead the Human Rights Council obviously dismayed many human rights advocates. Here was a man who had chaired the first ever complaint under the 1969 Human Rights Act, and now he was chairing the first complaint under the 1984 Human Rights Act. Not only had the Socreds appointed a throwback from the 1960s who had done nothing in the field of human rights for almost fifteen years, but the symbolism of a sexual harassment complaint – a form of discrimination that the Socreds had not recognized in their legislation – was telling. The case was eventually appealed, and the judge, who was shocked at Edgett's reasoning that harassment was acceptable if the employer harassed all women, overturned the decision. Fields eventually won $1,500 in damages in court (another irony, given that Hanne Jensen also won damages in court in 1971, even though human rights legislation was meant to provide a viable alternative to the courts).

The new structure did have one positive aspect: the Human Rights Council acted as a permanent tribunal, which allowed its members to develop an expertise in human rights. In the past, the individuals who chaired boards of inquiry were replaced by others over time, albeit many of the same people were often reappointed. Otherwise, the situation was bleak. There were 333 unresolved cases from the Human Rights Branch, and another 504 were received within a year. Of these 837 cases, 130 were sent for a hearing and the rest were either withdrawn, dismissed, or pending an investigation (a few were settled informally). By June 1984, inquiries from the public had dropped 63 percent; newly opened files dropped 54 percent; and files the council managed to close had dropped 59 percent. Complainants could appeal to the courts as Andrea Fields had done, but within the first two years only three people had taken that route.[106] Not a single case was sent to the minister to appoint a formal hearing.

The Human Rights Act did not become a precedent. The human rights state remained relatively unchanged outside British Columbia, and a new NDP government introduced legislation in 1996. For those intervening years, 1984 to 1996, British Columbia's human rights state was the black sheep in Canada. Whereas the province had boasted a progressive and innovative system for human rights adjudication under the Human Rights Code, no one sought to emulate the seriously flawed Human Rights Act. The politics surrounding the human rights legislation was as significant as the law itself in defining the scope and breath of the human rights state.

Conclusion

ROSEMARY BROWN (NDP): *There isn't a member on the floor of this House who hasn't had, coming through their constituency office door or over their constituency telephone, representations from welfare recipients who have told them that they have been refused accommodation because they are in receipt of income assistance.*

JACK KEMPF (SOCIAL CREDIT): *Wrong again.*

ROSEMARY BROWN: *You're never up in your riding. How can they ever reach you? I get mail from your riding asking if you're still alive. They never see him, Mr. Chairman. There's a big ad running in his constituency newspaper asking if anyone knows the whereabouts of the member for Omineca, he hasn't been seen up there in so long. They describe him as being a tall, slim, handsome gentleman. They've even forgotten what he looks like.*

– Debates of the Legislative Assembly
(*4 May 1984*)

The history of the human rights state in British Columbia is that of two competing visions for human rights law. The Opposition NDP labour critic captured the spirit of this philosophical divide with a private member's bill in 1984 that offered an alternative to the Socred

Human Rights Act. The proposed bill would have replicated the Human Rights Code with some notable additions: a more expansive education mandate; prohibiting discrimination on the basis of sexual orientation, income, language proficiency, and sexual harassment; reporting directly to the legislature, which would also be responsible for appointments to the Human Rights Commission; and empowering the Human Rights Branch to appoint boards of inquiry.[1]

The Socreds' vision was partly a product of their neo-liberal economic policies. From their point of view, human rights policies threatened legitimate business interests and imposed an unnecessary burden on employers. Such policies constituted an excessive form of state regulation that exposed business to unfounded and costly attacks.[2] Under neo-liberalism, as Alex Kirkup and Tony Evans suggest, "legitimate human rights can only be defined as that set of rights that require government abstention from acts that violate the individual's freedom to invest time, capital, and resources in processes of production and exchange."[3] In essence, the Socreds sought to privatize the human rights state. According to one report, the minister of labour suggested that the Better Business Bureau, rather than the government, should educate the public on human rights. In 1984, the government claimed that its new measures would save on costs, but this was doubtful. "Essentially what this government is doing," insisted the editors of the *Vancouver Sun,* "is making a philosophical statement diminishing the freedom of its constituents. It isn't really saving money. The amount of money involved is peanuts in a multibillion-dollar budget, and it's arguable that any small saving in administrative expenses will be more than overtaken by other costs, perhaps not so overt but none the less expensive to society."[4]

The Socred vision was premised on the limited concept of rights that had informed the original anti-discrimination laws of the 1940s and 1950s, and that had long since been abandoned in other jurisdictions. *Vancouver Sun* columnist Vaughn Palmer wrote one of the most insightful analyses of these competing visions amidst the debate surrounding the 1984 legislation.[5] He argued that the two political parties were fundamentally divided over three issues: what constituted an offence, how the law would be enforced, and how complaints should be resolved. For the Socreds, discrimination was a product of individual behaviour that should be penalized. Discrimination was easily identified, clearly delineated, and blatant or outspoken. For this reason, the government insisted on enumerating all potential grounds for discrimination, creating an agency to receive and adjudicate complaints, and resolving complaints through mediation or a quickly imposed settlement. It is likely, given the predominance of complaints directed at employers, that the Socreds saw human rights legislation as simply another form of labour law.

In contrast, the NDP saw the human rights state as grounded in a unique form of law for people who lacked the resources to seek redress in the courts. Discrimination was largely unseen, rooted in everyday practices, and evolving over time. The NDP vision conceived of an expansive law that lacked loopholes and was proactive and capable of genuine social change; it sought for an enforcement mechanism that was truly independent. Human rights legislation would be capable of confronting systemic discrimination and would focus on prevention rather than punishment. The NDP and the Socreds may have found common ground on a few small issues, such as streamlining procedures to reduce delays, but otherwise, their visions were irreconcilable.

Another distinction between the two parties was in their responses to the international human rights movement. On the one hand, the Socreds and the NDP both used international developments to justify implementing human rights law. The Socreds introduced the original Human Rights Act during the International Year for Human Rights, which was the twentieth anniversary of the Universal Declaration of Human Rights. The NDP marked the declaration's twenty-fifth anniversary with the Human Rights Code. The Socreds cited the International Year for the Disabled (1981) in explaining the inclusion of disability as a prohibited ground for discrimination in the Human Rights Act.[6] Moreover, as noted in Chapter 1, the Socreds initiated several legislative reforms to comply with the United Nations Convention on the Elimination of All Forms of Discrimination against Women.

Still, the Socreds were less responsive than the NDP to international developments. Canada was unable to ratify the United Nations convention until each province agreed to it, and British Columbia was among the last to consent. True, it did enact legal reform to comply with the convention, but it retained several obviously discriminatory statutes until the Charter of Rights and Freedoms forced it to enact additional reforms. During International Women's Year (IWY) in 1975, the NDP introduced several policies to advance women's equality: it established the Office of the Provincial Coordinator for the Status of Women and the Ministry of Education Provincial Advisory Committee on Sex Discrimination, while at the same time committing extensive funding for women's centres, transition houses, rape crisis centres, and research studies on the status of women. The government approved a budget of $200,000 for initiatives associated with IWY.[7] IWY also generated some debate in the legislature on the failure of equal pay laws in the province and contributed to a heightened awareness of the need to improve its human rights legislation. But before the New Democrats could enact legislative change, they lost the 1975 election, and the Socreds subsequently did nothing. The Status of Women Action Group (SWAG) later criticized the Socreds for refusing even to acknowledge the Federal Advisory Council's IWY Plan for Action.[8] SWAG was especially disappointed with the lack of any legal reform in British Columbia arising from IWY.[9] Moreover, within a year, the Socreds abolished the coordinator and the Advisory Committee, and later reduced funding for services. According to SWAG, the years 1975 to 1978 saw "a diminishing emphasis placed by the BC government on ensuring equal opportunity and rights for women in our society."[10]

In this way, international developments had an impact in British Columbia, but the domestic political context was a crucial determining factor. During IWY, SWAG held a march in Victoria to call for human rights legal reform. In 1976, the VSW used International Human Rights Day (10 December) to organize a day of mourning to protest government interference with human rights enforcement. The Socreds, however, dismissed these and similar actions. In 1984, they ignored the federal government's warnings that the proposed Human Rights Act might violate Canada's international human rights treaty commitments. Nowhere else in Canada were two competing views of the human rights state more polarized than in British Columbia.

These conflicting visions raise an interesting question: Why was the NDP's human rights regime more effective at responding to human rights violations? The Socreds' 1969 Human Rights Act depended on an unwieldy enforcement mechanism. In contrast, the Human Rights Code created a government branch dedicated to advancing human rights, which facilitated the expansion of the human rights state. It also incorporated an educational mandate for prevention, which was lacking in the Socreds' 1969 and 1984 statutes. It is also worth noting the predominance of sex discrimination complaints after 1972. The Socreds' precedent-setting ban on sex discrimination applied only to employment, and as Hanne Jensen quickly discovered, it was a poor vehicle for addressing even the most blatant forms of workplace discrimination against women. Under the Human Rights Code, however, complaints involving sex discrimination dominated the branch's operations. Social developments during the period help explain this change. By the 1970s, mobilization among feminists had reached a historic high, and the women's movement had become immensely influential. As more women entered the workforce and politics, the issue of sex discrimination gained greater prominence. Many feminist social movement organizations were responsible for legal reform, complaints to the branch, and promoting awareness of the law.

Finally, perhaps the most significant factor was the selection of those who administered human rights law. At their best, the Socreds appointed a career civil servant, Jack Sherlock, who had little interest in human rights and no experience with discrimination, either professionally or personally. At worst, the Socreds recruited individuals such as Jim Edgett who were indifferent, if not opposed, to the law. In contrast, Kathleen Ruff and Shelagh Day were instrumental in overhauling the human rights legal system and inviting women (and men) to file complaints. Both had been active in the women's movement, and they brought their passion, experience, and commitment to the job. After replacing Sherlock, Ruff acted quickly to negotiate an equal pay settlement with the Department of Health. This was the first class-action human rights case in British Columbia. Ruff did not share Sherlock's passive approach to the human rights state. Rather, she guided the branch toward complaints that would have a widespread impact. Human rights, she believed, were about social justice, not individual complaints. For years she resisted intense pressure and criticism from the Socreds. When the attorney general refused to provide legal counsel for the Gay Alliance Towards Equality case, Ruff went behind his back and convinced a private lawyer to work for the branch pro bono. She also resisted pressure from the minister of health to speak at a meeting of female hospital workers and, in the end, convinced them to submit an equal pay complaint. Unlike Sherlock, Ruff occasionally initiated complaints, often against employers who refused to hire women or who paid them less than male staff who did similar work. Ruff encouraged the Human Rights Commission to be proactive, and when the Socreds stocked it with lame ducks, she publicly criticized its members. She also laid the groundwork for expanding the human rights state by creating a wide-ranging infrastructure: she opened field offices and hired dozens of investigators, simplified complaint forms, reached out to employers' associations and advocacy groups, promoted the branch and the principles of the legislation through the radio, print, and television media, and directed the branch to develop its own educational materials when the Human Rights Commission failed to produce a human rights program.

Moreover, Ruff's decision to hire equally committed human rights investigators was as pivotal as her own appointment. Shelagh Day, the first human rights officer in the province, was at the forefront of developing new procedures for receiving and investigating complaints. The legislation was new, and Day worked with Ruff to encourage others to interpret it broadly. During this formative period for the human rights state, key precedents were established. Day contributed to how the branch defined discrimination, trained human rights officers, interpreted the law, implemented policies, and applied analytical models. Branch officers pursued complaints and provided boards of inquiry with cases to clarify the law on issues such as neutral practices. They were also responsible for resolving thousands of informal complaints that never went to a board of inquiry. Unlike industrial relations officers, Day was committed to working with complainants to challenge discriminatory practices. And many other lesser-known individuals, such as Alan Andison, Hugh McLeod, and Linda Sproule-Jones, were also essential to this process. The turnover rate among investigators was low. As April Katz discovered soon after arriving in Victoria, the staff at the Human Rights Branch were among the most dedicated civil servants working for a human rights agency in Canada.

Human Rights as State Policy

Vancouver's Lone Star Hotel had a reputation for not serving Aboriginals in its bar. Fred Arrance and Veronica Butler, both Aboriginal, decided to test its ban and file a human rights complaint. Their first attempt was on 15 July 1982. When they tried to enter the bar, they were blocked by the doorman, who told them that there was a five-dollar cover charge. They left and documented the incident. Five days later, they returned, accompanied this time by Arrance's sister Lorraine and his white friend John Turvey. Turvey stood across from the hotel to observe the other three enter it. The entire episode took only five minutes.

Although it was a quiet afternoon and the bar was almost empty, the doorman hurried over to intercept the Arrances and Butler. He insisted that the bar was reserved for members and that they should return the next day to speak to the manager. Lorraine Arrance spoke briefly with him, but he soon asked brusquely, "Are you going to go or do I have to throw you out?" At this point, John Ferry, who was seated near the entrance and who had witnessed the incident, attempted to intervene. He suggested that the Arrances and Butler join him at his table, but Lorraine Arrance shook her head and said they were not allowed to come in. The three left the bar. Ferry, who was white, also happened to be a journalist for the *Vancouver Province*. He had agreed to participate in the test case. Identifying himself as a reporter, he asked the doorman why he had refused entry to the three Aboriginals. The doorman replied that "the guy was so drunk he couldn't stand up." Ferry pointed out that this was not accurate, but the doorman retorted that drunken Indians were not welcome in the bar, which was trying to clean up its image.

A board of inquiry was held two months later in Vancouver. Ferry confirmed Arrance and Butler's testimony: he himself had entered the bar without hindrance; the three Aboriginals were told they must be members; they had left after the doorman, who was a large individual, threatened to throw them out; and the entire episode had been staged. In his closing testimony, Ferry stated "that the barman was perfectly friendly to me. It struck me how friendly he was to me and how discourteous he was to the Indians." When asked how she felt about the incident, Butler said that the experience had been painful even though she had expected it: "I knew that I was going to feel bad but it never occurred to me that I would feel so terrible ... And people got to watch us be treated that way ... Like they didn't care I was a person, that just because I'm an Indian means it's ok. They can throw me out of a bar." Fred Arrance was even more blunt: "I didn't feel good at all. Because I didn't feel these people had any right refusing me entry in that place because I was a native Indian and I wasn't drunk." When asked why they went to such lengths to organize a test case and pursue a complaint, Butler stated that she did not want the hotel to be punished: "Not necessarily punished. I want them to realize because I'm a native is no reason to have them act in this way. The colour of my skin should not make any difference in the way they treat me as a human being."

A human rights officer had initially attempted conciliation, but the Lone Star manager, Merwyn Tyer, fought the charge. His defence at the hearing was that the Arrances and Butler were poorly dressed and thus transgressed the bar's dress code. (All three had been casually dressed; Fred wore jeans, boots, a white shirt that was tucked in, and a jean jacket.) As was true of so many complaints, Tyer did not fit the stereotype of an unthinking racist. Witnesses testified that the bar did sometimes serve Aboriginal people, and there had never been a complaint against it. Tyer insisted that he believed in treating everyone equally, regardless of his or her race or ethnicity. He even produced a character reference from a high officer with B'nai Brith International. The inquiry chairman, Eric D. Powell, quickly discounted the dress code defence and concluded that, though the hotel did not demonstrate a systematic bias against Aboriginal people, it had rejected the Arrances and Butler because they were Aboriginal. He ordered the hotel to stop refusing service to Aboriginals and awarded the complainants a symbolic five hundred dollars in damages.[11]

Forcing a recalcitrant hotel to serve Aboriginals in its bar was hardly a ground-breaking achievement. And yet, the actions of the Arrances and Butler had profound implications and offer some insight into the fundamental nature of the human rights state. The three complainants went to great lengths to organize a test case and to work within the boundaries of the law. Lorraine Arrance stated at the hearing that they were indifferent to a financial award. In addition to recruiting a journalist, they dedicated time and effort – and suffered the humiliation of rejection – to test the bar. Why? Because, as Fred Arrance explained during the hearing, "I didn't feel these people had any right refusing me entry in that place because I was a native Indian." Arrance was asserting his human rights through the law, and what he sought was not material gain but recognition of his dignity as a human being. In fact, almost no one identified in this book pursued a human rights case for financial gain or, in many cases, even for their own benefit. Norene Warren had rented another house by the time her complaint had been processed. Jean Tharpe had quit her job with Lornex. Rather, they sought social justice. The symbolism of the Lone Star case, and the potential message it would convey to others, motivated Fred and Lorraine Arrance to walk into a bar with their friend Veronica Butler, knowing that they would be thrown out.

In this way, human rights legislation was innovative law. The original anti-discrimination statutes, which were poorly enforced, addressed only racial, ethnic, and religious discrimination. Still, they were important first steps in developing social policy premised on a new role for the state. Walter Tarnopolsky, the first Canadian scholar who systematically studied human rights law, offered a philosophical foundation to justify expanding state regulation through anti-discrimination law:

> If one asserts unlimited freedom of contract, and right to property, then clearly one enjoys the privilege of choosing whom to work with, whom to hire and whom to associate with. As long as one's choice is limited to purely private relationships, the law cannot interfere. However, when a private feeling of prejudice shifts to the realm of discriminatory practices in such public activities as employment, public accommodation, and even rental and sale of real property, then the law has the right to require compliance with certain standards of fair play. In other words, human rights legislation cannot eliminate bigotry and prejudice, but it can put an end to the public manifestation of such feelings which result in discrimination.[12]

Many politicians and legal experts in the 1950s believed that discrimination was not a social problem or that the state was incapable of legislating "morality." Soon, it became painfully apparent that anti-discrimination legislation was ineffective in practice. As Tarnopolsky explains, these laws continued

> to place the whole emphasis of promoting human rights legislation upon the individual who has suffered the most, and who is often in the least advantageous position to help himself. It does place the administrative machinery of the state at the disposal of the victim of discrimination, but it approaches the whole problem as if it were solely his problem and his responsibility.[13]

As a result, few complaints were received, and there was little enforcement. For this reason, a more robust human rights state was created, beginning in the 1960s.

Human rights legislation produced an adjudication system for complaints that was more accessible, affordable, and efficient than that of earlier anti-discrimination laws. And British Columbia led many of these innovations. Boards of inquiry established key precedents and, in doing so, created new law. Thousands of informal settlements were negotiated under the Human Rights Code. The scope of the human rights state expanded far beyond race, religion, and age to include sex, place of origin, nationality, physical and mental disability, sexual harassment, pregnancy, marital status, pardoned criminal conviction, sexual orientation, and family status. Even when the NDP found it politically unpalatable to ban discrimination on the basis of sexual orientation, a board of inquiry used the reasonable cause section to do it anyway. Human rights law therefore facilitated legal reform when, in the context of the 1970s, it was impossible politically. That the human rights state was designed to promote tolerance, rather than to be solely punitive, is evidenced in the education mandate. Instead of focusing solely on punishing individuals, human rights law sought to encourage tolerance and understanding through education and conciliation.

It is impressive that, with no real enforcement mechanism, the seemingly minor anti-discrimination laws of the 1950s evolved so dramatically. In fact, Canada eventually produced the most sophisticated human rights legal regime in the world. Its human rights laws applied to both state policy and private social practice. Each jurisdiction had a mandate for education. The human rights state moved beyond the major urban areas. In British

Columbia, human rights officers worked throughout the province, from Prince Rupert in the north to rural areas in the West Kootenays. Resistance to human rights legislation certainly did occur, especially in organizations that represented employers, but opposition to the principle of human rights legislation was generally muted. Even the Social Credit government never contemplated eliminating the legislation altogether.

The success of the human rights state relied a great deal on non-state actors. Social movement groups played multiple roles in implementing human rights law: campaigning for human rights legislation and, later, for reforms (or against regressive reforms); drafting legislation; enforcing the law; promoting awareness of the legislation and the issues; keeping the government accountable; acting as a liaison between human rights agencies and the community; and training human rights staff or providing a pool of recruits for human rights agencies. Studies of human rights commissions in Newfoundland, Nova Scotia, Ontario, and Saskatchewan have reached similar conclusions.[14] According to Rosanna Langer, the Ontario Human Rights Commission has historically relied on social movement organizations "to carry out field research and bring instances of discrimination to its attention. These groups continued to provide human rights expertise and play a collaborative role in advancing rights discourse in the community at large."[15]

Social movement associations, especially the Vancouver Status of Women, were implicated in almost every aspect of the human rights state. The Human Rights Branch and boards of inquiry were staffed by individuals who were recruited from advocacy groups, and officers in rural areas actively sought out community organizations. Social movement bodies also shaped the legislation. The Vancouver Civic Unity Council probably convinced the government to create the first Human Rights Act in 1969. When the NDP decided to overhaul the legislation, it depended heavily on the British Columbia Civil Liberties Association to draft the Human Rights Code. A decade later, most of the Human Rights Commission's recommendations for legal reform were based on what it heard from social movement organizations throughout the province. In fact, the commission was so convinced that social movement groups were integral to the human rights state that it provided them with thousands of dollars in funding for awareness and education programs. It initiated a few programs itself, but by and large it decided to work through social movement organizations to fulfill its education mandate.

If there is any doubt regarding the significance of human rights law as social policy, one need only consider how forcefully women mobilized around the human rights state. Legal and social discrimination, as documented in Chapter 1, was clearly widespread. When the first human rights laws banned sex discrimination, federal and provincial law was rife with inequitable provisions, from forcing married women to use their husband's surname to bans on military service. Employment discrimination, whether in refusing to hire women as taxi drivers or assuming that they could not operate a bus, was common. Canadian women used human rights law to fight discrimination, and it became overwhelmingly associated with gender during this period. In 1976, the Human Rights Branch conducted a survey of newspaper stories relating to human rights law since 1974. It examined even the smallest, most remote papers in the province as well as major papers across Canada. It found that when the media wrote about human rights, they were almost always writing about women's issues.[16] During this period, it was impossible to dissociate human rights from women's rights. The largest number of complaints and boards of inquiry dealt with sex discrimination, and they were often successful: between 1956 and 1984, the success rate for sex discrimination complaints that reached boards of inquiry in Canada was 66.4 percent (and 75.0 percent for cases involving pregnancy).[17] Women used the law to extend its protections to women who were pregnant, unmarried, single mothers, or sexually harassed. For some women, the complaints process provided an affirmation of their legitimate demands for equality. Human rights law also had symbolic value. Initially, the media mocked attempts to legislate bans on sex discrimination, but over time it was increasingly accepted as a genuine social problem. True, most of those who benefitted from the law were white-collar women living in urban centres. Nevertheless, there were many women like Jean Tharpe and Janice Foster – working in sparsely populated northern towns – who benefitted from the human rights state. At the very least, invoking a human rights law was far better than depending on the courts.

In a sense, the human rights state was revolutionary: it replaced a legal system that explicitly discriminated against women with one that banned discrimination in the private and public spheres. Thousands of individuals used it to end inequitable practices.

The Human Rights State and Social Change: Systemic Discrimination

However, the human rights state was not transformative. In other words, human rights law had some notable limitations. The success of the human rights state should be measured against its deficiencies in practice. Perhaps the most visible manifestation of its shortfalls was the Socreds' abuse of the law. The Human Rights Branch and Human Rights Commission became marginal departments subsumed within the Ministry of Labour. No board of inquiry could be called without the consent of the minister. When the Social Credit Party was in power, it refused to appoint boards until public pressure forced it to do so. The Socreds reduced staff, closed field offices, were recalcitrant in appointing people to the Human Rights Commission, and cut budgets. The human rights state under the Social Credit administration is a case study of how a government can inhibit the application of law.

Even the NDP's vision for the human rights state was imperfect. Although a human rights investigator could conciliate a dispute in a single day, the more difficult cases might take years. Successful complainants rarely received adequate compensation. The Human Rights Code allowed up to $5,000 in damages, in addition to costs associated with the complaint, but boards of inquiry rarely offered anywhere near that amount. Not all citizens enjoyed equal access. The human rights state continually suffered from lack of resources, especially in rural areas and the North. The relationship between the branch and commission, strained for most of the 1970s, was essentially dysfunctional, and in the end the commission never determined a role for itself. Aboriginal people were poorly represented.[18] Many Aboriginals, such as Yvonne Bill, did employ the machinery of the human rights state to challenge discrimination, but provincial human rights laws did not apply to reserves, which were under federal jurisdiction. Aboriginal people were exempted from the federal Human Rights Act until 2011. The Human Rights Code contained numerous exemptions, including for philanthropic, charitable, religious, and educational institutions. Finally, the weakness of its equal pay section was all the evidence anyone needed to see that the law had limits.

In this regard, British Columbia differed little from other jurisdictions in Canada. Delays, lack of funding, weak remedies, and a focus on individual complaints characterized the human rights state throughout the country.[19] Certainly, the BC Socreds did not have a monopoly on making ridiculous appointments. Writing in the late 1980s, Ruff described appointees to many human rights commissions in Canada as "cheering parties for the powerful and privileged, not defenders of the disadvantaged."[20] During the 1980s, appointees to the federal Human Rights Commission had strong ties to the Progressive Conservative Party, and although they had no expertise at all in human rights, Ruff wryly pointed out that many of them did "profess to have excellent health and a record of athletic accomplishments."[21] And British Columbia was hardly alone in refusing to prohibit discrimination on the basis of sexual orientation. Except in Quebec, bitter debates raged in the provinces – especially Alberta, Newfoundland, and Ontario – regarding whether sexual orientation should be added to the human rights law.[22]

Among the most controversial aspects of the Human Rights Code was the process for selecting boards of inquiry. Most jurisdictions assigned this task to the minister of labour. In Alberta, politics shaped the Lougheed government's 1971 decision that the commission would report to a minister. The Lougheed Conservatives had recently come to power and were concerned about the Opposition Social Credit Party's hostility to human rights legislation. As Premier Peter Lougheed later explained, "We made a commitment of our government on human rights. We wanted to be in control of the process and that would include the question of the appointment of the people to serve, so we felt it should be in the government, not within the orbit of the Legislature."[23] Years afterward, Ron Ghitter, the minister who had introduced the legislation, lamented that it did not require the commission to report to the legislature, because subsequent governments had interfered with its operations. To be sure, no government in Canada had ever abused its power as much as the Socreds did in British Columbia. In fact, during the 1980s, several provinces shifted the responsibility for appointing formal inquiries to an independent body.[24]

Such procedural failures restricted the potential of the human rights state to enable transformative social change. But an even more fundamental flaw existed from the beginning: its inability to fully address systemic discrimination. Initially, anti-discrimination legislation required proof of intent, and it applied only in cases of declared and explicit acts of discrimination (for instance, an employment centre that posted advertisements for whites only). Later, under human rights legislation, intent became irrelevant. Individuals were found guilty if their actions had a discriminatory effect. Moreover, discrimination was no longer restricted to direct acts.[25] Seemingly neutral policies, such as arbitrary height and weight requirements, were also inequitable because they indirectly excluded entire classes of people.[26]

Systemic discrimination, however, is far more insidious. Consider, for example, women in the legal profession. Jean Leiper's study abounds with what she calls "unwritten codes" that affect them. She describes a set of factors, such as "expectations about hours on the job, access to the best files, informal meetings, or unspoken views about pregnancy and childbirth," that serve to exclude them from positions of influence. Leiper recounts a story of how pregnant female lawyers were obliged to pool the robes of an obese male lawyer for their appearances in a Toronto courthouse because no one made robes to fit pregnant women. This was a telling instance of exclusionary practices that were neither discriminatory on the surface nor even intentional. Nonetheless, their effect on a group of people solely due to their gender was the same.[27] Discrimination is systemic when a

> person who is most often discriminated against as a member of a group, encumbered by the stereotypes and assumptions of his or her society about that group ... encounters behaviour which has become systematized and institutionalized, and who cannot be equal unless the negative burdens of this social and political context are removed. Nor can the burdens, according to this view, be removed for one individual; because of their nature, they must be removed for the group as a whole.[28]

Systemic inequalities "are endemic to the social, economic, and political order ... Dominant groups, their world views and their interests are entrenched and normalized as unstated standards against which Otherness is (re) marked as different."[29] Sex discrimination also emerges from patriarchal norms, stereotypes, and common sense notions about gender. For example, the Human Rights Code prohibited school boards from refusing to hire women as janitors – it did not prohibit schools from using textbooks in which only men were portrayed as janitors. Women were therefore excluded from opportunities available to men, partly because people refused to hire them as janitors (or lawyers, engineers, soldiers), but also because they themselves were not applying for jobs that they identified as reserved for men. Discrimination, even when directed at an individual in an identifiable group, also affects those members of the group who observe or know of the behaviour. Every incident compounds and affects the group, and resonates among its members because the treatment is familiar and common. In this way, the human rights state did not address the root causes of gender inequality. Shelagh Day offers a similar point about social norms, discrimination, and rights:

> Stereotypes and assumptions about particular groups have become embedded in practices. Left unchallenged, these practices perpetuate the exclusion of the group from opportunities which should be available to them ... Discrimination against these groups is ubiquitous. It occurs in the family,

Conclusion

in school, in culture, in employment, in politics, in personal interactions, and in the justice system, forming layers of oppression.[30]

A main reason why Canadian human rights legislation failed to address systemic discrimination was because it was constructed to respond to individual complaints. The Human Rights Code allowed the commission to initiate complaints, but this rarely occurred, and most of the branch's work involved responding to individual complaints. Human rights legislation was not proactive. Kathleen Ruff was especially critical of it for being negative legislation:

> It lists what shall not be done. Human rights agencies are set up to come into action after discrimination has occurred and have as their role to find evidence to prove the violation and then to seek a settlement rectifying the matter. The disadvantages of this approach are manifold: One, the major efforts of human rights agencies are spent in a mop-up operation after discrimination has already occurred. Two, attitudes tend to polarize and a climate of confrontation to develop when an allegation of discrimination is filed ... Human rights legislation requires that substantial evidence be obtained to prove that discrimination did occur ... Great pressure is placed on the complainant.[31]

A genuine substantive equality approach designed to counteract systemic discrimination must provide ameliorative measures rather than simply offering redress to individuals.[32]

After serving as director of the Human Rights Branch, Ruff went on to have a distinguished career as a leading expert on human rights law in Canada. She continued to lament that Canadian laws were unable to address systemic discrimination and came to believe that the focus on individual complaints was a fundamental flaw of the human rights state:

> This has a number of negative consequences. It means that discrimination is envisioned and investigated as a particular incident or set of incidents affecting an individual, rather than a systemic, broad-based practice affecting a whole group. Likewise, the remedy tends to be individual based. In addition, persons from disadvantaged groups who file human rights complaints tend to be the ones who have more resources and knowledge. The average member of a protected group is likely to be more disadvantaged and consequently less likely to come forward to file a complaint. Few complaints

are filed from persons who are doubly disadvantaged, such as minority women or disabled women. Few complaints come forward from people who are poor. Few complaints come from members of First Nations. Yet we all know that these are the very people who encounter the severest and most frequent discrimination in our society.[33]

Shelagh Day was awarded the Order of Canada for her human rights work. Her extensive knowledge and experience with human rights law led her to conclude that its transformative potential was undermined by human rights agencies' passive approach to receiving complaints:

> As it functions today, our human rights law is a dispute resolution system which best serves individuals. It is not an active transformational mechanism, but a complaint-based one. The assumption underlying this complaint-based mechanism is that if the inequality is important enough, the victim of it will complain. Only the discrimination complained of requires redress; any other discrimination is insignificant. The complaint-based system also assumes that we have equality now. It is only the lapses from it which will be complained of and remedied by the law. Since, unfortunately, we do not have equality now, the current human rights system is rooted in error. By itself, then, the present human rights system is not a transformational mechanism and cannot achieve equality in Canada.[34]

In effect, the human rights state failed to address patterns of entrenched discrimination. It was grounded in a complaints-driven process that *reacted* to complaints brought by *individuals*.[35]

At the same time, social and economic inequities extended into the arbitration process. Formal inquiries were designed as neutral negotiations between complainants and the accused, but because the accused had the advantage of time, prestige, money, and resources to defend themselves, complainants found themselves in the same powerless position that had made them targets of discrimination in the first place. In effect, inquiries replicated the disparities of society. The apparent neutrality of the human rights state reproduced the same inequalities of the society that it served (this was precisely the branch's criticism of the decision in Yvonne Bill's case). Because there were no provisions for class-action human rights cases, the human rights state could not address job ghettos (such as all-white fire departments) or offer collective remedies. Boards of inquiry could not impose equal opportunity (affirmative action) programs or engage in a complaint on behalf of an entire category of people.[36]

The Vancouver Women's Caucus lobbied in 1969 to have childcare added to the Human Rights Act. Human rights legislation, though, was never designed to deal with the inequitable distribution of wealth.[37] Quebec was the only province to include economic and social rights in its human rights legislation, although in practice few people availed themselves of these sections. The British Columbia Human Rights Commission did not even address economic and social rights when it recommended extensive amendments to the Human Rights Code in 1983.[38] Poverty among Aboriginal people, the disabled, and single mothers, or lower educational attainment among African Canadians, were not violations of human rights law. And yet, the impact of economic and social inequalities was similar to that of discrimination prohibited under the law: individuals had fewer opportunities because they belonged to a certain class of people.

The failure of human rights law to address systemic inequality was exacerbated by its focus on individual complaints and a clearly defined list of grounds. Every board of inquiry in British Columbia throughout the period of this study focused on a single issue, such as sex or race, and never engaged with the intersection of these factors. In the 1980s, feminists began to advance a more nuanced understanding of discrimination – intersectionality – that further highlighted the weakness of the human rights state. An intersectional analysis recognizes that reducing discrimination to one factor, such as sex, fails to account for how some individuals experience it.[39] Someone might be discriminated against, not because she is a woman or disabled, but because she is a disabled woman.[40] This reality was exacerbated under human rights laws, which defined discrimination through a catalogue of independently enumerated grounds.[41] Adjudicators were encouraged to examine a case through a single lens (including cases that involved multiple grounds), and complainants were obliged to define themselves in narrow terms: "In essence, the categorical structure of equality rights requires those injured through relations of inequality to caricaturize both themselves and their experiences of inequality, in order to succeed with a legal claim."[42] As a result, inquiries might misunderstand the causes of discriminatory acts or the nature of the harm (harm is compounded as a result of multiple factors); remedies might be affected; victims might be forced to frame their complaints in ways that do not reflect their actual experiences; and the case might be dismissed because adjudicators fail to account for the underlying cause.[43] An intersectional approach would force human rights adjudicators to consider the socio-economic context and histories of oppression that lead to human rights violations. Such an approach would be better situated to address systemic discrimination.

Justice Rosalie Abella's 1984 royal commission report on employment equity affirmed a growing trend toward substantive equality. Abella was critical of the human rights legislative model as it existed in 1984:

> This approach to the enforcement of human rights, based as it is on individual rather than group remedies, and perhaps confined to allegations of intentional discrimination, cannot deal with the pervasiveness and subtlety of discrimination ... Neither, by itself, can education. Education has been the classic crutch upon which we lean in the hopes of coaxing change in prejudicial attitudes. But education is an unreliable agent, glacially slow in movement and impact, and often completely ineffective in the face of intractable views. It promises no immediate relief despite the immediacy of the injustice.[44]

Abella's report began with a plea for a broader approach to rights adjudication that addressed systemic discrimination: "The systemic approach acknowledges that by and large the systems and practices we customarily and often unwittingly adopt may have an unjustifiably negative effect on certain groups in society. The effect of the system on the individual or group, rather than its attitudinal sources, governs whether or not a remedy is justified."[45] She did not recommend quotas. Rather, she called for widespread reform to public and private employment practices to systemically eliminate barriers to marginalized groups.[46] A year later, the Supreme Court of Canada upheld the concept of systemic discrimination, and several provinces addressed it in their human rights legislation.[47] British Columbia, New Brunswick, and Saskatchewan had also begun to promote affirmative action programs through human rights legislation.

Several jurisdictions amended their human rights laws in the 1980s to incorporate a mandate to investigate systemic discrimination.[48] But the economic recession led to extensive government cutbacks. Investigations into systemic discrimination were long and costly, and during a period of fiscal restraint *individual* complaints dominated the human rights agenda. As Howe and Johnson note, "financial constraints are compelling some provincial commissions to re-evaluate their support of systemic initiatives ... The critical factor is held to be the amount of time, effort, and funding required to assess and demonstrate systemic discrimination."[49] Shelagh Day went even further. Writing in 1990, she attributed the failure to address systemic discrimination to a traditional focus on individual complaints and the difficulties in shifting directions; commissions bogged down in time-consuming individual complaints; lack of resources; lack of proper skills training (such as statistical analysis) to deal with the nature of systemic complaints; and a lack of interest on the part of the human rights bureaucracy.[50]

As Maxine Molyneux and Shahra Razavi observe, Western human rights norms have historically been based on a "false universalism": states have failed to recognize women's difference as a basis for unequal treatment.[51] Human rights legislation in Canada "did not acknowledge underlying factors such as socialization, family structures, and the like, which effectively excluded women from full and equal participation in the community ... [When] women's new rights were not accompanied by the conditions that allowed them to be exercised, they meant little in practice."[52] Prohibitions on employment discrimination, for example, were undermined by limited access to childcare (especially in rural areas). Human rights laws conceived of equality as equal treatment or treating people in the same manner. Equal pay is a perfect example of the flaw in this way of thinking. Human rights laws prohibited differential pay for similar work, even though most women did not do the same work as men, but were instead concentrated in separate professions with lower pay.[53] Recent scholarship on human rights law in Canada has also been critical of attempts to determine discrimination by employing universal (male) standards. The trend of using comparator groups has led to decisions where, for example, women on maternity leave have been denied benefits because they were compared with male workers who were also on leave. Such an analysis ignores the obvious reality that women alone carry the burden of bearing children.[54] The comparator approach focuses on universal standards rather than the particular circumstances of each case, and in doing so it often ignores substantive equality. As Andrea Wright explains,

> The comparator group approach is an artificial, formalist search for a comparable "other," which leads to unpredictable results, in part because there are myriad ways to reasonably articulate a basis of comparison, and in part because the approach often neglects the gravamen of the complaint and the objective of substantive equality. Put simply, it is easy to get the choice of comparator group wrong, it is easy to reasonably justify several different comparator group choices, and it is easy to lose sight of the objective of substantive equality when searching for comparisons based on formalistic assessments of sameness and difference.[55]

Legal equality is insufficient. It does not change the legacy of generations of discrimination or its inter-generational effects. In 1980, a survey conducted by Gene Errington of approximately two hundred women, which focused on sexual harassment in the workplace, found that the subjects had little faith in the human rights state. Of all the possible solutions to harassment at work, legislation was less popular than education and encouraging women to be more assertive at work.[56] Janet Beebe, in a report for the Vancouver Status of Women in 1978, warned women about placing too much faith in legal reform: "People who expect [law] to change the status of women in society or alter their socio-economic status are insane ... What is necessary is an overall change in the attitude of people and that has to be done through education and through women actually doing their jobs people thought they would never do."[57] A transformational human rights agenda would go beyond formal equality and change institutional structures and practice.

This is not to say that the human rights state was a failure. The life stories recounted in this book are a testament to how human rights law affected women's lives in British Columbia. Rather than a failure, it was simply limited in its inability to prompt the state to promote a transformative human rights agenda. Abstract legal rights have the potential to mobilize a broad range of advocates for social change, but as Judy Fudge argues, "the significance of the assertion of a right depends upon the social vision or politics which informs it."[58] A transformative human rights jurisprudence "acknowledges rather than ignores the significant disparities in power, resources, social capital, and normative legitimacy that skew workplace disputes between complainant employees and respondent employers, and hold deeply embedded social inequalities in place."[59] The NDP's Women's Rights Committee lamented that its own party implemented virtually no policies for women while it was in office. In fact, the committee could think of just one major legislative initiative for women that the NDP had introduced between 1972 and 1975: the Human Rights Code.[60]

A society organized around principles of justice and equality cannot realize these principles solely through human rights law. Significant advances for women's equality were gained through the human rights state, but they were limited, restricted, and open to abuse. Human rights law is the first step toward a solution, not the solution itself.

Human rights are the beginning, not the end.

Notes

Introduction

1. University of British Columbia Rare Books and Special Collections, Vancouver (UBC RBSC), Vancouver Status of Women (VSW), v.2, f.33, Jacqueline Frances Culley and the Canadian Airline Flight Attendants Association v Canadian Pacific Airlines, 1976.
2. In addition, men were paid more money, and even the most junior male attendant was given priority over the most senior female employee. UBC RBSC, VSW, v.1, f.4, Air Canada Stewardesses fact sheet, 7 February 1974.
3. Joan Sangster, "Debating Maternity Rights: Pacific Western Airlines and Flight Attendants' Struggle to 'Fly Pregnant' in the 1970s," in *Work on Trial: Canadian Labour Law Struggles*, ed. Judy Fudge and Eric Tucker (Toronto: University of Toronto Press, 2010), 283-58.
4. *R. v. Pacific Western Ltd.*, [1975] 58 B.C.J. 2.
5. Sangster, "Debating Maternity Rights," 294-95.
6. *Canada Labour Code*, R.S.C. 1970, c. L-I, s. 59.4.
7. Sangster, "Debating Maternity Rights," 298.
8. *Culley and Canadian Airline Flight Attendants Association v. Canadian Pacific Airlines*, [1977] 1 W.W.R. 393.
9. Sangster, "Debating Maternity Rights," 302-3.
10. Jack Donnelly, *Universal Human Rights in Theory and Practice* (New York: Cornell University Press, 2003), 1.
11. This definition of human rights was offered in E.J. Hobsbawm, "Labour and Human Rights," in *Worlds of Labour: Further Studies in the History of Labour*, ed. E.J. Hobsbawm (London: Weidenfeld and Nicolson, 1984), 297.
12. For a detailed discussion of universal human rights principles, see Chapter 1 of Evelyn Kallen, *Ethnicity and Human Rights in Canada: A Human Rights Perspective on Ethnicity, Racism and Systemic Inequality* (Don Mills: Oxford University Press, 2003). Henry Shue makes a case for a set of "basic rights" – from which all other rights are derived or made possible – that includes physical security and subsistence, as well as freedom of movement

and participation. Henry Shue, *Basic Rights: Subsistence, Affluence and US Foreign Policy* (Princeton: Princeton University Press, 1996).

13 See, for instance, Nitya Duclos, "Disappearing Women: Racial Minority Women in Human Rights Cases," *Canadian Journal of Women and the Law* 6 (1993): 25-51; Diane Pothier, "Connecting Grounds of Discrimination to Real People's Real Experiences," *Canadian Journal of Women and the Law* 13 (2001): 37-73; and Kamini Steinberg, "The Ontario Human Rights Code: Implications for an Intersectional Approach to Human Rights Claims" (Master's thesis, University of Toronto, 2009).

14 Becki L. Ross, *Burlesque West: Showgirls, Sex and Sin in Postwar Vancouver* (Toronto: University of Toronto Press, 2009).

15 R. Brian Howe, "Incrementalism and Human Rights Reform," *Journal of Canadian Studies* 28 (1993): 29-44.

16 James W. St. G. Walker, "The 'Jewish Phase' in the Movement for Racial Equality in Canada," *Canadian Ethnic Studies* 34 (2002): 1.

17 Mary Cornish, Fay Faraday, and Jo-Anne Pickel, *Enforcing Human Rights in Ontario* (Aurora: Canada Law Books, 2009), 39.

18 Doris Anderson, *Rebel Daughter: An Autobiography* (Toronto: Key Porter Books, 1996), 173.

19 For an explanation of this, see Chapter 1 of Samuel Moyn, *The Last Utopia: Human Rights in History* (Boston: Belknap Press of Harvard University Press, 2010).

20 Nelson Lichtenstein, "The Rights Revolution," *New Labor Forum* 12 (2003): 61-73; Joseph A. McCartin, "Democratizing the Demand for Workers' Rights," *Dissent* 1 (Winter 2005): 61-68.

21 McCartin, "Democratizing the Demand," 63. According to Nelson Lichtenstein, industrial democracy was premised on the idea that "unionism would bring to the shop and office floor those procedures and standards that had long been venerated in the courts, the legislatures, and at the ballot box." Lichtenstein, "The Rights Revolution," 69.

22 Lichtenstein, "The Rights Revolution," 69. Lichtenstein also states that "in the contemporary American workplace, employers use their free speech rights to hire psychologically sophisticated antiunion consultants, organize procompany employee groups, hold mandatory captive audience meetings, tell workers that the factory will close or wages will decrease if they vote for a union, and spend millions of dollars on all sorts of antiunion propaganda ... Employer antiunionism has become increasingly oriented toward the ostensible protection of the individual rights of workers as against undemocratic unions and restrictive contracts that hamper the free choice of employees." Ibid.

23 Ibid., 68-69, 71.

24 Judy Fudge, "The Effect of Entrenching a Bill of Rights upon Political Discourse: Feminist Demands and Sexual Violence in Canada," *International Journal of the Sociology of Law* 17 (1989): 454.

25 Ibid., 458-59.

26 Dorothy L. Hodgson draws a similar conclusion in the context of gender-based violence: "We need to be alert to the ways in which discourses about gender-based violence and the suffering of women create particular cultural and political subjects, which often accompany and can come to subvert some of the other powerful enabling ideas of human rights. Human Rights positions itself as a neutral field of equality for all. Such a claim of neutrality, however, denies the myriad ways in which ideas about what it means to be a woman, about the proper relations between men and women, about the existence of a private and

a public sphere, for example, structure the demands and expectations of rights." Pamela Scully, "Gender, History, and Human Rights," in *Gender and Culture at the Limits of Rights*, ed. Dorothy L. Hodgson (Philadelphia: University of Pennsylvania Press, 2011), 17.
27 Fudge, "The Effect of Entrenching," 449.
28 Due to this comment, Barrett won the Vancouver Status of Women's first Male Chauvinist Pig Award. UBC RBSC, VSW, v.2, f.1, Male chauvinist pig awards, 1972; Rosemary Brown, *Being Brown: A Very Public Life* (Toronto: Random House, 1989), 131. In 1991, however, the NDP created the first stand-alone Ministry of Women's Equality.
29 There is an extensive literature on how men have exploited the Charter's equality provisions. In many cases, litigation has put feminists on the defensive rather than advancing women's equality. Wiegers's article on custody disputes is an especially fascinating analysis of how a shift toward gender neutrality in law can benefit biological fathers. Wanda Wiegers, "Gender, Biology, and Third Party Custody Disputes," *Alberta Law Review* 47 (2009): 1-37; See also Gwen Brodsky, *Canadian Charter Equality Rights for Women: One Step Forward or Two Steps Back?* (Ottawa: Canadian Advisory Council on the Status of Women, 1989); Hester Lessard, "Mothers, Fathers, and Naming: Reflections on the Law Equality Framework and Trociuk v. British Columbia (Attorney General)," *Canadian Journal of Women and the Law* 16 (2004): 165-211; Susan Boyd, "Is Equality Enough? Fathers' Rights and Women's Rights Advocacy," in *Rethinking Equality Projects in Law: Feminist Challenges*, ed. Rosemary Hunter (Oxford: Hart, 2008), 59-79; Lori Chambers, "Newborn Adoption: Birth Mothers, Genetic Fathers, and Reproductive Autonomy," *Canadian Journal of Family Law* 26 (2010): 339-93; and Lori Chambers, "'In the Name of the Father': Children, Naming Practices, and the Law in Canada," *UBC Law Review* 43 (2010-11): 1-45.
30 Lessard, "Mothers, Fathers, and Naming."
31 Virginia A. Leary pursues a similar argument in the context of workers' rights: "The concept of workers' rights has been given too narrow a focus. We have excluded workers' rights in practice from the broader realm of human rights and we have narrowed the concept of human rights to exclude social rights including workers' rights." Virginia A. Leary, "The Paradox of Human Rights and Workers' Rights," in *Human Rights, Labor Rights, and International Trade*, ed. Lance A. Compa and Stephen F. Diamond (Philadelphia: University of Pennsylvania Press, 2003), 42.
32 As Sally Engel Merry explains, the idea of women's rights (and indigenous rights) indicates how the concept of human rights has changed over time. Women's rights challenge the separation of public and private life. More than any other issue, Merry explains, violence against women instigated the movement to define women's rights as a distinct form of human rights. The state's failure to protect women from violence was construed as a violation of women's human rights. Merry notes that "women's rights are a relatively recent addition to the domain of human rights. Their importance began with the first meetings on women and development in the 1970s. The right to protection from violence is one of the most recently articulated. First discussed as a human rights violation in the late 1980s, this issue expanded enormously in the 1990s. It grew from a focus on rape and battering in intimate relationships to rape and gender violence enacted by states in warfare, torture, and imprisonment as well as during interethnic violence. Trafficking of sex workers, the AIDS pandemic, and particular social practices that have an impact on women such as female genital cutting have recently been defined as instances of violence against women. Thus, the content of women's rights has changed dramatically since 1948, as have human rights more generally." Sally Engel Merry, "Women, Violence, and the Human Rights

System," in *Women, Gender and Human Rights: A Global Perspective,* ed. Marjorie Agosin (Piscataway: Rutgers University Press, 2001), 83.

33 As Marjorie Agosin points out, "most governments as well as nongovernmental organizations (NGOs) define human rights in terms of male models and patterns of thinking. For example, they fail to take issues of health and reproductive freedom, which are often a matter of life and death, into separate account. In the late twentieth century, gender rarely played a role in decisions over the granting of asylum. Gender-based discrimination in times of war or peace has been systematically violated, from rape to being barred from holding high office." Marjorie Agosin, "Introduction," in *Women, Gender and Human Rights: A Global Perspective,* ed. Marjorie Agosin (Piscataway: Rutgers University Press, 2001), 2-3.

34 Wanda Wiegers, "Feminist Protest and the Regulation of Misogynist Speech: A Case Study of *Saskatchewan Human Rights Commission v Engineering Students' Society*," *Ottawa Law Review* 24 (1992): 434.

35 See Paul Gordon Lauren, *The Evolution of International Human Rights: Visions Seen* (Philadelphia: University of Pennsylvania Press, 2011).

36 See Dominique Clément, *Canada's Rights Revolution: Social Movements and Social Change, 1937-82* (Vancouver: UBC Press, 2008).

37 Thomas Risse, Stephen C. Ropp, and Kathryn Sikkink, eds., *The Power of Human Rights: International Norms and Domestic Change* (Cambridge: Cambridge University Press, 1999), 266. The authors show how a process of "normalization" or "socialization" occurred wherein human rights principles became an integral part of international politics.

38 Kenneth Cmiel, "The Recent History of Human Rights," *American Historical Review* 109, 1 (2004): 117-35; Moyn, *The Last Utopia,* 5.

39 Carmela Patrias attributes the dearth of studies on the 1947 Saskatchewan Bill of Rights to the legislation's overall ineffectiveness, its origin as a state-based initiative rather than a product of social mobilization, and the paucity of source material surrounding a measure that lacked any public campaign. Carmela Patrias, "Socialists, Jews, and the 1947 Saskatchewan Bill of Rights," *Canadian Historical Review* 87 (2006): 266.

40 The few book-length studies of Canadian human rights law include Andrée Côté and Lucie Lemonde, *Discrimination et commission des droits de la personne* (Montreal: Éditions Saint-Martin, 1988); Rainer Knopff, *Human Rights and Social Technology: The New War on Discrimination* (Ottawa: Carleton University Press, 1989); Didi Herman, *Rights of Passage: Struggles for Lesbian and Gay Legal Equality* (Toronto: University of Toronto Press, 1994); R. Brian Howe and David Johnson, *Restraining Equality: Human Rights Commissions in Canada* (Toronto: University of Toronto Press, 2000); and Rosanna L. Langer, *Defining Rights and Wrongs: Bureaucracy, Human Rights, and Public Accountability* (Vancouver: UBC Press, 2007).

41 Christopher MacLennan, *Toward the Charter: Canadians and the Demand for a National Bill of Rights, 1929-1960* (Montreal and Kingston: McGill-Queen's University Press, 2003); Janet Ajzenstat, *The Canadian Founding: John Locke and Parliament* (Montreal and Kingston: McGill-Queen's University Press, 2007); Clément, *Canada's Rights Revolution;* Michel Ducharme, *Le concept de liberté au Canada à l'époque des révolutions atlantiques, 1776-1838* (Montreal and Kingston: McGill-Queen's University Press, 2010).

42 Ruth A. Frager and Carmela Patrias, "'This Is Our Country, These Are Our Rights': Minorities and the Origins of Ontario's Human Rights Campaigns," *Canadian Historical Review* 82 (2001): 1-35; Ross Lambertson, "The Dresden Story: Racism, Human Rights,

and the Jewish Labour Committee of Canada," *Labour/Le travail* (Spring 2001): 43-82; Walker, "The 'Jewish Phase'"; Ross Lambertson, *Repression and Resistance: Canadian Human Rights Activists, 1930-1960* (Toronto: University of Toronto Press, 2005); Stephanie Bangarth, *Voices Raised in Protest: Defending North American Citizens of Japanese Ancestry, 1942-49* (Vancouver: UBC Press, 2008). See also Dominique Clément, "An Exercise in Futility? Regionalism, State Funding, and Ideology as Obstacles to the Formation of a National Social Movement Organization in Canada," *BC Studies* 146 (Summer 2005): 63-91; Clément, *Canada's Rights Revolution;* Dominique Clément, "'I Believe in Human Rights, Not Women's Rights': Women and the Human Rights State, 1969-1984," *Radical History Review* 101 (2008): 107-29; Dominique Clément, "Generations and the Transformation of Social Movements in Post-War Canada," *Histoire sociale/Social History* 42 (2009): 361-88; and Shirley Tillotson, "Human Rights Law as Prism: Women's Organizations, Unions, and Ontario's Female Employees Fair Remuneration Act, 1951," *Canadian Historical Review* 72, 4 (1991): 532-57.

43 James W. St. G. Walker, *"Race," Rights and the Law in the Supreme Court of Canada: Historical Case Studies* (Toronto: Wilfrid Laurier University Press, 1997); Miriam Smith, *Lesbian and Gay Rights in Canada: Social Movements and Equality-Seeking, 1971-1995* (Toronto: University of Toronto Press, 1999); Ross Lambertson, "The Black, Brown, White and Red Blues: The Beating of Clarence Clemons," *Canadian Historical Review* 85 (2004): 755-76; Miriam Smith, "Social Movements and Judicial Empowerment: Courts, Public Policy, and Lesbian and Gay Organizing in Canada," *Politics and Society* 33 (2005): 327-53; Patrias, "Socialists, Jews"; Carmela Patrias, "Race, Employment Discrimination, and State Complicity in Wartime Canada, 1939-1945," *Labour/Le travail* 59 (2007): 9-42; Ross Lambertson, "The BC Court of Appeal and Civil Liberties," *BC Studies* 163 (2009): 81-110; Carmela Patrias, *Jobs and Justice: Fighting Discrimination in Wartime Canada, 1939-1945* (Toronto: University of Toronto Press, 2012).

44 Julie A. Mertus, *Human Rights Matters: Local Politics and National Human Rights Institutions* (Stanford: Stanford University Press, 2008), 1.

45 David J. Mitchell, *W.A.C. Bennett and the Rise of British Columbia* (Vancouver: Douglas and McIntyre, 1995), 271.

46 Jean Barman, *The West beyond the West: A History of British Columbia* (Toronto: University of Toronto Press, 1991), 278.

47 On the political history of British Columbia, see Philip Resnick, "Social Democracy in Power: The Case of British Columbia," *BC Studies* 34 (1977): 3-20; Barman, *The West beyond the West,* 272-80, 293-96, 322-27; and Patricia E. Roy and John Herd Thompson, *British Columbia: Land of Promises* (Toronto: Oxford University Press, 2005), 151-70.

48 R. Brian Howe's comparative study of human rights programs in British Columbia and Ontario demonstrates the usefulness of examining provincial programs in a local context. His study is a good example of the need to avoid broad generalizations about the applicability of human rights law in Canada. Howe argues that, in the midst of economic restraint in the 1980s, "Ontario continued to provide a modicum of anti-discrimination protection despite the restraint," whereas the BC system "was dismantled and replaced by the weakest program of human rights protection in Canada. The different developments may be explained by the use of an incrementalist approach to human rights reform in Ontario as opposed to a non-incrementalist one in British Columbia, each in turn reflecting the different political cultures in the two provinces." Howe, "Incrementalism and Human Rights Reform," 29.

49 Ben Isitt, *Militant Minority: British Columbia Workers and the Rise of a New Left, 1948-1972* (Toronto: University of Toronto Press, 2010), 40.
50 Angus McLaren and Arlene Tigar McLaren, *The Bedroom and the State: The Changing Practices and Politics of Contraception and Abortion in Canada, 1880-1997* (Toronto: Oxford University Press, 1997), 58-59.
51 Margaret Hillyard Little, "Claiming a Unique Place: The Introduction of Mothers' Pensions in British Columbia," *BC Studies* 105-6 (1995): 93.
52 Barman, *The West beyond the West*, 303.
53 McLaren and McLaren, *The Bedroom and the State*, 58-59.
54 Clément, "An Exercise in Futility?" On anti-war protests in British Columbia, see Isitt, *Militant Minority*, 124-31.
55 Isitt, *Militant Minority*, 169, 192.
56 Margaret Hillyard Little argues that BC women's groups filled the vacuum left by churches, which were far more active in Ontario in the administration of mothers' allowances. Little, "Claiming a Unique Place," 101.
57 McLaren and McLaren, *The Bedroom and the State*, 58-59.
58 Clément, "'I Believe in Human Rights.'"
59 Jill Vickers, "The Intellectual Origins of the Women's Movements in Canada," in *Challenging Times: The Women's Movement in Canada and the United States*, ed. Constance Backhouse and David H. Flaherty (Montreal and Kingston: McGill-Queen's University Press, 1992), 44.
60 Brown, *Being Brown*, 98. Brown added, "There is a certain political recklessness about British Columbia that is manifest in its ability to support far right and far left parties with equal fervour. The only thing that it lacks is the ability to be middle-of-the-road. The women's movement was no different, and the aggressiveness of the Vancouver Status of Women Council was accepted by British Columbians as quite normal." Ibid.

Chapter 1: Sex Discrimination in Canadian Law

1 The history of women's suffrage in the nineteenth century is complex. For example, New Brunswick regulations explicitly barred them from voting in 1785, but a law passed ten years later did not regulate female voting. In 1832, the Assembly of Lower Canada prohibited women from exercising the franchise, but the law was disallowed. Depending on the jurisdiction and the period in history, women were either explicitly excluded from voting, did not vote though there were no legal impediments, or voted only in small numbers and often only if they owned property. For a useful overview, see Gail Cuthbert Brandt et al., *Canadian Women: A History* (Toronto: Nelson Education, 2011), 113-17.
2 The relevant amendment to BC law omitted married women by specifying that only single or widowed women could vote. *An Act to Amend the "Municipality Act 1872,"* S.B.C. 1873, c. 5.
3 *An Act further to amend the Public Schools Act*, S.B.C. 1913, c. 67; *An Act to amend the Public Schools Act*, S.B.C. 1922, c. 64.
4 Between 1885 and 1898, the federal government had its own criteria for voting eligibility. Under the Electoral Franchise Act, women were still denied the right to vote, as were persons of Mongolian or Chinese descent. *Dominion Elections Act*, R.S.C. 1906, c. 6; *Electoral Franchise Act*, S.C. 1885, c. 40.
5 *Re Mable French*, [1905] 27 N.B.R. 366.

6 By 1920, women could vote everywhere in Canada (and in Newfoundland if they were twenty-five years old), except in Quebec, where they were denied the provincial vote until 1940. At least fifteen legislative bills were introduced in Quebec between 1915 and 1940 before it granted female suffrage in 1940.
7 Barbara M. Hanley was the first woman to be elected mayor, of Webbwood, Ontario, in 1936.
8 Although women could not work underground, BC mining companies were permitted to hire them for clerical positions or to perform domestic duties in hotels, residences, and boarding houses associated with the mine. The provisions in the 1877 legislation were repealed in 1892, reinstated in 1897, and removed again from the statute by 1948. Ontario also banned women from working in mines (and as newspaper vendors in Toronto), passing legislation to that effect in 1890. In 1886, Manitoba prohibited women from working in bars and also severely restricted the ability of married women to own a liquor licence. Constance Backhouse, *Petticoats and Prejudice: Women and Law in Nineteenth-Century Canada* (Toronto: Women's Press, 1991), 290-91.
9 Ruth A. Frager and Carmela Patrias, *Discounted Labour: Women Workers in Canada, 1870-1939* (Toronto: University of Toronto Press, 2005), 39.
10 In 1895, after a prolonged battle with Ontario's law society, Clara Brett Martin became the first woman to be admitted to the bar (a first for both Canada and the entire Commonwealth).
11 Robert J. Sharpe and Patricia L. McMahon, *The Persons Case: The Origins and Legacy of the Fight for Legal Personhood* (Toronto: University of Toronto Press, 2007).
12 Lori Chambers, *Married Women and Property Law in Victorian Ontario* (Toronto: University of Toronto Press, 1997), 3.
13 Women who were sole heads of the household and who had dependent children were exempt from this law. Sarah Carter, "'Daughters of British Blood' or 'Hordes of Men of Alien Race': The Homesteads-for-Women Campaign in Western Canada," *Great Plains Quarterly* 29, 4 (2009): 267-68.
14 Frager and Patrias, *Discounted Labour*, 7-8.
15 Quebec's Civil Code was only somewhat less draconian than these strictures. Under New France's law, the Coutume de Paris, which was carried forth to Lower Canada and then Quebec, a woman held property jointly with her husband. He was the acknowledged head of the household, but he had a legal obligation to support his wife and children, and he could not sell her dower without her permission. The automatic right to dower existed in common law as well: a one-third interest in a husband's property inherited after his death. However, dower rights were restricted in Lower Canada under the Registry Act of 1841 and in the North-West Territories (the Prairies and parts of Ontario) in 1886. Quebec's Civil Code (1866) prohibited a married woman from entering into a contract or appearing before the courts; she could not engage in a profession separate from that of her husband or in commerce without his permission; and she could not discipline their children unless he defaulted in his duty. New France's law, the Coutume de Paris, specified all the rules relating to marriage: "Under this law, married women had a status inferior to that of their husbands ... The law clearly regarded the man as the head of the household. Widows sometimes could not even exercise guardianship over their own children. But the same law did afford some important economic protection to both married women and widows. Spouses were seen to have mutual obligations toward each other. The community of property that came into being at a marriage imposed some legal restrictions on the husband:

whatever property his wife brought into the marriage, he was to administer with care, and he could not dispose of it without his wife's permission. Furthermore, he was to use whatever property the couple acquired after marriage to support his wife and children; indeed, any property acquired after marriage belonged equally to both spouses. On the death of her husband, the widow could choose to continue the community of property or, if the debts exceeded the assets, to renounce it and with it any accumulated debt. By virtue of her dower rights, the widow was entitled to receive half the income generated by the communal property until her own death." Brandt et al., *Canadian Women*, 50; Backhouse, *Petticoats and Prejudice*. Dower complicated business transactions. It was based on landownership, and someone who purchased land might later discover that it was protected by dower rights. The Civil Code of 1866 required couples to register dower rights or lose them. Brandt et al., *Canadian Women*, 103, 144-45. Parliament also prohibited women, in 1872, from homesteading on their own unless they had children. Ibid., 145.

16 Quoted in Helen Gregory MacGill, *Daughters, Wives and Mothers in British Columbia* (Vancouver: Moore Printing, 1913), 18.
17 In certain cases, New Brunswick (1851) and Ontario (1859) granted women nominal control over their wages, free from their husband's authority.
18 *An Act to Protect the Property of a Wife Deserted by her Husband*, S.B.C. 1862, c. 116. Chris Clarkson explains that "the bill permitted a deserted wife to apply to the courts for a protection order declaring her a *femme sole*, with the right to hold property, contract, sue, and be sued as if she were a single woman. The order also explicitly freed her property from the claims of her husband or his creditors." The act was not insignificant at a time when men often fled the colonies to avoid imprisonment for debt. However, because most women lacked the means to apply for a court order, it had a limited impact. In addition, it applied only to deserted wives, and not, for instance, to those who were abused or neglected. Chris Clarkson, *Domestic Reforms: Political Visions and Family Regulation in British Columbia, 1862-1940* (Vancouver: UBC Press, 2007), 28, 30-31.
19 Ibid., 35-37.
20 *An Act to Extend the Rights of Property of Married Women*, S.B.C. 1873, c. 117.
21 Chambers, *Married Women and Property Law*, 4. In 1884, Ontario became the first jurisdiction to provide formal legal equality for wives (Married Women's Property Act). Over time, other provinces followed suit with similar legislation, although Quebec did not grant married women greater control over property until 1931. Backhouse, *Petticoats and Prejudice*, Chapter 6.
22 MacGill, *Daughters, Wives and Mothers*, 32.
23 Backhouse, *Petticoats and Prejudice*, 201.
24 *An Act to Consolidate and Amend the Law Relating to the Custody and Care of Infants*, R.S.B.C. 1897, c. 96. The 1855 Ontario legislation included similar provisions regarding the age of children (it applied only to children under twelve) and adultery. They were removed in 1887 because judges continued to favour fathers in custody battles.
25 *An Act Respecting the Maintenance of Wives Deserted by their Husbands*, R.S.B.C. 1911, c. 61.
26 Helen Gregory MacGill, *Laws for Women and Children in British Columbia* (Vancouver: privately printed, 1925), 17.
27 *Equal Guardianship Act*, S.B.C. 1917, c. 97. In 1922, the province also passed the Parents Maintenance Act, which required children to provide support for their impoverished parents. *Parents Maintenance Act*, S.B.C. 1922, c. 57.

28 The administration of mothers' allowances/pensions was rife with the biases of middle-class reformers. In most jurisdictions, investigators visited women's homes to confirm that they conformed to acceptable modes of behaviour, from cleanliness to avoiding alcohol. Deserted wives, unwed mothers, and widows with one child were ineligible (the widows were expected to find work as domestics). It is interesting to note that, in another precedent, British Columbia was the first province, in 1927, to pass enabling legislation to put federal old age pensions into effect.
29 Women with one child received $42.50 per month and $7.50 for each additional child. *An Act to Provide Pensions for Mothers*, S.B.C. 1920, c. 61. Margaret Hillyard Little, "Claiming a Unique Place: The Introduction of Mothers' Pensions in British Columbia," *BC Studies* 105-6 (1995): 93-94.
30 Margaret Hillyard Little, "'A Fit and Proper Person': The Moral Regulation of Single Mothers in Ontario, 1920-1940," in *Gendered Pasts: Historical Essays in Femininity and Masculinity in Canada,* ed. Kathryn McPherson, Cecilia Morgan, and Nancy M. Forestell (Toronto: Oxford University Press, 1999), 123-38; Nancy Christie, *Engendering the State: Family, Work, and Welfare in Canada* (Toronto: University of Toronto Press, 2000).
31 Although the province did have a Dower Act, it virtually undermined all rights to dower. Husbands could dispose of a wife's property as they wished, and creditors could confiscate any assets.
32 *Testator's Family Maintenance Bill,* S.B.C. 1920, c. 94.
33 *Amendment to the Administration Act,* S.B.C. 1924, c. 6.
34 *An Act to Provide for the Maintenance of Children of Unmarried Parents,* S.B.C. 1922, c. 9.
35 *An Act Respecting the Employment of Women Before and After Childbirth,* R.S.B.C. 1924, c. 155.
36 Backhouse, *Petticoats and Prejudice,* 267.
37 Women represented 13 percent of the paid labour force in 1901, 17 percent in 1931, and 20 percent in 1941. Their numbers were highest in major urban centres, where they constituted approximately 20 to 25 percent of the workforce by the late 1930s. Frager and Patrias, *Discounted Labour,* 25.
38 Ibid., 32.
39 Gillian Creese, "The Politics of Dependence: Women, Work and Unemployment in the Vancouver Labour Movement before World War II," in *British Columbia Reconsidered: Essays on Women,* ed. Gillian Creese and Veronica Strong-Boag (Vancouver: Press Gang, 1992), 368.
40 As Alison Prentice et al. note, "Alberta was the first province to adopt a minimum wage law for women in 1917. Most provinces followed suit: British Columbia and Manitoba in 1918, Saskatchewan and Quebec in 1919, and Nova Scotia and Ontario in 1920. By the end of the decade, only New Brunswick and Prince Edward Island had still not passed such laws. But it took Alberta until 1924 to set up a permanent wage board, and minimum wage legislation was not actually put into force in Quebec until 1972, and 1930 in Nova Scotia." Alison Prentice et al., *Canadian Women: A History* (Toronto: Harcourt Brace, 1996), 227.
41 *An Act Respecting a Minimum Wage for Women,* S.B.C. 1918, c. 173.
42 In 1930, only 155 women were on Vancouver's unemployment relief rolls, compared to 4,513 married men and 5,244 single men. Overall, legislators did little to address women's concerns during the Depression: "Lawmakers denied that single women's unemployment constituted a serious problem, even though many more young women would have been out working during more normal times. Even the limited efforts to create work and hostels

for single, unemployed men did not extend to their female counterparts." The federal government provided tax credits as an incentive to help mothers enter the workforce throughout the Second World War, only to immediately rescind the credits when it ended. Frager and Patrias, *Discounted Labour*, 85.
43 Creese, "The Politics of Dependence," 378.
44 Ibid., 380.
45 Frager and Patrias, *Discounted Labour*, 96.
46 Ibid., 105.
47 *An Act for the Protection of Persons Employed in Factories*, R.S.B.C. 1908, c. 15.
48 A 1927 amendment to the law removed references to permissible employment for children and imposed a blanket prohibition on employing them unless an inspector approved the work. *An Act to Amend the Factories Act*, S.B.C. 1927, c. 22.
49 Quoted in Susan Wade, "Helena Gutteridge: Votes for Women and Trade Unions," in *In Her Own Right: Selected Essays on Women's History in BC*, ed. Barbara Latham and Cathy Kess (Victoria: Camosun College, 1980), 193.
50 Frager and Patrias, *Discounted Labour*, 106.
51 *An Act to Prevent the Employment of Female Labour in Certain Capacities*, S.S. 1912, c. 17. The act was later amended to apply solely to the Chinese; in 1919, the reference to race was replaced with the requirement that employers must obtain a municipal licence to hire white women. See James W. St. G. Walker, *"Race," Rights and the Law in the Supreme Court of Canada: Historical Case Studies* (Toronto: Wilfrid Laurier University Press, 1997), 52.
52 *Municipal Act*, R.S.B.C. 1919, c. 63.
53 *An Act for the Protection of Women and Girls in Certain Cases*, R.S.B.C. 1924, c. 309. Walker writes that "the law was indifferently enforced until the mid-1930s, when a violent crime involving a Chinese suspect and a white female victim prompted Vancouver city officials to begin warning Chinese restaurants they must dismiss their white female employees or lose their licences." Walker, *"Race," Rights and the Law*, 113-14.
54 Brandt et al., *Canadian Women*, 292.
55 Josie Bannerman, Kathy Chopik, and Ann Zurbrigg, "Cheap at Half the Price: The History of the Fight for Equal Pay in BC," in *Not Just Pin Money: Selected Essays on the History of Women's Work in British Columbia*, ed. Barbara K. Latham and Roberta J. Pazdro (Victoria: Camosun College, 1984), 300.
56 Timothy J. Stanley, *Contesting White Supremacy: School Segregation, Anti-Racism, and the Making of Chinese Canadians* (Vancouver: UBC Press, 2011), 64.
57 Amanda Glasbeek argues that, in Toronto, police targeted interracial couples, especially those involving white women and Chinese men. The woman might be arrested for vagrancy, with the intent of "disciplining [her] for her choice of lovers." Amanda Glasbeek, *Feminized Justice: The Toronto Women's Court, 1913-1934* (Vancouver: UBC Press, 2009), 103.
58 Backhouse, *Petticoats and Prejudice*, 241.
59 Constance Backhouse, "Nineteenth Century Canadian Prostitution Law: Reflection of a Discriminatory Society," *Histoire sociale/Social History* 18 (1985): 420-22. The Indian Act was amended in 1884 to extend the prohibition from houses to "tents and wigwams." Also in that year, Ottawa imposed a more lenient standard for prosecuting Aboriginal men for frequenting prostitutes, although this provision was removed in 1887.
60 Frager and Patrias, *Discounted Labour*, 44.
61 Ibid., 71-73.
62 Little, "Claiming a Unique Place."

63 Backhouse, *Petticoats and Prejudice*, 8. In an earlier publication, Backhouse describes the 1865 Contagious Diseases Act in Upper and Lower Canada as "a blatant form of sex discrimination." Under this law, women who were suspected of being prostitutes with a venereal disease were forced to accept medical inspections and treatment. Backhouse, "Nineteenth Century Canadian," 391. On criminal law and the regulation of female sexuality, see Joan Sangster, "Incarcerating 'Bad Girls': The Regulation of Sexuality through the Female Refugees Act in Ontario, 1920-1945," *Histoire sociale/Social History* 7 (1996): 239-75; Joan Sangster, "Girls in Conflict with the Law: Exploring the Construction of Female 'Delinquency' in Ontario, 1940-1960," in *Through Feminist Eyes: Essays on Canadian Women's History*, ed. Joan Sangster (Edmonton: Athabasca University Press, 2011), 251-92; and Joan Sangster, "'Pardon Tales' from Magistrate's Court: Women, Crime, and the Court in Peterborough County, 1920-1950," in Sangster, *Through Feminist Eyes*, 173-212.

64 Walker, *"Race," Rights and the Law*, 82.

65 Sandra Burt, "The Changing Patterns of Public Policy," in *Changing Patterns: Women in Canada*, 2nd ed., ed. Sandra Burt, Lorraine Code, and Lindsay Dorney (Toronto: McClelland and Stewart, 1993), 214.

66 By 1915, almost a third of the Canadian Expeditionary Force was infected with a venereal disease, compared with 5 percent of British troops. The Canadian army insisted that at least a quarter of those infected had caught the disease in Canada. Robert A. Campbell, "Ladies and Escorts: Gender Segregation and Public Policy in British Columbia Beer Parlours, 1925 to 1945," *BC Studies* 105-6 (1995): 125.

67 Glasbeek, *Feminized Justice*, Chapter 3. See also Sangster, "'Pardon Tales.'"

68 Beverley Baines states that "according to the higher court judge, prostitution referred to 'activities which can only be engaged in by females.' It followed, therefore, that the law could treat women more harshly than men, at least in the context of prostitution." Beverley Baines, "Law, Gender, Equality," in Burt, Code, and Dorney, *Changing Patterns*, 260.

69 Brandt et al., *Canadian Women*, 99.

70 Under Quebec law, as of 1871, women convicted of vagrancy for the second time were liable to five years in prison; no such provision applied to men. As Backhouse writes, "Between 1869 and 1892 an explosion of federal enactments had attempted to place sweeping prohibitions on all prostitution activity. Parliament made it criminal to procure the defilement of women under the age of twenty-one by false pretences, representations, or other fraudulent means. Householders were prohibited from allowing women under the age of sixteen to resort there for the purpose of 'unlawful carnal knowledge.' It was an offence to entice a woman to a brothel for the purpose of prostitution, or to knowingly conceal her in such a house. It made criminal to procure women for unlawful carnal knowledge, or for parents or guardians to encourage the defilement of their daughters. A new offence, 'conspiracy to defile,' had also been created." Backhouse, *Petticoats and Prejudice*, 255.

71 Glasbeek, *Feminized Justice*, 106.

72 Backhouse, *Petticoats and Prejudice*, 111.

73 Ibid., 42. In cases where a woman was seduced and became pregnant, families had to demonstrate in court that the pregnancy resulted in a material loss to the family. In Upper Canada in 1837, and soon afterward in other jurisdictions during the late nineteenth century, the requirement for proving loss of a daughter's services was removed. The objective was to extend the opportunity to sue to working-class families in cases where the unmarried pregnant daughter was not living at home and providing a direct service to the family (but

the family was still financially supporting her). Backhouse notes that "juries would regularly rule for the plaintiffs, and defendants would then appeal to the full bench of judges to set aside the verdict. On balance, their success at this stage was well known. The judges overturned about half of these verdicts on points of law." Ibid., 56.

74 As Backhouse explains, "In 1890 the law would reach out to encompass guardians who seduced their wards and employers or supervisors in factories, mills and workshops who seduced young female employees. And in 1892, the seduction of female ship passengers by ship-masters, officers, and other seamen would be added." Ibid., 74-75. Keepers of immoral houses, their landlords, and property owners could avail themselves of numerous legal defences. Penalties for living off the avails of prostitution were low and often less severe than those for property offences. If an employer seduced a female employee who was under twenty-one, he could go to jail for two years; however, if she stole from him, she could go to jail for fourteen years. Glasbeek, *Feminized Justice*, 48-50.

75 In its original seventeenth-century British incarnation, "concealment of birth" was a crime punishable by death. It was usually applied to single women, but it rarely resulted in convictions. In 1803, the law was changed to allow the substitution of a verdict of concealment if the woman were acquitted of murder. Soon afterward, its scope was extended to married women and their accomplices. The original law was highly unusual: it presumed the accused guilty rather than innocent, and courts were encouraged to convict unless the mother could produce a witness to prove that the child was stillborn. Lower Canada, New Brunswick, and Nova Scotia adopted the 1803 British precedent within the following decade, although Upper Canada retained the original draconian version until 1836. Ibid., Chapter 4.

76 Ibid., 133.

77 Ibid., 162-63, 166.

78 British Columbia also implemented legislation to protect or provide relief to families of alcoholics. Although the law did not apply solely to men, it was intended (and enforced) primarily for them. Under the 1887 Habitual Drunkards Act, the court could assign a trustee to take control of a man's property to prevent him from spending the family income. The Liquor Control Act allowed a judge to prohibit any establishment from selling liquor to a drunkard, and the court could distribute a notice to all licensed vendors. A woman could use the legislation to stop merchants from selling liquor to her husband (the law also banned the sale of liquor to Indians and prostitutes). *Habitual Drunkards Act*, S.B.C. 1887, c. 11; *An Act Respecting the Sale by Retail of Fermented and Spirituous Liquors*, S.B.C. 1897, c. 124; *An Act Respecting Liquor Licences and the Traffic in Intoxicating Liquors*, S.B.C. 1910, c. 30.

79 Brandt et al., *Canadian Women*, 103.

80 Of the five divorces granted by the Legislature of Upper Canada before Confederation, none were on behalf of women. New France's law, the Coutume de Paris, allowed men and women to separate and divide property or determine room and board. The law did not permit divorce and remarriage, although the couple could live apart (the royal administration, which was keen to encourage young people to marry, provided twenty livres from the Crown to a young woman who married before the age of twenty). Separation was difficult to obtain, and women often justified their request for it on the grounds that the husband was an alcoholic, irresponsible, and/or abusive. In addition, under the Coutume, those few women who reached twenty-five without marrying were deemed to

have the same legal status as men, except they could not hold public office. Ibid., 44-45.
81 Interestingly, women in the Maritime provinces could apply for divorce on the basis of adultery alone, and divorce courts were established in New Brunswick (1758), Nova Scotia (1791), and Prince Edward Island (1833) to provide accessible venues for divorce. The situation remained largely unchanged after Confederation. From 1900 to the 1960s, divorce rates were highest in Alberta, British Columbia, and Ontario, a trend that continued in the immediate aftermath of the 1968 Divorce Act. In 1971, for example, divorce rates in Alberta and British Columbia were double those of Saskatchewan. Robert Pike, "Legal Access and the Incidence of Divorce in Canada: A Sociohistorical Analysis," *Canadian Review of Sociology and Anthropology* 12 (1975): 115-33.
82 Clarkson, *Domestic Reforms*, 9. As the authors of the leading textbook on women's history conclude, the laws "affecting sexuality, marriage and motherhood might be regarded as evidence of new kinds of intrusions into women's lives, as male lawgivers attempted to reinforce or reinterpret traditional male controls over, as well as their protection of, women in a changing world." Brandt et al., *Canadian Women*, 107.
83 Until 1954, women in Newfoundland could not vote until they were twenty-five, whereas men could vote at twenty-one.
84 *An Act Respecting the Removal of Disqualifications on Account of Sex*, S.B.C. 1931, c. 55.
85 Burt, "The Changing Patterns of Public Policy," 228.
86 Joan Brockman, *Gender in the Legal Profession: Fitting in or Breaking the Mould* (Vancouver: UBC Press, 2006), 8-9.
87 Full-Time University Enrolment, by Sex, Canada and Provinces, Selected Years, 1920 to 1975 (Table W340-438), in Statistics Canada, *Historical Statistics of Canada*, Catalogue no. 11-516-XWE (Ottawa: Statistics Canada, 1983).
88 *An Act Respecting the Industrial Home for Girls*, S.B.C. 1912, c. 11.
89 Jana Grekul, "The Right to Consent? Eugenics in Alberta, 1928-1972," in *A History of Human Rights in Canada: Essential Issues*, ed. Janet Miron (Toronto: Canadian Scholars' Press, 2009), 135-54.
90 Quoted in Prentice et al., *Canadian Women*, 400.
91 The Quebec government successfully lobbied Ottawa to send allowances to fathers. Quebec also retained a ban on female jury duty until 1976, and even then "domestic obligations" were a ground for exemption.
92 Maternity-leave provisions were added to the federal Unemployment Insurance Act in 1971. The law provided pregnant women with eleven weeks of paid leave and automatic job reinstatement at the same pay and seniority when they returned to work. Women were paid through the national unemployment insurance scheme, although they received less money than when they were working. Burt, "The Changing Patterns of Public Policy," 222.
93 *An Act Respecting Training Schools for Children*, S.B.C. 1963, c. 50, s. 13; *An Act to Amend and Repeal Certain Provisions of the Statute Law*, S.B.C. 1968, c. 53, s. 29.
94 *Family Relations Act*, S.B.C. 1972, c. 20.
95 By this time, visible minority women in British Columbia had the right to vote and were no longer barred from immigrating to Canada or working in certain professions. But, at a time when male homosexuality was criminalized (until 1969), lesbians led largely hidden lives and could not hope to adopt children, marry, or gain custody of their own children after a divorce. For further details on lesbians and the law, see Didi Herman, *Rights of Passage: Struggles for Lesbian and Gay Legal Equality* (Toronto: University of Toronto Press,

1994); and Becki L. Ross, *The House That Jill Built: A Lesbian Nation in Formation* (Toronto: University of Toronto Press, 1995). On police and court treatment of lesbians, see Elise Chenier, "Rethinking Class in Lesbian Bar Culture: Living the 'Gay Life' in Toronto, 1955-1965," in *Rethinking Canada: The Promise of Women's History,* ed. Mona Gleason and Adele Perry (Toronto: Oxford University Press, 2006), 301-22.

96 *An Act to Amend the Indian Act,* S.C. 1887, c. 33, ss.72, 73.
97 For a detailed list of the consequences faced by Aboriginal women who lost their status, see Sally Weaver, "First Nations Women and Government Policy, 1970-92: Discrimination and Conflict," in Burt, Code, and Dorney, *Changing Patterns,* 93-94.
98 Ibid., 108-10. See also Canada, Indian and Northern Affairs, *The Elimination of Sex Discrimination from the Indian Act* (Ottawa: Queen's Printer, 1982).
99 *Divorce Act,* S.C. 1968, c. 24.
100 Brandt et al., *Canadian Women,* 485.
101 Lynne Pearson, *Women in British Columbia: Issues, Resources and Services* (Victoria: Provincial Coordinator for the Status of Women's Office, 1975), 5. In 1977, the provinces began to pass legislation recognizing that women's work at home enabled wage earners to make money and buy property for the family, a fact that contributed to more equitable settlements in divorce cases. Brandt et al. note that "some fifteen years later, the Supreme Court completed the process of legal change when it established in the Beblow case that, under the new legislation, wives in common-law as well as formal marriages owned half the household assets when the relationship ended." Brandt et al., *Canadian Women,* 440, 560.
102 Canada, *Report of the Royal Commission on the Status of Women* (Ottawa: Queen's Printer, 1970), 365.
103 Between 1950 and 1966, women represented approximately 12.5 percent of all persons convicted of indictable offences, though rarely for violent crimes. Twenty-nine convictions for various offences related to their child-bearing function. Ibid., 365-66.
104 Some of the act's notable provisions were as follows: the Immigration Act no longer specified husbands as the head of the family; the Public Service Employment Act banned discrimination on the basis of marital status; the National Defence Act no longer barred women from joining the cadets; the Unemployment Insurance Act provided fifteen weeks of maternity leave with paid benefits; the Civilian War Pensions and Allowances Act afforded pensions to women; the Canada Elections Act required the same residency provisions for husbands of female temporary workers as it did for wives of male workers; and wide-ranging revisions to the Pension Act eliminated, among other things, discrepancies in the treatment of male and female children, restrictions on providing pensions to females in the armed forces, and restrictions on children or women benefitting from the pension of a deceased male (there was also a new section that allowed housewives to contribute to the Canada Pension Plan). Before 1974, female immigrants who married Canadian males were granted citizenship after one year of residence, compared with five years for men married to Canadian women; and legitimate children of Canadian women were denied the same rights as children of Canadian men. *An Act to Amend Certain Statutes to Provide Equality of Status Thereunder for Male and Female Persons,* S.C. 1975, c. 66.
105 For a useful overview of legal reforms based on the RCSW's recommendations, see Canada, Status of Women, *The Royal Commission on the Status of Women: An Overview 25 Years Later* (Ottawa: Status of Women Canada, 1995).
106 In 1978, the Supreme Court of Canada had "ruled that it was permissible to deny unemployment insurance benefits to pregnant women because 'any inequality between the

sexes in this area is not created by legislation but by nature.'" Baines, "Law, Gender, Equality," 261.
107 Judy Fudge, "The Effect of Entrenching a Bill of Rights upon Political Discourse: Feminist Demands and Sexual Violence in Canada," *International Journal of the Sociology of Law* 17 (1989): 451.
108 *Employment Equity Act*, S.C. 1986, c. 31.
109 University of Victoria Archives, Victoria (UVA), Status of Women Action Group (SWAG), AR119, 2004-017, f.1.3, SWAG open letter to MLAs in British Columbia, 1978. Forty-five recommendations from the RCSW applied explicitly to the provinces. An additional twenty-three, which dealt with federal programs such as Canada Employment, could have been applied to the provinces.
110 Janet Beebe, *Update on the Status of Women in British Columbia* (Vancouver: Vancouver Status of Women, 1978).
111 Ibid., 38-40.
112 For example, unlike the federal government, which implemented equal pay for work of equal value in 1977, British Columbia did not incorporate this principle in human rights legislation.
113 Several other legal reforms in British Columbia were consistent with the RCSW recommendations. In 1977, the government repealed legislation that dealt with succession duties following the dissolution of marriage; created a unified Family Court based on the recommendations of the Berger commission; passed a 1972 Family Relations Act in which both parents, not just the father, were responsible for maintaining their children; and repealed the requirement for unmarried mothers of illegitimate children to seek an order of affiliation to receive welfare. Ibid., 82-83, 95-97.
114 In Newfoundland, for instance, women working in the civil service and at Memorial University, until 1979, were required to quit if they married (unless the minister gave a special exemption); female civil servants received lower pensions than their male counterparts, could not claim a pension until they reached sixty-five (sixty for men), and could not receive compensation if they were injured on the job; women were prohibited from changing their name while married; unmarried girls under the age of sixteen were banned from employment without parental consent; married women's place of residence for elections was based on that of their husband; the Family Relief Act implied that being an unmarried female was a disability; and the Limitations of Actions Act placed married women in the same category as persons of unsound mind. Dominique Clément, "Equality Deferred: Sex Discrimination and the Newfoundland Human Rights State," *Acadiensis* 41 (2012): 102-27.
115 British Columbia Archives, Victoria, Department of Labour, Acc. 880057, box 3730, f. United Nations Convention on Elimination of All Forms of Discrimination against Women, Gilbert D. Kennedy to Jack Heinrich, 15 March 1982.
116 British Columbia was not the only jurisdiction to place gender restrictions on legal names. In 1985, a challenge under the Charter of Rights and Freedoms forced Yukon to amend its laws prohibiting a married woman from changing her name, and in 1985 a married woman successfully challenged Ontario's vital statistics law that denied her the right to give her child her surname. Baines, "Law, Gender, Equality," 266-67.
117 This regulation mirrored similar laws in Ontario that required welfare officials to discontinue support payments if female recipients were found to be living with a man. The same regulation did not apply to men.

118 Several laws provided special exemptions to women but not to men. For instance, the Elections Act (s. 24.2) allowed the wife of a member of the Executive Council to place her name on the same voters' list as his. The Homesteaders Act (s. 5.2) exempted a property from seizure for repayment of debt during a widow's "unmarried state" (it also required a husband to seek his wife's permission to sell, mortgage, or dispose of the land but did not impose similar obligations on her). The Insurance Act (s. 110.0) prevented a company from lending money to a director or executive of a company and his wife. Several other statutes specified "widow" rather than "spouse"; this applied to refunds under the Motor Vehicle Act (s. 26) and determining residence under the Residence and Responsibility Act (s. 1) and the Vancouver Charter (s. 9).

119 One immediate effect of s. 15 was to oblige the provinces to remove provisions in statute law requiring married women to take their husband's name. Michael Mandel, *The Charter of Rights and the Legislation of Politics in Canada* (Toronto: Thompson Educational, 1994), 399.

120 *Charter of Rights Amendments*, R.S.B.C. 1985, c. 6. Ontario was the first province, in 1978, the remove the concept of the illegitimacy of children from its statutes.

121 Nat Cole, "Barmaids for BC Still a Pub Dream," *Vancouver Sun*, 1 March 1969; Campbell, "Ladies and Escorts," 121, 131, 136.

122 Unlike their Ontario counterparts, BC judges did not use common law rules of interpretation to severely restrict the application of property law. Clarkson, *Domestic Reforms*, 12, 63-75.

123 Sangster, "Incarcerating 'Bad Girls,'" 240. In her analysis of Ontario's Female Refugees Act, Sangster argues that it was "an attempt to preserve the prevailing form of nuclear, patriarchal family in which the wife was monogamous and played a domestic role and the daughter a dutiful and chaste apprentice. The protection of these roles, which had both material and social power attached to them, was inextricably linked to the regulation of women's sexuality. Moreover, the sexual nonconformity of these women triggered other anxieties linked to class, race, and eugenic concerns ... Also, police, social workers and judges had clear suppositions about what constituted a moral home." Ibid., 274.

124 In essence, judicial interpretation of statute law became "a club to assail women and girls who dared to seek criminal sanction against men accused of sexual offences ... The doctrine of corroboration made a mockery of the ideals of even-handed justice and gender parity." Constance Backhouse, "The Doctrine of Corroboration in Sexual Assault Trials in Early 20th Century Canada and Australia," in *From Subjects to Citizens: A Hundred Years of Citizenship in Australia and Canada*, ed. Pierre Boyer, Linda Cardinal, and David Headon (Ottawa: University of Ottawa Press, 2004), 148.

125 As Baines notes, "In effect, the judiciary denied every claim in which women relied on the guarantee of sex equality in the Canadian Bill of Rights ... Thus, from the perspective of women, the judiciary effectively emptied the guarantee of sex-equality in the Canadian Bill of Rights of any meaning." Baines, "Law, Gender, Equality," 259.

126 *Murdoch v. Murdoch*, [1975] 1 S.C.R. 423.

127 Quoted in T. Brette Dawson, *Relating to Law: A Chronology of Women and Law in Canada* (Toronto: Captus Press, 1994), 10.

128 Ibid., 12.

129 Ibid., 13.

130 Baines, "Law, Gender, Equality," 258.

Chapter 2: "No Jews or Dogs Allowed"

1 Ross Lambertson, "Suppression and Subversion," in *A History of Human Rights in Canada,* ed. Janet Miron (Toronto: Canadian Scholars' Press, 2009), 33; Gerald Tulchinsky, *Canada's Jews: A People's Journey* (Toronto: University of Toronto Press, 2008): 172.
2 Carmela Patrias, "Race, Employment Discrimination, and State Complicity in Wartime Canada, 1939-1945," *Labour/Le travail* 59 (2007): 54. "Achat chez nous" translates to "buying from us."
3 Pierre Berton, "No Jews Need Apply," *Maclean's Magazine,* 1 November 1948.
4 Herbert A. Sohn, "Human Rights Legislation in Ontario: A Study of Social Action" (PhD diss., University of Toronto, 1975), 134.
5 Quoted in Library and Archives Canada (LAC), Jewish Labour Committee (JLC), MG28, V75, v.23, f.6, A Brief from the Association for Civil Liberties to the Premier of Ontario, 1951.
6 The party's opposition to discrimination was a product of several factors, including its members' dedication to secular humanism, the social gospel, and economic and social equality. Carmela Patrias, "Socialists, Jews, and the 1947 Saskatchewan Bill of Rights," *Canadian Historical Review* 87 (2006): 271.
7 James W. St. G. Walker, "The 'Jewish Phase' in the Movement for Racial Equality in Canada," *Canadian Ethnic Studies* 34 (2002): 4-5.
8 Ibid., 6.
9 Ibid.; Ruth A. Frager and Carmela Patrias, "'This Is Our Country, These Are Our Rights': Minorities and the Origins of Ontario's Human Rights Campaigns," *Canadian Historical Review* 82 (2001): 1-35.
10 On Kaplansky and the JLC, see Ross Lambertson, "The Dresden Story: Racism, Human Rights, and the Jewish Labour Committee of Canada," *Labour/Le travail* (Spring 2001): 43-82.
11 According to Margaret Hillyard Little, whereas other jurisdictions implemented mothers' *allowances,* rights discourse informed British Columbia's decision to implement mothers' *pensions* in 1920. During the hearings regarding the legislation, the debates in the legislature, and the subsequent administration of the law, people framed mothers' pensions as legal rights. Little suggests that "the discourse surrounding the BC policy implies that it was considered a right rather than a privilege." However, as she also notes, the discourse was not one of universal human rights. Racial minorities were denied mothers' pensions. Margaret Hillyard Little, "Claiming a Unique Place: The Introduction of Mothers' Pensions in British Columbia," *BC Studies* 105-6 (1995): 97.
12 Michael Dawson, "Leisure, Consumption, and the Public Sphere: Postwar Debates over Shopping Regulations in Vancouver and Victoria during the Cold War," in *Creating Postwar Canada: Community, Diversity, and Dissent, 1945-75,* ed. Magda Fahrni (Vancouver: UBC Press, 2007), 205.
13 Shirley Tillotson, "Time, Swimming Pools, and Citizenship: The Emergence of Leisure Rights in Mid-Twentieth-Century Canada," in *Contesting Canadian Citizenship: Historical Readings,* ed. Robert Adamoski, Dorothy E. Chunn, and Robert Menzies (Peterborough: Broadview Press, 2002), 199-224.
14 "Fair Employment Bill," *Toronto Globe and Mail,* 27 February 1951; "Equal Pay for Women," *Toronto Globe and Mail,* 10 March 1951; "Why the Opposition?" *Toronto Globe and Mail,* 14 March 1951.

15 *Unemployment Relief Act*, S.B.C. 1931, c. 65; *Unemployment Relief Act*, S.B.C. 1932, c. 58.
16 *The Insurance Act*, R.S.O. 1970, c. 224.
17 Quoted in Walter Tarnopolsky, *Discrimination and the Law in Canada* (Toronto: De Boo, 1982), 26.
18 James W. St. G. Walker, *"Race," Rights and the Law in the Supreme Court of Canada: Historical Case Studies* (Toronto: Wilfrid Laurier University Press, 1997); Constance Backhouse, *Colour-Coded: A Legal History of Racism in Canada, 1900-1950* (Toronto: University of Toronto Press, 1999); Patrias, "Race, Employment Discrimination."
19 Sohn, "Human Rights Legislation," 40; Walker, "The 'Jewish Phase'"; Carmela Patrias, *Jobs and Justice: Fighting Discrimination in Wartime Canada, 1939-1945* (Toronto: University of Toronto Press, 2012), 62-64.
20 Patrias, "Race, Employment Discrimination."
21 Some of these groups included the Hungarian Mutual Benefit Federation, the Lithuanian Club, the Rosedale Civil Club, the Slovenian Club, and the Society of Democratic Hungarians in Niagara Falls. According to Frager and Patrias, Aboriginals, Chinese Canadians, Roman Catholics, and southern and eastern Europeans were largely absent from anti-discrimination campaigns during the 1940s. Many of these groups justifiably distrusted the Canadian state, and their numbers were often too small to organize effective lobbies. Frager and Patrias, "'This Is Our Country,'" 11-12.
22 For a history of the early civil liberties movement, see Ross Lambertson, *Repression and Resistance: Canadian Human Rights Activists, 1930-1960* (Toronto: University of Toronto Press, 2005).
23 Walker, *"Race," Rights and the Law*, Chapter 3.
24 Christopher Moore, *The British Columbia Court of Appeal: The First Hundred Years, 1910-2010* (Vancouver: UBC Press, 2010), 82.
25 *Social Assistance Act*, S.B.C. 1945, c. 62.
26 *The Racial Discrimination Act, 1944*, S.O. 1944, c. 51; O. Reg. 67/44, *The Community Halls Act, 1920*, 1944.
27 *The Bill of Rights Act*, S.A. 1946, c. 11; *Reference re Alberta Bill of Rights Act*, [1947] 2 W.W.R. 401 (JCPC).
28 Patrias, "Socialists, Jews," 282.
29 Tarnopolsky, *Discrimination and the Law*, 27.
30 Patrias, "Socialists, Jews," 284.
31 Ibid., 283.
32 *The Labour Relations Act, 1950*, S.O. 1950, c. 34; *The Conveyancing and Law of Property Amendment Act, 1950*, S.O. 1950, c. 11. The 1950 ban on restrictive covenants, however, was not retroactive.
33 *The Fair Employment Practices Act, 1951*, S.O. 1951, c. 24; *The Fair Accommodation Practices Act, 1954*, S.O. 1954, c. 28.
34 *An Act respecting the legal capacity of married women*, S.Q. 1964, c. 66, s. 1; *Fair Employment Practices Act Amendment Act, 1964*, S.B.C. 1964, c. 19; *The Age Discrimination Act, 1966*, S.O. 1966, c. 3; LAC, A Brief from the Association for Civil Liberties to the Premier of Ontario, 1951.
35 Tarnopolsky, *Discrimination and the Law*, 35-36.
36 R. Brian Howe and David Johnson, *Restraining Equality: Human Rights Commissions in Canada* (Toronto: University of Toronto Press, 2000), 4.
37 Quoted in Walker, "The 'Jewish Phase,'" 5.

38 LAC, JLC, MG28, V75, v.38, f.1, discours pronounce par Michael Rubinstein, à la conférence provinciale pour un code des droits de l'homme tenue à Montréal, 2 December 1972.
39 Sohn, "Human Rights Legislation," 64-65.
40 "Blow to Discrimination," *Toronto Globe and Mail*, 18 February 1947.
41 A 1949 *Vancouver Sun* editorial reflected a similar perception that discrimination was not a social problem: "Except for very rare incidents involving Negroes, Vancouver has been happily free of racial discrimination." "He Ought to Be Ashamed of Himself," *Vancouver Sun*, 12 May 1949.
42 Patrias, "Socialists, Jews," 282.
43 Walker, "The 'Jewish Phase,'" 8.
44 Ibid., 4.
45 Maureen Riddell, *The Evolution of Human Rights Legislation in Alberta, 1945-1979* (Edmonton: Government of Alberta, 1978-79), 6.
46 T.M. Eberlee and D.G. Hill, "The Ontario Human Rights Code," *University of Toronto Law Journal* 15 (1964): 453.
47 Shirley Tillotson, "Human Rights Law as Prism: Women's Organizations, Unions, and Ontario's Female Employees Fair Remuneration Act, 1951," *Canadian Historical Review* 72, 4 (1991): 532-57. Frager and Patrias offer several compelling examples of how Fine undermined the enforcement of the equal pay law. Ruth A. Frager and Carmela Patrias, "Human Rights Activists and the Question of Sex Discrimination in Postwar Ontario," *Canadian Historical Review* 93 (2012): 1-28.
48 Sohn, "Human Rights Legislation," 78-82.
49 LAC, Senate Committee on Industrial Relations, RG14-20, Acc. 1987-88/146, box 63, list of organizations, 1952-53.
50 Sohn, "Human Rights Legislation," 158.
51 Walker, "The 'Jewish Phase,'" 5-7.
52 LAC, A Brief from the Association for Civil Liberties to the Premier of Ontario, 1951.
53 Sidney Katz, "Jim Crow Lives in Dresden," *Maclean's Magazine*, 1 November 1949, 9.
54 The referendum question read "Do you approve of the Council passing a by-law licensing restaurants in Dresden and restraining the owner or owners from refusing service regardless of race, color or creed?" Quoted in Walker, "The 'Jewish Phase,'" 12.
55 Lambertson, "The Dresden Story."
56 Katz, "Jim Crow Lives," 52.
57 According to Herbert Sohn, many activists dedicated their energies to convincing key members of the bureaucracy to enact anti-discrimination legislation: "[Thomas] Eberlee recalls that it was through the human rights conferences and the contacts generally with the activists that he learned discrimination in Ontario was an issue with which to be reckoned." Civil servants, in turn, were another important force in the campaign for human rights legislation. Sohn, "Human Rights Legislation," 171.
58 Lambertson, "The Dresden Story," 72-73.
59 Sohn, "Human Rights Legislation," 48.
60 LAC, JLC, MG28, V75, v.23, f.6, case study reports on discrimination and unions, 1952.
61 Lambertson, "The Dresden Story," 54.
62 "Present Brief on Equal Pay, Equal Work," *Montreal Star*, 23 April 1953; "Labour, Social Groups Hail Anti-Discrimination Bill," *Montreal Star*, 23 April 1953; LAC, JLC, MG28, V75, v.23, f.6, Report of the BC Federation of Labour Human Rights Committee, n.d.
63 LAC, Canadian Labour Congress (CLC), MG28 I103, H-266, f.7, report on activities, 20 March 1959.

64 LAC, CLC, MG28 I103, H-433, f.2, report on activities, November 1960 to March 1961; LAC, CLC, MG28 I103, H-93, f.13, convention – report of the executive council, 18 March 1959.
65 LAC, CLC, MG28 I103, H-266, f.9, brief to Premier Lesage, n.d. The JLC's Quebec affiliate, the United Council for Human Rights, organized at least four major delegations leading up to the 1964 Act Respecting Discrimination in Employment, with forty to fifty delegates each visit. LAC, JLC, MG28, V75, UCHR Comprehensive Report to the Executive Council, 16 November 1966.
66 House of Commons, *Hansard*, no. 4 (1952-53), 3762.
67 LAC, CLC, MG28 I103, H-266, f.6, report on activities, November 1960 to March 1961. On the campaign in Nova Scotia, see Erica Colter, "A State of Affairs Most Common: Black Nova Scotians and the Stanfield Government's Interdepartmental Committee on Human Rights, 1959-1967" (Master's thesis, Dalhousie University, 2006).
68 LAC, Convention – report of the executive council, 18 March 1959.
69 Canada, Department of Labour, *Canadian Labour in the Struggle against Employment Discrimination* (Ottawa: Queen's Printer, 1960), 5. The JLC files suggest that, at the very least, the organization's affiliates were involved in almost every initiative to introduce or amend anti-discrimination laws in British Columbia, Manitoba, Nova Scotia, Ontario, and Quebec. See LAC, Ontario Labour Committee for Human Rights, MG28, I173, v.5, f.13, David Orlikow to Alan Borovoy, 9 January 1964.
70 "Discrimination and the Law," *Toronto Star*, 3 August 1961; Eberlee and Hill, "The Ontario Human Rights Code," 451; Rosanna L. Langer, *Defining Rights and Wrongs: Bureaucracy, Human Rights, and Public Accountability* (Vancouver: UBC Press, 2007), 4.
71 Tarnopolsky, *Discrimination and the Law*, 30.
72 LAC, JLC, MG28, V75, v.23, f.6, employment discrimination case studies.
73 R. Brian Howe and D. Johnson, "Variations in Enforcing Equality: A Study of Provincial Human Rights Funding," *Canadian Public Administration* 38 (1995): 245.
74 William W. Black, *Reassessing Statutory Human Rights Legislation Thirty Years Later: Human Rights Enforcement in British Columbia: A Case Study* (Ottawa: Human Rights Research and Education Centre, 1995), 3.
75 House of Commons, *Hansard*, no. 4 (1952-53), 3763.
76 "Racial Bias in Cafe Jobs?" *Winnipeg Free Press*, 2 September 1960; "Race Prejudice Case Dismissed," *Winnipeg Free Press*, 19 November 1960.
77 LAC, CLC, MG28 I103, H-93, f.13, National Committee on Human Rights reports of activities, 1967 to 1968.
78 LAC, JLC, MG28, V75, v.36, f.15, Comments on an Act concerning Discrimination in Employment, n.d.
79 LAC, JLC, MG28, V75, v.40, f.15, David Orlikow to Alan Borovoy, 3 October 1966; LAC, JLC, MG28, V75, v.40, f.10, memorandum to the Halifax Advisory Committee on Human Relations, n.d.
80 Frager and Patrias, "Human Rights Activists," 9.
81 LAC, Kalmen Kaplansky, v.16, f.1, "Human Rights Commission – The Next Phase," Address delivered by Bora Laskin to the 19th Annual Conference of Commissions for Human Rights, 6 July 1967.
82 Dan Hill, the first chairman of the Ontario Human Rights Commission, emphasized this point in 1969: "Immigration also affects the Commission's work. Almost overnight a new

heterogeneity is developing in Ontario's population structure. At least 500,000 of the two million inhabitants of Metropolitan Toronto are newcomers who are primarily Italian, German, European and Moroccan Jews, French, Polish, Hungarian, Greek, Dutch, Portuguese, Negro, and Asian in origin. There has been a large increase, particularly in Toronto and Hamilton, of West Indian Negroes in the case load. There also is a distinct rise in complaints from Asian immigrants, primarily from India and Pakistan and the Commission now works more closely with the new Filipino and Portuguese communities." Daniel G. Hill, "The Role of a Human Rights Commission: The Ontario Experience," *University of Toronto Law Journal* 19 (1969): 397.
83 Leo Driedger, *Race and Ethnicity: Finding Identities and Equalities,* 2nd ed. (Toronto: Oxford University Press, 2003), 57.
84 Ruth A. Frager and Carmela Patrias, *Discounted Labour: Women Workers in Canada, 1870-1939* (Toronto: University of Toronto Press, 2005), 153.
85 Colter, "A State of Affairs," 78.

Chapter 3: Gender and Canada's Human Rights State

1 Doris Anderson, *Rebel Daughter: An Autobiography* (Toronto: Key Porter Books, 1996), 124.
2 Josie Bannerman, Kathy Chopik, and Ann Zurbrigg, "Cheap at Half the Price: The History of the Fight for Equal Pay in BC," in *Not Just Pin Money: Selected Essays on the History of Women's Work in British Columbia,* ed. Barbara K. Latham and Roberta J. Pazdro (Victoria: Camosun College, 1984), 299.
3 Quoted in Gillian Creese, "The Politics of Dependence: Women, Work and Unemployment in the Vancouver Labour Movement before World War II," in *British Columbia Reconsidered: Essays on Women,* ed. Gillian Creese and Veronica Strong-Boag (Vancouver: Press Gang, 1992), 372.
4 Anderson, *Rebel Daughter,* 89.
5 Quoted in Judy Rebick, *Ten Thousand Roses: The Making of a Feminist Revolution* (Toronto: Penguin Canada, 2005), 201.
6 Anderson, *Rebel Daughter,* 89.
7 Ruth A. Frager and Carmela Patrias, *Discounted Labour: Women Workers in Canada, 1870-1939* (Toronto: University of Toronto Press, 2005), 154. LiLynn Wan argues that the rights of racial minorities overshadowed any discussion of women's rights in debates surrounding British Columbia's ban on white women working for Chinese men. LiLynn Wan, "'Out of Many Kindreds and Tongues': Racial Identity and Rights Activism in Vancouver, 1919-1939" (PhD diss., Dalhousie University, 2011), 265.
8 Dean Beeby, "Women in the Ontario C.C.F., 1940-1950," *Ontario History* 74 (1982): 267.
9 John C. Bagnall, "The Ontario Conservatives and the Development of Anti-Discrimination Policy" (PhD diss., Queen's University, 1984), 273.
10 Carmela Patrias, "Socialists, Jews, and the 1947 Saskatchewan Bill of Rights," *Canadian Historical Review* 87 (2006): 280.
11 Ruth A. Frager and Carmela Patrias, "Human Rights Activists and the Question of Sex Discrimination in Postwar Ontario," *Canadian Historical Review* 93 (2012): 10-15.
12 House of Commons, *Hansard,* no. 4 (1952-53), 3761-79.

13 Ibid., 3769.
14 Quoted in Ruth A. Frager and Carmela Patrias, "'This Is Our Country, These Are Our Rights': Minorities and the Origins of Ontario's Human Rights Campaigns," *Canadian Historical Review* 82 (2001): 4.
15 Ibid.
16 On women and discrimination in BC unions, see Marie Campbell, "Sexism in British Columbia Trade Unions, 1900-1920," in *In Her Own Right: Selected Essays on Women's History in BC*, ed. Barbara Latham and Cathy Kess (Victoria: Camosun College, 1980), 167-86; Gail Cuthbert Brandt et al., *Canadian Women: A History* (Toronto: Nelson Education, 2011), 304-7, 462-70.
17 Joan Sangster, "Radical Ruptures: Feminism, Labor, and the Left in the Long Sixties in Canada," *American Review of Canadian Studies* 40 (2010): 5.
18 "Present Brief on Equal Pay, Equal Work," *Montreal Star*, 23 April 1953.
19 Library and Archives Canada, Ottawa (LAC), Senate Committee on Industrial Relations, RG14-20, Acc. 1987-88/146, box 63, Cora Woloszyn to Don F. Brown, 16 March 1953.
20 Ross Lambertson, "The Dresden Story: Racism, Human Rights, and the Jewish Labour Committee of Canada," *Labour/Le travail* (Spring 2001): 43-82; James W. St. G. Walker, "The 'Jewish Phase' in the Movement for Racial Equality in Canada," *Canadian Ethnic Studies* 34 (2002): 1-29.
21 On this point, see Shirley Tillotson, "Human Rights Law as Prism: Women's Organizations, Unions, and Ontario's Female Employees Fair Remuneration Act, 1951," *Canadian Historical Review* 72, 4 (1991): 532-57.
22 Campbell, "Sexism in British Columbia Trade Unions, 1900-1920," 177.
23 Frager and Patrias, *Discounted Labour*, 82-83.
24 LAC, Senate Committee on Industrial Relations, RG14-20, Acc. 1987-88/146, box 63, correspondence from the IODE (7 April 1953), University Women's Club (16 February 1953), and National Council of Jewish Women (5 November 1953).
25 Frager and Patrias, "Human Rights Activists," 16-17.
26 The resolution read as follows: "Fair Accommodation. WHEREAS there is concern caused by the practice of some proprietors, withholding service from groups or individuals because of race, colour, religion or national origin, and WHEREAS it is desirable that democratic nations make a concerted effort to remove every vestige of discrimination, and WHEREAS it is increasingly apparent that the law has a role in combating discrimination THEREFORE BE IT RESOLVED: That the Vancouver Council of Women request the Provincial Council of Women, to petition the British Columbia legislature to introduce appropriate legislation to prohibit discrimination in places supplying accommodation and services to the general public." British Columbia Archives, Victoria, Provincial Council of Women of British Columbia, box 4, f.3, "Submission to Cabinet, 1959."
27 Legislation for equal pay was introduced for the first time in Ontario in 1949 by the CCF but defeated in the legislature. Beeby, "Women in the Ontario C.C.F."; *The Female Employees Fair Remuneration Act*, S.O. 1951, c. 26; *The Equal Pay Act, 1952*, S.S. 1952, c. 104; *Equal Pay Act*, S.B.C. 1953, c. 6; *Equal Pay Act*, S.N.S. 1956, c. 5; *Equal Pay Act*, S.M. 1956, c. 18; *Female Employees Equal Pay Act*, S.C. 1956, c. 38; *An Act to amend The Alberta Labour Act*, S.A. 1957, c. 38; *The Equal Pay Act*, S.P.E.I. 1959, c. 11; *Female Employees Fair Remuneration Act*, S.N.B. 1961, c. 7; Tillotson, "Human Rights Law," 535.
28 Frager and Patrias, *Discounted Labour*, 153.

29 Marjorie Griffin Cohen, "Paid Work," in Ruth Roach Pierson and Marjorie Griffin Cohen, *Canadian Women's Issues,* vol. 2, *Bold Visions* (Toronto: James Lorimer, 1995), 86-87.
30 As Tillotson suggests, "the history of FEFRA [Female Employees Fair Remuneration Act] also reminds us of how organized extra-parliamentary interventions determine the meaning of human rights law." Tillotson, "Human Rights Law," 557.
31 Bannerman, Chopik, and Zurbrigg, "Cheap at Half the Price," 305.
32 Alison Prentice et al., *Canadian Women: A History* (Toronto: Harcourt Brace, 1996), 332-33.
33 Ibid., 333. The Canadian Business and Professional Women's Clubs in Alberta, British Columbia, New Brunswick, and Ontario (and the federal executive) were among the most vocal critics of the 1953 federal Fair Employment Practices Act for not including sex.
34 Ibid., 334. Tillotson concludes that "had there been no pressure from women's groups, however, labour's interest in pay equity would not have led to legislation." Tillotson, "Human Rights Law," 542.
35 Tillotson, "Human Rights Law," 536-37.
36 Beeby, "Women in the Ontario C.C.F.," 267-68.
37 Prentice et al., *Canadian Women,* 379.
38 Tillotson, "Human Rights Law," 545.
39 Quoted in ibid., 544.
40 Frager and Patrias, "Human Rights Activists," 22.
41 Beverley Baines, "Law, Gender, Equality," in *Changing Patterns: Women in Canada,* ed. Sandra Burt, Lorraine Code, and Lindsay Dorney (Toronto: McClelland and Stewart, 1993), 259.
42 Duane Lockard, *Toward Equal Opportunity: A Study of State and Local Antidiscrimination Laws* (New York: Macmillan, 1968).
43 For a survey of Australian human rights law, see Nick O'Neill, Simon Rice, and Roger Douglas, *Retreat from Injustice: Human Rights Law in Australia* (Sydney: Federation Press, 2004); and Louise Chappell, John Chesterman, and Lisa Hill, *The Politics of Human Rights in Australia* (Cambridge: Cambridge University Press, 2009).
44 Linda Reif, "Building Democratic Institutions: The Role of National Human Rights Institutions in Good Governance and Human Rights Protection," *Harvard Human Rights Journal* 13 (2000): 1-69; Thomas Pegram, "Diffusion across Political Systems: The Global Spread of National Human Rights Institutions," *Human Rights Quarterly* 32, 3 (2010): 729-60.
45 Pegram, "Diffusion across Political Systems," 731-32.
46 Eric Adams, "The Idea of Constitutional Rights and the Transformation of Canadian Constitutional Law, 1930-1960" (Phd diss., University of Toronto, 2009), 170. Christopher MacLennan forwards a similar argument in his study of the 1960 Canadian Bill of Rights: "Organizations across the country studied the [UDHR] and passed resolutions demanding various responses from the government. The demands from these human rights advocates ranged from asking Ottawa to make a symbolic gesture in support of the UN initiative to outright calls for a national bill of rights based on the contents of the declaration ... Newspapers, organized labour, civil liberties associations, women's groups, and ethnic organizations all pressured the federal government to explain why, in light of its apparent support for the UN program, it balked at suggestions for a national bill of rights." Christopher MacLennan, *Toward the Charter: Canadians and the Demand for a*

National Bill of Rights, 1929-1960 (Montreal and Kingston: McGill-Queen's University Press, 2003), 79.

47 John C. Bagnall, "The Ontario Conservatives and the Development of Anti-Discrimination Policy" (PhD diss., Queen's University, 1984), 307, 371. In addition to citing the UDHR, Frost argued that human rights were a part of the Cold War conflict, a sentiment that was shared by many advocates for anti-discrimination legislation. As Rabbi Abraham Feinberg pointed out to Frost during a delegation to the premier, "It is a sham to attempt to defend western democracy against communism if a man or woman is prevented from getting a job because of discrimination against race, religion or colour." Quoted in ibid., 122.

48 Quoted in William Schabas and Stéphane Beaulac, *International Human Rights and Canadian Law: Legal Commitment, Implementation and the Charter* (Toronto: Thompson Carswell, 2007), 36. Federal legislators also referred to the UDHR when they introduced the first federal anti-discrimination law in 1952. House of Commons, *Hansard*, no. 4 (1952-53), 3761-79.

49 On human rights legislation in Alberta, British Columbia, Manitoba, and Quebec, see Dominique Clément, *Canada's Rights Revolution: Social Movements and Social Change, 1937-82* (Vancouver: UBC Press, 2008); Dominique Clément, "'I Believe in Human Rights, Not Women's Rights': Women and the Human Rights State, 1969-1984," *Radical History Review* 101 (2008): 107-29; and Dominique Clément, "Human Rights Law and Sexual Discrimination in British Columbia, 1953-1984," in *The West and Beyond*, ed. Sara Carter, Alvin Finkel, and Peter Fortna (Edmonton: Athabasca University Press, 2010), 297-325. On human rights legislation in New Brunswick and Newfoundland, see Alan D. Reid, "The New Brunswick Human Rights Act," *University of Toronto Law Journal* 18 (1968): 394-400; Shannon Williams, "Human Rights in Theory and Practice: A Sociological Study of Aboriginal Peoples and the New Brunswick Human Rights Commission, 1967-1997" (Master's thesis, University of New Brunswick, 1998); Fred W. Coates, interview by Dominique Clément, 11 March 2002; Théo Gagnon, interview by Dominique Clément, 20 June 2004; and Dominique Clément, "Equality Deferred: Sex Discrimination and the Newfoundland Human Rights State," *Acadiensis* 41 (2012): 102-27.

50 Williams, "Human Rights in Theory," 30.

51 The Newfoundland Human Rights Association was a key player in working with the government to secure, and later expand, the human rights code. Minister of Manpower and Industrial Relations Edward Maynard stated that he "would single-out the Newfoundland-Labrador Human Rights Association and the Newfoundland Status of Women Council for their tremendous assistance in providing comprehensive briefs relating to the Amendments" (he later acknowledged the Newfoundland Federation of Labour's role as well). Newfoundland Legislative Library, Press Clippings, press release from Edward Maynard (Minister of Manpower and Industrial Relations), 20 December 1974.

52 Even by 1991, 99 percent of Newfoundland's population spoke English as a first language, and only 1.5 percent was foreign-born. Statistics Canada, *Canada Year Book*, 1967; Leo Driedger, *Race and Ethnicity: Finding Identities and Equalities*, 2nd ed. (Toronto: Oxford University Press, 2003), 73.

53 Of the Jews, Frager and Patrias write that "their greater integration into Canadian society, as well as sheer numbers, allowed them to be the most influential and effective campaigners against discrimination. By the 1940s many of them were English-speaking, and their ranks included academics and lawyers who undertook to do the necessary human rights research and become spokespersons for the campaigns for human rights. While most Jews lived in

larger urban areas, some Jews (mostly small-business owners) could be found throughout Ontario. Frequently active members of the Canadian Jewish Congress, the small-town Jews provided the Jewish community with a province-wide communication network unparalleled by any other minority group." Frager and Patrias, "'This Is Our Country,'" 17.

54 The Human Rights Commission was, in fact, created in 1961 to enforce the legislation that predated the Human Rights Code, which was passed a year later.
55 By the mid-1970s, legislation in Alberta, Manitoba, Nova Scotia, and Ontario included provisions for human rights commissions to initiate complaints.
56 Daniel G. Hill, "The Role of a Human Rights Commission: The Ontario Experience," *University of Toronto Law Journal* 19 (1969): 390-401; R. Brian Howe, "Incrementalism and Human Rights Reform," *Journal of Canadian Studies* 28 (1993): 35-36.
57 "Another Unworkable Law," *Toronto Globe and Mail*, 11 March 1966; "The Act Is Also on Trial," *Toronto Globe and Mail*, 18 May 1968; "Human Rights – At All Costs," *Toronto Globe and Mail*, 20 June 1968.
58 In 1970, the Canada Fair Employment Practices Act and the Female Employees' Equal Pay Act were incorporated into the new Canadian Labour Code. Ottawa also had provisions in the Public Service Employment Act that prohibited discrimination in hiring practices and promotion for the federal civil service. The Unemployment Insurance Act mandated that the minister of employment and immigration not discriminate when referring workers to employment opportunities. The National Housing Loan Regulations in 1978 required the Central Housing and Mortgage Corporation to ensure that borrowers with insured loans not discriminate on the basis of sex, marital status, race, colour, religion, or national origin in the sale or lease of a home. Federal law also applied to the territories until they enacted their own human rights legislation. For a more detailed discussion of federal law and policies, see Walter Tarnopolsky, *Discrimination and the Law in Canada* (Toronto: De Boo, 1982), 35-37.
59 On human rights laws in Nova Scotia, see W.A. MacKay, "Recent Developments in the Field of Human Rights in Nova Scotia," *University of Toronto Law Journal* 17 (1967): 176-86; and Erica Colter, "A State of Affairs Most Common: Black Nova Scotians and the Stanfield Government's Interdepartmental Committee on Human Rights, 1959-1967" (Master's thesis, Dalhousie University, 2006).
60 University of Victoria Archives, Victoria (UVA), Human Rights Boards of Inquiry Collection (BOIs), AR017, box 1, f.18, Jane Gawne v Richard Chapman & Associates 1979.
61 British Columbia, "Human Rights Board of Inquiry: Refusal to Hire," *Labour Research Bulletin* (February 1979): 35-36; UVA, BOIs, AR017, box 1, f.18, Jane Gawne v Richard Chapman & Associates 1979.
62 Hill, "The Role of a Human Rights Commission," 392. Hill added, "However, since the enactment of this legislation in 1962, of approximately 2,000 formal cases investigated, only about 50 have required resort to this procedure [board of inquiry]. Since 1962 the Commission has investigated, settled, dismissed or referred over 12,000 formal, informal, and miscellaneous complaints and inquiries." Ibid.
63 Ibid., 393.
64 T.M. Eberlee and D.G. Hill, "The Ontario Human Rights Code," *University of Toronto Law Journal* 15 (1964): 451.
65 Blair Mason, a future chairman of the Alberta Human Rights Commission, insisted that education was a central feature of human rights law: "Education is the greatest form of prevention because what you understand you don't fear. Every time you're able to establish

teamwork with different cultures and you begin to realize the uniformity of human nature regardless of our race, creed, whatever, and the richness of that diversity, you begin to appreciate how strong a society could be if all of that was integrated." Quoted in Jim Gurnett, "Oral Histories," in *Alberta Legacies,* ed. Dominique Clément and Gerry Gall (Edmonton: John Humphrey Centre for Peace and Human Rights, 2011), 152.

66 Bill Black, *BC Human Rights Review: Report on Human Rights in British Columbia* (Vancouver: Government of British Columbia, 1994), 71.

67 Newfoundland Human Rights Commission private office files, St. John's, f. History of the Human Rights Commission, "Newfoundland and Labrador Human Rights Commission," n.d. Also in this file, see Fred Coates to Joseph Rousseau (Minister of Manpower), 11 May 1973; and Fred Coates to Edward Maynard (Minister of Manpower and Industrial Relations), 22 October 1974.

68 Williams, "Human Rights in Theory," 32.

69 Reid, "The New Brunswick Human Rights Act," 399.

70 For a detailed study of the post-war human rights movement, see Clément, *Canada's Rights Revolution.*

71 Dominique Clément, "Searching for Rights in the Age of Activism: The Newfoundland-Labrador Human Rights Association, 1968-1982," *Newfoundland Studies* 19 (2003): 347-72; Clément, "Equality Deferred."

72 "Human Rights Association Influences Legislation," *National Newsletter/Bulletin nationale* (Canadian Federation of Civil Liberties and Human Rights Associations) 1, 1 (June 1972).

73 "A Free Flow of Information and Experience," *National Newsletter/Bulletin nationale* 1, 2 (August 1972).

74 Clément, *Canada's Rights Revolution,* Chapter 5.

75 In British Columbia, for instance, the labour federation participated in the International Year for Human Rights committee that lobbied the Social Credit government to introduce its 1969 Human Rights Act.

76 Jewish Public Library, Montreal, JLC, f. 98, United Council for Human Rights press releases, 22 August 1972, 22 March 1973.

77 Arnold Bruner, "The Genesis of Ontario Human Rights Legislation: A Study in Law Reform," *University of Toronto Faculty Law Review* 31 (1979): 249-50.

78 Valerie Korinek, "'The Most Openly Gay Person for at Least a Thousand Miles': Doug Wilson and the Politicization of a Province," *Canadian Historical Review* 84 (2003): 548-49.

79 Université du Québec à Montréal, Montreal, Service des archives et de gestion des documents, Fond Ligue des droits et libertés, 24P12/8, declaration from the Conseil du Patronat du Québec, October 1973; Clément, "Equality Deferred"; LAC, Jewish Labour Committee (JLC), MG28, V75, v.41, f.1, Brief of the NSAACP to the Bill Amendments Committee re. Bill no. 1, 11 March 1969; LAC, JLC, MG28, V75, v.47, f.5, Human rights committee of the BC Federation of Labour, Memorandum submitted to the provincial cabinet, 12 December 1964.

80 Although the law is fundamentally similar in every Canadian jurisdiction, there are variations in current human rights law. Saskatchewan's Human Rights Act prohibits discrimination in the contracting process and has a section on education (other provinces consider education as part of the provision on public services). Criminal conviction, political belief, and gender identity are prohibited grounds of discrimination in some jurisdictions but not others. British Columbia offers a blanket exemption for Bona Fide Occupational

Requirements, whereas Saskatchewan restricts Bona Fide Occupational Qualification to sex, ability, or age. British Columbia also provides a general exemption for charitable and religious organizations, whereas the exemption in other jurisdictions is based on specific circumstances. Ontario refers to undue hardship in the context of duty to accommodate, but not British Columbia (albeit the courts have interpreted the BC statute to include the same principle). Mary Anne Waldron, *Free to Believe: Rethinking Freedom of Conscience and Religion in Canada* (Toronto: University of Toronto Press, 2013), 129.

81 The first board of inquiry under Alberta's human rights legislation involved an Aboriginal woman named Frances Weaselfat, who filed a grievance against Denny's Shell Service, which required all "Indians" to pay in advance before pumping gas. The complaint was sustained, and the gas station owner was ordered to publish an apology and end the practice. Dominique Clément, "Human Rights Milestones: Alberta's Rights Revolution," in *Alberta's Human Rights Story: The Search for Equality and Justice*, ed. Dominique Clément and Renée Vaugeois (Edmonton: John Humphrey Centre for Peace and Human Rights, 2012), 1-40.

82 University of British Columbia Rare Books and Special Collections, Vancouver, Vancouver Status of Women, v.3, f.2, Jean Sam v Paul Tymchischin and the Tweedsmuir Hotel, 1975.

83 "Rights Board Awards $1250 to Indian Refused Hotel Room," *Vancouver Sun*, 6 February 1976.

84 Williams, "Human Rights in Theory," Chapter 4.

85 Except for Alberta, Canada, and New Brunswick, all jurisdictions exempted exclusively religious, philanthropic, educational, fraternal, and social organizations operating not-for-profit. Only British Columbia, Canada, and New Brunswick applied the employment provisions of human rights law to domestics working in private homes. Ontario removed the exemption for the government in 1965 and British Columbia in 1973.

86 Clément, "Equality Deferred."

87 *Vancouver Rape Relief Society v. Nixon et al.*, 2003 BCSC 1936 (B.C.S.C.). The BC Court of Appeal sustained the lower court's decision, and the Supreme Court of Canada refused in 2007 to consider Nixon's appeal. See also *Gould v. Yukon Order of Pioneers*, [1996] 1 S.C.R. 571. In *Gould*, a woman was refused membership in the Yukon Order of Pioneers, a private organization dedicated to promoting Yukon and preserving its heritage. The Yukon Human Rights Commission determined that the refusal constituted sex discrimination because the organization was offering a service normally available to the public. The Supreme Court of the Yukon Territory, however, set aside the decision, and both the Court of Appeal and the Supreme Court of Canada dismissed the appeal. The Supreme Court of Canada held that the refusal did not constitute discrimination under the legislation, because the Yukon Order was a social (rather than economic) association that did not provide a public service.

88 Tarnopolsky, *Discrimination and the Law*, 31.

Chapter 4: Women and Anti-Discrimination Law

1 "Legislature Rejects BC Bill of Rights," *Vancouver Sun*, 22 April 1948; "Bill of Rights Unnecessary, House Feels," *Vancouver Province*, 31 March 1950; University of British Columbia Rare Books and Special Collections, Vancouver (UBC RBSC), Vancouver Joint Labour Committee to Combat Racial Discrimination, box 4, Report on Activities, April 1951, and box 2, A resume of the Vancouver Labour Committee for Human Rights, n.d.

2 The JLC affiliate was also responsible for drafting a Vancouver bylaw banning discrimination in businesses licensed by the city.
3 UBC RBSC, Vancouver Joint Labour Committee to Combat Racial Discrimination, box 5, Report of Progress, 1952. Section 1 of City of Vancouver, Bylaw no. 4429, *Racial Discrimination By-law to amend bylaw no 3846* (17 June 1969), states, "No person holding or required to hold a license for the carrying on of any trade, business or occupation under the provisions of any bylaw of the City of Vancouver shall refuse to sell any goods or furnish any service or supply any accommodation to a person by reason only of such person's race, creed or colour."
4 John C. Bagnall, "The Ontario Conservatives and the Development of Anti-Discrimination Policy" (PhD diss., Queen's University, 1984), 289.
5 Library and Archives Canada, Ottawa (LAC), Canadian Labour Congress (CLC), MG28 I103, H-93, f.13, report of activities, September and October 1960.
6 British Columbia, Department of Labour, *Annual Report* (Victoria: Queen's Printer, 1967).
7 British Columbia, Department of Labour, *Annual Report* (Victoria: Queen's Printer, 1953).
8 British Columbia, Department of Labour, *Annual Report* (Victoria: Queen's Printer, 1953-69).
9 Marjorie Griffin Cohen, "Paid Work," in Ruth Roach Pierson and Marjorie Griffin Cohen, *Canadian Women's Issues*, vol. 2, *Bold Visions* (Toronto: James Lorimer, 1995), 86-87.
10 Joan Sangster, "Invoking Experience as Evidence," *Canadian Historical Review* 92 (2011): 148.
11 Ibid., 149.
12 Ibid., 153 (emphasis in original).
13 "Report of the Women's Bureau," in British Columbia, Department of Labour, *Annual Report* (Victoria: Queen's Printer, 1967), 37.
14 *An Act Respecting a Minimum Wage for Women*, R.S.B.C. 1924, c. 173.
15 British Columbia Archives, Victoria (BCA), Status of Women Action Group, v.3, f.32, Report on discrimination in the retail trades, 1972.
16 Linda Sproule-Jones, "A Brief Concerning the British Columbia Human Rights Act by the Victoria Voice of Women and the Victoria Labour Council," October 1972, private collection (Linda Sproule-Jones).
17 LAC, Senate Committee on Industrial Relations, RG14-20, Acc. 1987-88/146, box 63, Margaret Campbell to A.F. Macdonald, 20 February 1953.
18 BCA, Provincial Council of Women, box 4, f.6, "Mrs. Rex Eaton Presidential Address, 1950."
19 *An Act to Ensure Fair Remuneration for Female Employees*, S.B.C. 1953, c. 6.
20 "Tilly's Last Act to Help BC Women," *Vancouver Sun*, 14 October 1953.
21 "Council Seeks Changes in Bill for Equal Pay," *Vancouver Sun*, 6 October 1953.
22 British Columbia, Department of Labour, *Annual Report*, 1953-69.
23 "Equal Pay Only if Women 'Beef,'" *Vancouver Sun*, 30 December 1953.
24 April D. Katz, Chief of Compliance, Human Rights Branch, Ministry of Labour, "Human Rights and Employment in British Columbia," n.d., private collection (April Katz); UBC RBSC, VLCHR, box 1, Report on Activities, December 1955.
25 UBC RBSC, VLCHR, box 5, Report of Progress, 1952; box 1, Monthly Progress Reports, 1960-71; box 2, A resume of VLCHR, n.d.
26 Herbert A. Sohn, "Human Rights Legislation in Ontario: A Study of Social Action" (PhD diss., University of Toronto, 1975), 194.

27 UBC RBSC, VLCHR, box 1, Report on Activities, October 1959.
28 Instead of inquiring about race, job application forms commonly asked for photographs. UBC RBSC, VLCHR, box 1, survey of application forms, n.d., and Monthly Progress Reports, 1960-71.
29 LAC, Dan Hill, MG31, H155, v.16, f.17, Submission by the Human Rights Committee of the BC Federation of Labour, 1964 and 1969.
30 UBC RBSC, Monthly Progress Reports, 1960-71; LAC, Jewish Labour Committee (JLC), v.23, f.6, Report of the British Columbia Federation of Labour Human Rights Committee, 1961.
31 UBC RBSC, VLCHR, box 1, Reports on Activities (1952-71), January 1967.
32 The British Columbia government added age as a prohibited ground for discrimination in a 1964 amendment to the Fair Employment Practices Act.
33 British Columbia, Department of Labour, *Annual Report,* 1953-69.
34 UBC RBSC, British Columbia Federation of Labour, v.52, f.8, Edgar complaint, 1967.
35 UBC RBSC, British Columbia Federation of Labour, v.52, f.8, Thomas Berger to J. McNevin, 7 August 1967.
36 "Human Rights Committee Report," in British Columbia Federation of Labour, *Summary of Proceedings, Annual General Meeting* (Burnaby: British Columbia Federation of Labour, 1972).
37 LAC, Dan Hill, MG31, H155, v.16, f.17, Submission by the Human Rights Committee of the BC Federation of Labour, 1964.
38 LAC, JLC, MG28, V75, v.23, f.6, Report of the BC Federation of Labour Human Rights Committee, n.d.
39 UBC RBSC, VLCHR, box 4, Report on activities, July 1956.
40 British Columbia Commission for International Year for Human Rights, "Report" (1968); "Report Urges Human Rights Act for BC," *Vancouver Province,* 11 December 1968.
41 For further information on the International Year for Human Rights in Canada, refer to Clément, *Canada's Rights Revolution.*
42 Dominique Clément, "Rights in the Age of Protest: A History of the Human Rights and Civil Liberties Movement in Canada, 1962-1982" (PhD diss., Memorial University of Newfoundland, 2005), Appendix; Clément, *Canada's Rights Revolution,* Chapter 8.
43 The Vancouver Civic Unity Association also held four meetings a year in a Vancouver "ethnic hall" and encouraged residents to attend and learn about the diverse cultures in the community. LAC, Walter Tarnopolsky, MG31, E55, v.31, f.7, International Year for Human Rights – Vancouver United Association, December 1958; Giesbrecht, Clément interview.
44 Among the organizations represented at the conference were the BC Association for the Advancement of Coloured People, Canadian Association for Adult Education, Canadian Committee on Christians and Jews, Council of Churches, Provincial Council of Women or the Catholic Women's League, the Sikh Temple, United Nations Association (Vancouver branch), Vancouver Area B'nai Brith Women, Vancouver Citizenship Council, Vancouver Council of Women, Vancouver Indian Centre Society, YMCA, and the YWCA.
45 A important recommendation was that the Fair Employment Practices Act apply to civil servants and businesses employing fewer than five people.
46 Donald Anderson, "The Development of Human Rights Protections in British Columbia" (Master's thesis, University of Victoria, 1986), 69-70.

CHAPTER 5: JACK SHERLOCK AND THE FAILED HUMAN RIGHTS ACT

1 Women constituted 34.2 percent of university undergraduate students in 1967-68 and 53.5 percent in 1992-93 (however, they remained underrepresented in engineering and sciences). They earned 21.4 percent of all master's degrees in 1930-31 and 20.6 percent in 1966-67. In 1930-31, they secured 15.2 percent of doctorates, a figure that had declined to 7.6 percent by 1966-67. Their workforce participation rates transformed dramatically in Canada after the war, from 20 percent in 1941 to 34 percent in 1971 and 40 percent in 1981. Sixty-five percent of Canadian families replicated the traditional male breadwinner model in 1961; less than 12 percent did so by 1986. Married women's workforce participation rate jumped from 11 percent in 1951 to 61 percent in 1991 (from 30 to 64 percent of the total female workforce). And by the 1980s, for the first time in history, women with small children remained in their jobs, belying the stereotype that they left the workforce to raise a family. Ruth Roach Pierson, "Education and Training," in Ruth Roach Pierson and Marjorie Griffin Cohen, *Canadian Women's Issues*, vol. 2, *Bold Visions* (Toronto: James Lorimer, 1995), 164-65, 195n192. Ruth A. Frager and Carmela Patrias, *Discounted Labour: Women Workers in Canada, 1870-1939* (Toronto: University of Toronto Press, 2005), 153.
2 The Department of Labour's Women's Bureau, which was established in 1966, listed a number of factors to account for the rise in female workers during the 1960s: "Apart from the strong demand for women's labour, the growth of new industries in British Columbia's dynamic economy and expanded activities in others, such as commerce and trade, have opened doors for women. Participation rates appear to be affected by favourable economic conditions. Other factors are lighter home responsibilities because children are in school and technological advances that have simplified home chores." Only one person worked in the Women's Bureau, which did little more than conduct some research on women in the workforce, participate in conferences, liaise with community groups, and stock a reference library. "Report of the Women's Bureau," in British Columbia, Department of Labour, *Annual Report* (Victoria: Queen's Printer, 1968), 35. On the federal Women's Bureau, refer to Sandra Burt, "The Changing Patterns of Public Policy," in *Changing Patterns: Women in Canada*, 2nd ed., ed. Sandra Burt, Lorraine Code, and Lindsay Dorney (Toronto: McClelland and Stewart, 1993), 220-21.
3 Marguerite Andersen, ed., *Feminist Journeys* (Ottawa: Feminist History Society, 2010).
4 Gail G. Campbell, "Perhaps I Arrived at the Best of Times," in ibid., 88.
5 Margaret Conrad, "From the Age of Four," in Andersen, *Feminist Journeys*, 92.
6 Audrey Hozack, "Upstairs and Downstairs," in Andersen, *Feminist Journeys*, 177.
7 Joan Gilroy, "A Long Process," in Andersen, *Feminist Journeys*, 151.
8 Lorraine Greaves, "The Politics of Housework," in Andersen, *Feminist Journeys*, 159.
9 Margaret McCrae, "Teaching Sex Education," in Andersen, *Feminist Journeys*, 243.
10 *An Act for the Promotion and Protection of the Fundamental Rights of the People of British Columbia*, S.B.C. 1969, c. 2.
11 University of Northern British Columbia Archives, Prince George, Women's Resource Centre collection, 2006.5.1, "Discrimination – BC Civil Liberties Association Handbook on the 1969 Human Rights Act," n.d.
12 William W. Black, *Reassessing Statutory Human Rights Legislation Thirty Years Later: Human Rights Enforcement in British Columbia: A Case Study* (Ottawa: Human Rights Research and Education Centre, 1995), 4-5.

13 "Members Names to Act as Rights Commission," *Vancouver Province,* 11 June 1969.
14 Black, *Reassessing Statutory Human Rights Legislation,* 4-5.
15 Jean Barman, *The West beyond the West: A History of British Columbia* (Toronto: University of Toronto, 1991), 279. W.A.C. Bennett's biographer suggests that he had little interest in or knowledge of women's issues and that his female appointments to cabinet (three, without portfolio) in 1966 were largely window dressing. David J. Mitchell, *W.A.C. Bennett and the Rise of British Columbia* (Vancouver: Douglas and McIntyre, 1995), 373.
16 Library and Archives Canada, Ottawa, Dan Hill, MG31, H155, v.16, f.17, Submission by the Human Rights Committee of the BC Federation of Labour, 1964.
17 In her informal survey of the history of anti-discrimination laws in British Columbia, April Katz credits the Vancouver Civic Unity Association with successfully lobbying the government to introduce the 1969 Human Rights Act. April D. Katz, Chief of Compliance, Human Rights Branch, Ministry of Labour, "Human Rights and Employment in British Columbia," n.d., private collection (April Katz).
18 "Cabinet OK's $42,429 Ad Payments," *Vancouver Sun,* 31 October 1969; Donald Anderson, "The Development of Human Rights Protections in British Columbia" (Master's thesis, University of Victoria, 1986), 66.
19 Donna Vogel, *Challenging Politics: COPE, Electoral Politics and Social Movements* (Halifax: Fernwood Press, 2003), 57-58.
20 University of British Columbia Rare Books and Special Collections, Vancouver (UBC RBSC), Vancouver Status of Women (VSW), v.2, f.1, male chauvinist pig awards, 1972.
21 "Inadequate Rights Bill," *Democratic Commitment: Newsletter of the British Columbia Civil Liberties Association* 10 (June 1969): 3.
22 "Human Rights Act Full of Holes – Federation," *Vancouver Province,* 10 April 1969.
23 Anderson, "The Development of Human Rights," 64.
24 The following discussion of Jensen's case and the events surrounding the complaint is based on a series of newspaper articles as well as interviews, including, "Employer, Employees Claim Rights Law Helps Neither," *Vancouver Sun,* 14 November 1972; and Kathleen Ruff, interview by Dominique Clément, 14 April 2010.
25 "Employer, Employees Claim Rights Law Helps Neither."
26 The legislation also did not cover discrimination on the basis of political belief. Nor did the prohibition on age discrimination apply to retirement, pension, insurance plans, or anyone who was younger than forty-five.
27 B.C. Civil Servant, "Human Rights ... but Not for Women," *The Pedestal* 1, 1 (Fall 1969): 1.
28 Nat Cole, "Barmaids for BC Still a Pub Dream," *Vancouver Sun,* 1 March 1969.
29 Anderson, "The Development of Human Rights," 62-64.
30 "Members Names to Act."
31 "Poverty 'Explosion' Feared," *Vancouver Province,* 4 December 1969.
32 Ruff, Clément interview.
33 UBC RBSC, VSW, v.33, f.22, A Brief Presented to David Barrett, October 1972.
34 Black, *Reassessing Statutory Human Rights Legislation,* 4-5.
35 The data on investigations between 1969 and 1973 are based on two sources: annual reports from the Department of Labour and documents in the collection of Bill Black. Black produced a survey of cases in the mid-1970s, when Kathleen Ruff gave him access to the Human Rights Branch files.
36 UBC RBSC, Renate Shearer, v.1, f.3, Ralph Loffmark to William Bennett, 12 March 1970.

37 UBC RBSC, A Brief Presented to David Barrett, October 1972.
38 Anderson, "The Development of Human Rights," 69.
39 British Columbia, *Debates of the Legislative Assembly* (5 November 1973), 1264.

Chapter 6: Kathleen Ruff and the Human Rights Code

1 Day also served as president of the Women's Legal Education and Action Fund, vice-president of the National Action Committee on the Status of Women, a founding member of the Court Challenges Program, special adviser on human rights to the National Association of Women and the Law, and the publisher of the *Canadian Human Rights Reporter*.
2 Iain Hunter and Jes Odam, "Charter for Women Detailed," *Vancouver Sun*, 28 February 1969.
3 "Veils for Female Job-Seekers?" *Vancouver Province*, 25 March 1969.
4 Dominique Clément, "An Exercise in Futility? Regionalism, State Funding, and Ideology as Obstacles to the Formation of a National Social Movement Organization in Canada," *BC Studies* 146 (Summer 2005): 63-91.
5 University of British Columbia Rare Books and Special Collections, Vancouver (UBC RBSC), Vancouver Status of Women (VSW), Grant Applications to the Provincial Secretary of BC, 1 April 1977 to 31 March 1978.
6 Rosemary Brown, *Being Brown: A Very Public Life* (Toronto: Random House, 1989), 98.
7 University of Victoria Archives, Victoria (UVA), Victoria Status of Women Action Group (SWAG), AR119, 2004-005, f.1.1, Status of Women Action Group, n.d.
8 UVA, SWAG, AR119, 2004-005, f.1.5, Challenge 86 grant application (includes history of SWAG), n.d.
9 Major revisions to human rights laws were implemented in New Brunswick (1973), Quebec (1977), Alberta (1980), Ontario (1981), British Columbia (1984), Canada (1985), Manitoba (1987), Newfoundland (1988), Prince Edward Island (1988), and Nova Scotia (1989). R. Brian Howe and D. Johnson, "Variations in Enforcing Equality: A Study of Provincial Human Rights Funding," *Canadian Public Administration* 38 (1995): 249; Dominique Clément, Will Silver, and Dan Trottier, *The Evolution of Human Rights in Canada* (Ottawa: Canadian Human Rights Commission, 2012).
10 Dominique Clément, *Canada's Rights Revolution: Social Movements and Social Change, 1937-82* (Vancouver: UBC Press, 2008), 121-23. For a detailed review of human rights legislation in Quebec, see Andrée Côté and Lucie Lemonde, *Discrimination et commission des droits de la personne* (Montreal: Éditions Saint-Martin, 1988).
11 Philip Resnick, "Social Democracy in Power: The Case of British Columbia," *BC Studies* 34 (1977): 3-20.
12 For King's useful overview of the NDP critique of the 1969 Human Rights Act, see British Columbia, *Debates of the Legislative Assembly* (5 November 1973), 1256-57.
13 Donald Anderson, "The Development of Human Rights Protections in British Columbia" (Master's thesis, University of Victoria, 1986), 154; Bill Black, interview by Dominique Clément, 20 June 2002.
14 Dominique Clément, "'I Believe in Human Rights, Not Women's Rights': Women and the Human Rights State, 1969-1984," *Radical History Review* 101 (2008): 107-29.

15 Simon Fraser Rare Books and Special Collections, Burnaby, Frances Wasserlein, f.162-3-3-0-4, Vancouver Women's Caucus Brief to the Human Rights Commission, 3 December 1969; Canadian Women's Movement Archives, University of Ottawa, Ottawa, British Columbia Federation of Women, vols. 5-6, materials on the British Columbia human rights code and commission, 1979; Anderson, "The Development of Human Rights," 69-70; UBC RBSC, Rosemary Brown, v.8, f.9, briefs and correspondence by the Vancouver Young Women's Christian Association, British Columbia Federation of Labour Women's Rights Committee, and the University of British Columbia Women's Action Group.

16 Shelagh Day described the investigation process as follows: "The investigating officer gathers available information relating to the complaint from all parties and, on the basis of this information, determines whether a contravention of the Code has occurred. If the officer has evidence that discrimination has occurred, he or she makes a recommendation that the complaint be settled by the respondent. On the other hand, if there is no evidence of discrimination, the officer recommends to the Director that no further action be taken." Shelagh Day, "Recent Developments in Human Rights," *Labour Research Bulletin* (June 1977): 16-24.

17 Unlike in the courts, this innovation would ensure that employers, who had more resources than a recently dismissed employee, would not have an unfair advantage. Victims of discrimination, including racial minorities and women, often struggled on the margins of the labour market. The law was designed to make the process accessible to everyone.

18 British Columbia, *Debates of the Legislative Assembly* (5 November 1973), 1257.

19 UVA, Human Rights Boards of Inquiry (BOIs), AR017, Acc. 97-159, f.2.21, Norene Warren v F.A. Cleland and Son, and David Fowler, 1975; Kathleen Ruff, interview by Dominique Clément, 14 April 2010.

20 The one exception to the clause was tenants – it did not apply to people seeking to rent. During second reading of the bill, Rosemary Brown suggested that this was because the Law Reform Commission was currently considering the issue. British Columbia, *Debates of the Legislative Assembly* (5 November 1973), 1260.

21 Rainer Knopff states that "Manitoba has similar reasonable cause provisions regarding tenancy and public facilities. Until 1987 Manitoba also had a similar but somewhat weaker formulation for employment, by which stipulated forms of discrimination were prohibited 'without limiting the generality of the foregoing.' This has been replaced by a prohibition of employment discrimination 'unless the discrimination is based upon bona fide and reasonable requirements or qualifications.' The cases brought under the former section in Manitoba were resolved through adjudication, except one, and this case was sustained in the courts." Rainer Knopff, *Human Rights and Social Technology: The New War on Discrimination* (Ottawa: Carleton University Press, 1989), 39.

22 H.W.'s full name appears in the official transcript, but in its final report, the board of inquiry notes that she asked to be identified only by her initials. In withholding her name, I have chosen to honour her request.

23 Shelagh Day notes, "This is the first case in Canada to deal with employment discrimination against a pregnant woman and the BC human rights legislation is singularly able to provide protection to pregnant women because Section 8 prohibits discrimination without reasonable cause." Day, "Recent Developments in Human Rights," 21. See also British Columbia, "Human Rights Boards of Inquiry: Rights of Pregnant Women," *Labour Research Bulletin* (July 1976): 69-71; British Columbia, "Human Rights Boards of Inquiry: Warren

v Becket, Nadon & Creditel of Canada Limited," *Labour Research Bulletin* (January 1977): 62-63; Peter Comparelli and Glen Schaefer, "Two Women Sexually Harassed, Inquiries Rule," *Vancouver Sun,* 28 July 1984; and *Julie Webb v. Cyprus Pizza,* [1985] 6 C.H.R.R. D/2794.

24 Jan O'Brien, "Employer Surprised His Woman-Grabbing Unwanted," *Vancouver Province,* 29 November 1979.

25 Constance Backhouse and Leah Cohen, *The Secret Oppression: Sexual Harassment of Working Women* (Toronto: Macmillan, 1978).

26 Doris Anderson, *Rebel Daughter: An Autobiography* (Toronto: Key Porter Books, 1996), 173.

27 In their study, Backhouse and Cohen briefly discuss why sexual harassment was a "recent" phenomenon in the 1970s: "One [reason] is that since more women are working there are more instances of sexual harassment, and this has brought the problem to a head. Another is that middle-class women have begun to recognize they will continue to work outside their homes for the majority of their lives. This, it is argued, causes them to take threats to their working status – such as sexual harassment – more seriously." Backhouse and Cohen also suggest that the efforts of women activists to raise awareness of rape have also led to greater awareness of sexual harassment. Backhouse and Cohen, *The Secret Oppression,* 1-2, 71-72.

28 *Carignan v. Mastercraft Publications Limited,* [1984] 5 C.H.R.R. D/2282.

29 Ibid.

30 For a list of the specific decisions on the reasonable cause section, see R. Brian Howe, "Incrementalism and Human Rights Reform," *Journal of Canadian Studies* 28 (1993): 35-36.

31 "Report of the Human Rights Branch," in British Columbia, Department of Labour, *Annual Report* (Victoria: Queen's Printer, 1974), X58.

32 As described in Day, "Recent Developments in Human Rights," 16.

33 UBC RBSC, VSW, v.6, f.15, memorandum by Carol Pfeifer, 3 December 1976; UBC RBSC, VSW, v.10, f.2, Kathleen Ruff to Carol Pfeifer, 15 December 1976; UVA, BOIs, AR017, Acc. 97-159, f.2.19, Linda Ward v Pilgrim House Penticton, n.d.

34 After 1979, the Human Rights Commission's reports no longer appeared in the annual reports of the Ministry of Labour but were submitted directly to the legislature through the minister. British Columbia, Ministry of Labour, *Annual Report* (Victoria: Queen's Printer, 1970-82); British Columbia, Human Rights Commission, *Annual Report* (Victoria: Queen's Printer, 1979-82).

35 Of the 709 formal complaints in 1978, 73 percent dealt with employment discrimination, 20 percent with services, and 6 percent with tenancy. In total, 379 cases were closed: of these, 62 percent dealt with employment, 15 percent were dismissed, 9 percent were withdrawn, 10 percent were not pursued, 1 percent fell outside the scope of the law, and 3 percent were referred to the minister. British Columbia, Ministry of Labour, *Annual Report, Human Rights (Industrial Relations Division)* (Victoria: Queen's Printer, 1975), 58-59 (source available at the Legislative Library of British Columbia).

36 Howe, "Incrementalism and Human Rights Reform."

37 "Report of the Human Rights Branch," in British Columbia, Department of Labour, *Annual Report* (Victoria: Queen's Printer, 1973), BB40.

38 Ruff, Clément interview.

39 Shelagh Day, interview by Dominique Clément, 12 May 2009.

40 There were only twenty-six IROs in the mid-1960s and forty in 1970 scattered throughout the province. British Columbia, Department of Labour, *Annual Report* (Victoria: Queen's Printer, 1963), 33; UBC RBSC, Vancouver Labour Committee for Human Rights, box 1, John C. Sherlock to Bill Giesbrecht, 20 October 1970; University of Northern British Columbia Archives, Prince George, Women's Resource Centre collection, v.5, f.1, "Discrimination – BC Civil Liberties Association Handbook on the 1969 Human Rights Act," n.d.
41 Day, Clément interview.
42 UBC RBSC, VSW, v.10, f.2, Kathleen Ruff to Carol Pfeifer, 15 December 1976.
43 Day, Clément interview.
44 Linda Sproule-Jones, interview by Dominique Clément, 5 May 2009.
45 Part of the investigation process involved securing access to documents. For instance, a human rights officer might review company files relating to its hiring practices. The Human Rights Code authorized the branch to require employers to provide all relevant documents. Each officer was given a badge.
46 Ruff, Clément interview.
47 Day, Clément interview.
48 Sproule-Jones, Clément interview. The Capital Regional District agreed to pay Jewsbury $2,000 and to offer her the next available position as a waste water technician. Although the case went to a board of inquiry, the two parties reached a settlement at the beginning of the hearing and agreed to adjourn it without airing arguments. UVA, BOIs, AR017, Acc. 97-159, f.2.2, Gail Jewsbury v Capital Regional District, 1978.
49 Sproule-Jones, Clément interview.
50 Ruff, Clément interview.
51 Attorney General's Office, Victoria, British Columbia Human Rights Branch (AG HRB), Acc. 1989-699-02, case summaries by Reginald Newkirk, 1976 to 1981.
52 UBC RBSC, VSW, v.2, f.31, Bonnie Bukwa vs Lornex Mining Corporation, 1976.
53 British Columbia, "Human Rights Boards of Inquiry: Aggravated Damage," *Labour Research Bulletin* (February 1976): 85-86; UVA, BOIs, AR017, Acc. 97-159, Jean Tharpe v Lornex Mining Corporation, 1976.
54 Day, Clément interview.
55 "Discrimination and Rights," *Penticton Herald*, 28 February 1977.
56 UBC RBSC, VSW, v.2, f.27, Dutchie Mathison to human rights branch, n.d.
57 AG HRB, Acc. 1989-699-07, report on sexual harassment and the Human Rights Code by the Human Rights Branch, 8 August 1980.
58 Several briefs prepared by the VSW dealing with the status of women in British Columbia are available in UBC RBSC, VSW, v.8, f.29, and v.13, f.9 to f.11. See also UBC RBSC, VSW, v.6, f.15, day of mourning for the human rights code, December 1976; British Columbia, *Debates of the Legislative Assembly* (16 February 1984), 3292.
59 UBC RBSC, VSW, v.13, f.22, A Two-Fold Proposal to Improve the Status of Women in British Columbia: Brief Presented to David Barrett, October 1972.
60 Heather Conn and Peter Menyasz, "Women Gear Up for EUS Battle," *The Ubyssey*, 28 February 1980. See also Terry Gould, "The Engineers of Dumb Behavior," *Vancouver Magazine*, May 1991; Ruth Roach Pierson, "The Politics of the Body," in Ruth Roach Pierson et al., *Canadian Women's Issues*, vol. 1, *Strong Voices* (Toronto: James Lorimer, 1993), 171; and Hester Lessard, "Backlash in the Academy: The Evolution of Campus Sexual Harassment Regimes," in *Reaction and Resistance: Feminism, Law, and Social Change*, ed. Dorothy E. Chunn, Susan B. Boyd, and Hester Lessard (Vancouver: UBC Press, 2007), 173.

61 "Charge Claimed Unfounded," *Vancouver Province*, 29 February 1980.
62 Wanda Wiegers, "Feminist Protest and the Regulation of Misogynist Speech: A Case Study of *Saskatchewan Human Rights Commission v Engineering Students' Society*," *Ottawa Law Review* 24 (1992): 363-435. The Lady Godiva ride was a staple on many university campuses. The tradition was meant to pay homage to an eleventh-century English noblewoman who rode naked through the streets of Coventry to force her husband to eliminate oppressive taxation.
63 Christabelle Sethna, "'Chastity Outmoded': *The Ubyssey*, Sex, and the Single Girl, 1960-1970," in *Creating Postwar Canada: Community, Diversity and Dissent, 1945-75*, ed. Magda Fahrni and Robert Rutherdale (Vancouver: UBC Press, 2007), 308.
64 Wiegers, "Feminist Protest," 386-96.
65 Lessard, "Backlash in the Academy," 173.
66 British Columbia Archives, Victoria (BCA), Victoria Status of Women Action Group, v.3, f.32, Report on discrimination in the retail trades, 1972; Linda Sproule-Jones to David Barrett, 12 December 1973, and Linda Sproule-Jones to William Black, 15 January 1974, private collection (Linda Sproule-Jones); UBC RBSC, VSW, v.10, f.2, Kathleen Ruff to Carol Pfeifer, 15 December 1976; Library and Archives Canada, Ottawa, Dan Hill, MG31 H155, v.16, f.17, Victoria Human Rights Council Brief to the Human Rights Commission, 1979; BCA, Department of Labour, G84-079, box 5, SWAG report on the Human Rights Code, 1981; UBC RBSC, British Columbia Federation of Women, v.1, f.28, human rights policy, n.d.
67 Day, "Recent Developments in Human Rights."

Chapter 7: Struggling to Innovate

1 *Grafe v. Sechelt Building Supplies*, unreported (17 May 1979), BC Board of Inquiry; "Human Rights Is B.S.," *Kinesis* 8, 6 (June 1979): 11.
2 Alison Prentice et al., *Canadian Women: A History* (Toronto: Harcourt Brace, 1996), 378.
3 Ibid., 379.
4 Men reported an average pension in 1981 income of $5,613, compared with $3,663 for women. Peter Bartlett, "Sexual Distinctions in Pensions," *Osgoode Hall Law Journal* 24 (1986): 835.
5 Ibid., 838.
6 Gender-based mortality tables used by insurance companies became a controversial public issue in Canada and the United States during the 1980s. Ibid., 849-65.
7 Lynne Pearson, *Women in British Columbia: Issues, Resources and Services* (Victoria: Provincial Coordinator for the Status of Women's Office, 1975), 5.
8 Ibid.
9 British Columbia Archives, Victoria (BCA), Department of Labour, G85-168, box 8, Acc. 8800573718, Women and Youth in Northwest BC Labour Markets, Summary Report, Associated Economic Consultants Ltd., December 1982.
10 Ibid., 8.
11 British Columbia Human Rights Commission, *I'm Okay; We're Not So Sure about You: A Report of the BC Human Rights Commission on Extensions to the Code* (Victoria: British Columbia Human Rights Commission, 1983), 37-42.
12 University of British Columbia Rare Books and Special Collections, Vancouver (UBC RBSC), Vancouver Status of Women (VSW), v.1, f.32, BCTF Task Force on Women in Education and Work Report, 1974.

13 Ibid.
14 The following account demonstrates how the segregation of male and female teachers in primary and secondary schools was informed by a gender bias: "One former UBC Education student, now graduated, and substitute teaching in Vancouver, reported that he registered in the primary section of the Education Department and found that he had been changed to the intermediate section. On questioning this he was told that he would have difficulty getting work in the primary area. It was also assumed that he had wanted [to be] in the primary area because his marks were too low to handle any other grade level. On checking, the Department was surprised to find that his marks were perfectly satisfactory." Ibid.
15 Ibid.
16 Linda Goulden et al., *Report of the Task Force on the Status of Women in the Government and in Education in B.C.* (Vancouver: British Columbia Teachers' Federation, 1973).
17 Attorney General's Office, Victoria, British Columbia Human Rights Branch (AG HRB), Acc. 1989-700-14, memorandum on community organizations, 1981.
18 Alan Andison, interview by Dominique Clément, 19 August 2010.
19 April Katz, interview by Dominique Clément, 17 August 2010.
20 British Columbia, *Debates of the Legislative Assembly* (27 July 1977), 4125.
21 The offices covered the following areas: "Terrace serving the northwest of the province including Prince Rupert and Stewart, south to Ocean Falls and east almost to Vanderhoof. Prince George picks up the northeast including Port Nelson and Dawson Creek, west to Vanderhoof and south to 100 Mile House and Revelstoke, while the Kamloops officer covers the central interior from Chase west to Lillooet and south through the Okanagan to Osoyoos. Finally, Nelson takes the Kootenays north to Golden and east to the Alberta border." AG HRB, Acc. 1989-699-31, regional offices breakdown, 1975, and Human Rights Branch staff list, 1983.
22 AG HRB, Acc. 1989-699-31, Vehicle Distance for 1983.
23 BCA, Department of Labour, G85-168, Acc. 880057-3714, box 4, f. H-5-L, memorandum from D.H. Cameron to W. Mitchell, 25 March 1981; UBC RBSC, Renate Shearer, v.2, f.1, memorandum strategic plan 1983-84, 13 July 1982.
24 This trend persisted in 1982. Another sample of complaints – 373 investigated between January and September of that year – resulted in 10 percent unsettled, 15 percent withdrawn, 17 percent not pursued, and 58 percent resolved or settled. Statistics on case complaints and closures were compiled from monthly reports produced by the Human Rights Branch, which are available in AG HRB, Acc. 1989-700-14, and Acc. 1989-699-05, complaint closures 1982; and UBC RBSC, Renate Shearer, v.1, f.13, complaint closures 1982-83.
25 BCA, Department of Labour, G85-158, box 5, Acc. 880057-3715, Human Rights Case – Kathleen Strenja v United Cabs-Comox Taxi, 1981.
26 AG HRB, Acc. 1989-699-63, Remi B. De Roo to Manager of SuperValu, 17 July 1975.
27 AG HRB, Acc. 1989-699-0, Margaret Strongitharm to Kathleen Ruff, 23 March 1979.
28 Landucci described the situation when she arrived in Victoria as walking into "a two-year public and private war between the commission and the branch." According to reporter Ros Oberlyn, "each side through the other was trying to undermine its credibility." Ros Oberlyn, "Socreds Have No Clear Policy on Human Rights," *Vancouver Sun,* 23 November 1981.
29 The following is a sample of Human Rights Commission grants in 1980 and 1981: Association of Disabled Persons ($1,500); British Columbia Human Rights Coalition ($5,000); Canadian Council of Christians and Jews ($5,000); Lesbian Information Line ($7,750); National Association of Women in the Law ($500); North Shore Women's Centre ($20,000);

Okanagan Women's Coalition ($1,500); and West Kootenay Multicultural Society ($3,000). AG HRB, Acc. 1989-699-27, and Acc. 1989-699-6, lists of grants provided by the Human Rights Commission.
30 UBC RBSC, Renate Shearer, v.1, f.15, lists of grants from the Human Rights Commission, 1979-83.
31 "Andy Chelsea v Sportsman's Motel," in British Columbia Human Rights Commission, *Reasons for Decisions* (Victoria: BC Human Rights Commission, 1980-82).
32 AG HRB, Acc. 1989-699-31, Henry Jay to Bill King, 28 November 1975.
33 AG HRB, Acc. 1989-699-31, memorandums to staff (field offices), n.d.
34 In Andison's first week, no less than the deputy minister of labour dropped by to visit. IROs who had worked for the department for decades had never even met a deputy minister. According to Andison, the deputy minister wanted to warn him that the job was politically sensitive and that he should avoid embarrassing the government. Andison, Clément interview.
35 At one point, Prince George had two human rights officers, but following budget cuts in 1980-81, only one remained. BCA, Department of Labour, G85 168, Acc. 880057-3714, box 4, f. H-5-L, memorandum from D.H. Cameron to W. Mitchell, 25 March 1981.
36 Andison, Clément interview.
37 AG HRB, Acc. 1989-699-10, newspaper index, 1976.
38 AG HRB, Acc. 1989-700-40, intake files for Prince George, Kamloops, Vancouver, and Victoria, 1979.
39 Andison, Clément interview.
40 Ibid.
41 Ibid.
42 AG HRB, newspaper index, 1976.
43 BCA, Department of Labour, G85-168, box 8, Acc. 880057-3718, Women and Youth in Northwest BC Labour Markets, Summary Report, Associated Economic Consultants Ltd., December 1982.
44 BCA, Department of Labour, G85-168, Acc. 880057-3714, box 4, f. H-5-L, memorandum from D.H. Cameron to W. Mitchell, 25 March 1981.
45 Ros Oberlyn, "Pregnancy 'Big Cause' of Sex Discrimination," *Vancouver Sun*, 29 November 1979; AG HRB, Acc. 1989-699-02, Working Women Unite Brief to the Human Rights Commission, March 1980; BCA, Department of Labour, G84-079, box 5, f. Human Rights Commission Correspondence 1981, SWAG review of the Human Rights Code, 22 June 1981.
46 AG HRB, Acc. 1989-700-42, BCCLA: Recommendations for Legislative Change, 1981.
47 In connection with amending the code, the Human Rights Commission consulted a wide range of social movement organizations in 1981: BC Association for the Mentally Retarded; BC Coalition of the Disabled; BC School Trustees Association; BCCLA; British Columbia Teachers' Federation; Canadian National Institute for the Blind; Greater Vancouver Association of the Deaf; Okanagan Women's Coalition; Social Planning and Review Council of BC; Society for Education Action Research and Counseling on Homosexuality; Vancouver Labour Council; and Working Women Unite.
48 AG HRB, Acc. 1989-701-09, Brief Presented to the British Columbia Human Rights Commission by the Victoria Human Rights Coalition, 17 July 1979.
49 UBC RBSC, VSW, v.2, f.20, Board of Inquiry: Nechiporenko v Tye Hardware, 1975. See also Shelagh Day, "Recent Developments in Human Rights," *Labour Relations Bulletin* (June 1977): 16-24.

50 University of Victoria Archives, Victoria (UVA), Human Rights Boards of Inquiry (BOIs), AR017, Acc. 97-159, Diane Davies, Eileen Hickford and Hildegard Toews v District of Abbotsford, 1977.
51 UVA, BOIs, AR017, Acc. 97-159, f.2.20, Loraine Warren v D. Becket and Credit of Canada Ltd., 1977; British Columbia, "Human Rights Boards of Inquiry: Warren v Becket, Nadon & Creditel of Canada Limited," *Labour Research Bulletin* (January 1977): 62-63.
52 British Columbia, *Debates of the Legislative Assembly* (24 July 1980), 3493; Marjorie Griffin Cohen, "Paid Work," in Ruth Roach Pierson and Marjorie Griffin Cohen, *Canadian Women's Issues*, vol. 2, *Bold Visions* (Toronto: James Lorimer, 1995), 138.
53 Day, "Recent Developments in Human Rights."
54 UVA, BOIs, AR017, Acc. 97-159, f.2.6, Billie Linton v Nabob Foods Ltd., 1977; British Columbia, "Human Rights Boards of Inquiry: Linton v Nabob Foods Ltd.," *Labour Research Bulletin* (October 1978): 32-33.
55 Ibid.
56 Day, "Recent Developments in Human Rights," 17-18.
57 British Columbia, Ministry of Labour, *Annual Report* (Victoria: Queen's Printer, 1977-82); UBC RBSC, Renate Shearer, v.2, f.7, and v.1, f.13, complaint closures.
58 For a useful definition of systemic discrimination in the context of equal pay, see *CN v. Canada (Canadian Human Rights Commission)*, [1987] 1 S.C.R. 1145; and Aileen McColgan, *Women under the Law: The False Promise of Human Rights* (New Baskerville: Longman, 2000), 187.
59 Day, "Recent Developments in Human Rights," 17.
60 Statistics on women in the labour force are available in Women's Program British Columbia, *Women in British Columbia, 1971-1981* (Victoria: Ministry of Labour, 1984).
61 British Columbia Human Rights Commission, *I'm Okay*, 37.
62 BCA, Department of Labour, G84-079, Acc. 880057-1812, f. United Nations Convention, J. Gretzinger to Jack Heinrich, 11 December 1981.
63 BCA, Department of Labour, G84-079, Acc. 880057-1812, f. United Nations Convention, Department of Labour memorandum on equal pay, Pieta Van Dyke to S.R. Stackhouse, 29 October 1981.
64 BCA, Department of Labour, G84-079, Acc. 880057-1809, v.5, f. human rights correspondence, Submission regarding Proposed Legislative Changes to the Human Rights Code by the Employers Council of British Columbia, June 1982.
65 UBC RBSC, Renate Shearer, v.1, f.13, J.D. Allan to Robert McClelland, 15 February 1983.

CHAPTER 8: MAKING NEW LAW UNDER THE HUMAN RIGHTS CODE

1 British Columbia, "Human Rights Code – Board of Inquiry Decision: Garnett v Kompleat Industries Incorporated," *Labour Research Bulletin* (April 1979): 52-53.
2 Alan Andison, interview by Dominique Clément, 19 August 2010.
3 Two cases were dismissed on technical rather than substantive grounds. In one of these, the complaint had been submitted after the six-month period permitted under the law; in the other, the individual had moved to England before the case finally reached an inquiry. The complaints were dismissed due to technicalities, even though the chairman had initially upheld them. They are included among the 58 cases that were upheld. Most of the dismissed cases fell into the reasonable cause category; because the reasonable cause section of the Human Rights Code was new law, it was the most contested.

4 University of Victoria Archives, Victoria (UVA), BC Human Rights Boards of Inquiry (BOIs), AR017, box 97-159, Jane Gawne v Richard Chapman and Associates, 1979. McLachlin noted that two previous boards of inquiry had awarded $375 and $500 in damages.
5 Attorney General's Office, Victoria, British Columbia Human Rights Branch (AG HRB), Acc. 1989-699-05, Human Rights Boards of Inquiry, 1977-79: For Human Rights Officers' Use Only.
6 As Rosanna Langer explains, "A historical review indicates that the early dispute resolution approach is well established, and was based on the prototype in the field of labour relations, where parties often have ongoing relations and seek remedies crafted to individual circumstances. It has also been found that providing an effective remedy or accommodation to the complainant was more important than punishing a delinquent respondent." Rosanna L. Langer, *Defining Rights and Wrongs: Bureaucracy, Human Rights, and Public Accountability* (Vancouver: UBC Press, 2007), 9.
7 Kathleen Ruff stated, "I think it is quite common – not in all of the cases – but in a lot of the cases, the individual could see it is not worth the hassle. And in many cases, they do not want to stay because of the way they were treated. But they believe that this is wrong and it is not going to change and someone is going to stand up to it. And by God, they think it's wrong. They don't want others to suffer what they suffered. They want to open the door to others. That was the spirit in which we tried to run the Human Rights Branch. It was not the individualism. It was about trying to have a just society where all groups were treated fairly." Kathleen Ruff, interview by Dominique Clément, 14 April 2010.
8 Ibid.
9 University of British Columbia Rare Books and Special Collections, Vancouver (UBC RBSC), Vancouver Status of Women (VSW), v.2, f.46, Yvonne Bill v J.R. Trailer Sales, 1977.
10 British Columbia Archives, Victoria, Department of Labour, G85-168, box 20, Human Rights Cases: Picard v Dunn Lehman Trucking, 1980.
11 UBC RBSC, VSW, v.2, f.7, Murray Block v University of British Columbia, 1982.
12 UBC RBSC, VSW, v.2, f.32, Burns v Piping Industry, 1977.
13 UBC RBSC, Yvonne Bill v J.R. Trailer Sales, 1977.
14 AG HRB, Acc. 1989-699-05, boards of inquiry list, 1977 to 1979.
15 One inquiry board attempted to expand the scope of reasonable cause beyond discrimination. It concluded that Aberdeen Hospital did not treat Filomena Lopetrone fairly when it interviewed her for employment (hospital administrators were "careless, hasty and unfair in their hiring practices"; in one instance, they lost the candidate's job application). However, the Supreme Court ruled that this application of the Human Rights Code was improper because the code was concerned only with discrimination. UBC RBSC, VSW, v.2, f.29, Lopetrone and Bilga v Juan de Fuca Hospital, 1975.
16 UBC RBSC, VSW, v.3, f.12, Oram and McLaren v Pho, 1975.
17 The ad read as follows: "Subs. To GAY TIDE, gay lib paper $1.00 for 6 issues. 2146 Yew Street, Vancouver." The *Vancouver Sun* challenged the ruling in the British Columbia Supreme Court, where the presiding judge concluded that reasonable cause was a question of fact for the board of inquiry and could not be interfered with by a court. The Court of Appeal did not agree. In a two-to-one decision, Justices Branca and Robertson addressed the scope of the reasonable cause section and the legislation. They rejected the argument that the courts could not review board decisions, and they chastised the board for relying on a subjective analysis of the *Sun* editor's motives rather than employing a finding of fact,

as the legislation required. The inquiry should have focused on how a gay advertisement could potentially have affected the *Sun*'s reputation instead of on the editor's possible bias. GATE appealed to the Supreme Court of Canada, which sustained the appeal court decision in a six-to-three decision. Speaking for the majority, Justice Ronald Martland argued that newspapers were protected and had the right to express whatever opinions they saw fit. This protection, according to Martland, extended to refusing to publish an ad. (The *Sun* agreed to voluntarily publish the ad in 1980.) *Vancouver Sun v. Gay Alliance Towards Equality*, [1976] W.W.R. 160 (B.C.S.C.); *Vancouver Sun v. Gay Alliance*, [1977] 77 D.L.R. 487 (B.C.C.A.); *Gay Alliance Towards Equality v. Vancouver Sun*, [1979] 2 S.C.R. 435.
18 UBC RBSC, VSW, v.2, f.29, Human Rights Commission v Board of School Trustees, 1977.
19 For the two boards, see *Carignan v. Mastercraft Publications Limited*, [1984] 5 C.H.R.R. D/2282; and *Sheri Zarankin v. Ian Johnstone, Wessex Inn*, [1984] 5 C.H.R.R. D/2274. The first sexual harassment decision, *Bell v. Ladas*, was in Ontario in 1980; during the following year, the province amended the legislation so that it explicitly recognized sexual harassment.
20 *Brooks v. Canada Safeway Ltd.*, [1989] 1 S.C.R. 1219; *Janzen v. Platy Enterprises*, [1989] 1 S.C.R. 1252.
21 R. Brian Howe, "Incrementalism and Human Rights Reform," *Journal of Canadian Studies* 28 (1993): 29-44.
22 *Insurance Corporation of British Columbia v. Heerspink*, [1982] 3 C.H.R.R. D/1163 (S.C.C.); William W. Black, *Reassessing Statutory Human Rights Legislation Thirty Years Later: Human Rights Enforcement in British Columbia: A Case Study* (Ottawa: Human Rights Research and Education Centre, 1995), 8-9.
23 *Nelson v. Gubbins*, [1979] 17 B.C.L.R. 259 (B.C.C.A.).
24 AG HRB, Acc. 1989-699-97, memorandum from Maurice Guilbault to Jack Heinrich, 28 November 1979.
25 *Nelson v. Byron Price and Associates*, [1981] 122 D.L.R. (3d) 284 (B.C.C.A.).
26 For a more detailed discussion of the honest belief defence in BC human rights cases, see Rainer Knopff, *Human Rights and Social Technology: The New War on Discrimination* (Ottawa: Carleton University Press, 1989), 111-14.
27 *British Columbia Forest Products Limited v. Foster*, [1980] 2 W.W.R. 289 (B.C.S.C.). In this case the judge was offering only a commentary and ultimately rejected the appeal in Foster's favour.
28 *Vancouver Sun v. Gay Alliance*, [1977] 77 D.L.R. 487 (B.C.C.A.).
29 However, in *Holloway v. Clairco Foods Lot* (1983) and *Paton v. Brouwer and Co.* (1984), the boards of inquiry found that discrimination due to pregnancy could also be considered sex discrimination.
30 Nitya Duclos, "Disappearing Women: Racial Minority Women in Human Rights Cases," *Canadian Journal of Women and the Law* 6 (1993): 37-38.
31 Under the Human Rights Act, the Human Rights Council could ask the minister to appoint a board of inquiry, but it never did. Instead, it endeavoured to negotiate settlements, not unlike the approach favoured by IROs in the early 1970s.

Chapter 9: The Politics of (Undermining) Human Rights

1 For information relating to the Zarankin case, see University of Northern British Columbia Archives, Prince George, Women's Resource Centre collection, v.5, f.1, Sheri Zarankin v Ian Johnstone board of inquiry decision, 16 July 1984.

2 At the time, only federal, Newfoundland, Ontario, and Quebec law recognized sexual harassment in human rights legislation.
3 Regional offices were distributed as follows (there were none in Prince Edward Island or Newfoundland): Alberta (two), British Columbia (six), Manitoba (one), New Brunswick (three), Nova Scotia (three), Ontario (fourteen), Quebec (one), and Saskatchewan (two). Attorney General's Office, Victoria, British Columbia Human Rights Branch (AG HRB), Acc. 1989-700-42, Report on human rights commissions in Canada, 1980.
4 AG HRB, Acc. 1989-700-37, report on human rights commissions in Canada, 2 November 1982.
5 Dominique Clément, "Equality Deferred: Sex Discrimination and the Newfoundland Human Rights State," *Acadiensis* 41 (2012): 102-27.
6 R. Brian Howe and David Johnson, *Restraining Equality: Human Rights Commissions in Canada* (Toronto: University of Toronto Press, 2000), 12-22.
7 British Columbia, *Debates of the Legislative Assembly* (2 August 1977), 4198.
8 University of Victoria Archives, Victoria (UVA), Status of Women Action Group (SWAG), AR119, 2004-005, f.1.2, "Human Rights Commission Unfit to Serve," letter to membership, 7 April 1979.
9 "Report of the Human Rights Branch," in British Columbia, Department of Labour, *Annual Report* (Victoria: Queen's Printer, 1975), 63-64, 80-81.
10 Quoted in Bob Plecas, *Bill Bennett: A Mandarin's View* (Vancouver: Douglas and McIntyre, 2006), 194.
11 "Report of the Human Rights Branch," in British Columbia, Ministry of Labour, *Annual Report* (Victoria: Queen's Printer, 1980), 17-26.
12 British Columbia Archives, Victoria (BCA), Department of Labour, G85-168, Acc. 880057-3714, box 4, f. H-5-L, memorandum from D.H. Cameron to W. Mitchell, 25 March 1981.
13 BCA, Department of Labour, G85-168, Acc. 880057-3714, box 4, f. H-5-L, Memorandum from Stephen Stackhouse to Jack Heinrich, 5 February 1982.
14 BCA, Department of Labour, G84-079, Acc. 880057-1809, box 5, f. Human Rights Commission 1981, Margaret Strongitharm to Jack Heinrich, 23 July 1981.
15 Dale Gibson (letter to the editor), "Meeting Critical of BC Rights Law," *Vancouver Sun*, 13 June 1984.
16 Howe and Johnson, *Restraining Equality*, 78-79.
17 BCA, Department of Labour, G84-079, Acc. 880057-1809, box 5, f. Human Rights Commission 1981, memorandum from Hanne Jensen to Stephen Stackhouse, 4 August 1981.
18 Clément, "Equality Deferred."
19 The New Brunswick Human Rights Commission (NBHRC) offers a comparable example of what an education program might accomplish: "Some examples of the NBHRC's 'proactive approaches' are the production of educational materials including printed material and videos; the presentation of public workshops; involvement in community development activities; assisting employers with policy development; and the annual presentation of the Human Rights Award recognizing individuals who have promoted human rights in New Brunswick." Shannon Williams, "Human Rights in Theory and Practice: A Sociological Study of Aboriginal Peoples and the New Brunswick Human Rights Commission, 1967-1997" (Master's thesis, University of New Brunswick, 1998), 32.
20 Quoted in Donald Anderson, "The Development of Human Rights Protections in British Columbia" (Master's thesis, University of Victoria, 1986), 82. As the NDP minister of labour, Bill King delegated the responsibility for board of inquiry appointments to his staff, who chose one or two individuals from a list of candidates (in fact, King solicited

suggestions for possible candidates from various community groups). In contrast, Socred appointments came directly through the minister of labour on an ad hoc basis.

21 "Report of the Human Rights Branch," in British Columbia, Ministry of Labour, *Annual Report* (Victoria: Queen's Printer, 1981), 9, 22-31.

22 "Alan Fotheringham" (self-titled column), *Vancouver Sun*, 2 September 1978.

23 Jock Smith was chairman of the Surrey school board when it was found guilty of violating the code by advertising for a school principal who adhered to "Judeo-Christian principles." Smith was also a respondent as a school board trustee on another case involving refusal to provide pay benefits to teachers with pregnancy-related illnesses. According to reporter Stephen Hume, "Smith was a vocal opponent of allowing pregnant women to have disability benefits." Smith's reaction to the discrimination decision was to insist that "we aren't discriminating against anybody because I don't know any man who can get pregnant." Stephen Hume, "Decision on Quitting Up to Them," *Victoria Times-Colonist*, 13 April 1979; Stephen Hume, "Rights Appointee Involved in Two Violation Cases," *Victoria Times-Colonist*, 11 April 1979.

24 She was director of the National Multiple Sclerosis Society, chair of the Vancouver Island Health Board, and vice-president for Western Canada for the Canadian Federation of University Women. "Rights Commission Enlarged," *Vancouver Sun*, 31 August 1978.

25 As the newspaper explained, "Commission member Ted Pearce is quoted suggesting that the commission set up a 'take-a-gay-to-lunch-day' and that men should have the right to throw women reporters in locker rooms 'the hell out of there.'" Jan O'Brien, "Williams Not Too Happy with Rights Commission," *Vancouver Express*, 11 April 1979. See also Stephen Hume, "Rights Meeting 'Like Boys' Locker Room,'" *Victoria Times-Colonist*, 4 April 1979; Stephen Hume, "Rights Panel Resignation Clamor Rises," *Victoria Times-Colonist*, 12 April 1979; "13 Groups Calling for Resignation," *Victoria Times-Colonist*, 21 April 1979; Stephen Hume, "Candidates Berate Rights Body," *Victoria Times-Colonist*, 2 May 1979; and UVA, SWAG, "Human Rights Commission Unfit to Serve," 7 April 1979. The second female commissioner, Mildred Gottfriedson, had attended only two meetings in 1979 before resigning due to ill health. Ros Oberlyn, "Gentlemanly Gesture Asked of Human Rights Commission," *Vancouver Sun*, 5 March 1980.

26 Stephen Hume, "Rights Official Backs Members," *Victoria Times-Colonist*, 25 April 1979.

27 British Columbia, *Debates of the Legislative Assembly* (1 April 1980), 1787; Oberlyn, "Gentlemanly Gesture"; Damian Inwood, "Human Rights Commission to Be Cut," *Vancouver Province*, 14 September 1980.

28 "Homosexual Teachers Get Backing from Ruff," *Vancouver Express*, 18 April 1978.

29 These groups included the British Columbia Federation of Women, FLAG, Gay Alliance Towards Equality, Pacific Life Community, Prime Time, SEARCH, University of Victoria Gay Focus Club, Vancouver Transition House, Victoria Civil Liberties Association, Victoria Jewish Information Committee, Victoria Rape/Assault Centre, Status of Women Action Group, Voice of Women, and the Women's Action Group (University of Victoria). Canadian Women's Movement Archives, University of Ottawa, Ottawa, British Columbia Federation of Women, v.28, f. Feminist Lesbian Action Group, n.d. Karen Sandford, an NDP Opposition MLA, also attacked the government's choice of appointees. British Columbia, *Debates of the Legislative Assembly* (23 July 1980), 3473.

30 AG HRB, Acc. 1989-699-99, Doris Anderson to Bill Bennett, 12 July 1979.

31 Ontario Human Rights Commission, *Life Together: A Report on Human Rights in Ontario* (Toronto: Ontario Human Rights Commission, 1977), 10; Manitoba Human Rights Commission, *Annual Report* (Winnipeg: Manitoba Human Rights Commission, 1979).

32 British Columbia, *Debates of the Legislative Assembly* (28 June 1977), 4147-48.
33 Writing to the labour minister, Carol Pfeifer noted, "Ms. Ruff states in a letter regarding the Ward case that 'because of their responsibilities and work load in the Labour Standards Branch, IRO's are not able to go back a second time on a Human Rights case.' Yet, in a letter addressed to a member of VSW, you state that it is 'because of their availability for work of this kind for which they are eminently suited' that IRO's are used. The conflict in these two statements is obvious and leads us to question the suitability and availability of IROs for cases relating to the Human Rights Code." University of British Columbia Rare Books and Special Collections, Vancouver (UBC RBSC), Vancouver Status of Women (VSW), v.5, f.30, Carol Pfeifer to Allan Williams, 28 February 1977.
34 British Columbia, *Debates of the Legislative Assembly* (2 August1977), 4198.
35 AG HRB, Acc. 1989-699-10, memorandum boards of inquiry, 11 May 1981.
36 British Columbia, *Debates of the Legislative Assembly* (19 March1981), 4646; AG HRB, Acc. 1989-700-13, human rights branch case statistics, 1982; AG HRB, Acc. 1989-700-2, Human Rights Program Annual Report, 1983.
37 BCA, Department of Labour, Cameron to Mitchell, 25 March 1981.
38 UBC RBSC, VSW, v.6, f.15, day of mourning for the human rights code, December 1976.
39 AG HRB, Acc. 1989-699-05, box 5 (petitions file), Linda J. Brandie to Margaret Strongitharm, 28 August 1979.
40 *Newsletter* (British Columbia Federation of Labour) 1, 7 (June 1975).
41 *The Rally Story* (Vancouver: Press Gang, 1976).
42 Anderson, "The Development of Human Rights," 81.
43 Quoted in Ros Oberlyn, "Socreds Have No Clear Policy on Human Rights," *Vancouver Sun,* 23 November 1981.
44 Quoted in Miguel Moya, "Former Rights Chief Says She Has No Resentments," *Vancouver Sun,* 26 February 1984.
45 BCA, Department of Labour, G84-079, Acc. 880057-1809, box 5, f. Human Rights Commission 1981, Margaret Strongitharm to Jack Heinrich, 22 July 1981; Anderson, "The Development of Human Rights," 82.
46 AG HRB, Acc. 1989-700-38, Charles Paris to Robert McClelland, 3 February 1983; McClelland to Paris, 9 February 1983; McClelland to Paris, 11 February 1983.
47 Anderson, "The Development of Human Rights," 111; Kathleen Ruff, interview by Dominique Clément, 14 April 2010.
48 Shelagh Day, interview by Dominique Clément, 12 May 2009.
49 James Matkin to Kathleen Ruff, 10 February 1976 (emphasis added), private collection (Kathleen Ruff); Ruff, Clément interview.
50 Ruff, Clément interview.
51 BCA, Department of Labour, G84-079, Acc. 880057-1809, box 5, f. Human Rights Cases – General, 1980-81; BCA, Department of Labour, G85-168, Acc. 880057-3715, box 5, f. Unsettled Cases, n.d.
52 UBC RBSC, VSW, v.10, f.2, Kathleen Ruff to Carol Pfeifer, 15 December 1976.
53 AG HRB, Acc. 1989-700-3, Karl Friedman to Robert McClelland, 27 October 1982.
54 Quoted in Moya, "Former Rights Chief."
55 British Columbia, *Debates of the Legislative Assembly* (2 May 1984), 4463.
56 Bill Black, "Human Rights in British Columbia: Equality Postponed," in *Canadian Human Rights Yearbook, 1984-85,* ed. William Pentney and Daniel Proulx (Toronto: Carswell, 1985), 232.

57 British Columbia Human Rights Commission, *Recommendations for Changes to the Human Rights Code of British Columbia* (Victoria: Human Rights Commission of British Columbia, 1981); British Columbia Human Rights Commission, *How to Make It Work: A Report of the BC Human Rights Commission on Strengthening the Statutory Protection of Human Rights* (Victoria: British Columbia Human Rights Commission, 1983); British Columbia Human Rights Commission, *I'm Okay; We're Not So Sure about You: A Report of the BC Human Rights Commission on Extensions to the Code* (Victoria: British Columbia Human Rights Commission, 1983).

58 "Hunky" and "bohunk" had been used in the past as terms of ridicule for Ukrainian settlers on the prairies. BCA, G84-079, box 5, f. HRC General Correspondence, Mir Huculak to William Bennett, 11 May 1981.

59 Allen Garr wrote several columns in the *Vancouver Province,* criticizing the government for its treatment of the human rights officers. For instance, see Allen Garr, "Socred Hitmen Swoop on Rights Workers," *Vancouver Province,* 12 July 1983; and Allen Garr, "Main Issue Is Treatment of Employees," *Vancouver Province,* 14 July 1983; See also Black, "Human Rights in British Columbia," 220-21.

60 British Columbia, *Debates of the Legislative Assembly* (20 September 1983), 1659.

61 AG HRB, Acc. 1989-700-38, Robert McClelland to Charles Paris, 11 February 1983.

62 As Bryan Palmer puts it, "Few were more willing in the early 1980's to take up the cause of dismantling the welfare state and curbing the 'excessive' power of the trade unions than the populist neo-conservatives of the Canadian hinterland, the petty commodity hucksters, interest magnates and speculators of British Columbia's Social Credit Party, recently re-elected to rule in a 1983 parliamentary contest." Bryan Palmer, *Solidarity: The Rise and Fall of an Opposition in British Columbia* (Vancouver: New Star Books, 1987), 19. Palmer provides a detailed discussion of the restraint package and the movement against the reforms.

63 *Human Rights Act,* S.B.C. 1984, c. 22.

64 In addition, because the legislation required complainants to exhaust other legislative avenues for redress, it could force them to complete a lengthy labour arbitration process before filing a human rights complaint. For a detailed review and critique of the Human Rights Act, refer to Bill Black, "BC's Bill 27 – Fact Sheet," *Rights and Freedoms* 43 (November-December 1983): 12-13; and Black, *BC Human Rights Review.*

65 UBC RBSC, Renate Shearer, v.2, f.13, Text to the minister of labour of British Columbia, 8 May 1984.

66 Ontario, Human Rights Commission, *Annual Report* (Toronto: Queen's Printer, 1981-82); Anderson, "The Development of Human Rights," 84.

67 Bill Black wrote, "My conclusion that conciliation will be de-emphasized is based in part on the intention to reduce staff sharply and partly on the wording of the Act. The Act provides that the Council can recommend a settlement at the end of the investigation, but indications are that conciliation efforts will not go beyond this settlement proposal." Black, "Human Rights in British Columbia," 227.

68 "A Sweeping Change," *Vancouver Sun,* 26 July 1984.

69 "Grits' Lee Joins Critics, Argues Bill Should Die," *Toronto Globe and Mail,* 7 May 1984.

70 Howe and Johnson, *Restraining Equality,* 158.

71 R. Brian Howe, "Incrementalism and Human Rights Reform," *Journal of Canadian Studies* 28 (1993): 38.

72 "Preserving Human Rights," *Vancouver Sun,* 16 July 1983.

73 Black, "Human Rights in British Columbia," 231.

74 British Columbia, *Debates of the Legislative Assembly* (11 August 1983), 769.
75 BCA, Department of Labour, G85-168, Acc. 880057-3730, box 20, cabinet submission, The Human Rights Code of British Columbia, 15 May 1982.
76 Ibid. According to the memorandum, single-parent families and welfare recipients would benefit from "expanded housing opportunities," but the document does not explain how this would be realized in the proposed legislation.
77 *Sisterhood* (publication of the NDP Women's Rights Committee) 7, 2 (August 1983).
78 UBC RBSC, Solidarity Coalition, v.2, f.12, SWAG – Brief to the People's Commission on Social and Economic Policy Alternatives, 7 December 1984.
79 UBC RBSC, Solidarity Coalition, v.5, f.6, Nanaimo Women's Resources Society – Brief Submitted to the People's Commission for Policy Alternatives, September 1984. The VSW was a key member of the Solidarity Coalition and a staunch opponent of the Social Credit government's so-called austerity package. British Columbia, *Debates of the Legislative Assembly* (3 May 1984), 4471-72.
80 On opposition from women's groups to the 1984 Human Rights Act, see *Sisterhood* 7, 2 (August 1983); UBC RBSC, Solidarity Coalition, v.2, briefs to the People's Commission on Social and Economic Policy Alternatives, 1984; see also *Vancouver Sun,* 24 November 1984; *Vancouver Sun,* 27 November 1984; *Vancouver Sun,* 29 November 1984; and *Vancouver Sun,* 12 December 1984.
81 "Angry Crowd Wants Anti-Gov't Protest," *Vancouver Province,* 13 July 1983; Marc Edge, "Thousands Join Call to Battle Socreds' Budget," *Vancouver Province,* 24 July 1983.
82 UBC RBSC, Renate Shearer, v.2, f.13, Joint Statements on Bill 11, 12 April 1984.
83 "Human Rights Bill: Called a 'Sham and a Fraud,'" *Vancouver Courier,* 18 April 1984. Emery Barnes, the NDP labour critic, listed some of the organizations that were openly hostile to the legislation: "the Human Rights Coalition, the Organization to Fight Racism, the Coalition of the Disabled, the Federation of Labour, the Civil Liberties Association, the Association of Social Workers, the Sikh Solidarity Association, Vancouver Status of Women, the Gay Rights Union, the Vancouver Gay Community Centre, the Solidarity coalition, the Committee for Racial Justice, Black Solidarity, Vancouver Rape Relief, Gay Men in Solidarity, the lower mainland Solidarity coalition, Lesbians Against the Budget, the Canadian Farmworkers' Union, former chairman of the Human Rights Commission, Dr. Charles Paris, who is presently director of the Canadian Council of Christians and Jews, and Loui Rudland of Vancouver Status of Women." British Columbia, *Debates of the Legislative Assembly* (3 May 1984), 4471-72.
84 Donna Vogel, *Challenging Politics: COPE, Electoral Politics and Social Movements* (Halifax: Fernwood Press, 2003), 75.
85 "Preserving Human Rights." The *Sun* added that "the new act would replace a process of conciliation and negotiation with an adversarial and confrontational system of handling complaints, a change that can only heighten hostility to human rights rather than further public acceptance of the concept." Ibid.
86 For more on the Solidarity Coalition, see Palmer, *Solidarity.*
87 Quoted in "Critics Rap Socreds over Rights Record," *Vancouver Sun,* 22 September 1984. Fairweather, who believed that the reforms set the stage for American-style social polarization, lamented attempts to "import this kind of thinking in Canada." Quoted in "BC Rights Move Rapped in Ottawa," *Vancouver Province,* 9 September 1983.
88 UBC RBSC, Solidarity Coalition, f.19-1, Ken Norman to William Bennett, 2 July 1983.
89 Vaughn Palmer, "A Strong Defence of the New Rights Act," *Vancouver Sun,* 5 June 1984; "Rights Activists Deplore BC Loss," *Vancouver Sun,* 12 July 1983.

90 "BC Rights Move Rapped in Ottawa"; "Five Provinces Reject Call," *Vancouver Sun,* 10 September 1983.
91 Ann Silversides, "Four Federal Ministers Ask BC to Reconsider Its Human Rights Bill," *Toronto Globe and Mail,* 9 May 1984.
92 UBC RBSC, Solidarity Coalition, f.19-1, Serge Joyal to R.H. McClelland, 7 October 1983.
93 Ed Ratushney, "BC's Giant Step Backward in Human Rights," *Toronto Globe and Mail,* 19 August 1983.
94 UBC RBSC, Solidarity Coalition, f.19-1, Press Release, CASHRA, 14 July 1983. CASHRA added that it "deplores this ill-advised proposal and urges the Government of British Columbia to reconsider it. If it were implemented the powerless would be deprived of an advocate in the struggle against racism and bigotry ... To disband an organization that has proven expertise in providing such protection would be tragic." Ibid. See also "Ottawa Steps Up Rights Pressure on BC," *Vancouver Province,* 17 July 1983; and Palmer, "A Strong Defence."
95 UBC RBSC, Press Release, CASHRA.
96 UBC RBSC, Solidarity Coalition, f.19-1, Press Release, Canadian Advisory Council on the Status of Women, 25 July 1983; Nancy Knickerbocker, "Lawyers Urge Delay," *Vancouver Sun,* 26 September 1983. The Canadian Bar Association often participated in debates regarding human rights violations, from government restrictions on civil liberties during the Second World War to the negotiations surrounding the creation of the Canadian Charter of Rights and Freedoms. Dominique Clément, "Rights in the Age of Protest: A History of the Human Rights and Civil Liberties Movement in Canada, 1962-1982" (PhD diss., Memorial University of Newfoundland, 2005), 141-43.
97 Quoted in Anderson, "The Development of Human Rights," 88.
98 Nancy Knickerbocker and Peter Comparelli, "Harassment Complainant to Fight Ruling," *Vancouver Sun,* 27 November 1984.
99 Allen Garr, *Tough Guy: Bill Bennett and the Taking of British Columbia* (Toronto: Key Porter Books, 1985), 181.
100 The British Columbia Federation of Labour condemned the council's decision in the Fields case and demanded that its members resign. Marjorie Griffin Cohen, "Paid Work," in Ruth Roach Pierson and Marjorie Griffin Cohen, *Canadian Women's Issues,* vol. 2, *Bold Visions* (Toronto: James Lorimer, 1995), 157-58.
101 Quoted in Nancy Knickerbocker, "Sex Bias Ruling Hit by Ex-Rights Officer," *Vancouver Sun,* 24 November 1984; Vaughn Palmer, "Waitress's Allegations Were Substantially Unproven," *Vancouver Sun,* 27 November 1984.
102 Knickerbocker and Comparelli, "Harassment Complainant to Fight"; UBC RBSC, Rosemary Brown, v.51, f.5, Colin Gableman to Robert McClelland, 26 November 1984; UBC RBSC, Rosemary Brown, v.51, f.5, press release, 26 November 1984.
103 "All Too Familiar," *Vancouver Sun,* 28 November 1984; "Worrying Messages from the Fields Case," *Victoria Times-Colonist,* 28 November 1984.
104 "Sex Harassment Needs Definition," *Vancouver Province,* 28 November 1984.
105 UBC RBSC, Renate Shearer, v.2, f.8, BC Human Rights Coalition Press Release, 26 November 1984. One of the more comical responses was a 1984 letter to Edgett endorsed by over a dozen organizations, congratulating him for advancing the cause of sexual harassment. The letter asked whether employers could be officially authorized to hug, kiss, touch, and write crude notes to their employees, and whether habitual harasser accreditation could be granted. RBSC, Renate Shearer, v.1, f.8, open letter from community groups to

Jim Edgett, 4 December 1984. For a copy of the British Columbia Federation of Labour resolution, see Cohen, "Paid Work," 157-58.
106 AG HRB, Acc. 1989-700-15, April Katz to Graham Leslie, 19 June 1984; UVA, Evelyn Hammond, v.2, f.5, "837 Cases Handled in Two Years," n.d.

Conclusion

1 "'More Power' to Act in Revised Rights Bill," *Victoria Times-Colonist,* 11 April 1984.
2 According to W.A.C. Bennett's biographer, the premier's philosophy for governing was based on four principles: "(1) The individual is the most important factor in any organized society; (2) The major function of democratic government is to give the people the results they want in the management of their affairs; (3) The individual must be guaranteed economic security without the sacrifice of his personal freedom; (4) That which is physically possible, and desirable, and morally right can and should be made financially possible." David J. Mitchell, *W.A.C. Bennett and the Rise of British Columbia* (Vancouver: Douglas and McIntyre, 1995), 169.
3 Alex Kirkup and Tony Evans, "The Myth of Western Opposition to Economic, Social, and Cultural Rights? A Reply to Whelan and Donnelly," *Human Rights Quarterly* 31, 1 (2009): 225.
4 "Rights Still Wronged," *Vancouver Sun,* 6 June 1984.
5 Vaughn Palmer, "Rights: The New Democrats' Alternative Philosophy," *Vancouver Sun,* 7 June 1984.
6 British Columbia, *Debates of the Legislative Assembly* (4 December 1980), 4219.
7 Ibid. (10 March 1977), 1763-64.
8 University of Victoria Archives, Victoria (UVA), Victoria Status of Women Action Group (SWAG), AR119, 2004-017, f.1.3, SWAG open letter to MLAs in British Columbia, 1978.
9 UVA, SWAG, AR119, 1995-052, f.1.4, SWAG Newsletter, President's Report, 15 March 1976, 3, 1.
10 UVA, SWAG, SWAG open letter to MLAs in British Columbia, 1978.
11 *Veronica Butler, Judy Minchinton, Fred Arrance, Lorraine Arrance, Jimmy Stewart, John Turvey v. Lone Star Hotel,* 4 CHRR [1983] D/1694.
12 Walter Tarnopolsky, "The Iron Hand in the Velvet Glove: Administration and Enforcement of Human Rights Legislation in Canada," *Canadian Bar Review* 56 (1978): 567.
13 Ibid., 568.
14 Ruth A. Frager and Carmela Patrias, "'This Is Our Country, These Are Our Rights': Minorities and the Origins of Ontario's Human Rights Campaigns," *Canadian Historical Review* 82 (2001): 1-35; Erica Colter, "A State of Affairs Most Common: Black Nova Scotians and the Stanfield Government's Interdepartmental Committee on Human Rights, 1959-1967" (Master's thesis, Dalhousie University, 2006); Carmela Patrias, "Socialists, Jews, and the 1947 Saskatchewan Bill of Rights," *Canadian Historical Review* 87 (2006): 265-92; Dominique Clément, "'I Believe in Human Rights, Not Women's Rights': Women and the Human Rights State, 1969-1984," *Radical History Review* 101 (2008): 107-29; Dominique Clément, "Equality Deferred: Sex Discrimination and the Newfoundland Human Rights State," *Acadiensis* 41 (2012): 102-27.
15 Rosanna L. Langer, *Defining Rights and Wrongs: Bureaucracy, Human Rights, and Public Accountability* (Vancouver: UBC Press, 2007), 9. Langer adds, "Thus armed with an

expansive interpretation of rights and the legal machinery to advance their law reform agenda in individual cases, special interest advocacy groups have become forceful participants and stakeholders in the human rights complaint process in Ontario." Ibid., 111.

16 Attorney General's Office, Victoria, British Columbia Human Rights Branch, Acc. 1989-699-63, newspaper index and outline, 1974 to 1976.

17 In a survey of human rights cases in Canada involving pregnancy and sex discrimination between 1980 and 1987, Andiappan, Reavley, and Silver found that "tribunals have refused to accept employers' arguments of increased costs of training alternate employees and negative attitudes of customers toward pregnant employees as justifiable grounds for refusing to promote pregnant employees. They have held that not being pregnant is not a bona fide occupational qualification in most jobs ... Boards of inquiry have held the view that if a female employee is absent from work for reasons related to her pregnancy, then she is normally not entitled to sick leave benefits. However, if some form of disability or abnormal condition accompanies the pregnancy, the employee should be entitled to these benefits." P. Andiappan, M. Reavley, and S. Silver, "Discrimination against Pregnant Employees: An Analysis of Arbitration and Human Rights Tribunal Decisions in Canada," *Journal of Business Ethics* 9 (1990): 146, 148.

18 There are no sustained studies of Aboriginal people and human rights law in Canada. However, two studies (based largely on interviews) do offer some insights into why Aboriginals have not engaged extensively with the human rights state in Canada. See Allan McChesney, "Aboriginal Communities, Aboriginal Rights, and the Human Rights System," in *Human Rights in Cross-Cultural Perspectives: A Quest for Consensus*, ed. Abdullahi Ahmed An-Na'im (Philadelphia: University of Pennsylvania Press, 1992), 221-52; and Shannon Williams, "Human Rights in Theory and Practice: A Sociological Study of Aboriginal Peoples and the New Brunswick Human Rights Commission, 1967-1997" (Master's thesis, University of New Brunswick, 1998).

19 For a useful critique of human rights law in Canada during this period, see Kathleen Ruff, "A Critical Survey of Human Rights Acts and Commissions in Canada," in *Discrimination in the Law and the Administration of Justice*, ed. Walter S. Tarnopolsky, Joyce Whitman, and Monique Ouellette (Toronto: Canadian Institute for the Administration of Justice, 1992), 25-37. Similar deficiencies in Ontario's human rights legislation led to a major policy review in 1975. For an analysis of the review, see Jennifer Tunnicliffe, "The Ontario Human Rights Code Review, 1975-1981: A New Understanding of Human Rights and Its Meaning for Public Policy" (Master's thesis, University of Waterloo, 2006).

20 Ruff, "A Critical Survey," 30.

21 Ibid., 31. Ruff elaborated: "One of the appointees to the Canadian Human Rights Commission, Gerald Kambeitz, put it baldly. When questioned by a parliamentary committee as to what his qualifications were for being appointed to the Human Rights Commission, he stated that his qualifications were that he had never had any involvement or interest in human rights. Kambeitz said this made him neutral and qualified." Ibid.

22 For examples of the debate in Newfoundland and Ontario, see Didi Herman, *Rights of Passage: Struggles for Lesbian and Gay Legal Equality* (Toronto: University of Toronto Press, 1994); Tunnicliffe, "The Ontario Human Rights Code"; and Clément, "Equality Deferred." For a survey of other provinces, see Tom Warner, *Never Going Back: A History of Queer Activism in Canada* (Toronto: University of Toronto Press, 2002).

23 Quoted in Jim Gurnett, "Oral Histories," in *Alberta Legacies,* ed. Dominique Clément and Gerry Gall (Edmonton: John Humphrey Centre for Peace and Human Rights, 2011), 47.

24 On changing policies for appointing boards of inquiry, see R. Brian Howe and David Johnson, *Restraining Equality: Human Rights Commissions in Canada* (Toronto: University of Toronto Press, 2000), 56-57.
25 Rainer Knopff describes systemic inequality in terms of intent and notes that it may also be "the unintentional effect of a requirement on a target group." Rainer Knopff, *Human Rights and Social Technology: The New War on Discrimination* (Ottawa: Carleton University Press, 1989), 46. And yet, many examples still exist of neutral policies and practices that unfairly affect groups of people. Vesting provisions for pensions, for instance – which require employees to work a certain number of years before they can collect a pension – have always disproportionately discriminated against women, who overwhelmingly leave the workforce earlier than men. On pensions and sex discrimination, see Peter Bartlett, "Sexual Distinctions in Pensions," *Osgoode Hall Law Journal* 24 (1986): 833-65.
26 The Royal Commission on Equality in Employment (1984) defined discrimination as follows: "'Discrimination ... means practices or attitudes that have, whether by design or impact, the effect of limiting an individual's or a group's right to the opportunities generally available because of attributed rather than actual characteristics. It is not a question of whether this discrimination is motivated by an intentional desire to obstruct someone's potential or whether it is the accidental byproduct of innocently motivated practices or systems. If the barrier is affecting certain groups in a disproportionately negative way, it is a signal that the practices that lead to adversity may be discriminatory. This is why it is important to look at the results of a system.' In other words, discrimination is not only the indirect impact of certain actions, but it is directed towards an individual because they belong to an identifiable group." Royal Commission on Equality in Employment, *Report of the Royal Commission on Equality in Employment* (Ottawa: Supply and Services Canada, 1984), 2.
27 Jean McKenzie Leiper, *Bar Codes: Women in the Legal Profession* (Vancouver: UBC Press, 2006), 6.
28 Shelagh Day, *A Report on the Status of Women at the University of British Columbia* (Vancouver: Women's Action Group UBC, 1973), 39.
29 Sheila McIntyre, "Studied Ignorance and Privileged Innocence: Keeping Equity Academic," *Canadian Journal of Women and the Law* 12 (2000): 160.
30 Day, *A Report on the Status*, 21, 23.
31 Library and Archives Canada, Ottawa, Walter S. Tarnopolsky, v.31, f.14, Conference of Human Rights Ministers, 7 November 1974.
32 The issue of substantive equality in human rights law, and the need to be proactive and to offer remedies, is explored in Karen Schucher, "Contesting Women's Solidarity: Human Rights Law and the FWTAO Membership Case" (PhD diss., York University, 2007).
33 Ruff, "A Critical Survey," 27.
34 Shelagh Day, "Impediments to Achieving Equality," in *Equality and Judicial Neutrality*, ed. Sheilah L. Martin and Kathleen E. Mahoney (Toronto: Carswell, 1987), 403.
35 In 1973, 324 practical nurses filed complaints alleging that they were doing the same work as orderlies but were paid less. The legislation, however, required complaints to be dealt with individually. As Human Rights Branch director, Kathleen Ruff stepped in and successfully negotiated a settlement with the Department of Health that eliminated discrimination against women in the health industry. The success of this class-action complaint was therefore a result of Ruff's efforts *in spite of* the legislation. Shelagh Day, "Recent Developments in Human Rights," *Labour Relations Bulletin* (June 1977): 17-18.

36 A useful example of the failure of human rights legislation to proactively address systemic discrimination, and its tendency to ignore the role of affirmative action, is the 1994 Federation of Women Teachers' Associations of Ontario membership case. An Ontario board of inquiry focused its decision narrowly on the direct effect of excluding men from the federation rather than on the systemic discrimination in the labour force that necessitated an organization exclusively representing women. For an analysis of the case, see Emily Grabham, "Substantive Equality: A Comparative Analysis of UK, EC and Canadian Law" (Master's thesis, Queen's University, 2000).

37 Daiva Stasiulis makes a similar point in her study of the Ontario Human Rights Commission (OHRC) and racial minorities: "The OHRC is provided with neither the mandate nor resources to deal with the inequitable distribution of wealth and power which perpetuates the structure of racial inequality. The limitations of the Commission's interventions in mediating discrimination have important consequences for those visible minority organizations which attempt to work with or through the OHRC. The Commission channels racial grievances and anti-racist efforts into a quasi-official body, whose own constraints dictate caution and compromise, rather than the strong advocacy of human and minority rights. Because of its critically limited resources, conciliatory bent, and cumbersome methods of investigation, the organization has not been efficient in achieving even its limited aims of finding solutions for individual cases of discrimination." Daiva Kristina Stasiulis, "Race, Ethnicity and the State: The Political Structuring of South Asian and West Indian Communal Action in Combating Racism" (Master's thesis, University of Toronto, 1982), 275.

38 British Columbia Human Rights Commission, *I'm Okay; We're Not So Sure about You: A Report of the BC Human Rights Commission on Extensions to the Code* (Victoria: British Columbia Human Rights Commission, 1983). In its second report, titled *How to Make It Work*, the commission recommended that legislation be revised to deal with the health and safety of farm labourers and a minimum wage for household workers, which could certainly be categorized as economic and social rights. Significantly, however, the commission did not recommend that the relevant alterations be made in the Human Rights Code. Instead, it called for amendments to the minimum wage legislation and for changes to the Workers' Compensation Board. British Columbia Human Rights Commission, *How to Make It Work: A Report of the BC Human Rights Commission on Strengthening the Statutory Protection of Human Rights* (Victoria: British Columbia Human Rights Commission, 1983). See also British Columbia Human Rights Commission, *Recommendations for Changes to the Human Rights Code of British Columbia* (Victoria: Human Rights Commission of British Columbia, 1981).

39 As Martha Minow explains, "each person is alone at the unique crossroad of each intersecting group. Each of us is a unique member of the sets of endless groupings that touch us, whether called racial, gender, disability, family, ethnicity, or nationality." Martha Minow, *Not Only for Myself: Identity, Politics, and the Law* (New York: New Press, 1997), 39.

40 For a personal narrative that more fully explains this point, see Diane Pothier, "Connecting Grounds of Discrimination to Real People's Real Experiences," *Canadian Journal of Women and the Law* 13 (2001): 64. As Nitya Duclos notes, "it is not hard to see that stereotypes arising from particular combinations of race and gender are often the source of the discriminatory treatment that gives rise to the complaint ... Stereotypes which combine race and gender are common to everyday experience. Race and gender are equally apparent and, together with other visible characteristics, are likely to form part of our initial generalizations about people. It is only when one becomes immersed in the world of law that

race and gender are extracted from the whole person and become mutually exclusive categories of discrimination." Nitya Duclos, "Disappearing Women: Racial Minority Women in Human Rights Cases," *Canadian Journal of Women and the Law* 6 (1993): 33.
41 Minow notes that intersectionality "refers to the way in which any particular individual stands at the crossroads of multiple groups. All women also have a race; all whites also have a gender. The individuals stand in different places as gender and racial politics converge and diverge. Moreover, the meanings of gender are inflected and informed by race, and the meanings of racial identity are similarly influenced by images of gender." Minow, *Not Only for Myself,* 38.
42 Nitya Iyer, "Categorical Denials: Equality Rights and the Shaping of Social Identity," *Queen's Law Journal* 19 (1993): 181. Iyer refers to the *Mossop* case to demonstrate her argument. Brian Mossop, a federal civil servant, was denied bereavement leave to attend the funeral of his partner's father because his partner was male. Eventually, he appealed to the Supreme Court of Canada. According to Iyer, his appeal failed because the judges defined family status in terms of variations on the heterosexual family and insisted that Mossop's case fell under the category of sexual orientation, which at the time was not recognized in the federal Human Rights Act. In other words, by resorting to categories of discrimination, and defining each category in terms of how it differed from an assumed norm, the court was blind to Mossop's experience of discrimination. Ibid., 194-97.
43 For example, a landlord who refused to rent to an inter-racial couple and was therefore accused of racism might defeat the complaint by showing that he had rented other premises to racial minorities. If he objected to inter-racial sexual relationships, only an approach that considered both race and sex would adequately identify the underlying cause and justify the complaint. According to Nitya Duclos (who also writes under the name of Nitya Iyer), "as a complainant departs from the norm in an increasing number of directions, it is less and less likely that the conduct complained of will be held to constitute discrimination in law. If the complainant straddles too many categories, she is increasingly likely to lose her balance and fall through the cracks: it is no longer discrimination, it is 'just her.'" Duclos, "Disappearing Women," 42. In 1998, the federal Human Rights Act was amended to recognize that "a discriminatory practice includes a practice based on ... the effect of a combination of prohibited grounds." *An Act to Amend the Canada Evidence Act and the Criminal Code in Respect of Persons with Disabilities, to Amend the Canadian Human Rights Act in Respect of Persons with Disabilities and Other Matters and to make Consequential Amendments to Other Acts,* S.C. 1998, c. 9, s. 11.
44 Royal Commission on Equality in Employment, *Report,* 8.
45 Ibid., 9.
46 Her recommendations addressed issues such as training, childcare, equal pay for work of equal value, creating educational institutions and programs aimed at minorities, generating programs to help integrate new immigrants (such as language training), and monitoring hiring practices or trends.
47 Howe and Johnson, *Restraining Equality,* 25.
48 See, for instance, the Ontario Human Rights Code Review Task Force report on the need to investigate systemic discrimination. Ontario Human Rights Code Review Task Force, *Achieving Equality: A Report on Human Rights Reform* (Toronto: Ministry of Citizenship, 1992).
49 Howe and Johnson, *Restraining Equality,* 126. The authors also found that the most common complaint among advocacy groups was that human rights commissions failed to

adequately address systemic discrimination. Ibid., 142-44. For other recent criticisms of this shortcoming, see Grabham, "Substantive Equality"; Langer, *Defining Rights and Wrongs;* Schucher, "Contesting Women's Solidarity"; and Kamini Steinberg, "The Ontario Human Rights Code: Implications for an Intersectional Approach to Human Rights Claims" (Master's thesis, University of Toronto, 2009).

50 Shelagh Day, "The Process for Achieving Equality," in *Human Rights in Canada: Into the 1990s and Beyond,* ed. Ryszard I. Cholewinski (Ottawa: Human Rights Research and Education Centre, 1990), 22-23.

51 Maxine Molyneux and Shahra Razavi, *Gender, Justice, Development and Rights* (New York: United Nations Research Institute for Social Development, 2003), 5-6.

52 Ibid., 6, 109.

53 Most jurisdictions had introduced a form of equal pay for work of equal value by the 1990s. Pay equity benefitted many female workers, especially in the public service, but did not have a transformative impact. On average, women continue to earn significantly less than men.

54 See, for instance, Andrea Wright, "Formulaic Comparisons: Stopping the Charter at the Statutory Human Rights Gate," in *Making Equality Rights Real: Securing Substantive Equality under the Charter,* ed. Fay Faraday, Margaret Denike, and M. Kate Stephenson (Toronto: Irwin Law, 2006), 409-41. For an example of a successful challenge to standards based on male performance in the workplace, see Judy Fudge and Hester Lessard, "Challenging Norms and Creating Precedents: The Tale of a Woman Firefighter in the Forests of British Columbia," in *Challenging Norms and Creating Precedents,* ed. Judy Fudge and Eric Tucker (Toronto: University of Toronto Press, 2010), 315-54.

55 Wright, "Formulaic Comparisons," 417.

56 B. Gene Errington, "Sexual Harassment in the Workplace: A Discussion Paper" (British Columbia Federation of Labour and the Vancouver Women's Research Centre, 1980), 3-4.

57 Quoted in Janet Beebe, *Update on the Status of Women in British Columbia* (Vancouver: Vancouver Status of Women, 1978), 12.

58 Judy Fudge, "The Effect of Entrenching a Bill of Rights upon Political Discourse: Feminist Demands and Sexual Violence in Canada," *International Journal of the Sociology of Law* 17 (1989): 448.

59 Fudge and Lessard, "Challenging Norms and Creating Precedents," 346.

60 University of British Columbia Rare Books and Special Collections, Vancouver, Rosemary Brown, v.1, f.5, NDP Women's Committee: Herstory and Policy, 1977.

Bibliography

There is no single collection of BC human rights board of inquiry decisions. Most of the decisions cited in this book are available by case name in the University of Victoria Archives' Human Rights Board of Inquiry Collection (UVA, BOIs) or the Human Rights Branch office files currently located with the Ministry of the Attorney General (AG HRB), which were secured through an application under the Freedom of Information and Protection of Privacy Act. Case summaries are also available in the *Labour Research Bulletin* and the *Canadian Human Rights Reporter*. A few cases appear in archival records, including the Vancouver Status of Women and Renate Shearer fonds at University of British Columbia Rare Books and Special Collections.

For additional content related to this book, please visit www.HistoryOfRights.com.

Archival Sources

British Columbia Archives, Victoria (BCA)
British Columbia Voice of Women
Department of Labour
Provincial Council of Women

Canadian Women's Movement Archives, University of Ottawa, Ottawa
British Columbia Federation of Women
Status of Women Action Group

Library and Archives Canada, Ottawa (LAC)
Dan Hill
Jewish Labour Committee (JLC)
Kalmen Kaplansky
Voice of Women
Walter S. Tarnopolsky

Bibliography

Ministry of Attorney General of British Columbia
Human Rights Branch and Commission

Simon Fraser Rare Books and Special Collections, Burnaby
British Columbia Federation of Women
Frances Wasserlein
W.A.C. Bennett

University of British Columbia Rare Books and Special Collections, Vancouver (UBC RBSC)
British Columbia Federation of Labour
British Columbia Federation of Women
British Columbia Voice of Women
Dave Barrett
NDP Women's Rights Committee
Renate Shearer
Rosemary Brown
Solidarity Coalition
Vancouver Labour Committee for Human Rights (VLCHR)
Vancouver Status of Women (VSW)

University of Northern British Columbia Archives, Prince George
Women's Resource Centre collection

University of Victoria Archives, Victoria (UVA)
Human Rights Boards of Inquiry Collection (BOIs)
Status of Women Action Group (SWAG)

Interviews

Andison, Alan. 19 August 2010.
Black, Bill. 20 June 2002 and 15 May 2009.
Coates, Fred W. 11 March 2002.
Day, Shelagh. 12 May 2009.
Flood, Cynthia. 10 May 2009.
Katz, April. 17 August 2010.
Preston, Norrie. 8 May 2009.
Ruff, Kathleen. 14 April 2010.
Sproule-Jones, Linda. 5 May 2009.
Vivian, Gladys. 4 August 2004.

Secondary Sources

Adams, Eric. "The Idea of Constitutional Rights and the Transformation of Canadian Constitutional Law, 1930-1960." PhD diss., University of Toronto, 2009.

Ajzenstat, Janet. *The Canadian Founding: John Locke and Parliament.* Montreal and Kingston: McGill-Queen's University Press, 2007.
Andersen, Marguerite, ed. *Feminist Journeys.* Ottawa: Feminist History Society, 2010.
Anderson, Donald. "The Development of Human Rights Protections in British Columbia." Master's thesis, University of Victoria, 1986.
Anderson, Doris. *Rebel Daughter: An Autobiography.* Toronto: Key Porter Books, 1996.
Andiappan, P., M. Reavley, and S. Silver. "Discrimination against Pregnant Employees: An Analysis of Arbitration and Human Rights Tribunal Decisions in Canada." *Journal of Business Ethics* 9 (1990): 143-51.
Bachman, Cindy. "A Satisfaction Survey on the BC Human Rights Commission's Dispute Resolution Process." Master's thesis, Royal Roads University, 2003.
Backhouse, Constance. *Colour-Coded: A Legal History of Racism in Canada, 1900-1950.* Toronto: University of Toronto Press, 1999.
–. "The Doctrine of Corroboration in Sexual Assault Trials in Early 20th Century Canada and Australia." In *From Subjects to Citizens: A Hundred Years of Citizenship in Australia and Canada,* ed. Pierre Boyer, Linda Cardinal, and David Headon, 123-59. Ottawa: University of Ottawa Press, 2004.
–. "Nineteenth Century Canadian Prostitution Law: Reflection of a Discriminatory Society." *Histoire sociale/Social History* 18 (1985): 387-423.
–. *Petticoats and Prejudice: Women and Law in Nineteenth-Century Canada.* Toronto: Women's Press, 1991.
Backhouse, Constance, and Leah Cohen. *The Secret Oppression: Sexual Harassment of Working Women.* Toronto: Macmillan, 1978.
Backhouse, Constance, and David H. Flaherty, eds. *Challenging Times: The Women's Movement in Canada and the United States.* Montreal and Kingston: McGill-Queen's University Press, 1992.
Bagnall, John C. "The Ontario Conservatives and the Development of Anti-Discrimination Policy." PhD diss., Queen's University, 1984.
Baines, Beverley. "Law, Gender, Equality." In *Changing Patterns: Women in Canada,* ed. Sandra Burt, Lorraine Code, and Lindsay Dorney, 243-78. Toronto: McClelland and Stewart, 1993.
Bakan, Abigail B., and Audrey Kobayashi. "Backlash against Employment Equity: The British Columbia Experience." *Atlantis* 29 (2004): 61-70.
Bangarth, Stephanie. *Voices Raised in Protest: Defending North American Citizens of Japanese Ancestry, 1942-49.* Vancouver: UBC Press, 2008.
Bannerman, Josie, Kathy Chopik, and Ann Zurbrigg. "Cheap at Half the Price: The History of the Fight for Equal Pay in BC." In *Not Just Pin Money: Selected Essays on the History of Women's Work in British Columbia,* ed. Barbara K. Latham and Roberta J. Pazdro, 297-313. Victoria: Camosun College, 1984.
Barman, Jean. *The West beyond the West: A History of British Columbia.* Toronto: University of Toronto Press, 1991.
Bartlett, Peter. "Sexual Distinctions in Pensions." *Osgoode Hall Law Journal* 24 (1986): 833-65.
Beebe, Janet. *Update on the Status of Women in British Columbia.* Vancouver: Vancouver Status of Women, 1978.
Beeby, Dean. "Women in the Ontario C.C.F., 1940-1950." *Ontario History* 74 (1982): 258-83.

Black, Bill. *BC Human Rights Review: Report on Human Rights in British Columbia.* Vancouver: Government of British Columbia, 1994.

–. "Human Rights in British Columbia: Equality Postponed." In *Canadian Human Rights Yearbook, 1984-85,* ed. William Pentney and Daniel Proulx, 219-36. Toronto: Carswell, 1985.

Boyd, Susan. "Is Equality Enough? Fathers' Rights and Women's Rights Advocacy." In *Rethinking Equality Projects in Law: Feminist Challenges,* ed. Rosemary Hunter, 59-79. Oxford: Hart, 2008.

Brandt, Gail Cuthbert, Naomi Black, Paula Bourne, and Magda Fahrni. *Canadian Women: A History.* Toronto: Nelson Education, 2011.

British Columbia Commission for International Year for Human Rights. *Report.* Victoria: Queen's Printer, 1968.

British Columbia Human Rights Commission. *How to Make It Work: A Report of the BC Human Rights Commission on Strengthening the Statutory Protection of Human Rights.* Victoria: British Columbia Human Rights Commission, 1983.

–. *I'm Okay; We're Not So Sure about You: A Report of the BC Human Rights Commission on Extensions to the Code.* Victoria: British Columbia Human Rights Commission, 1983.

–. *Recommendations for Changes to the Human Rights Code of British Columbia.* Victoria: Human Rights Commission of British Columbia, 1981.

Brockman, Joan. *Gender in the Legal Profession: Fitting in or Breaking the Mould.* Vancouver: UBC Press, 2006.

Brodsky, Gwen. *Canadian Charter Equality Rights for Women: One Step Forward or Two Steps Back?* Ottawa: Canadian Advisory Council on the Status of Women, 1989.

Brown, Rosemary. *Being Brown: A Very Public Life.* Toronto: Random House, 1989.

Bruner, Arnold. "The Genesis of Ontario Human Rights Legislation: A Study in Law Reform." *University of Toronto Faculty Law Review* 31 (1979): 236-53.

Buckley, Melinda. "Towards Transformative Human Rights Practices: A Reconsideration of the Role of Legal Institutions in Achieving Justice." PhD diss., University of British Columbia, 2002.

Burt, Sandra. "The Changing Patterns of Public Policy." In *Changing Patterns: Women in Canada.* 2nd ed., ed. Sandra Burt, Lorraine Code, and Lindsay Dorney, 212-41. Toronto: McClelland and Stewart, 1993.

Campbell, Marie. "Sexism in British Columbia Trade Unions, 1900-1920." In *In Her Own Right: Selected Essays on Women's History in BC,* ed. Barbara Latham and Cathy Kess, 167-86. Victoria: Camosun College, 1980.

Campbell, Robert A. "Ladies and Escorts: Gender Segregation and Public Policy in British Columbia Beer Parlours, 1925 to 1945." *BC Studies* 105-6 (1995): 120-38.

Canada. *Report of the Royal Commission on the Status of Women.* Ottawa: Queen's Printer, 1970.

Canada, Indian and Northern Affairs. *The Elimination of Sex Discrimination from the Indian Act.* Ottawa: Queen's Printer, 1982.

Canada, Status of Women. *The Royal Commission on the Status of Women: An Overview 25 Years Later.* Ottawa: Status of Women Canada, 1995.

Cardenas, Sonia. "Transgovernmental Activism: Canada's Role in Promoting National Human Rights Commissions." *Human Rights Quarterly* 25, 3 (2003): 775-90.

Carter, Sarah. "'Daughters of British Blood' or 'Hordes of Men of Alien Race': The Homesteads-for-Women Campaign in Western Canada." *Great Plains Quarterly* 29, 1 (2009): 267-86.

Cassin, A. Marguerite. "Human Rights, Culture and Everyday Lives." *British Journal of Canadian Studies* 19 (2006): 279-304.

Chambers, Lori. "'In the Name of the Father': Children, Naming Practices, and the Law in Canada." *UBC Law Review* 43 (2010-11): 1-45.

–. *Married Women and Property Law in Victorian Ontario.* Toronto: University of Toronto Press, 1997.

–. "Newborn Adoption: Birth Mothers, Genetic Fathers, and Reproductive Autonomy." *Canadian Journal of Family Law* 26 (2010): 339-93.

Chappell, Louise, John Chesterman, and Lisa Hill. *The Politics of Human Rights in Australia.* Cambridge: Cambridge University Press, 2009.

Chenier, Elise. "Rethinking Class in Lesbian Bar Culture: Living the 'Gay Life' in Toronto, 1955-1965." In *Rethinking Canada: The Promise of Women's History,* ed. Mona Gleason and Adele Perry, 301-22. Toronto: Oxford University Press, 2006.

Christie, Nancy. *Engendering the State: Family, Work, and Welfare in Canada.* Toronto: University of Toronto Press, 2000.

Clarkson, Chris. *Domestic Reforms: Political Visions and Family Regulation in British Columbia, 1862-1940.* Vancouver: UBC Press, 2007.

Clément, Dominique. "Alberta's Rights Revolution." *British Journal of Canadian Studies* 26 (2013): 59-79.

–. *Canada's Rights Revolution: Social Movements and Social Change, 1937-82.* Vancouver: UBC Press, 2008.

–. "Equality Deferred: Sex Discrimination and the Newfoundland Human Rights State." *Acadiensis* 41 (2012): 102-27.

–. "An Exercise in Futility? Regionalism, State Funding, and Ideology as Obstacles to the Formation of a National Social Movement Organization in Canada." *BC Studies* 146 (Summer 2005): 63-91.

–. "Generations and the Transformation of Social Movements in Post-War Canada." *Histoire sociale/Social History* 42 (2009): 361-88.

–. "Human Rights in Canadian Domestic and Foreign Politics: From 'Niggardly Acceptance' to Enthusiastic Embrace." *Human Rights Quarterly* 34, 3 (2012): 751-78.

–. "Human Rights Law and Sexual Discrimination in British Columbia, 1953-1984." In *The West and Beyond,* ed. Sara Carter, Alvin Finkel, and Peter Fortna, 297-325. Edmonton: Athabasca University Press, 2010.

–. "'I Believe in Human Rights, Not Women's Rights': Women and the Human Rights State, 1969-1984." *Radical History Review* 101 (2008): 107-29.

–. "Rights in the Age of Protest: A History of the Human Rights and Civil Liberties Movement in Canada, 1962-1982." PhD diss., Memorial University of Newfoundland, 2005.

–. "Searching for Rights in the Age of Activism: The Newfoundland-Labrador Human Rights Association, 1968-1982." *Newfoundland Studies* 19 (2003): 347-72.

Clément, Dominique, Will Silver, and Dan Trottier. *The Evolution of Human Rights in Canada.* Ottawa: Canadian Human Rights Commission, 2012.

Clément, Dominique, and Renée Vaugeois, eds. *Alberta's Human Rights Story: The Search for Equality and Justice.* Edmonton: John Humphrey Centre for Peace and Human Rights, 2012.

Cohen, Marjorie Griffin. "Paid Work." In Ruth Roach Pierson and Marjorie Griffin Cohen, *Canadian Women's Issues.* Vol. 2, *Bold Visions,* 83-116. Toronto: James Lorimer, 1995.

Bibliography

Colter, Erica. "A State of Affairs Most Common: Black Nova Scotians and the Stanfield Government's Interdepartmental Committee on Human Rights, 1959-1967." Master's thesis, Dalhousie University, 2006.

Cornish, Mary, Fay Faraday, and Jo-Anne Pickel. *Enforcing Human Rights in Ontario.* Aurora: Canada Law Books, 2009.

Côté, Andrée, and Lucie Lemonde. *Discrimination et commission des droits de la personne.* Montreal: Éditions Saint-Martin, 1988.

Creese, Gillian. "The Politics of Dependence: Women, Work and Unemployment in the Vancouver Labour Movement before World War II." In *British Columbia Reconsidered: Essays on Women,* ed. Gillian Creese and Veronica Strong-Boag, 364-90. Vancouver: Press Gang, 1992.

Dawson, Michael. "Leisure, Consumption, and the Public Sphere: Postwar Debates over Shopping Regulations in Vancouver and Victoria during the Cold War." In *Creating Postwar Canada: Community, Diversity, and Dissent, 1945-75,* ed. Magda Fahrni, 193-216. Vancouver: UBC Press, 2007.

Dawson, T. Brette. *Relating to Law: A Chronology of Women and Law in Canada.* Toronto: Captus Press, 1994.

Day, Shelagh. "Impediments to Achieving Equality." In *Equality and Judicial Neutrality,* ed. Sheilah L. Martin and Kathleen E. Mahoney, 402-9. Toronto: Carswell, 1987.

–. "The Process for Achieving Equality." In *Human Rights in Canada: Into the 1990s and Beyond,* ed. Ryszard I. Cholewinski, 17-30. Ottawa: Human Rights Research and Education Centre, 1990.

–. *Reassessing Statutory Human Rights Legislation Thirty Years Later: Affirmative Action and Equality Concepts.* Ottawa: Human Rights Research and Education Centre, 1995.

–. "Recent Developments in Human Rights." *Labour Research Bulletin* (June 1977): 16-24.

–. *A Report on the Status of Women at the University of British Columbia.* Vancouver: Women's Action Group UBC, 1973.

Day, Shelagh, Ken Norman, and Lucie Lamarche, eds. *14 Arguments in Favour of Human Rights Institutions.* Toronto: Irwin Law, 2014.

Donnelly, Jack. *Universal Human Rights in Theory and Practice.* New York: Cornell University Press, 2003.

Driedger, Leo. *Race and Ethnicity: Finding Identities and Equalities.* 2nd ed. Oxford University Press, 2003.

Ducharme, Michel. *Le concept de liberté au Canada à l'époque des révolutions atlantiques, 1776-1838.* Montreal and Kingston: McGill-Queen's University Press, 2010.

Duclos, Nitya. "Disappearing Women: Racial Minority Women in Human Rights Cases." *Canadian Journal of Women and the Law* 6 (1993): 25-51.

Duhaime, Bernard. "Strengthening the Protection of Human Rights in the Americas: A Role for Canada?" In *Human Rights in the Americas,* ed. Monica Serrano and Vesselin Popovski, 84-113. New York: United Nations University Press, 2010.

Eberlee, T.M., and D.G. Hill. "The Ontario Human Rights Code." *University of Toronto Law Journal* 15 (1964): 448-55.

Eliadis, Pearl. *Speaking Out on Human Rights: Debating Canada's Human Rights System.* Montreal and Kingston: McGill-Queen's University Press, 2014.

Errington, B. Gene. "Sexual Harassment in the Workplace: A Discussion Paper." British Columbia Federation of Labour Women's Committee and the Vancouver Women's Research Centre, 1980.

Flanagan, Thomas. "The Manufacture of Minorities." In *Minorities and the Canadian State*, ed. Neil Nevitte and Allan Kornberg, 107-22. Oakville: Mosaic Press, 1985.
Flanagan, Thomas, Rainer Knopff, and Keith Archer. "Selection Bias in Human Rights Tribunals: An Exploratory Study." *Canadian Public Administration* 31 (1988): 483-500.
Frager, Ruth A., and Carmela Patrias. *Discounted Labour: Women Workers in Canada, 1870-1939*. Toronto: University of Toronto Press, 2005.
–. "Human Rights Activists and the Question of Sex Discrimination in Postwar Ontario." *Canadian Historical Review* 93 (2012): 1-28.
–. "'This Is Our Country, These Are Our Rights': Minorities and the Origins of Ontario's Human Rights Campaigns." *Canadian Historical Review* 82 (2001): 1-35.
Frideres, James S., and William J. Reeves. "The Ability to Implement Human Rights Legislation in Canada." *Canadian Review of Sociology and Anthropology* 26 (1989): 311-32.
Fudge, Judy. "The Effect of Entrenching a Bill of Rights upon Political Discourse: Feminist Demands and Sexual Violence in Canada." *International Journal of the Sociology of Law* 17 (1989): 445-63.
Fudge, Judy, and Hester Lessard. "Challenging Norms and Creating Precedents: The Tale of a Woman Firefighter in the Forests of British Columbia." In *Challenging Norms and Creating Precedents*, ed. Judy Fudge and Eric Tucker, 315-54. Toronto: University of Toronto Press, 2010.
Garcia-Ricci, Diego. "Human Rights Protection in Canada: A Unique, Multi-Dimensional Approach." Master's thesis, University of Toronto, 2007.
Garr, Allen. *Tough Guy: Bill Bennett and the Taking of British Columbia*. Toronto: Key Porter Books, 1985.
Gill, Amy. "In Their Finest Hour: Deciphering the Role of the Canadian Women's Movement in the Formulation of the Charter of Rights and Freedoms." Master's thesis, University of Ottawa, 2010.
Glasbeek, Amanda. *Feminized Justice: The Toronto Women's Court, 1913-1934*. Vancouver: UBC Press, 2009.
Godfrey, Stuart. *Human Rights and Social Policy in Newfoundland, 1832-1982*. St. John's: Harry Cuff, 1985.
Gould, Terry. "The Engineers of Dumb Behavior." *Vancouver Magazine*, May 1991, 29-40, 109-10.
Grabham, Emily. "Substantive Equality: A Comparative Analysis of UK, EC and Canadian Law." Master's thesis, Queen's University, 2000.
Grekul, Jana. "The Right to Consent? Eugenics in Alberta, 1928-1972." In *A History of Human Rights in Canada: Essential Issues*, ed. Janet Miron, 135-54. Toronto: Canadian Scholars' Press, 2009.
Gupta, P.A. Neena. "Reconsidering Bhaduria: A Re-Examination of the Roles of the Ontario Human Rights Commission and the Courts in the Fight against Discrimination." Master's thesis, University of Toronto, 1993.
Gurnett, Jim. "Oral Histories." In *Alberta Legacies*, ed. Dominique Clément and Gerry Gall, 41-58. Edmonton: John Humphrey Centre for Peace and Human Rights, 2011.
Herman, Didi. *Rights of Passage: Struggles for Lesbian and Gay Legal Equality*. Toronto: University of Toronto Press, 1994.
Hesler, Nicole Duval. "Human Rights Adjudication." In *Discrimination in the Law and the Administration of Justice*, ed. Walter S. Tarnopolsky, Joyce Whitman, and Monique Ouellette, 509-18. Toronto: Canadian Institute for the Administration of Justice, 1992.

Hill, Daniel G. "The Role of a Human Rights Commission: The Ontario Experience." *University of Toronto Law Journal* 19 (1969): 390-401.

Hobsbawm, E.J. "Labour and Human Rights." In *Worlds of Labour: Further Studies in the History of Labour,* ed. E.J. Hobsbawm, 297-316. London: Weidenfeld and Nicolson, 1984.

Hodgson, Dorothy L. "Introduction: Gender and Culture at the Limits of Rights." In *Gender and Culture at the Limits of Rights,* ed. Dorothy L. Hodgson, 1-14. Philadelphia: University of Pennsylvania Press, 2011.

Howe, R. Brian. "The Evolution of Human Rights Policy in Ontario." *Canadian Journal of Political Science/Revue canadienne de science politique* 24 (1991): 783-802.

–. "Human Rights in Hard Times: The Post-War Canadian Experience." *Canadian Public Administration* 35 (1992): 464-84.

–. "Human Rights Policy in Ontario: The Tension between Positive and Negative State Laws." PhD diss., University of Toronto, 1989.

–. "Incrementalism and Human Rights Reform." *Journal of Canadian Studies* 28 (1993): 29-44.

Howe, R. Brian, and Malcolm J. Andrade. "The Reputations of Human Rights Commissions in Canada." *Canadian Journal of Law and Society* 9 (1994): 1-20.

Howe, R. Brian, and David Johnson. *Restraining Equality: Human Rights Commissions in Canada.* Toronto: University of Toronto Press, 2000.

–. "Variations in Enforcing Equality: A Study of Provincial Human Rights Funding." *Canadian Public Administration* 38 (1995): 242-62.

Hucker, John. "Antidiscrimination Laws in Canada: Human Rights Commissions and the Search for Equality." *Human Rights Quarterly* 19, 3 (1997): 547-71.

Hunter, Ian A. "The Development of the Ontario Human Rights Code: A Decade in Retrospect." *University of Toronto Law Journal* 22 (1972): 237-57.

–. "Liberty and Equality: A Tale of Two Codes." *McGill Law Journal* 29 (1983): 1-24.

–. "The Origin, Development and Interpretation of Human Rights Legislation." In *The Practice of Freedom: Canadian Essays on Human Rights and Fundamental Freedoms,* ed. John P. Humphrey and R. St. J. Macdonald, 77-110. Toronto: Butterworth, 1979.

Isitt, Ben. *Militant Minority: British Columbia Workers and the Rise of a New Left, 1948-1972.* Toronto: University of Toronto Press, 2010.

Iyer, Nitya. "Categorical Denials: Equality Rights and the Shaping of Social Identity." *Queen's Law Journal* 19 (1993): 179-207.

Kallen, Evelyn. *Ethnicity and Human Rights in Canada: A Human Rights Perspective on Ethnicity, Racism and Systemic Inequality.* Don Mills: Oxford University Press, 2003.

Kirkup, Alex, and Tony Evans. "The Myth of Western Opposition to Economic, Social, and Cultural Rights? A Reply to Whelan and Donnelly." *Human Rights Quarterly* 31, 1 (2009): 221-38.

Knopff, Rainer. *Human Rights and Social Technology: The New War on Discrimination.* Ottawa: Carleton University Press, 1989.

Korinek, Valerie. "'The Most Openly Gay Person for at Least a Thousand Miles': Doug Wilson and the Politicization of a Province." *Canadian Historical Review* 84 (2003): 516-51.

Lambertson, Ross. "The BC Court of Appeal and Civil Liberties." *BC Studies* 163 (2009): 81-110.

–. "The Black, Brown, White and Red Blues: The Beating of Clarence Clemons." *Canadian Historical Review* 85 (2004): 755-76.

–. "The Dresden Story: Racism, Human Rights, and the Jewish Labour Committee of Canada." *Labour/Le travail* (Spring 2001): 43-82.
–. *Repression and Resistance: Canadian Human Rights Activists, 1930-1960*. Toronto: University of Toronto Press, 2005.
–. "Suppression and Subversion." In *A History of Human Rights in Canada*, ed. Janet Miron, 27-42. Toronto: Canadian Scholars' Press, 2009.
Langer, Rosanna L. *Defining Rights and Wrongs: Bureaucracy, Human Rights, and Public Accountability*. Vancouver: UBC Press, 2007.
Lauren, Paul Gordon. *The Evolution of International Human Rights: Visions Seen*. Philadelphia: University of Pennsylvania Press, 2011.
Leary, Virginia A. "The Paradox of Human Rights and Workers' Rights." In *Human Rights, Labor Rights, and International Trade*, ed. Lance A. Compa and Stephen F. Diamond, 22-47. Philadelphia: University of Pennsylvania Press, 2003.
Leiper, Jean McKenzie. *Bar Codes: Women in the Legal Profession*. Vancouver: UBC Press, 2006.
Lessard, Hester. "Backlash in the Academy: The Evolution of Campus Sexual Harassment Regimes." In *Reaction and Resistance: Feminism, Law, and Social Change*, ed. Dorothy E. Chunn, Susan B. Boyd, and Hester Lessard, 164-95. Vancouver: UBC Press, 2007.
–. "Mothers, Fathers, and Naming: Reflections on the Law Equality Framework and Trociuk v. British Columbia (Attorney General)." *Canadian Journal of Women and the Law* 16 (2004): 165-211.
Lichtenstein, Nelson. "The Rights Revolution." *New Labor Forum* 12 (2003): 61-73.
Little, Margaret Hillyard. "Claiming a Unique Place: The Introduction of Mothers' Pensions in British Columbia." *BC Studies* 105-6 (1995): 80-102.
–. "'A Fit and Proper Person': The Moral Regulation of Single Mothers in Ontario, 1920-1940." In *Gendered Pasts: Historical Essays in Femininity and Masculinity in Canada*, ed. Kathryn McPherson, Cecilia Morgan, and Nancy M. Forestell, 123-38. Toronto: Oxford University Press, 1999.
Lockard, Duane. *Toward Equal Opportunity: A Study of State and Local Antidiscrimination Laws*. New York: Macmillan, 1968.
Lui, Andrew. *Why Canada Cares: Human Rights and Foreign Policy in Theory and Practice*. Montreal and Kingston: McGill-Queen's University Press, 2012.
MacGill, Helen Gregory. *Daughters, Wives and Mothers in British Columbia*. Vancouver: Moore Printing, 1913.
–. *Laws for Women and Children in British Columbia*. Vancouver: privately printed, 1925.
MacKay, W.A. "Recent Developments in the Field of Human Rights in Nova Scotia." *University of Toronto Law Journal* 17 (1967): 176-86.
MacLennan, Christopher. *Toward the Charter: Canadians and the Demand for a National Bill of Rights, 1929-1960*. Montreal and Kingston: McGill-Queen's University Press, 2003.
Mandel, Michael. *The Charter of Rights and the Legislation of Politics in Canada*. Toronto: Thompson Educational, 1994.
McCartin, Joseph A. "Democratizing the Demand for Workers' Rights." *Dissent* 1 (Winter 2005): 61-68.
McChesney, Allan. "Aboriginal Communities, Aboriginal Rights, and the Human Rights System." In *Human Rights in Cross-Cultural Perspectives: A Quest for Consensus*, ed. Abdullahi Ahmed An-Na'im, 221-52. Philadelphia: University of Pennsylvania Press, 1992.

McColgan, Aileen. *Women under the Law: The False Promise of Human Rights.* New Baskerville: Longman, 2000.
McIntyre, Sheila. "Studied Ignorance and Privileged Innocence: Keeping Equity Academic." *Canadian Journal of Women and the Law* 12 (2000): 147-96.
McLaren, Angus, and Arlene Tigar McLaren. *The Bedroom and the State: The Changing Practices and Politics of Contraception and Abortion in Canada, 1880-1997.* Toronto: Oxford University Press, 1997.
Merry, Sally Engle. "Women, Violence, and the Human Rights System." In *Women, Gender and Human Rights: A Global Perspective,* ed. Marjorie Agosin, 83-98. Piscataway: Rutgers University Press, 2001.
Mertus, Julie A. *Human Rights Matters: Local Politics and National Human Rights Institutions.* Stanford: Stanford University Press, 2008.
Minow, Martha. *Not Only for Myself: Identity, Politics, and the Law.* New York: New Press, 1997.
Mitchell, David J. *W.A.C. Bennett and the Rise of British Columbia.* Vancouver: Douglas and McIntyre, 1995.
Molyneux, Maxine, and Shahra Razavi. *Gender, Justice, Development and Rights.* New York: United Nations Research Institute for Social Development, 2003.
Moore, Christopher. *The British Columbia Court of Appeal: The First Hundred Years, 1910-2010.* Vancouver: UBC Press, 2010.
Moore, Dorothy Emma. "Multiculturalism: Ideology or Social Reality?" PhD diss., Boston University, 1980.
Morel, André. "Le Charte Québécoise: un document unique dans l'histoire législative canadienne." *Revue juridique themis* 21 (1987): 1-23.
Moyn, Samuel. *The Last Utopia: Human Rights in History.* Boston: Belknap Press of Harvard University Press, 2010.
Nevitte, Neil, and Allan Kornberg. *Minorities and the Canadian State.* Oakville: Mosaic Press, 1985.
Nixon, Charles David. "Resolving Human Rights Complaints in a Unionized Environment: A Blueprint for Reform." Master's thesis, Royal Roads University, 2000.
Nolan, Cathal J. "Reluctant Liberal: Canada, Human Rights and the United Nations." *Diplomacy and Statecraft* 2 (1990): 281-305.
Norman, Ken. "Problems in Human Rights Legislation and Administration." In *Equality and Judicial Neutrality,* ed. Sheilah L. Martin and Kathleen E. Mahoney, 391-401. Toronto: Carswell, 1987.
O'Neill, Nick, Simon Rice, and Roger Douglas. *Retreat from Injustice: Human Rights Law in Australia.* Sydney: Federation Press, 2004.
Ontario Human Rights Commission. *Life Together: A Report on Human Rights in Ontario.* Toronto: Ontario Human Rights Commission, 1977.
Palmer, Bryan. *Solidarity: The Rise and Fall of an Opposition in British Columbia.* Vancouver: New Star Books, 1987.
Patrias, Carmela. *Jobs and Justice: Fighting Discrimination in Wartime Canada, 1939-1945.* Toronto: University of Toronto Press, 2012.
–. "Race, Employment Discrimination, and State Complicity in Wartime Canada, 1939-1945." *Labour/Le travail* 59 (2007): 9-42.
–. "Socialists, Jews, and the 1947 Saskatchewan Bill of Rights." *Canadian Historical Review* 87 (2006): 265-92.

Pearson, Lynne. *Women in British Columbia: Issues, Resources and Services.* Victoria: Provincial Coordinator of the Status of Women's Office, 1975.
Pegram, Thomas. "Diffusion across Political Systems: The Global Spread of National Human Rights Institutions." *Human Rights Quarterly* 32, 3 (2010): 729-60.
Pierson, Ruth Roach. "Education and Training." In Ruth Roach Pierson and Marjorie Griffin Cohen, *Canadian Women's Issues.* Vol. 2, *Bold Visions,* 162-202. Toronto: James Lorimer, 1995.
–. "The Politics of the Body." In Ruth Roach Pierson, Marjorie Griffin Cohen, Paula Bourne, and Philinda Masters, *Canadian Women's Issues.* Vol. 1, *Strong Voices,* 186-263. Toronto: James Lorimer, 1993.
Pierson, Ruth Roach, and Marjorie Griffin Cohen. *Canadian Women's Issues.* Vol. 2, *Bold Visions.* Toronto: James Lorimer, 1995.
Pike, Robert. "Legal Access and the Incidence of Divorce in Canada: A Sociohistorical Analysis." *Canadian Review of Sociology and Anthropology* 12 (1975): 115-33.
Plecas, Bob. *Bill Bennett: A Mandarin's View.* Vancouver: Douglas and McIntyre, 2006.
Pothier, Diane. "Connecting Grounds of Discrimination to Real People's Real Experiences." *Canadian Journal of Women and the Law* 13 (2001): 37-73.
Prentice, Alison, Paula Bourne, Gail Cuthbert Brandt, Beth Light, Wendy Mitchenson, and Naomi Black. *Canadian Women: A History.* Toronto: Harcourt Brace, 1996.
Pulkingham, Jane, ed. *Human Welfare, Rights, and Social Activism: Rethinking the Legacy of J.S. Woodsworth.* Toronto: University of Toronto Press, 2010.
Réaume, Denise G. "Of Pigeonholes and Principles: A Reconsideration of Discrimination Law." *Osgoode Hall Law Journal* 40 (2002): 113-44.
Rebick, Judy. *Ten Thousand Roses: The Making of a Feminist Revolution.* Toronto: Penguin Canada, 2005.
Reid, Alan D. "The New Brunswick Human Rights Act." *University of Toronto Law Journal* 18 (1968): 394-400.
Reif, Linda. "Building Democratic Institutions: The Role of National Human Rights Institutions in Good Governance and Human Rights Protection." *Harvard Human Rights Journal* 13 (2000): 1-69.
Resnick, Philip. "Social Democracy in Power: The Case of British Columbia." *BC Studies* 34 (1977): 3-20.
Riddell, Maureen. *The Evolution of Human Rights Legislation in Alberta, 1945-1979.* Edmonton: Government of Alberta, 1978-79.
Risse, Thomas, Stephen C. Ropp, and Kathryn Sikkink, eds. *The Power of Human Rights: International Norms and Domestic Change.* Cambridge: Cambridge University Press, 1999.
Ross, Becki L. *Burlesque West: Showgirls, Sex and Sin in Postwar Vancouver.* Toronto: University of Toronto Press, 2009.
–. *The House That Jill Built: A Lesbian Nation in Formation.* Toronto: University of Toronto Press, 1995.
Roy, Patricia E., and John Herd Thompson. *British Columbia: Land of Promises.* Toronto: Oxford University Press, 2005.
Royal Commission on Equality in Employment. *Report of the Royal Commission on Equality in Employment.* Ottawa: Supply and Services Canada, 1984.
Ruff, Kathleen. "A Critical Survey of Human Rights Acts and Commissions in Canada." In *Discrimination in the Law and the Administration of Justice,* ed. Walter S. Tarnopolsky,

Joyce Whitman, and Monique Ouellette, 25-37. Toronto: Canadian Institute for the Administration of Justice, 1992.

Sangster, Joan. "Debating Maternity Rights: Pacific Western Airlines and Flight Attendants' Struggle to 'Fly Pregnant' in the 1970s." In *Work on Trial: Canadian Labour Law Struggles*, ed. Judy Fudge and Eric Tucker, 283-314. Toronto: University of Toronto Press, 2010.

–. "Girls in Conflict with the Law: Exploring the Construction of Female 'Delinquency' in Ontario, 1940-1960." In *Through Feminist Eyes: Essays on Canadian Women's History*, ed. Joan Sangster, 251-92. Edmonton: Athabasca University Press, 2011.

–. "Incarcerating 'Bad Girls': The Regulation of Sexuality through the Female Refugees Act in Ontario, 1920-1945." *Histoire sociale/Social History* 7 (1996): 239-75.

–. "Invoking Experience as Evidence." *Canadian Historical Review* 92 (2011): 135-63.

–. "'Pardon Tales' from Magistrate's Court: Women, Crime, and the Court in Peterborough County, 1920-1950." In *Through Feminist Eyes: Essays on Canadian Women's History*, ed. Joan Sangster, 173-212. Edmonton: Athabasca University Press, 2011.

–. "Radical Ruptures: Feminism, Labor, and the Left in the Long Sixties in Canada." *American Review of Canadian Studies* 40 (2010): 1-21.

Schabas, William, and Stéphane Beaulac. *International Human Rights and Canadian Law: Legal Commitment, Implementation and the Charter*. Toronto: Thompson Carswell, 2007.

Schucher, Karen. "Contesting Women's Solidarity: Human Rights Law and the FWTAO Membership Case." PhD diss., York University, 2007.

Sethna, Christabelle. "'Chastity Outmoded': *The Ubyssey*, Sex, and the Single Girl, 1960-1970." In *Creating Postwar Canada: Community, Diversity and Dissent, 1945-75*, ed. Magda Fahrni and Robert Rutherdale, 289-314. Vancouver: UBC Press, 2007.

Sharpe, Robert J., and Patricia L. McMahon. *The Persons Case: The Origins and Legacy of the Fight for Legal Personhood*. Toronto: University of Toronto Press, 2007.

Shue, Henry. *Basic Rights: Subsistence, Affluence and US Foreign Policy*. Princeton: Princeton University Press, 1996.

Smith, Miriam. *Lesbian and Gay Rights in Canada: Social Movements and Equality-Seeking, 1971-1995*. Toronto: University of Toronto Press, 1999.

–. "Social Movements and Judicial Empowerment: Courts, Public Policy, and Lesbian and Gay Organizing in Canada." *Politics and Society* 33 (2005): 327-53.

Sohn, Herbert A. "Human Rights Legislation in Ontario: A Study of Social Action." PhD diss., University of Toronto, 1975.

Stanley, Timothy J. *Contesting White Supremacy: School Segregation, Anti-Racism, and the Making of Chinese Canadians*. Vancouver: UBC Press, 2011.

Stasiulis, Daiva Kristina. "Race, Ethnicity and the State: The Political Structuring of South Asian and West Indian Communal Action in Combating Racism." Master's thesis, University of Toronto, 1982.

Steinberg, Kamini. "The Ontario Human Rights Code: Implications for an Intersectional Approach to Human Rights Claims." Master's thesis, University of Toronto, 2009.

Tarnopolsky, Walter. *The Canadian Bill of Rights*. Toronto: Carswell, 1966.

–. *Discrimination and the Law in Canada*. Toronto: De Boo, 1982.

–. "The Iron Hand in the Velvet Glove: Administration and Enforcement of Human Rights Legislation in Canada." *Canadian Bar Review* 56 (1978): 565-91.

Thompson, Andrew S. *In Defence of Principles: NGOs and Human Rights in Canada*. Vancouver: UBC Press, 2010.

Tillotson, Shirley. "Human Rights Law as Prism: Women's Organizations, Unions, and Ontario's Female Employees Fair Remuneration Act, 1951." *Canadian Historical Review* 72, 4 (1991): 532-57.
–. "Time, Swimming Pools, and Citizenship: The Emergence of Leisure Rights in Mid-Twentieth-Century Canada." In *Contesting Canadian Citizenship: Historical Readings*, ed. Robert Adamoski, Dorothy E. Chunn, and Robert Menzies, 199-224. Peterborough: Broadview Press, 2002.
Tunnicliffe, Jennifer. "The Ontario Human Rights Code Review, 1975-1981: A New Understanding of Human Rights and Its Meaning for Public Policy." Master's thesis, University of Waterloo, 2006.
Vickers, Jill. "The Intellectual Origins of the Women's Movements in Canada." In *Challenging Times: The Women's Movement in Canada and the United States*, ed. Constance Backhouse and David H. Flaherty, 39-60. Montreal and Kingston: McGill-Queen's University Press, 1992.
Vogel, Donna. *Challenging Politics: Cope, Electoral Politics and Social Movements*. Halifax: Fernwood Press, 2003.
Wade, Susan. "Helena Gutteridge: Votes for Women and Trade Unions." In *In Her Own Right: Selected Essays on Women's History in BC,* ed. Barbara Latham and Cathy Kess, 187-204. Victoria: Camosun College, 1980.
Waldron, Mary Anne. *Free to Believe: Rethinking Freedom of Conscience and Religion in Canada*. Toronto: University of Toronto Press, 2013.
Walker, James W. St. G. "The 'Jewish Phase' in the Movement for Racial Equality in Canada." *Canadian Ethnic Studies* 34 (2002): 1-29.
–. *"Race," Rights and the Law in the Supreme Court of Canada: Historical Case Studies*. Toronto: Wilfrid Laurier University Press, 1997.
Wan, LiLynn. *Never Going Back: A History of Queer Activism in Canada*. Toronto: University of Toronto Press, 2002.
–. "'Out of Many Kindreds and Tongues': Racial Identity and Rights Activism in Vancouver, 1919-1939." PhD diss., Dalhousie University, 2011.
Weaver, Sally. "First Nations Women and Government Policy, 1970-92: Discrimination and Conflict." In *Changing Patterns: Women in Canada*, ed. Sandra Burt, Lorraine Code, and Lindsay Dorney, 92-147. Toronto: McClelland and Stewart, 1988.
Welsh, Sandy, and James E. Gruber. "Not Taking It Any More: Women Who Report or File Complaints of Sexual Harassment." *Canadian Review of Sociology and Anthropology* 36 (1999): 559-83.
Wiegers, Wanda. "Feminist Protest and the Regulation of Misogynist Speech: A Case Study of *Saskatchewan Human Rights Commission v Engineering Students' Society*." *Ottawa Law Review* 24 (1992): 363-435.
–. "Gender, Biology, and Third Party Custody Disputes." *Alberta Law Review* 47 (2009): 1-37.
Williams, Cynthia. "The Changing Nature of Citizen Rights." In *Constitutionalism, Citizenship and Society in Canada*, ed. Alan Cairns and Cynthia Williams, 99-132. Toronto: University of Toronto Press, 1985.
Williams, Shannon. "Human Rights in Theory and Practice: A Sociological Study of Aboriginal Peoples and the New Brunswick Human Rights Commission, 1967-1997." Master's thesis, University of New Brunswick, 1998.
Wingate, Andrew. "Discrimination against Pregnant Employees in Canada, 1988-2000." Master's thesis, University of Windsor, 2000.

Wright, Andrea. "Formulaic Comparisons: Stopping the Charter at the Statutory Human Rights Gate." In *Making Equality Rights Real: Securing Substantive Equality under the Charter,* ed. Fay Faraday, Margaret Denike, and M. Kate Stephenson, 409-41. Toronto: Irwin Law, 2006.

Yalden, Maxwell. *Transforming Rights: Reflections from the Front Lines.* Toronto: University of Toronto Press, 2009.

Index

Note: "(f)" after a page number indicates a figure; "(p)" after a page number indicates a photograph.

Abella, Rosalie, 214
Aboriginal peoples: denial of service, 202-4; franchise, 35; housing or tenancy, 83-84, 146-47, 163; Indian status, 37, 208; racism, 47, 243*n*81; on reserves, 84, 208; in rural BC, 149-50; sterilization of, 36; women, 30, 31, 34, 36-37
abortion laws, 33-34, 45
accommodation. *See* housing or tenancy
Act for the Protection of Women and Girls in Certain Cases (BC), 30
An Act Respecting the Employment of Women Before and After Childbirth (BC), 28
activism. *See* social movements; women's movements
Adamoski, Robert, 233*n*13
Adams, Eric, 75, 239*n*46
administrative justice model: burden of proof, 154-55, 188; compared to court system, 85, 162; complaint process, 61-62, 78-80; conciliation, 80, 114-15, 123-24; education programs, 121, 142-45; force of law, 115, 166; future of, xiii; investigators, 140-41, 146-51, 172; precedents, 162; pressure to settle, 101-4; third-party complaints, 77, 92. *See also* boards of inquiry; settlements
adoption, 12, 38-39
affirmative action programs, 77, 145, 152, 174, 212, 214
age discrimination: in ads, 77-78; of female workers, 4, 88; forced retirement, 184; laws, 77-78, 245*n*32, 247*n*26; as prohibited grounds, 9, 83, 152, 165; in training programs, 162, 164-65
Age Discrimination Act (Ontario), 77-78
Agosin, Marjorie, 219*n*32, 220*n*33
airline industry, 3-5
Ajzenstat, Janet, 14, 220*n*41
Alberta: bill of rights, 53, 78; equal pay law, 73(f); forced sterilization, 36; human rights law, 76, 78(f); maintenance laws, 38; minimum wage laws, 29, 36; political interference, 209; sex discrimination law, 74(f)
Alberta Human Rights and Civil Liberties Association, 82

Index

Allen, Nadine, 131
Andersen, Marguerite, 246*n*3, 246*nn*5-9
Anderson, Donald, 245*n*46, 247*n*18, 247*n*23, 247*n*29, 248*n*13, 248*n*38, 258*n*20, 260*n*42, 260*n*47
Anderson, Doris, 179, 218*n*18, 237*n*1, 237*n*4, 237*n*6, 250*n*26; on sexism, 10, 66, 67, 117
Anderson, Gail, 4
Andiappan, P., 265*n*17
Andison, Alan, 157, 202, 254*n*34; in rural BC, 140, 147-50
anti-discrimination laws: complaint-based, 211-13; discrimination defined, 266*n*26; history of, 50-65, 86-93; ineffectiveness of, 62-65; post-war advocates, 47-52; prohibited grounds, 83, 113, 116, 165, 186, 213; public education, 57-60; race-based activism, 46-50; reaction to, 52-53, 55-58; table of, 61(f); use of test cases, 58-59, 64, 202-4. *See also* human rights laws
Arrance, Fred, 202-4
Arrance, Lorraine, 202-4
Association for Civil Liberties (Toronto), 52
Austin, Helen, 133

Backhouse, Constance, 223*n*8, 224*n*21, 224*n*23, 225*n*36, 226*nn*58-59, 227*n*63, 227*n*70, 227*nn*72-73, 228*n*74, 232*n*124, 234*n*18, 250*n*25, 250*n*27; on legal system, 26, 32
Bagnall, John C., 237*n*9, 240*n*47, 244*n*4
Baines, Beverley, 74, 227*n*68, 230*n*106, 232*n*125, 232*n*130, 239*n*41
Bakan, Abigail, 14
Bangarth, Stephanie, 14, 220*n*42
Bannerman, Josie, 226*n*55, 237*n*2, 239*n*31
barbers, 43, 67
Barman, Jean, 18, 98, 221*n*46, 221*n*47, 222*n*52, 247*n*15
Barnes, Emery, 108
Barrett, David: about, 15-16; government of, 113-14; on human rights, 11, 219*n*28
Bartlett, Peter, 252*nn*4-5, 266*n*25

Beaulac, Stéphane, 240*n*48
Beebe, Janet, 216, 231*nn*110-11, 269*n*57
Beeby, Dean, 68, 237*n*8, 238*n*27, 239*n*36
Bennett, Bob, 142
Bennett, W.A.C., 15, 113
Berger, Thomas, 91
Berton, Pierre, 233*n*3
Bill, Yvonne, 163, 208
Bill of Rights (Canada, 1960), 44, 74, 75, 96
Bill of Rights (Saskatchewan, 1947), 53, 54, 56, 61(f), 68, 74(f), 220*n*39
bills of rights legislation: advocates, 49, 52, 53; enforcement issues, 54-55; shortfalls of, 208-9. *See also by jurisdiction*
Black, William W. (Bill), 236*n*74, 242*n*66, 246*n*12, 247*n*14, 247*n*34, 257*n*22, 260*n*56, 261*n*65, 261*n*67, 261*n*73; about, 97, 112, 114, 143, 159, 189; on discrimination, 62, 81
blacks: denial of service, 52-53, 54-55, 58, 87, 90; segregation, 47; and systemic discrimination, 48, 64-65
Blair, Charles, 54-55
Blum, Sid, 50, 52, 58
boards of inquiry: and enforcement, 61-65; force of law, 115, 166; lack of compensation, 161, 208; provincial variations, 174, 175(f); role of, 157-68, 172, 205-6; use of labour mediators, 101-2, 104, 180, 188. *See also* settlements; *specific commission or branch*
Boyd, Susan B., 219*n*29, 251*n*60
Boyer, Pierre, 232*n*124
Brandt, Gail Cuthbert, 222*n*1, 223*n*15, 226*n*54, 227*n*69, 228*n*79, 230*nn*100-1, 238*n*16
Bremer v. Board of School Trustees, 164, 166
British Columbia: competing visions, 15-16, 197-201; discriminatory policy, 43-44; early legal history, 27-32, 86-93; franchise in, 23-24, 222*n*2; local context, 14-15, 17-19, 221*n*48; mass rally in support of human rights, 181; minority rights, 31; political history, 15-16, 40-43, 86

British Columbia Civil Liberties Association (BCCLA), 82, 99, 111(p), 181, 206
British Columbia Federation of Labour, 60, 90, 92, 100
British Columbia Teachers' Federation, 41, 137
Broadbent, Ed, 192
Brockman, Joan, 229*n*86
Brodsky, Gwen, 219*n*29
Brown, Rosemary, 20, 197, 219*n*28, 222*n*60, 248*n*6, 249*n*29; about, 19, 41, 114, 130, 194
Bruner, Arnold, 242*n*77
Bukwa, Bonnie, 126, 127
burden of proof, 54, 62, 154-55, 188, 209
Burt, Sandra, 227*n*65, 229*n*85, 229*n*92, 230*nn*97-98, 239*n*41, 246*n*2
Butler, Veronica, 202-4

Caccia, Charles, 192
Cameron, D.H., 177
Camp, J.J., 159
Campbell, Gail G., 94, 246*n*4
Campbell, Marie, 238*n*16, 238*n*22
Campbell, Robert A., 227*n*66
Canada: and Aboriginal rights, 37, 84, 208; citizenship, 23, 38-39, 40, 165; criminal law, 32-35, 39-40, 43-44; discrimination in, 47-50; franchise in, 23, 222*n*4; law reform, 38-40, 241*n*58; sex discrimination law, 74(f); treaties and conventions, 13, 41-42, 75, 192, 199, 200. *See also* human rights state
Canadian Bill of Rights (1960), 44, 74, 75, 96
Canadian Charter of Rights and Freedoms, 9, 12, 43, 199, 219*n*29
Canadian Congress of Labour, 50
Canadian Council of Christians and Jews, 145
Canadian Federation of Business and Professional Women's Clubs, 70, 71
Canadian Human Rights Act (1977), 74(f), 82, 113
Canadian Human Rights Reporter, 174-75
Canadian Jewish Congress, 49, 52, 59

Canadian Labour Congress, 50, 70, 82
Cardenas, Sonia, 14
Carignan, Renee, 117-18
Carr, W.F., 91
Carson, Garry, 133
Carter, Sarah, 223*n*13, 240*n*49
Cass-Beggs, Barbara, 68
Cassidy, Aileen, 101-3, 105
censorship, 112, 131, 132
Chambers, Lori, 12, 219*n*29, 223*n*12, 224*n*21
Chapman, Richard, 79-80
Chappell, Louise, 239*n*43
Chappell, S., 128
Charlie, Rose, 143
Charlton, Susan, 147
Charter of Human Rights and Freedom (Quebec, 1975), 76, 82, 113
Charter of Rights and Freedoms (Canada), 9, 12, 43, 199, 219*n*29
chastity laws, 32-33
Chatelaine, 10, 66
Chelsea, Andy, 146-47
Chenier, Elise, 229*n*95
Chesterman, John, 239*n*43
children: child care, 213; custody disputes, 12, 26-27, 219*n*29; guardianship, 27, 42; and labour law, 29; seduction of, 33; sexual assault, 40; support of, 27-28, 38; working mothers, 88
Children of Unmarried Parents Act (BC), 28
Chinese: men and white women, 30; minority rights, 17, 31
Chopik, Kathy, 226*n*55, 237*n*2, 239*n*31
Christie, Fred, 52-53
Christie, Nancy, 225*n*30
Christie v. York decision, 53
Chunn, Dorothy E., 233*n*13, 251*n*60
citizenship: loss of, 38-39; rights of, 23, 40, 165
Citizenship Act (Canada), 40
civil liberties organizations, 52, 81-82, 99, 111, 112
Clarkson, Chris, 35, 224*n*18, 229*n*82, 232*n*122

Index

class-action, 201, 212, 266*n*35
Cleland, Frank, 116
Clément, Dominique, 220*n*36, 220*n*41, 220*n*42, 222*n*54, 222*n*58, 240*n*49, 241*n*65, 242*nn*70-71, 242*n*74, 242*n*79, 243*n*81, 243*n*86, 245*nn*41-43, 247*n*24, 247*n*32, 248*n*4, 248*nn*9-10, 248*n*14, 250*nn*38-39, 258*n*5, 258*n*18, 263*n*96, 264*n*14
Cmiel, Kenneth, 14, 220*n*38
Coates, Fred W., 240*n*49
Code, Lorraine, 227*n*65, 230*nn*97-98, 239*n*41, 246*n*2
Cohen, Leah, 250*n*25, 250*n*27
Cohen, Marcy, 100-1, 102
Cohen, Marjorie Griffin, 239*n*29, 244*n*9, 246*n*1, 263*n*100, 263*n*105
Cole, Nat, 232*n*121, 247*n*28
Collenette, David, 192
Colter, Erica, 236*n*67, 237*n*85, 241*n*59, 264*n*14
common law rights, 53, 56, 223*n*15
Communist Party of Canada, 52
Compa, Lance A., 219*n*31
Comparelli, Peter, 249*n*23, 263*n*98, 263*n*101
Conn, Heather, 251*n*60
Conrad, Margaret, 95, 246*n*5
Co-operative Commonwealth Federation (CCF), 47-48, 49, 52, 68, 72, 86
Cornish, Mary, 218*n*17
Côté, Andrée, 14, 220*n*40, 248*n*10
Council of Women, 19, 57, 70, 71, 72
court system: compared to commissions, 85, 158; judicial interpretation, 43-45; process, 54, 61-62; successful law suits, 195; testimony of females, 44; and women, 32-35, 39-40, 43-44
Creese, Gillian, 225*n*39, 226*nn*43-44, 237*n*3
Criminal Code (Canada), 33, 39-40
criminal conviction, 115, 161, 164; pardoned, 9, 113, 205
criminal law and women, 32-35, 39-40, 43-44
Culley, Jacqueline, 3-4, 5

Davies, Diane, 153
Dawson, Michael, 50, 233*n*12
Dawson, T. Brette, 232*nn*127-29
Day, Shelagh, 14, 249*n*16, 249*n*23, 250*n*32, 252*n*67, 254*n*49, 255*n*53, 255*n*56, 255*n*59, 266*n*28, 266*n*30, 266*nn*34-35, 269*n*50; on human rights, 155, 210-11, 212, 214-15; and the Human Rights Branch, 110, 120-22, 123, 125, 127, 183, 201-2
De Roo, Bishop Remi B., 143, 144(p)
Demarais, Lou, 159
denial of services: and long hair, 164; and race, 52-53, 54-55, 58, 87, 202-4
Deserted Wives Act (BC), 27
Dhaliwal v. British Columbia Timber, 165
Diamond, Stephen F., 219*n*31
Diefenbaker, John, 75
disability, physical or mental, 83, 164, 186, 188, 191, 199
discrimination. *See* anti-discrimination laws; human rights laws; prohibited grounds
dismissal, unlawful, 4, 67, 116-17
division of labour. *See* sexual division of labour
divorce. *See* family law
Divorce Act (Canada, 1968), 37
Dominion Election Act (1906), 23
Dominion Lands Act (Canada), 25
Donnelly, Jack, 217*n*10
Dorney, Lindsay, 227*n*65, 230*nn*97-98, 239*n*41, 246*n*2
Douglas, Roger, 239*n*43
Douglas, Tommy, 54, 55
Doukhobours, 24, 112
dress code defence, 203
Drew, George, 55
Driedger, Leo, 237*n*83, 240*n*52
Driedger v. Peace River Block News, 161
Ducharme, Michel, 14, 220*n*41
Duclos, Nitya (aka Iyer), 218*n*13, 257*n*30, 267*n*40, 268*nn*42-43
Duplessis, Maurice, 55-56

Eberlee, T.M. (Thomas), 80, 235*n*46, 235*n*57, 241*n*64

Edgar, Lawrence, 90-91
Edge, Marc, 262*n*81
Edgett, Jim, 103, 193, 195, 201
education: access to, 36, 94-95; job training, 136; reforms to, 41
education programs: of the commission, 121, 142-45; and community groups, 57-60, 139-40, 145; and funding reduction, 178; lack of in BC, 90, 91; as prevention, 81, 162, 201
employment applications, advertising or interview, 67, 77-78, 90, 100, 124-25, 188
Employment Equity Act (Canada, 1986), 40
employment practices, 239*n*31; and conciliation process, 90, 123-24; and discrimination, 28, 29-31, 48, 55, 94-97; and dismissal, 4, 67, 116-17; ineffectiveness of laws, 62-65, 87-91; male attitudes, 67, 68, 99; public education, 57-60; use of job classifications, 88, 117, 153-55; vicarious liability, 166-67. *See also* equal pay or wages; sexual division of labour
employment rights. *See* workers' rights
Equal Pay Act (BC, 1953), 73(f), 86, 87, 89, 90, 96, 154, 156
equal pay for work of equal value, 113, 115, 152, 155, 174, 269*n*53
equal pay laws: anti-discrimination, 55, 57; in BC, 87, 88, 115; in Canada, 71-75; minimum wage, 29, 36, 38, 41, 70-72, 88; table of, 73(f)
equal pay or wages: complaints, 151-56; differential, 28-29, 156; and division of labour, 12, 88; income disparities, 29, 66, 72, 135; Jensen case, 100-3, 105, 155, 158, 195; and job classifications, 88, 117, 153-55; pay scales, 41, 67, 68, 153-54; and systemic discrimination, 215-16
equality, formal, 9, 35-45, 205, 215-16
equality, substantive, 10. *See also* systemic discrimination
Erola, Judy, 192
Errington, Gene, 130, 136, 143, 216, 269*n*56

ethnicity, 9, 55, 76, 83
European Convention on Human Rights (1950), 75
Evans, Tony, 198, 264*n*3

Factories Act (BC), 29, 36, 42, 43
Fahrni, Magda, 233*n*12, 252*n*63
Fair Employment Practices Act (BC, 1956), 61(f), 89, 92
Fair Employment Practices Act (Canada, 1953), 55, 57, 60, 61(f), 63, 69, 71, 88
Fair Employment Practices Act (Nova Scotia), 61(f), 63-64
Fair Employment Practices Act (Ontario), 61(f), 64, 68
Fairclough, Ellen, 68-69
Fairweather, Gordon, 192
Family and Child Services Act (BC), 42
family law: child support, 27-28; custody disputes, 12, 26-27, 219*n*29; division of assets, 44; divorce laws, 34-35, 37-38; family allowance, 36; maintenance, 27, 36, 38; maternity leave, 18, 28, 36, 215; mothers' pensions, 18, 19, 27, 34, 36; reforms to, 231*n*113. *See also* children
Family Relations Act (BC), 36, 231*n*113
family status: as prohibited grounds, 205, 268*n*42; working mothers, 88
Faraday, Fay, 218*n*17, 269*n*54
Faulkes, Charles, 99
Fedy, Ross, 139
Feinberg, Abraham, 240*n*47
Female Employees Fair Remuneration Act (Ontario, 1951), 72, 73
feminism. *See* women's movements
Ferry, John, 202-4
Field, Debbie, 67
Fields, Andrea, 7, 193-94
Fine, Louis, 57
Finkel, Alvin, 240*n*49
First Nations. *See* Aboriginal peoples
Flaherty, David H., 222*n*59
Fortna, Peter, 240*n*49
Foster, Janice, 7, 157-58, 161, 167
Foster v. British Columbia Forest Products, 157-58, 165, 167, 168
Foulks, James, 112

Frager, Ruth A., 14, 29, 30, 68, 69, 72, 220*n*42, 223*n*9, 223*n*14, 225*n*37, 226*n*45, 226*n*50, 226*n*60, 233*n*9, 234*n*21, 235*n*47, 236*n*80, 237*n*7, 237*n*11, 237*n*84, 238*n*14, 238*n*23, 238*n*25, 238*n*28, 239*n*40, 240*n*53, 246*n*1, 264*n*14
franchise reform, 23-24, 222*n*1
French, Mabel, 24
Friedman, Karl, 184
frivolous complaints, 186-87
Frost, Leslie, 52, 56, 57, 71, 75
Fudge, Judy, 12, 216, 218*nn*24-25, 219*n*27, 231*n*107, 269*n*54, 269*nn*58-59
funding: education programs, 178; human rights programs, 172-73, 176-77

Gagnon, Théo, 240*n*49
Gall, Gerry, 241*n*65
Garr, Allen, 261*n*59, 263*n*99
Gawne, Jane, 78-79, 161
Gay Alliance Towards Equality v. Vancouver Sun, 164, 166, 167, 182, 201, 256*n*17
gender identity and expression, 6-7, 85, 219*n*29. *See also* sexual orientation
gender inequality. *See* men; sex discrimination; women
gender roles: entrenched in law, 22-23, 34; occupational, 99, 111, 210; rural BC, 136, 150-51; working mothers, 88
gendered language, 40, 41-43
George, Gloria, 145
Georgia Straight, 112
Ghitter, Ron, 209
Gibson, Dale, 258*n*15
Giesbrecht, William, 90, 91, 159
Gilroy, Joan, 95
Glasbeek, Amanda, 32, 226*n*57, 227*n*67, 227*n*71, 228*nn*74-77
Gleason, Mona, 229*n*95
Goldrick, Penny, 139
golf courses, 47, 60, 128-29, 185
Gottfriedson, Mildred, 178
Gould, Terry, 251*n*60
Goulden, Linda, 253*n*16
Grabham, Emily, 267*n*36, 268*n*49
Grafe, Kathleen, 134-35

Grafe v. Sechelt Building Supplies, 134-35, 165
Graydon, Shari, 96
Greenwood, Bruce, 170
Gregg, Milton, 69
Grekul, Jana, 229*n*89
Guardians Appointment Act (BC), 27
Gubbins, Loretta, 166
Guilbault, Maurice, 84, 121, 139, 183
Gurnett, Jim, 241*n*65, 265*n*23
Gutteridge, Helena, 30

Haley, Mildred, 65
Hanley, Barbara M., 223*n*7
hate speech, 145, 186
Heerspink v. ICBC, 164, 166
height and weight requirements, 8, 67, 135, 150-51, 157-58, 165, 209
Heinrich, Jack, 185
Herman, Didi, 220*n*40, 229*n*95, 265*n*22
Hewett, Philip, 112
Hill, Daniel G., 80, 235*n*46, 236*n*82, 241*n*56, 241*nn*62-64
Hill, Lisa, 239*n*43
Hobsbawm, E.J., 217*n*11
Hodgson, Dorothy L., 218*n*26
homosexuals. *See* sexual orientation
honest belief defence, 167
Hope, Alan, 163
Hope, Graham, 133
hospital industry, practical nurses, 87, 106-7, 153-54, 266*n*35
housing or tenancy: anti-discrimination law, 55, 60, 77, 89, 92; hotels, 83-84, 146; obtaining mortgage, 96; rental, 47, 55, 90-91, 115-16, 163, 249*n*20, 249*n*29; restrictive covenants, 48-49, 55; work site, 126-27
Howe, R. Brian, 9, 14, 55, 62, 189, 214, 218*n*15, 220*n*40, 221*n*48, 234*n*36, 236*n*73, 248*n*9, 250*n*30, 250*n*36, 257*n*21, 258*n*6, 258*n*16, 261*nn*70-71, 266*n*24, 268*n*49
Hozak, Audrey, 95, 246*n*6
Hughes, E.N., 159
Human Rights Act (BC, 1969): equal pay complaints, 152-53; implementation,

96-100; results, 105-8; and sex discrimination, 74(f), 93
Human Rights Act (BC, 1984): background, 186-88; failure of, 193-96; opposition to, 190-93; provisions, 188-90, 261*n*64
Human Rights Association (Newfoundland), 81, 240*n*51
human rights associations, 81-82
Human Rights Branch (BC, 1973-84): appointments, 178-79, 195; boards of inquiry, 157-68, 172, 205; directors, 110-11, 138, 143, 201; innovations, 115-19, 138-42, 200-1; investigators, 123-24, 129, 138-40; loss of credibility, 176-86; mandate, 114, 143-45; operation, 109-13, 119-29; political interference, 176-77, 182-84; regional offices, 140, 141, 146-51; and social movements, 137, 139-40; use of labour mediators, 101-2, 104-6, 120, 122, 180. *See also* settlements
Human Rights Code (BC, 1973): activist support, 130-33; administration of, 119-29; drafting of, 112-15; impact of, 113, 125-26, 168; innovations, 115-19; reform of, 151-53; undermining of, 168, 171
Human Rights Code (Ontario, 1962), 74, 75-78, 172
Human Rights Commission (BC, 1969-73): director, 96-97, 105, 108, 119, 201; Jensen case, 100-3, 105, 158; settlements, 77, 84; use of labour mediators, 101-2, 104
Human Rights Commission (BC, 1973-84): changes in 1984, 188-89; directors, 119-20, 143-45; loss of credibility, 176-86; mandate, 114, 138. *See also* Human Rights Branch (BC, 1973-84)
Human Rights Commission (New Brunswick), 81, 84
human rights commissions: government appointments to, 208-9; provincial variations, 83, 84-85, 174, 175(f), 205-6, 208-9. *See also by jurisdiction*
human rights laws: across jurisdictions, 83, 84-85, 242*n*80, 243*n*85; complaint-based, 211-13; and equal pay, 71-75; exemptions, 174, 208; and formal equality, 35-45, 215-16; as gender neutral, 11, 45; and intersectionality, 7, 213, 268*n*41; literature on, 14-15, 240*n*49; and public campaigns, 50, 57-60, 142-45; reasonable cause provision, 116, 118, 164, 165, 168; and sex discrimination, 5-8; tables of, 61(f), 73(f), 74(f), 78(f); types of complaints, 106-8, 141-42, 159-60, 175(f). *See also* anti-discrimination laws
human rights state: competing visions, 15-16, 197-201; complaint-based, 211-13; definitions, 8, 210, 266*n*26; and formal equality, 35-45; government obstruction, 176-86, 208-9; mass rally in support, 181; obligations of, 204-5; reform in rural BC, 149-50; and systemic discrimination, 8-13, 118, 202-5, 209-16
Hume, Stephen, 259*n*23, 259*nn*25-26
Hunky Bill, 186
Hunter, Iain, 248*n*2
Hunter, Rosemary, 219*n*29
H.W. v. Kroff, 116-17, 164
Hyndman, Margaret, 71, 72

immigration, 31, 38-39, 40, 47
Indian Act (Canada), 31, 34, 37, 226*n*59
Indo-Canadians, 17
Industrial Home for Girls Act (BC, 1912), 36
industrial relations officers (IRO): lack of training, 101, 120-21, 122; pressure to settle, 101-4; reintroduction of, 180, 188; settlements by, 105-6
infanticide, 33
inheritance laws, 27-28
international human rights movement, 199-200
international treaties, 13, 75-76, 92-93; obligations under, 41-42, 192, 199, 200
International Women's Year (IWY), 136, 199
International Year for Human Rights, 81, 92-93, 98, 178, 242*n*75, 245*n*41
International Year for the Disabled, 199
intersectionality, 7, 213, 268*n*41

investigators: caseloads, 140-41, 172; proactive, 123-29, 138-40; regional offices, 146-51
Inwood, Damian, 259*n*27
Isitt, Ben, 222*n*49, 222*n*55
Iyer, Nitya (aka Duclos), 218*n*13, 257*n*30, 267*n*40, 268*nn*42-43

Jamieson, Laura, 89
Japanese, 47
Jay, Henry, 147
Jefferson v. BC Ferries, 164
Jehovah's Witnesses, 48
Jensen, Hanne, 139(p); career, 138, 181-82, 184; case, 100-3, 105, 155, 158, 195
Jewish community, 48, 49-52, 58-59, 89-90, 92, 240*n*53
Jewish Labour Committee (JLC): campaigns, 49-50, 58-60, 63-64, 82, 86-87, 89-90, 92; posters, 51(p), 59(p)
Jewsbury, Gail, 123-24, 251*n*48
Johnson, David, 14, 55, 62, 189, 214, 220*n*40, 234*n*36, 236*n*73, 248*n*9, 258*n*6, 258*n*16, 261*n*70, 266*n*24, 268*n*49
Johnston, C.E., 68
Johnston, Rita, 19
Johnstone, Ian, 169-71
Joliffe, E.B., 64
Joyal, Serge, 192
jury duty, 36, 39

Kallen, Evelyn, 217*n*12
Kambeitz, Gerald, 265*n*21
Kaplansky, Kalmen, 50, 51(p), 52, 60, 69, 236*n*81
Katz, April D., 140, 202, 244*n*24, 247*n*17
Katz, Joseph, 8, 100, 178
Katz, Sidney, 58, 235*n*53, 235*n*56
Kellcher, S.F.D., 159
Kelly, James, 14
Kenny, Doug, 131
Kess, Cathy, 226*n*49, 238*n*16
Killam, Hayden, 134-35
Kinesis (newspaper), 19
King, Bill, 113, 114, 115
King, Emile, 52
King, Terry, 128

Kinghorn, Russ, 131
Kirkup, Alex, 198, 264*n*3
Knickerbocker, Nancy, 263*n*98, 263*nn*101-2
Knopff, Rainer, 249*n*21, 257*n*26, 266*n*25
Knowles, Stanley, 68
Konyk, William, 186
Korinek, Valerie, 242*n*78
Kroff, Jack, 116-17

labour law, 30-32, 40. *See also* workers' rights; working conditions
labour organizations: campaigns, 50, 60, 82; and female workers' wages, 67, 69-70; and higher wages for men, 107, 156; and individual rights, 11; and sex discrimination, 99; women in, 4-5, 17
Lady Godiva ride, 131-32, 252*n*62
Lamarche, Lucie, 14
Lambertson, Ross, 14, 220*n*42, 221*n*43, 233*n*1, 233*n*10, 234*n*22, 235*n*55, 235*n*58, 235*n*61, 238*n*20
Landucci, Nola, 138, 139(p), 144, 181, 253*n*28
Langer, Rosanna L., 14, 206, 220*n*40, 236*n*70, 256*n*6, 264*n*15, 268*n*49
language, gendered, 40, 41-43
language requirements, 32, 118, 165-66, 198
Laskin, Bora, 64, 167, 236*n*81
Latham, Barbara K., 226*n*49, 226*n*55, 237*n*2, 238*n*16
Lauren, Paul Gordon, 220*n*35
Lawrence, Alicia, 194
Leary, Virginia A., 219*n*31
Lecky, Carol, 159
Lecompte, Roger, 146
legal counsel, access to, 158, 188, 212
legal profession: access to, 24, 35; and human rights expertise, 159; and sex discrimination, 44, 209-10
legal status and gender. *See* sex discrimination
Leiper, Jean McKenzie, 209-10, 266*n*27
Lemonde, Lucie, 14, 220*n*40, 248*n*10
lesbians. *See* sexual orientation
Lessard, Hester, 12, 14, 219*nn*29-30,

251*n*60, 252*n*65, 269*n*54, 269*n*59
Lichtenstein, Nelson, 11, 218*nn*20-23
Linton, Billie, 154
liquor: sale of, 43, 228*n*78; serving of, 101
Little, Margaret Hillyard, 222*n*51, 222*n*56, 225*nn*29-30, 226*n*62, 233*n*11
Lockard, Duane, 239*n*42
Loffmark, Ralph R., 107
Lornex Mining Company, 7, 126-27
Lougheed, Peter, 209
Lucas, F.G.T., 25

Macdonald, M.A., 53
MacGill, Helen Gregory, 26, 32, 224*n*16, 224*n*22, 224*n*26
MacGregor, Gillian, 133
MacGuigan, Mark, 192
MacKay, W.A., 241*n*59
MacLennan, Christopher, 14, 220*n*41, 239*n*46
Macphail, Agnes, 69
Mandel, Michael, 232*n*119
Manitoba: anti-discrimination law, 52, 61(f), 63, 74(f); equal pay law, 73(f); franchise in, 24; human rights law, 78(f)
Mann, Marjory, 68
Manning, Ernest, 56-57
marital status: and loss of employment, 4, 29, 95, 116; and loss of rights, 25-29, 38; as prohibited grounds, 55, 83, 152, 205; single women, 29-30, 43; widows, 25, 27-28, 42
marriage: of Aboriginal women, 37; change of name laws, 38, 42, 232*n*119; of orphans, 42; and sexual abuse, 40. *See also* family law
Married Women's Property Act (BC), 26, 36, 43
Martin, Clara Brett, 223*n*10
Mason, Blair, 241*n*65
maternity leave, 18, 28, 36, 215
Mathison, Dutchie, 7, 128-29
Maynard, Edward, 240*n*51
McAuley, Heather, 122
McCann, Alan, 146

McCartin, Joseph A., 218*nn*20-21
McChesney, Allan, 265*n*18
McClelland, Robert, 176, 182, 189, 191(p), 193-94
McCord, Harley, 118-19, 127-28
McCrae, Margaret, 96
McDonald, Jim, 46, 47
McInnis, Grace, 19, 70
McIntyre, Sheila, 266*n*29
McKay, Morley, 58, 62
McLachlin, Beverley M., 79-80, 135, 159, 161
McLaren, Angus, 18, 222*n*50, 222*n*53, 222*n*57
McLaren, Arlene Tigar, 18, 222*n*50, 222*n*53, 222*n*57
McLaren, Joan, 164
McLeod, Hugh, 139, 202
McMahon, Patricia L., 223*n*11
McPherson, Kathryn, 225*n*30
media: and public education, 59(p), 81. *See also* newspapers
Mehat, Ajit, 139
men: backlash to human rights, 135; father's rights, 12, 219*n*29; male attitudes, 24, 67, 68, 89, 95; male privilege, 35, 131-32, 154-55; rights over family, 26-27, 33, 34-35
mentally ill, sterilization of, 36
Menyasz, Peter, 251*n*60
Menzies, Robert, 233*n*13
Merry, Sally Engel, 219*n*32
Mertus, Julie A., 15, 221*n*44
military service, 38, 40, 45
minimum wage laws, 29, 36, 38, 41, 70-71, 88
minority rights: visible, 24, 31, 35, 64, 190; and women, 31, 34, 46, 47, 71, 168, 229*n*95
Minow, Martha, 267*n*39, 268*n*41
Miron, Janet, 229*n*89, 233*n*1
Mitchell, David J., 221*n*45, 247*n*15, 264*n*2
Molyneux, Maxine, 215, 268*n*49, 269*nn*51-52
Moore, Christopher, 234*n*24
mothers' pensions, 18, 19, 27, 34, 36

Mou, Jonna Bruh, 184
Mowat, Douglas, 178
Moya, Miguel, 260*n*44, 260*n*54
Moyn, Samuel, 14, 218*n*19

Name Act (BC), 42
National Council of Women, 19, 57, 70, 71, 72
National Housing Act (Canada), 60, 92
national origin, 53, 55, 71
Nechiporenko, Gwen R., 151-52
Nelson, Alex and Nella, 166
Nelson v. Gubbins, 166
New Brunswick: anti-discrimination law, 60, 61(f), 74(f); education programs, 81; franchise in, 23, 222*n*1; human rights law, 76, 78(f)
New Democratic Party (NDP): Barrett government, 15, 113-14; ideology of, 86, 197-200; support of human rights, 176; Women's Rights Committee, 11, 190, 216
Newfoundland: about, 76, 85, 174; equal pay law, 73(f); franchise in, 223*n*6, 229*n*83; human rights law, 74, 78(f), 85; sex discrimination law, 74(f), 231*n*114
Newkirk, Reginald, 133, 135-36, 139, 194
newspapers: censorship, 112, 131, 132; feminist, 19; *Gay Alliance* case, 164, 166, 167, 182, 201, 256*n*17; job ads in, 77-78, 124-25; and public education, 59; survey of articles in, 149
Nixon, Kimberly, 85
Norman, Ken, 192
Northwest Territories, 61(f), 78(f)
Nova Scotia: anti-discrimination law, 60, 61(f); equal pay law, 73(f); franchise in, 23; human rights law, 78(f); sex discrimination law, 74(f)
Nunavut, 78(f)
nursing profession, 87, 106-7, 153-54, 266*n*35

Oberlyn, Ros, 253*n*28, 254*n*45, 259*n*27, 260*n*43
O'Brien, Jan, 250*n*24, 259*n*25

Odam, Jes, 248*n*2
Office Assistance Limited, 100, 101, 105
O'Halloran, Cornelius, 53
O'Neill, Nick, 239*n*43
Ontario: affirmative action, 267*n*36; anti-discrimination law, 52, 53, 54, 55, 61(f), 68; education campaigns, 57-60; equal pay law, 72-74; franchise in, 23; human rights reforms, 74, 76-78, 172; local context, 14, 220*n*48; sex discrimination law, 74(f), 76
Oram, Douglas, 164
Orlikow, David, 50, 63
Ostapchuck, Emily, 93
Owen-Flood, Dermod, 146

Palmer, Bryan, 261*n*62
Palmer, Vaughn, 198, 262*n*89, 263*n*94, 263*n*101, 264*n*5
pardoned conviction, 9, 113, 205
Paris, Charles, 145, 182, 186, 193
Park, Eamon, 64
Parkison, Bill, 147
paternalism: in court system, 44-45; in hiring, 124; and motherhood, 22-23, 30-31, 36, 88, 99; in sexual assault cases, 32-33
Patrias, Carmela, 14, 29, 30, 54, 68, 69, 72, 220*n*39, 220*n*42, 221*n*43, 223*n*9, 223*n*14, 225*nn*37-38, 226*n*45, 226*n*50, 226*n*60, 233*n*2, 233*n*6, 233*n*9, 234*nn*19-21, 234*n*28, 234*n*30, 235*n*42, 235*n*47, 236*n*80, 237*n*7, 237*nn*10-11, 238*n*14, 238*n*23, 238*n*25, 238*n*28, 239*n*40, 240*n*53, 246*n*1, 264*n*14
Pazdro, Roberta J., 226*n*55, 237*n*2
Pearson, Lynne, 37, 230*n*101, 252*n*7
Pegram, Thomas, 75, 239*nn*44-45
Penner, Roland, 192
pension and allowance laws, 18, 19, 27, 34, 36, 40, 53
pension plans, 39, 135
Perry, Adele, 229*n*95
Perry, W.C., 64
Pfeifer, Carol, 260*n*32
Picard, Clifford, 162
Pickel, Jo-Anne, 218*n*17

Pierson, Ruth Roach, 239*n*29, 246*n*1, 251*n*60, 263*n*100
place of origin, 205
Plecas, Bob, 258*n*10
political affiliation, 9, 52, 115, 164
politics: lack of access for women, 35, 70; right to hold office, 23, 24, 35
Pothier, Diane, 218*n*13, 267*n*40
poverty and inequality, 135, 186, 213
Powell, Eric D., 203
pregnancy: birth control movement, 19; and dismissal, 116-17, 164; and employment, 3-5, 265*n*17; as prohibited grounds, 205
Prentice, Alison, 225*n*40, 229*n*90, 239*nn*32-34, 239*n*37, 252*nn*2-3
Priestman, Jordan, 159
Prince Edward Island: equal pay law, 73(f); franchise in, 23; human rights law, 78(f); sex discrimination law, 74(f)
Prince George (BC), 148
prisons, 39, 150, 153
Prisons and Reformatories Act (Canada), 39
professions, access by women, 23-25, 35, 66, 67; and post-secondary education, 94-95
Progressive Conservative Party, 208
prohibited grounds: age, 9, 83, 152, 165; in Canadian law, 9, 152, 164, 165, 205; disability, 83, 164, 186, 188, 191, 199; ethnicity, 9, 55, 76, 83; family status, 205, 268*n*42; gender identity, 6-7, 85, 219*n*29; hate speech, 145, 186; height and weight, 8, 67, 135, 150-51; language, 32, 118, 165-66, 198; marital status, 55, 83, 152, 205; and multiple factors, 213; national origin, 53, 55, 71; in Ontario law, 76; pardoned conviction, 9, 113, 205; place of origin, 205; political affiliation, 9, 52, 115, 164; proposed for BC, 186; in Quebec law, 83, 113; race or colour, 53, 55, 83; and reasonable cause, 116; religion, 53, 83; sex, 55, 83, 152, 205; sexual harassment, 68, 117-18, 152; sexual orientation, 83, 164, 186; social condition, 3, 9, 11
proof, burden of, 119

property law: and franchise, 23; and married women, 25-26, 38; restrictive covenants, 48-49, 55; widow's rights, 25, 27-28
prostitution laws, 31, 32, 40, 227*n*70
Public Accommodation Practices Act (BC, 1961), 61(f), 89, 92
public facilities, use of, 183-84
public office: elected, 35, 70; jury duty, 36, 39; right to hold, 23, 24, 35; stereotyping of women, 99
public policy. *See* human rights state
public service employees, 136
purchase of property, 48-49, 55, 96

Quebec: activism, 82; anti-discrimination law, 60, 61(f), 83, 113; Civil Code, 223*n*15; commission, 174, 183; equal pay law, 73(f), 155; franchise in, 223*n*6; human rights law, 76, 78(f), 82, 84, 113, 174; marriage in, 228*n*80; sex discrimination law, 74(f)
Quebec Charter of Human Rights and Freedom (1975), 75, 82, 113

race and gender, as combined factors, 213, 267*n*40
race or colour: discrimination, 47-50, 91, 121, 146-47, 202-4; franchise, 24, 48; interracial couples, 87, 92, 268*n*43; in labour law, 30-32; as prohibited grounds, 53, 55, 83; visible minorities, 31, 34, 46, 47, 71, 168
Ranel, Tel, 99
Ratushney, Ed, 192, 263*n*93
Razavi, Shahra, 215, 269*nn*51-52
Reavley, M., 265*n*17
Rebick, Judy, 237*n*5
Red Eye (newspaper), 131, 132
Reid, Alan D., 240*n*49, 242*n*69
Reif, Linda, 239*n*44
religion, as prohibited grounds, 53, 83
religious minorities, 24, 47, 48
remedies. *See* settlements
Remondo, Frank, 123-24
rental, accommodations. *See* housing or tenancy

Index

Resnick, Philip, 221*n*47, 248*n*11
restrictive covenants, 48-49, 55
Rice, Simon, 239*n*43
Richardson, Maureen, 73-74
Riddell, Maureen, 56, 235*n*45
Risse, Thomas, 220*n*37
Rolston, Tilly, 70, 89
Ropp, Stephen C., 220*n*37
Ross, Becki L., 7, 218*n*14, 229*n*95
Rowell, Floyd, 99
Roy, Patricia E., 221*n*47
Royal Canadian Mounted Police (RCMP), 38, 40
Royal Commission on the Status of Women (RCSW) (1967), 38-40
Rubinstein, Michael, 235*n*38
Ruck, Calvin, 65
Ruff, Kathleen, 103, 163, 174, 247*n*24, 247*n*32, 247*n*35, 265*n*n19-21, 266*n*33; about, 110, 111(p), 112, 119; career, 201-2, 211; on human rights, 208-9, 211-12; and the Human Rights Branch, 119-20, 121-23, 124, 133, 138, 182, 184
rural communities, 136, 146-51
Rutherdale, Robert, 252*n*63
Ryan, Larry, 143

Sam, Jean, 83-84
Sanderson, Kenneth, 154
Sands, William H., 102
Sanger, Margaret, 18
Sangster, Joan, 217*n*3, 227*n*63, 227*n*67, 232*n*123, 238*n*17, 244*n*n10-12; on working women, 4, 5, 43, 87
Saskatchewan: anti-discrimination law, 53-55, 60, 61(f); equal pay law, 73(f); human rights law, 78(f), 220*n*39; sex discrimination law, 74(f)
Saskatchewan Bill of Rights. *See* Bill of Rights (Saskatchewan, 1947)
Saskatchewan Federation of Labour, 82
Schabas, William, 240*n*48
Schaefer, Glen, 249*n*23
Schucher, Karen, 266*n*32, 268*n*49
Scully, Pamela, 218*n*26
services, denial of: and long hair, 164; and race, 52-53, 54-55, 58, 87, 202-4

Sethna, Christabelle, 252*n*63
settlements: and fines, 77, 84; force of law, 115, 166; investigators, 123-29, 138-40, 140-41, 147-51, 172; lack of compensation, 161, 208; precedents, 162; types of, 118-19, 141, 160-61, 160(f), 185(f); unequal sides, 104, 188, 212. *See also* boards of inquiry
sex as prohibited grounds, 55, 152, 205
sex discrimination: awareness of issue, 200-1; banned in all forms, 116; and BC Human Rights Act, 94-108; complaints of, 149, 152, 207; equal pay, 71-75, 86-90; history of, 22-35; and human rights laws, 5-8, 75-85; lack of will to reform, 66-71, 92, 108; legal equality, 35-45. *See also by specific complainant name*
sexual assault, 32-33, 40, 44
sexual division of labour: income disparities, 86-89, 215; job classifications, 117, 153-54, 155; male attitudes, 24, 67, 89; managerial positions, 99; in the workforce, 28, 29-31
sexual harassment: conciliation approach, 129; systemic, 68, 117-18; Zarankin case, 169-71, 193, 257*n*1, 257*n*19
sexual orientation: and criminal law, 229*n*95; debate, 209; *Gay Alliance* case, 164, 166, 167, 182, 201, 256*n*17; gender identity, 6-7, 85, 219*n*29; as prohibited grounds, 83, 164, 186
sexuality, regulation of, 34, 35, 39-40, 43-44
Sharma, Bhan, 117
Sharpe, Robert J., 223*n*11
Shearer, Renate, 145, 192
Sherlock, Jack, 96-97, 105, 108, 119, 201
Shue, Henry, 217*n*12
Shumiatcher, Morris, 68
signs and advertising and notices: newspaper ads, 67, 77-78, 124-25; notices, 84; signs, 43
Sikhs, 150
Sikkink, Kathryn, 220*n*37
Silver, S., 265*n*17
Silver, Will, 248*n*9
Silversides, Ann, 263*n*91

single women: and social assistance, 43; and social policy, 29-30
Smith, Danny, 159
Smith, Jock, 178, 259*n*23
Smith, Lynn, 170, 171
Smith, Mary Ellen, 24, 30
Smith, Miriam, 14, 221*n*43
Smitz, Jerome, 99
social assistance: anti-discrimination in, 53; denial to single women, 43
Social Assistance Act (BC, 1945), 53
social condition, as prohibited grounds, 9, 113
Social Credit Party (Socreds) government: W.A.C. Bennett, 96, 98-99, 108, 113; ideology of, 15, 86, 197-201; political interference, 176-77, 182-84, 208; regressive reforms, 186-93; restraint package, 187-88; undermining human rights laws, 40-43, 168, 171
social movements: to celebrate UDHR anniversary, 92-93; civil liberties, 52, 81-82, 99, 111, 112; coalitions, 52, 69-71, 81-82, 191-92; and the Human Rights Branch, 137, 139-40; Jewish community, 49-52, 58-59, 89-90, 92, 240*n*53; and legal reform, 206-7; opposition to 1984 law, 191-93; post-war priorities, 47, 49-50; public education campaigns, 57-60, 144-45; race-based activism, 46-50. *See also* women's movements
social policy: barriers to change, 7-8, 25, 136, 150-51; equality or differential debate, 29; failure to address sex discrimination, 22-23, 29-30, 108; and law enforcement, 16-17, 43-45, 157-68; social inequalities, 213-16, 267*n*38. *See also* human rights state
Sohn, Herbert A., 233*n*4, 234*n*18, 235*n*39, 235*n*48, 235*n*50, 235*n*57, 235*n*59, 244*n*26
Solidarity Coalition, 191-92
Sproule-Jones, Linda, 109, 122, 124, 125, 202, 244*n*16
St. Jean, Steven, 52
Stanley, Timothy J., 31, 226*n*56
Stasiulis, Daiva, 267*n*37

Status of Women Action Group (SWAG), 41, 88, 111, 112, 130, 176, 181, 200
Statute Law (Status of Women) Amendment (Canada, 1974), 40, 230*n*104
Steinberg, Kamini, 218*n*13, 268*n*49
Stewart, Alistair, 68
Stinson, Arthur, 93
Strenja, Kathleen, 7, 142
Strong-Boag, Veronica, 225*n*39, 237*n*3
Strongitharm, Margaret, 143, 144, 145, 179, 182
Sunday shopping debate, 50
Supreme Court of Canada (SCC): on abortion law, 45; appointments to, 36; on division of assets, 44; on gay rights, 164, 166, 167; on personhood, 25; on sex discrimination, 165
Sylvia, Gerri, 63
systemic discrimination: and complaint-based laws, 211-13; definition, 210; and equal pay, 215-16; failure to address, 8-13, 199, 202-5, 209-16; and formal equality, 10, 12-13, 35-38; and racism, 48, 58-59, 64-65, 202-4

Tarnopolsky, Walter, 234*n*17, 234*n*29, 234*n*35, 236*n*71, 241*n*58, 264*n*12; on human rights law, 54, 85, 204-5
taxi business, 7, 142, 150
teaching profession, 94, 136-37
tenancy. *See* housing or tenancy
Tharpe, Jean, 7, 126-27, 161, 204
Thompson, John Herd, 221*n*47
Tillotson, Shirley, 14, 50, 57, 220*n*42, 233*n*13, 235*n*47, 238*n*21, 238*n*27, 239*n*30, 239*n*35, 239*nn*38-39
Toronto: activists, 52, 71, 76; human rights bylaw, 87; racism in, 48
Toronto Globe and Mail, 50, 56, 77
Trades and Labour Congress, 50
treaties and conventions, 13, 75; obligations under, 41-42, 192, 199, 200
Trociuk decision, 12
Trottier, Dan, 248*n*9
Tulchinsky, Gerald, 233*n*1

Tunnicliffe, Jennifer, 265*n*19, 265*n*22
Tyer, Merwyn, 203
Tymchischin, Paul, 83-84

UDHR. *See* Universal Declaration of Human Rights (UDHR)
Ueffing, Wilhelm, 193
unemployment insurance, 39, 40
Unemployment Insurance Act (Canada), 40
Unemployment Relief Act (BC, 1931), 50, 52
unions. *See* labour organizations
United States: activism, 11; laws, 6, 13, 75
Universal Declaration of Human Rights (UDHR), 13, 49, 75-76, 81, 92-93
universities: male attitudes, 131-32; women's experience of, 94-95
University of British Columbia, 130-32
University of Saskatchewan, 132
unmarried women: and social assistance, 43; and social policy, 29-30

vagrancy laws, 32, 40
Vancouver: activism, 18, 111-12; during Depression, 29; human rights bylaw, 87; immigrant population, 17
Vancouver Civic Unity Association, 86, 93, 98, 206
Vancouver Council of Women, 20, 28, 71, 89
Vancouver Status of Women (VSW), 20, 102, 105, 107, 111, 112, 130, 131, 132, 181, 200
Vancouver Sun, 31, 89, 106, 110-11, 124-25, 189, 191, 194, 198; *Gay Alliance* case, 164, 166, 182
Vancouver Women's Caucus, 19, 100, 102, 213
Vant, T. Neil, 179
Vaugeois, Renée, 243*n*81
vicarious liability, 166-67
Vickers, David, 124, 159
Vickers, Jill, 20, 222*n*59
Victoria, 88, 152; activists, 112-13
Victoria Times-Colonist, 195

violence, gender-based: and criminal law, 39-40; and human rights, 12, 218*n*26, 219*n*32; in marriage, 34; in pornography, 131; rape trials, 32-33
vital statistics and discrimination, 31, 42
Vogel, Donna, 247*n*19, 262*n*84
Voice of Women, 19, 107-8
vote, right to: of minorities, 23-24, 35, 48; of women, 222*n*1, 222*n*4, 223*n*6

Wade, Susan, 226*n*49
wage laws. *See* equal pay or wages
Waldron, Mary Anne, 242*n*80
Walker, James W. St. G., 9, 14, 49, 218*n*16, 220*n*42, 221*n*43, 226*n*51, 226*n*53, 227*n*64, 233*nn*7-9, 234*nn*18-19, 234*n*23, 234*n*37, 235*n*43, 235*n*51, 235*n*54, 238*n*20
Wallace, G. Scott, 180
Wan, LiLynn, 237*n*7
Ward, Linda, 118-19, 127-28
Warner, Tom, 265*n*22
Warren, Loraine, 153, 155, 161
Warren, Norene, 116, 204
Weaselfat, Francis, 243*n*81
Weaver, Sally, 230*nn*97-98
Wedepohl, Martin, 131
Who-Peng, Leigh, 147
widows, 25, 27-28, 42
Wiegers, Wanda, 12, 219*n*29, 220*n*34, 252*n*62, 252*n*64
Williams, Allan, 178, 179, 184
Williams, Shannon, 240*nn*49-50, 242*n*68, 243*n*84, 258*n*19, 265*n*18
Wills, Charles, 184
Wilson, Doug, 242*n*78
Woloszyn, Cora, 238*n*19
women: changing work force, 64, 72, 87, 94-96, 156; experiences of, 6-7, 87-88, 94-96, 128-29; and male privilege, 35, 131-32, 154-55; and motherhood, 22-23, 30-31, 36, 88, 99; multiple discrimination factors, 30-32, 213
Women and Girls Protection Act (BC), 36
women's movements: coalitions with reformist groups, 18-20, 114, 181; and equal pay law, 72; and the Human

Rights Branch, 130-33; impact in BC, 41, 88-89, 111-13, 200-1; and legal reform, 206-7; and sex discrimination, 70-71
Wood, Josiah, 159
Woodsworth, Ellen, 131
workers' rights: focus of, 219*n*31; and industrial democracy, 11; labour laws, 29-32; workers compensation laws, 39, 42. *See also* equal pay or wages
working conditions: division of labour, 24, 223*n*8; of female workers, 42, 67-68; and the labour movement, 11; and protection of women, 29-31; sexual harassment, 68, 117-18
Wright, Andrea, 215, 269*nn*54-55

Young Women's Christian Association (YWCA), 70, 71, 72
Yukon, 38, 78(f)

Zarankin, Sheri, 169-71, 193, 257*n*1, 257*n*19
Zurbrigg, Ann, 226*n*55, 237*n*2, 239*n*31

PUBLICATIONS OF THE OSGOODE SOCIETY FOR CANADIAN LEGAL HISTORY

2014 CHRISTOPHER MOORE, *A History of the Ontario Court of Appeal*
DOMINIQUE CLÉMENT, *Equality Deferred: Sex Discrimination and British Columbia's Human Rights State, 1953-84*
PAUL CRAVEN, *Petty Justice: Low Law and the Sessions System in Charlotte County, New Brunswick, 1785-1867*
THOMAS TELFER, *Ruin and Redemption: The Struggle for a Canadian Bankruptcy Law, 1867-1919*

2013 ROY MCMURTRY, *Memoirs & Reflections*
CHARLOTTE GRAY, *The Massey Murder: A Maid, Her Master and the Trial that Shocked a Nation*
C. IAN KYER, *Lawyers, Families, and Businesses: The Shaping of a Bay Street Law Firm, Faskens 1863-1963*
G. BLAINE BAKER and DONALD FYSON, eds., *Essays in the History of Canadian Law. Volume 11: Quebec and the Canadas*

2012 R. BLAKE BROWN, *Arming and Disarming: A History of Gun Control in Canada*
ERIC TUCKER, JAMES MUIR, and BRUCE ZIFF, eds., *Property on Trial: Canadian Cases in Context*
SHELLEY A.M. GAVIGAN, *Hunger, Horses, and Government Men: Criminal Law on the Aboriginal Plains, 1870-1905*
BARRINGTON WALKER, ed., *The African-Canadian Legal Odyssey: Historical Essays*

2011 ROBERT J. SHARPE, *The Lazier Murder: Prince Edward County, 1884*
PHILIP GIRARD, *Lawyers and Legal Culture in British North America: Beamish Murdoch of Halifax*
JOHN MCLAREN, *Dewigged, Bothered and Bewildered: British Colonial Judges on Trial*
LESLEY ERICKSON, *Westward Bound: Sex, Violence, the Law, and the Making of a Settler Society*

2010   Judy Fudge and Eric Tucker, eds., *Work on Trial: Canadian Labour Law Struggles*
Christopher Moore, *The British Columbia Court of Appeal: The First Hundred Years*
Frederick Vaughan, *Viscount Haldane: The Wicked Step-father of the Canadian Constitution*
Barrington Walker, *Race on Trial: Black Defendants in Ontario's Criminal Courts, 1850-1950*

2009   William Kaplan, *Canadian Maverick: The Life and Times of Ivan C. Rand*
R. Blake Brown, *A Trying Question: The Jury in Nineteenth-Century Canada*
Barry Wright and Susan Binnie, eds., *Canadian State Trials. Volume 3: Political Trials and Security Measures, 1840-1914*
Robert J. Sharpe, *The Last Day, the Last Hour: The Currie Libel Trial*

2008   Constance Backhouse, *Carnal Crimes: Sexual Assault Law in Canada, 1900-1975*
Jim Phillips, R. Roy McMurtry, and John Saywell, eds., *Essays in the History of Canadian Law. Volume 10: A Tribute to Peter N. Oliver*
Gregory Taylor, *The Law of the Land: Canada's Receptions of the Torrens System*
Hamar Foster, Benjamin Berger, and A.R. Buck, eds., *The Grand Experiment: Law and Legal Culture in British Settler Societies*

2007   Robert Sharpe and Patricia McMahon, *The Persons Case: The Origins and Legacy of the Fight for Legal Personhood*
Lori Chambers, *Misconceptions: Unmarried Motherhood and the Ontario Children of Unmarried Parents Act, 1921-1969*
Jonathan Swainger, ed., *The Alberta Supreme Court at 100: History and Authority*
Martin Friedland, *My Life in Crime and Other Academic Adventures*

2006   Donald Fyson, *Magistrates, Police and People: Everyday Criminal Justice in Quebec and Lower Canada, 1764-1837*
Dale Brawn, *The Court of Queen's Bench of Manitoba 1870-1950: A Biographical History*
R.C.B. Risk, *A History of Canadian Legal Thought: Collected Essays*, edited and introduced by G. Blaine Baker and Jim Phillips

2005   PHILIP GIRARD, *Bora Laskin: Bringing Law to Life*
       CHRISTOPHER ENGLISH, ed., *Essays in the History of Canadian Law. Volume 9: Two Islands, Newfoundland and Prince Edward Island*
       FRED KAUFMAN, *Searching for Justice: An Autobiography*

2004   JOHN D. HONSBERGER, *Osgoode Hall: An Illustrated History*
       FREDERICK VAUGHAN, *Aggressive in Pursuit: The Life of Justice Emmett Hall*
       CONSTANCE BACKHOUSE and NANCY BACKHOUSE, *The Heiress versus the Establishment: Mrs. Campbell's Campaign for Legal Justice*
       PHILIP GIRARD, JIM PHILLIPS, and BARRY CAHILL, eds., *The Supreme Court of Nova Scotia, 1754-2004: From Imperial Bastion to Provincial Oracle*

2003   ROBERT SHARPE and KENT ROACH, *Brian Dickson: A Judge's Journey*
       GEORGE FINLAYSON, *John J. Robinette: Peerless Mentor*
       PETER OLIVER, *The Conventional Man: The Diaries of Ontario Chief Justice Robert A. Harrison, 1856-1878*
       JERRY BANNISTER, *The Rule of the Admirals: Law, Custom and Naval Government in Newfoundland, 1699-1832*

2002   JOHN T. SAYWELL, *The Law Makers: Judicial Power and the Shaping of Canadian Federalism*
       DAVID MURRAY, *Colonial Justice: Justice, Morality and Crime in the Niagara District, 1791-1849*
       F. MURRAY GREENWOOD and BARRY WRIGHT, eds., *Canadian State Trials. Volume 2: Rebellion and Invasion in the Canadas, 1837-38*
       PATRICK BRODE, *Courted and Abandoned: Seduction in Canadian Law*

2001   ELLEN ANDERSON, *Judging Bertha Wilson: Law as Large as Life*
       JUDY FUDGE and ERIC TUCKER, *Labour before the Law: Collective Action in Canada, 1900-1948*
       LAUREL SEFTON MACDOWELL, *Renegade Lawyer: The Life of J.L. Cohen*

2000   BARRY CAHILL, *"The Thousandth Man": A Biography of James McGregor Stewart*
       A.B. MCKILLOP, *The Spinster and the Prophet: Florence Deeks, H.G. Wells, and the Mystery of the Purloined Past*
       BEVERLEY BOISSERY and F. MURRAY GREENWOOD, *Uncertain Justice: Canadian Women and Capital Punishment*

BRUCE ZIFF, *Unforeseen Legacies: Reuben Wells Leonard and the Leonard Foundation Trust*

1999 CONSTANCE BACKHOUSE, *Colour-Coded: A Legal History of Racism in Canada, 1900-1950*
G. BLAINE BAKER and JIM PHILLIPS, eds., *Essays in the History of Canadian Law. Volume 8: In Honour of R.C.B. Risk*
RICHARD W. POUND, *Chief Justice W.R. Jackett: By the Law of the Land*
DAVID VANEK, *Fulfilment: Memoirs of a Criminal Court Judge*

1998 SIDNEY HARRING, *White Man's Law: Native People in Nineteenth-Century Canadian Jurisprudence*
PETER OLIVER, *"Terror to Evil-Doers": Prisons and Punishments in Nineteenth-Century Ontario*

1997 JAMES W. ST. G. WALKER, *"Race," Rights and the Law in the Supreme Court of Canada: Historical Case Studies*
LORI CHAMBERS, *Married Women and Property Law in Victorian Ontario*
PATRICK BRODE, *Casual Slaughters and Accidental Judgments: Canadian War Crimes and Prosecutions, 1944-1948*
IAN BUSHNELL, *The Federal Court of Canada: A History, 1875-1992*

1996 CAROL WILTON, ed., *Essays in the History of Canadian Law. Volume 7: Inside the Law – Canadian Law Firms in Historical Perspective*
WILLIAM KAPLAN, *Bad Judgment: The Case of Mr. Justice Leo A. Landreville*
MURRAY GREENWOOD and BARRY WRIGHT, eds., *Canadian State Trials. Volume 1: Law, Politics and Security Measures, 1608-1837*

1995 DAVID WILLIAMS, *Just Lawyers: Seven Portraits*
HAMAR FOSTER and JOHN MCLAREN, eds., *Essays in the History of Canadian Law. Volume 6: British Columbia and the Yukon*
W.H. MORROW, ed., *Northern Justice: The Memoirs of Mr. Justice William G. Morrow*
BEVERLEY BOISSERY, *A Deep Sense of Wrong: The Treason, Trials and Transportation to New South Wales of Lower Canadian Rebels after the 1838 Rebellion*

1994 PATRICK BOYER, *A Passion for Justice: The Legacy of James Chalmers McRuer*

CHARLES PULLEN, *The Life and Times of Arthur Maloney: The Last of the Tribunes*
JIM PHILLIPS, TINA LOO, and SUSAN LEWTHWAITE, eds., *Essays in the History of Canadian Law. Volume 5: Crime and Criminal Justice*
BRIAN YOUNG, *The Politics of Codification: The Lower Canadian Civil Code of 1866*

1993   GREG MARQUIS, *Policing Canada's Century: A History of the Canadian Association of Chiefs of Police*
MURRAY GREENWOOD, *Legacies of Fear: Law and Politics in Quebec in the Era of the French Revolution*

1992   BRENDAN O'BRIEN, *Speedy Justice: The Tragic Last Voyage of His Majesty's Vessel* Speedy
ROBERT FRASER, ed., *Provincial Justice: Upper Canadian Legal Portraits from the* Dictionary of Canadian Biography

1991   CONSTANCE BACKHOUSE, *Petticoats and Prejudice: Women and Law in Nineteenth-Century Canada*

1990   PHILIP GIRARD and JIM PHILLIPS, eds., *Essays in the History of Canadian Law. Volume 3: Nova Scotia*
CAROL WILTON, ed., *Essays in the History of Canadian Law. Volume 4: Beyond the Law – Lawyers and Business in Canada 1830-1930*

1989   DESMOND BROWN, *The Genesis of the Canadian Criminal Code of 1892*
PATRICK BRODE, *The Odyssey of John Anderson*

1988   ROBERT SHARPE, *The Last Day, the Last Hour: The Currie Libel Trial*
JOHN D. ARNUP, *Middleton: The Beloved Judge*

1987   C. IAN KYER and JEROME BICKENBACH, *The Fiercest Debate: Cecil A. Wright, the Benchers and Legal Education in Ontario, 1923-1957*

1986   PAUL ROMNEY, *Mr. Attorney: The Attorney General for Ontario in Court, Cabinet and Legislature, 1791-1899*
MARTIN FRIEDLAND, *The Case of Valentine Shortis: A True Story of Crime and Politics in Canada*

1985   JAMES SNELL and FREDERICK VAUGHAN, *The Supreme Court of Canada: History of the Institution*

1984　Patrick Brode, *Sir John Beverley Robinson: Bone and Sinew of the Compact*
　　　David Williams, *Duff: A Life in the Law*

1983　David H. Flaherty, ed., *Essays in the History of Canadian Law. Volume 2*

1982　Marion MacRae and Anthony Adamson, *Cornerstones of Order: Courthouses and Town Halls of Ontario, 1784-1914*

1981　David H. Flaherty, ed., *Essays in the History of Canadian Law. Volume 1*

2014 Dale Brawn, *Paths to the Bench: The Judicial Appointment Process in Manitoba, 1870-1950*
       Irvin Studin, *The Strategic Constitution: Understanding Canadian Power in the World*

2013 Elizabeth A. Sheehy, *Defending Battered Women on Trial: Lessons from the Transcripts*
       Carmela Murdocca, *To Right Historical Wrongs: Race, Gender, and Sentencing in Canada*
       Donn Short, *"Don't Be So Gay!" Queers, Bullying, and Making Schools Safe*
       Melissa Munn and Chris Bruckert, *On the Outside: From Lengthy Imprisonment to Lasting Freedom*
       Emmett Macfarlane, *Governing from the Bench: The Supreme Court of Canada and the Judicial Role*
       Ron Ellis, *Unjust by Design: The Administrative Justice System in Canada*

2012 Shelley A.M. Gavigan, *Hunger, Horses, and Government Men: Criminal Law on the Aboriginal Plains, 1870-1905*
       David R. Boyd, *The Right to a Healthy Environment: Revitalizing Canada's Constitution*
       David Milward, *Aboriginal Justice and the Charter: Realizing a Culturally Sensitive Interpretation of Legal Rights*
       Steven Bittle, *Still Dying for a Living: Corporate Criminal Liability after the Westray Mine Disaster*
       Jacqueline D. Krikorian, *International Trade Law and Domestic Policy: Canada, the United States, and the WTO*
       Michael Boudreau, *City of Order: Crime and Society in Halifax, 1918-35*

2011 Lesley Erickson, *Westward Bound: Sex, Violence, the Law, and the Making of a Settler Society*

DAVID R. BOYD, *The Environmental Rights Revolution: A Global Study of Constitutions, Human Rights, and the Environment*
ELAINE CRAIG, *Troubling Sex: Toward a Legal Theory of Sexual Integrity*
LAURA DeVRIES, *Conflict in Caledonia: Aboriginal Land Rights and the Rule of Law*
JOCELYN DOWNIE and JENNIFER J. LLEWELLYN, eds., *Being Relational: Reflections on Relational Theory and Health Law and Policy*
GRACE LI XIU WOO, *Ghost Dancing with Colonialism: Decolonization and Indigenous Rights at the Supreme Court of Canada*
FIONA J. KELLY, *Transforming Law's Family: The Legal Recognition of Planned Lesbian Motherhood*
COLLEEN BELL, *The Freedom of Security: Governing Canada in the Age of Counter-Terrorism*

2010 ANDREW S. THOMPSON, *In Defence of Principles: NGOs and Human Rights in Canada*
AARON DOYLE and DAWN MOORE, eds., *Critical Criminology in Canada: New Voices, New Directions*
JOANNA R. QUINN, *The Politics of Acknowledgement: Truth Commissions in Uganda and Haiti*
PATRICK JAMES, *Constitutional Politics in Canada after the Charter: Liberalism, Communitarianism, and Systemism*
LOUIS A. KNAFLA and HAIJO WESTRA, eds., *Aboriginal Title and Indigenous Peoples: Canada, Australia, and New Zealand*
JANET MOSHER and JOAN BROCKMAN, eds., *Constructing Crime: Contemporary Processes of Criminalization*

2009 STEPHEN CLARKSON and STEPAN WOOD, *A Perilous Imbalance: The Globalization of Canadian Law and Governance*
AMANDA GLASBEEK, *Feminized Justice: The Toronto Women's Court, 1913-34*
KIMBERLEY BROOKS, ed., *Justice Bertha Wilson: One Woman's Difference*
WAYNE V. McINTOSH and CYNTHIA L. CATES, *Multi-Party Litigation: The Strategic Context*
RENISA MAWANI, *Colonial Proximities: Crossracial Encounters and Juridical Truths in British Columbia, 1871-1921*
JAMES B. KELLY and CHRISTOPHER P. MANFREDI, eds., *Contested Constitutionalism: Reflections on the Canadian Charter of Rights and Freedoms*

2008 CATHERINE E. BELL and ROBERT K. PATERSON, eds., *Protection of First Nations Cultural Heritage: Laws, Policy, and Reform*

Richard J. Moon, ed., *Law and Religious Pluralism in Canada*
Catherine E. Bell and Val Napoleon, eds., *First Nations Cultural Heritage and Law: Case Studies, Voices, and Perspectives*
Douglas C. Harris, *Landing Native Fisheries: Indian Reserves and Fishing Rights in British Columbia, 1849-1925*
Peggy J. Blair, *Lament for a First Nation: The Williams Treaties in Southern Ontario*

2007　Lori G. Beaman, *Defining Harm: Religious Freedom and the Limits of the Law*
Stephen Tierney, ed., *Multiculturalism and the Canadian Constitution*
Julie Macfarlane, *The New Lawyer: How Settlement Is Transforming the Practice of Law*
Kimberley White, *Negotiating Responsibility: Law, Murder, and States of Mind*
Dawn Moore, *Criminal Artefacts: Governing Drugs and Users*
Hamar Foster, Heather Raven, and Jeremy Webber, eds., *Let Right Be Done: Aboriginal Title, the Calder Case, and the Future of Indigenous Rights*
Dorothy E. Chunn, Susan B. Boyd, and Hester Lessard, eds., *Reaction and Resistance: Feminism, Law, and Social Change*
Margot Young, Susan B. Boyd, Gwen Brodsky, and Shelagh Day, eds., *Poverty: Rights, Social Citizenship, and Legal Activism*
Rosanna L. Langer, *Defining Rights and Wrongs: Bureaucracy, Human Rights, and Public Accountability*
C.L. Ostberg and Matthew E. Wetstein, *Attitudinal Decision Making in the Supreme Court of Canada*
Chris Clarkson, *Domestic Reforms: Political Visions and Family Regulation in British Columbia, 1862-1940*

2006　Jean McKenzie Leiper, *Bar Codes: Women in the Legal Profession*
Gerald Baier, *Courts and Federalism: Judicial Doctrine in the United States, Australia, and Canada*
Avigail Eisenberg, ed., *Diversity and Equality: The Changing Framework of Freedom in Canada*

2005　Randy K. Lippert, *Sanctuary, Sovereignty, Sacrifice: Canadian Sanctuary Incidents, Power, and Law*
James B. Kelly, *Governing with the Charter: Legislative and Judicial Activism and Framers' Intent*
Dianne Pothier and Richard Devlin, eds., *Critical Disability Theory: Essays in Philosophy, Politics, Policy, and Law*

SUSAN G. DRUMMOND, *Mapping Marriage Law in Spanish Gitano Communities*
LOUIS A. KNAFLA and JONATHAN SWAINGER, eds., *Laws and Societies in the Canadian Prairie West, 1670-1940*
IKECHI MGBEOJI, *Global Biopiracy: Patents, Plants, and Indigenous Knowledge*
FLORIAN SAUVAGEAU, DAVID SCHNEIDERMAN, and DAVID TARAS, with RUTH KLINKHAMMER and PIERRE TRUDEL, *The Last Word: Media Coverage of the Supreme Court of Canada*
GERALD KERNERMAN, *Multicultural Nationalism: Civilizing Difference, Constituting Community*
PAMELA A. JORDAN, *Defending Rights in Russia: Lawyers, the State, and Legal Reform in the Post-Soviet Era*
ANNA PRATT, *Securing Borders: Detention and Deportation in Canada*
KIRSTEN JOHNSON KRAMAR, *Unwilling Mothers, Unwanted Babies: Infanticide in Canada*
W.A. BOGART, *Good Government? Good Citizens? Courts, Politics, and Markets in a Changing Canada*
CATHERINE DAUVERGNE, *Humanitarianism, Identity, and Nation: Migration Laws in Canada and Australia*
MICHAEL LEE ROSS, *First Nations Sacred Sites in Canada's Courts*
ANDREW WOOLFORD, *Between Justice and Certainty: Treaty Making in British Columbia*

2004 JOHN MCLAREN, ANDREW BUCK, and NANCY WRIGHT, eds., *Despotic Dominion: Property Rights in British Settler Societies*
GEORGES CAMPEAU, *From UI to EI: Waging War on the Welfare State*
ALVIN J. ESAU, *The Courts and the Colonies: The Litigation of Hutterite Church Disputes*
CHRISTOPHER N. KENDALL, *Gay Male Pornography: An Issue of Sex Discrimination*
ROY B. FLEMMING, *Tournament of Appeals: Granting Judicial Review in Canada*
CONSTANCE BACKHOUSE and NANCY L. BACKHOUSE, *The Heiress vs the Establishment: Mrs. Campbell's Campaign for Legal Justice*
CHRISTOPHER P. MANFREDI, *Feminist Activism in the Supreme Court: Legal Mobilization and the Women's Legal Education and Action Fund*
ANNALISE ACORN, *Compulsory Compassion: A Critique of Restorative Justice*

2003 Jonathan Swainger and Constance Backhouse, eds., *People and Place: Historical Influences on Legal Culture*
Jim Phillips and Rosemary Gartner, *Murdering Holiness: The Trials of Franz Creffield and George Mitchell*
David R. Boyd, *Unnatural Law: Rethinking Canadian Environmental Law and Policy*
Ikechi Mgbeoji, *Collective Insecurity: The Liberian Crisis, Unilateralism, and Global Order*

2002 Rebecca Johnson, *Taxing Choices: The Intersection of Class, Gender, Parenthood, and the Law*
John McLaren, Robert Menzies, and Dorothy E. Chunn, eds., *Regulating Lives: Historical Essays on the State, Society, the Individual, and the Law*

2001 Joan Brockman, *Gender in the Legal Profession: Fitting or Breaking the Mould*

Printed and bound in Canada by Friesens
Set in Garamond by Artegraphica Design Co. Ltd.
Copy editor: Deborah Kerr
Proofreader: Francis Chow